Why Americans Hate Welfare

Studies in Communication, Media, and Public Opinion
A series edited by Susan Herbst and Benjamin I. Page

Why Americans Hate Welfare

RACE, MEDIA, AND THE POLITICS
OF ANTIPOVERTY POLICY

Martin Gilens

THE UNIVERSITY OF CHICAGO PRESS

*

Chicago and London

The University of Chicago Press, Chicago 60637
The University of Chicago Press, Ltd., London
© 1999 by The University of Chicago
All rights reserved. Published 1999
Paperback edition 2000

14 13 12 11 10 09   5 6 7 8

ISBN: 0-226-29364-5 (cloth)
ISBN: 0-226-29365-3 (paperback)

Library of Congress Cataloging-in-Publication Data

Gilens, Martin
    Why Americans hate welfare : race, media, and the politics of
antipoverty policy / Martin Gilens.
      p. cm.—(Studies in communication, media, and public opinion)
    Includes bibliographical references and index.
    ISBN 0-226-29364-5 (cloth : alk. paper)
    1. Public welfare in mass media.   2. Racism in mass media.   3. Mass
media and public opinion—United States.   4. Racism—United States.
5. Public welfare—United States.   6. Public opinion—United States.
I. Title. II. Series
P96.P842 U654   1999
070.4'493616—dc21   98-48866
                                          CIP

⊚ The paper used in this publication meets the minimum requirements of the
American National Standard for Information Sciences—Permanence of Paper
for Printed Library Materials, ANSI Z39.48-1992.

For Janet, my love

Contents

Preface

The topics I explore in this book—why Americans hate welfare, and what they would prefer to see in its place—are just a small part of a much larger question: How should an affluent society respond to poverty? For most of human history, most people struggled just to obtain the basic necessities of life. But America at the turn of the twenty-first century is among the richest societies ever to exist. Today we possess the means to provide all our citizens not only with life's necessities, but with material abundance that would have astounded our nation's founders. Yet in the midst of this wealth live many who suffer material deprivation. Millions of Americans lack sufficient food, clothing, and shelter. A hundred thousand families with children are homeless, and hundreds of thousands of poor families that do have homes lack such basic amenities as indoor plumbing. According to government statistics, one out of five American children is living in poverty—a proportion that is higher now than it was thirty years ago.

The pages that follow are not really about poor Americans, at least not directly. My focus instead is on what Americans in general *think* about the poor: their images of poverty, their beliefs about its causes, and especially their notions of what the government should and should not do in its efforts to help the poor. I care about the public's attitudes toward welfare and poverty because I believe that these attitudes have shaped (and continue to shape) government antipoverty policy. But I also care about public attitudes toward welfare and poverty because I think they tell us something important about the nature of our society and the passions and concerns that animate Americans' political views.

Many of the findings in this book confirm what most people already believe: that Americans oppose welfare, that they hold cynical views of welfare recipients, and that their thinking about poverty and welfare is permeated by their beliefs about blacks. But just as important, although less widely understood, is that Americans are committed to helping the poor—they donate their own time and money to charitable causes, they want their government to do more to help the poor, and they consistently express a willingness to pay higher taxes to help poor people and welfare recipients obtain better wages, better housing, medical care, child care, education, and job training.

When I began this research I thought public attitudes toward welfare would be a narrow and clearly circumscribed topic. But I soon came to realize that, even in this one small domain, the public's views are a complex amalgam of competing, though not incompatible, considerations. This book represents my effort to understand the complexities of Americans' welfare attitudes and to describe the contours of this one aspect of the public's political thinking.

This book grew out of my dissertation at the University of California, Berkeley, where I had the good fortune to meet up with an exceptional group of faculty and graduate students studying American politics and society. In the sociology department—where I was formally enrolled—I benefited greatly from the guidance of my faculty advisors Neil Smelser and Michael Hout. More surprising, to me at least, was the generosity of the political science professors, who took me under their wings (despite their initial misgivings about my suspect origins in sociology). Raymond Wolfinger and Merrill Shanks introduced me to the study of American public opinion and, along with Henry Brady, gave generously of their time and expertise. Paul Sniderman, affiliated with both Stanford University and the Survey Research Center at UC Berkeley, contributed enormously to my work as a graduate student and to my subsequent research. In the past decade, Paul has been the principal force behind three national telephone surveys of Americans conducted by the Survey Research Center. Each has been a collaborative effort among faculty from around the country, and I am fortunate to have been involved in them all. (All of the analyses in chapter 4, as well as results presented in chapters 2, 3, 6, and 8, are based on these surveys.)

Berkeley is a hard place to leave, but joining Yale's unusually collegial and stimulating political science department eased the pain. My colleagues here at Yale have supported my work, challenged my ideas, broadened my understanding, and showed me by example what distinguished social science research looks like. I am especially grateful to Alan Gerber, Donald Green, David Mayhew, Eric Patashnik, and Rogers Smith for both their criticisms and their encouragement.

Over the years, many people have read one or another part of this work, and it is a far better piece of research (and writing) as a result. For their comments, I am indebted to Henry Brady, Denis Chong, Cathy Cohen, Janet Felton, Herbert Gans, Alan Gerber, James Glaser, Marissa Martino Golden, Donald Green, Michael Hagen, Michael Hout, Ian Hurd, James Kuklinski, David Mayhew, Benjamin Page, Eric Patashnik, Mark Peffley, Robert Shapiro, Neil Smelser, Rogers Smith, Paul Sniderman, Davida Weinberger, and Raymond Wolfinger. I owe a particularly large debt to my graduate school colleague, occasional coauthor, and—most importantly—good friend Jim Glaser. Over the years, Jim has been a keen critic and an ardent supporter, and he possesses that rare ability to discern the logic lurking beneath pages of rambling prose.

In addition to good mentors, colleagues, and friends, I was fortunate to have able research assistance in many aspects of this work, not least the painstaking process of coding hundreds of newsmagazine and television news stories. I am happy to thank Daniel Dowd, Michael Ebeid, Jane Han, Ian Hurd, Andrew Rich, Simon Rodberg, Peter Stein, and Linda Stork for their help. The television news stories I analyzed were obtained from the Vanderbilt Television News Archive, and I am indebted to the VTNA's director, John Lynch, for his considerable assistance in making these materials more accessible.

Financial support for this research was provided by a grant from the Social Science Research Council's Program for Research on the Urban Underclass and by a variety of programs and institutions at Yale University, including the Block Fund for research on politics and the media, the Social Science Faculty Research Fund, the Institution for Social and Policy Studies, the Center for the Study of Race, Inequality and Politics, and the Hilles Publication Fund.

The University of Chicago Press, and especially my editor John Tryneski, have been wonderful to work with, and I am indebted as well to Benjamin Page and Susan Herbst, the series editors, and to an anonymous reviewer for their very helpful suggestions.

This project began on one side of the country and ended, many years later, on the other. My wife, Janet Felton, put up with our geographical upheaval and my constantly revised research "schedule" with less grumbling and more patience than I had any right to expect. As every parent knows, geographical upheaval cannot hold a candle to the arrival of children into one's life. During the course of this research my own two little upheavals arrived, my daughter Naomi and my son Joshua. They have added immensely not only to the tumult, but to the richness, of my life.

Writing is a hard and lonely task. The long nights sitting in front of a computer were made bearable by the love of my family. For that love I am truly blessed.

Introduction

For thirty years now, "welfare bashing" has been a popular staple of American politics. "The current welfare system," President Nixon proclaimed, "has become a monstrous, consuming outrage—an outrage against the community, against the taxpayer, and particularly against the children it is supposed to help."[1] Reclaiming antiwelfare politics from the Republicans, President Carter described welfare as "anti-work, anti-family, inequitable in its treatment of the poor and wasteful of taxpayers' dollars," while President Clinton ran for office with the pledge to "end welfare as we know it."[2] Of course, politicians vilify welfare because welfare bashing strikes a chord with the American public.

Americans' opposition to welfare does not seem hard to understand. For one thing, the welfare state is widely viewed as a European invention, thoroughly at odds with Americans' preferences for small government, personal freedom, and individual responsibility. And of the many aspects of the welfare state, "welfare" itself—that is, cash benefits paid to the working-age, able-bodied poor—conflicts most flagrantly with Americans' beliefs that individuals should take responsibility for their own betterment and not rely on the government for support. Furthermore, Americans are thought to reject welfare for practical as well as principled reasons. As national economic growth has slowed over the past decades, it is said that middle-class Americans have increasingly resented paying taxes to support the able-bodied poor. For most Americans, then, interests and ideology point clearly in the same direction: welfare is a violation of America's cherished values and an unwelcome claim upon its economic resources.

The purpose of this book is to subject these popular claims to empirical scrutiny. What I find, in a nutshell, is that much of what is widely believed about Americans' attitudes toward welfare is wrong. Despite their individualistic inclinations, Americans do not oppose the welfare state; in fact, they strongly support it. The American public consistently expresses a desire for more government effort, and higher levels of spending, for almost every aspect of the welfare state. Year after year, surveys show that most Americans think the government is not doing enough (or not spending enough) for education, health care, child care, the elderly, the homeless, and the poor.

To be sure, individualism is alive and well in America. But the public's commitment to individual effort and responsibility is subtler than is commonly assumed. Most Americans do believe that taking responsibility for yourself and "pulling yourself up by your own bootstraps" is an important part of what being an American is all about. But at the same time most believe that government can and should play a central role in providing both the means for individuals to better themselves and a cushion for times when individuals' own efforts are not enough.

Americans' individualism does not stand in the way of strong public support for the welfare state. Nor, it appears, do the economic concerns of the middle class lead them to oppose government programs for the poor. Politics is often viewed, by elites at least, as a process centered on the question "who gets what." For ordinary Americans, however, politics is more often about "who *deserves* what," and the welfare state is no exception. When they evaluate government policy, the question foremost in their minds is "what policy is best," not "what policy is best for me." Like much of politics, support or opposition to the various programs of the welfare state turns on issues of merit and deservedness, and on questions of how to most effectively realize Americans' shared values. Most middle-class Americans think welfare spending should be cut, but this desire does not stem from a self-interested reluctance to pay for welfare. Indeed, most of these same people oppose spending cuts for other programs designed to help the poor, including public housing, Head Start, job training, Medicaid, legal aid, or government-funded day care for poor children.

Am I claiming, then, that despite appearances Americans really *like* welfare? That might be going a bit too far. But I do believe that most Americans see welfare as a necessary and desirable function of government. That is not to say, however, that Americans are particularly happy with the current welfare system. But the source of their unhappiness, indeed the focus of considerable public anger and resentment, is not the *principle* of government support for the needy, but the perception that most people currently receiving welfare are undeserving. While no one factor can fully account for the public's opposition to welfare, the most important single component is this widespread belief that most welfare recipients would rather sit home and collect benefits than work hard to support themselves.

In large measure, Americans hate welfare because they view it as a program that rewards the undeserving poor. To understand public opposition to welfare, then, we need to understand the public's perceptions of welfare recipients, and here two important and related factors stand out. First, the American public thinks that most people who receive welfare are black, and second, the public thinks that blacks are less committed to the work ethic than are other Americans. There exists now a widespread perception that welfare has become a "code word" for race. Although this is too simple a formulation, I will show that white Americans' attitudes toward welfare can only be understood in connection with their beliefs about blacks—especially their judgments about the causes of racial inequality and the extent to which blacks' problems stem from their own lack of effort.

In this book I argue that racial stereotypes play a central role in generating opposition to welfare in America. In particular, the centuries-old stereotype of blacks as lazy remains credible for large numbers of white Americans. This stereotype grew out of, and was used to defend, slavery, and it has been perpetuated over the years by the continuing economic disparities between black and white Americans. In a culture in which economic failure is often attributed to lack of effort, blacks' economic problems themselves reinforce the stereotype of laziness. And over the past decades this problem has been exacerbated by the emergence of a highly visible black urban underclass that has exerted an inordinate influence over popular images of blacks, even though it constitutes only a small fraction of African Americans. Finally, as analyses of the news media will show, the stereotype of blacks as lazy has been reinforced by biased coverage of both black people and poor people in the popular press.

Racial stereotypes constitute an obstacle to public support for antipoverty programs. Yet the obstacle is not as formidable as it might seem. For most white Americans, race-based opposition to welfare is not fed by ill will toward blacks, nor is it based on whites' desire to maintain their economic advantages over African Americans. Instead, race-based opposition to welfare stems from the specific perception that, as a group, African Americans are not committed to the work ethic. Because the racial attitudes that are most responsible for white opposition to welfare are narrowly focused, the impact of those attitudes on antipoverty policy preferences is limited. Antipoverty programs that evoke the stereotype of blacks as lazy are opposed by most

white Americans, but programs that are viewed as helping the deserving poor to better support themselves are quite popular, even if those
programs are strongly associated with blacks. Whites oppose welfare
not because they think it primarily benefits blacks, but because they
think it benefits blacks who prefer to live off the government rather than
work. Yet programs such as job training and Head Start, which are just
as strongly associated with African Americans as is welfare, are overwhelmingly popular because they are viewed as helping the deserving
poor to better support themselves.

Although the public is quite cynical about the true needs and moti-
vations of welfare recipients, most Americans do want to help those
poor people, whether on welfare or not, who are genuinely trying to
make it on their own. Thus the public strongly favors time limits and
work requirements for welfare recipients but simultaneously wants to
spend more for job training, child care, transportation, and other services to help welfare recipients become self-supporting. And this desire to help the deserving poor extends to poor deserving blacks as
well. Americans express strong but complex attitudes toward government antipoverty policy. Despite their cynical (and often misinformed)
views of both blacks and welfare recipients, most Americans believe we
should be doing more, not less, to help the poor.

In the following pages I examine the nature, causes, and consequences
of Americans' attitudes toward the welfare state (understood as the
broad array of government programs to assist individuals—including
pensions, medical care, education, housing, unemployment insurance,
and antipoverty programs) and toward "welfare" in particular (referring to cash or cash-like assistance for the able-bodied, working-age
poor). In chapter 1, I briefly describe America's current social welfare
programs and examine the differing levels of support they receive from
the public. Consistent with popular beliefs, I find that Americans overwhelmingly think we are spending too much on welfare. But I also
find that welfare, and to a lesser extent food stamps, are the exception:
Americans think spending should be *increased* for most welfare-state
programs, including not only programs that benefit the middle class,
like education or Social Security, but efforts to help the poor as well.

In chapter 2, I explore two popular explanations for Americans' dislike of welfare: economic self-interest and individualism. I argue that
self-interest plays little role in explaining Americans' opposition to welfare. Careful comparison shows that public support for means-tested
programs that benefit only the poor is just as high as support for similar

universal programs that also benefit the middle class and the affluent. Moreover, contrary to popular perceptions, public support for welfare spending does not decline during economic downturns. Hard times, I show, do not elicit from the middle class a self-interested concern with minimizing taxes or a resentment over paying for welfare. On the contrary, national economic adversity leads to a greater sense that poor people are the victims of circumstances beyond their control and hence to greater support for welfare.

Individualism—that is, a commitment to the values of hard work and individual responsibility—has long been an important element of American culture. But most Americans temper their commitment to individualism with the understanding that people cannot always support themselves, and most believe that when individuals are in need the government has a responsibility to help. Americans' attraction to individualist values is important in understanding opposition to welfare. I argue, however, that individualism does not lead to a principled rejection of government support for the poor, but rather to a strong demand that welfare recipients, like everyone else, share a commitment to individual effort and responsibility.

The third chapter examines two additional explanations for opposition to welfare: cynicism toward welfare recipients and attitudes toward blacks. I show that the majority of Americans think most welfare recipients are taking advantage of the system and would rather sit home and collect benefits than work. I also show in chapter 3 that whites' cynical views of welfare recipients are paralleled by their negative stereotypes of blacks. Most white Americans believe that blacks are less committed to the work ethic than are whites, and this belief is strongly related to opposition to welfare.

In chapter 4, I use more sophisticated statistical tools to compare the relative importance of each of the alternative explanations for Americans' opposition to welfare. Taking into account individualism, self-interest, racial attitudes, and perceptions that welfare recipients are undeserving, along with a variety of other attitudinal and demographic characteristics, I find that racial attitudes have a profound impact on opposition to welfare, both directly and by shaping perceptions of the deservingness of welfare recipients. Despite the fact that African Americans constitute only 36 percent of welfare recipients and only 27 percent of all poor Americans, whites' attitudes toward poverty and welfare are dominated by their beliefs about blacks.

The fifth chapter looks at the historical circumstances surrounding the "racialization" of welfare and poverty in the American mind. Using analyses of newsmagazines and television news broadcasts, I trace changes in popular images of the poor from the 1950s to the 1990s. Poverty emerged as a subject of scientific inquiry in the late nineteenth century. Yet poor African Americans were almost wholly ignored until the mid-1960s, when public images of poverty shifted dramatically and came to focus disproportionately on blacks. In an effort to explain this striking shift in perceptions of the poor, I examine the roles of African American migration from southern states to the industrial cities of the North and West, President Johnson's War on Poverty, changes in the Aid to Families with Dependent Children (AFDC) program, shifts in the focus of the civil rights movement, and the urban riots that occupied the nation during the summers of 1965 through 1968. Each of these factors played some role in the racialization of poverty images in America; my analyses suggest, however, that changes in the complexion of poverty coverage stemmed from the news media's increasingly negative discourse on poverty and welfare and its consistent tendency to associate African Americans with the least sympathetic aspects of poverty.

In chapter 6, I argue that racial distortions in the media's coverage of poverty are largely responsible for public misperceptions of the poor. Furthermore, these misperceptions have important consequences for Americans' political preferences: whites with the most exaggerated misperceptions of the extent to which blacks compose the poor express the most cynical attitudes toward welfare recipients and the greatest opposition to welfare.

Racially biased coverage of poverty, I argue, cannot be explained either by the logistics of news production or by the concentration of poor blacks in large urban centers. Instead, the overly racialized images of poverty and the association of blacks with the least sympathetic subgroups of the poor reflect news professionals' own racial stereotypes, which operate as an unconscious influence on the content of the news they produce. Despite the generally liberal political orientations of individual news workers, the racialization of welfare and poverty in the mid-1960s did not reflect a sympathetic effort to draw attention to the black poor. Instead, blacks began to appear in poverty coverage only as that coverage turned a critical eye toward the country's poor and toward the War on Poverty in particular. Similarly, the pattern of poverty coverage over the ensuing decades reveals a tendency to portray the black poor more negatively than the nonblack poor; pictures of poor blacks are abundant when poverty coverage is most negative, while pictures of nonblacks dominate the more sympathetic coverage that accompanies periods of national economic hardship.

In chapter 7, I look in more detail at the nature and history of racial stereotypes. I describe stereotypes as exaggerated or wholly erroneous generalizations about specific social groups. Although stereotypes can reflect and embody both prejudice and material group interests, I argue that whites' belief that blacks are lazy and the opposition to welfare that grows out of this belief do not primarily reflect either a general animus toward African Americans or racial conflict over tangible resources. As a consequence, antipoverty programs that are not seen as rewards for the lazy can gain widespread approval among white Americans, even if these programs are strongly identified with blacks.

In chapter 8, I turn from public opinion to public policy, exploring the lessons that state welfare policy and federal welfare reform hold for our understanding of the politics of the American welfare state. The importance of race emerges once again, as we see that states with similar levels of income and education but with larger proportions of blacks among their welfare populations provide lower welfare benefits than states with fewer blacks on welfare. The history of welfare reform at the federal level also provides alternative evidence to complement what surveys tell us about Americans' views on welfare. Thirty years of welfare reform efforts have, for the most part, been consistent with the public's desires. Work requirements for welfare recipients, time limits on welfare receipt, job training and "work readiness" programs, and social supports such as child care, health care, and transportation have been used in the effort to move people from welfare to work. Surveys show that Americans strongly support both the "carrots" and the "sticks" of welfare reform, and are more concerned with helping the poor to become self-supporting than with saving taxpayer dollars.

Finally, I conclude by examining the policy implications of Americans' attitudes toward blacks and toward the poor. I argue that a reservoir of public support exists for increasing government efforts to help the poor. Furthermore, the perception that a program's beneficiaries are largely, or even primarily black, does not preclude overwhelming public support. As long as blacks remain disproportionately poor, it is unlikely that antipoverty policy can ever be divorced from racial politics, but even programs strongly associated with African Americans can enjoy broad support among the white public as long as they are seen as helping the deserving poor to better their lot.

The popularity of universal social programs such as Social Security has led some to conclude that public support for antipoverty efforts can be gained only by "hiding" such efforts within the framework of a program that provides benefits for all Americans, whether poor or not.

The findings in this book strongly challenge that notion. Means-tested programs that help only the poor can receive broad support from the American public, as long as those programs are consistent with the public's desire to help the needy to support themselves. Efforts to assist the poor need not depend on the costly stratagem of providing benefits to the large number of nonpoor as well.

Welfare has never been popular in America. Even as he established the first federal welfare programs in 1935, Franklin Roosevelt called welfare "a narcotic" and "a subtle destroyer of the human spirit" and proclaimed that "continued dependence upon relief induces a spiritual and moral disintegration fundamentally destructive to the national fiber."[3] In the intervening years Americans have come to accept, and indeed to demand, an array of government social services that would have been hard to imagine in the dawning years of the American welfare state. But welfare itself remains the most talked about and least liked of America's social welfare programs. The public's opposition to welfare is fed by the potent combination of racial stereotypes and misinformation about the true nature of America's poor. But the very real and widespread opposition to welfare evident among the American people is accompanied by an equally widespread desire to do more to help the poor. And the view among white Americans that blacks lack commitment to the work ethic is accompanied not by ill will toward blacks but by a willingness to assist all needy Americans, black and white, who are trying to improve their lot through hard work.

The American public is often characterized as simple-minded and inattentive when it comes to politics, and to some degree this charge is fair. Most Americans are not knowledgeable about the details of public policy or the nuances of partisan political arguments. But welfare is an enduring political issue that touches on the central values that animate public life. On such issues, Americans are often more sophisticated in their thinking and more nuanced in their preferences than they are given credit for. When we look closely, we find that Americans express a stable, coherent, and complex set of preferences toward antipoverty policy—preferences that reflect a balance between the desire to help the deserving poor and a concern with undermining their work ethic or rewarding those who prefer government support to self-support.

If we insist on a simple story about the politics of antipoverty policy, we will fail in the task of understanding the public's views. Whites tend to stereotype African Americans as lazy, yet most want to increase assistance for those blacks who are trying to make it on their own. Most

Americans reject the view that welfare is a "right" and that welfare recipients are victims of the economic system, but they dismiss just as strongly the idea that government already does too much in trying to help the poor. Americans are neither mean-spirited in their opposition to welfare nor indiscriminate in their desire to do more for the poor; their attitudes attest both to the complexity of the issue and to the sophistication of the public's views about government antipoverty policy.

1

The American Welfare State:
Public Opinion and Public Policy

The relationship between the prosperous and the poor is a central concern in all but the simplest societies. Although disparities in wealth vary by degree, every society contains some who are more privileged than others. How a society feels and acts toward its less fortunate members tells us much, not only about the society's social and political arrangements, but also the beliefs, values, and inner lives of its population. Are the sick made well? Are the destitute cared for? Do the frail, the disabled, and those too old to work have the means to live on? Are the fortunate concerned or indifferent to the plight of the less well-off? Is assistance given generously, grudgingly, or not at all?

The social and economic needs of a nation are not met solely through any one channel. Individuals rely on themselves and their families, on their friends and their communities, on their government, and often on strangers—through organized charities or personal kindnesses. In industrial societies, however, government social welfare programs have become an indispensable source of assistance to both the needy and the more privileged. In every developed country, government programs are central in providing education, health care, and housing for the general populace, as well as income support for the poor, the elderly, and the disabled. Indeed, government social spending—or "the welfare state" for short—now accounts for the majority of government expenditures in most economically advanced countries.[1]

In this chapter I briefly sketch the development of the American welfare state and the various government programs that make it up, and I then examine Americans' varying levels of support for those programs. I show that, contrary to popular image, Americans are not individualistic opponents of the welfare state; in fact, the American public strongly supports most aspects of the welfare state and in most cases believes that government should be doing more to assist its citizens. Large majorities of Americans, for example, think the government should be spending more money to fight poverty and homelessness, to improve our nation's education and health care, and to assist displaced workers and the elderly. One exception stands out, however: when it comes to "welfare" itself, widespread support turns to widespread opposition. The aim of this book is to understand why Americans seem to hate welfare even while they embrace most other elements of the welfare state.

The first step in studying Americans' attitudes toward welfare is to identify the subject of our inquiry. This is not a trivial exercise, since none of the dozens of different government antipoverty programs bears the title "welfare." Like many other terms, welfare has a fairly clear "center" but rather fuzzy "borders"—it is easier to point to clear examples of welfare than to identify the full set of criteria that would define the boundaries of the concept. Nevertheless, as it is usually understood, the term "welfare" refers to a subset of government assistance programs that share the following characteristics: First, benefits are means-tested, meaning that only individuals with incomes or assets below a set level are eligible. Second, benefits are provided in cash or in a near-cash form. Food stamps are the best example of a near-cash "welfare" program because food stamp coupons can be used in place of money to purchase approved foodstuffs. In addition, food stamps resemble cash in that they can be sold or traded, unlike other in-kind benefits such as medical care or public housing. Nevertheless, because food stamps are intended to purchase only a single (and particularly important) commodity, this program might better be considered a "quasi-welfare program" that differs slightly from the "core" welfare programs that provide cash benefits. Finally, "welfare" is usually understood to refer to programs that assist the working-age, able-bodied poor. Thus disability and retirement programs are not typically thought of as welfare, even if those programs limit their benefits to poor members of those populations.

Understood in this way, the term "welfare" refers most clearly to the state-run General Assistance (GA) programs for the poor and the federal/state program now called Temporary Assistance for Needy Families (TANF), and formerly known as Aid to Families with Dependent Children (AFDC). These programs provide cash benefits to the able-bodied, working-age poor. As already mentioned, food stamps can be considered a somewhat less typical example of "welfare," while even

further out on the boundaries of the category lies the federal Supplemental Security Income program (SSI), a means-tested program that
provides cash benefits to poor people who are aged, blind, or otherwise
disabled.

Such a loosely defined concept as welfare might seem a poor subject
for study. If our concern was with public policy alone, we might ignore
the amorphous term "welfare" and simply identify the specific government programs of interest. But in studying public attitudes, we must
adopt the language and concepts that the public employs. The lack of
an "official" definition has not kept the American public from devel-
oping clear and strong views about welfare, nor has this lack dissuaded
political elites and the mass media from talking about welfare. Even the
most casual acquaintance with recent public discussions of antipoverty
policy makes clear that the central referent in these debates is "welfare."

I will use the term "welfare" to refer to means-tested cash benefit
programs available to able-bodied, working-age adults. Welfare, in this
narrow sense, is distinguished from "the welfare state," which refers to
the broad array of government social programs that assist poor and
nonpoor Americans of all ages and economic conditions. Despite a certain unavoidable ambiguity, my focus in this book is public attitudes
toward "welfare," and my central goal is to understand the often bois-
terous opposition to welfare expressed by the American public. Before
turning to public attitudes, however, I look briefly at the nature and
history of the American welfare state.

Industrialization and the Birth of the Welfare State

The welfare state emerged in the nineteenth century as a response to
the new problems and opportunities created by industrialization and
economic growth. After centuries of stasis, the industrial revolution
had reformed the social and economic landscape of much of the Western world. New jobs arose as technology transformed the making of
textiles, clothing, shoes, iron, and steel and the mining of coal and met-
als. New technologies, including the coal-fired steam engine, the blast
furnace, the power loom, and the railroad, transformed the economies
of Europe and North America.

In the meantime, agriculture was shifting from subsistence farming
to market production to feed the growing populations of the cities, and
new agricultural technologies were reducing the demand for farm labor. In combination, the pull of new opportunities in manufacturing
and the decline of employment in agriculture (aided by the social

reorganization of agricultural production such as the enclosure movement in England) led to a dramatic shift of population from rural to
urban areas and from subsistence farming to wage employment. In
1850 only 16 percent of the U.S. workforce was employed in manufacturing and construction, while 64 percent worked in agriculture.[2] By
1870 manufacturing and construction employed 23 percent of the labor
force, and by 1920 this figure had risen to 31 percent. In the meantime
the proportion of agricultural workers declined to 58 percent by 1870
and 27 percent by 1920.[3] In the span of seventy years, an economy
dominated by agriculture was transformed into a modern industrial
economy in which a majority of workers were employed in manufacturing, mining, construction, trade, finance, and transportation.

Among the social consequences of industrialization and urbanization
was a decline in birth rates and the demise of the extended, multigener-
ational family. Birth rates declined in part because children were less
valuable economically for urban workers than for farmers, while extended families were harder to maintain as workers became more mo-
bile in search of employment. As the birth rate declined, the population
aged, since each successive generation contained fewer children to replace the aging adults. In addition, because the elderly were less likely
to be living with their children, the population of older adults trying to
scrape by with limited economic resources grew.

The welfare state emerged in the late nineteenth century as a response to the social problems created by the industrial revolution and
its demographic repercussions. The uncertainties of industrial employment and the collapse of the extended family gave rise to the first widespread government social programs: industrial accident insurance, old-
age pensions, unemployment insurance, and health care. By the end of
the nineteenth century, Denmark and Germany had national workers'
compensation (for industrial injuries), pensions, and sickness insurance
programs, and by 1913 Britain, Sweden, and the Netherlands had all of
these programs as well.[4] In most aspects of the welfare state, the United
States lagged behind the more advanced western European nations.
With the exception of a pension program for Northern Civil War veterans, which stretched into the first two decades of the twentieth century, Americans had to wait until the New Deal for government old-age
pensions, and not until the 1960s did broad government-funded health
insurance programs arrive in the United States (and unlike the universal insurance programs established in European countries, America's
government-funded health care remains limited to veterans, the elderly, the disabled, and the poor). Overall, the United States continues
to devote less of its resources to social welfare than do most other

developed countries. According to the Organization for Economic Cooperation and Development, the United States ranks twelfth out of thirteen industrial nations in the percentage of GNP devoted to government social expenditures.[5]

This account of industrialization is not intended to be an indictment; the change from an agricultural to an industrial economy brought not only new problems but many benefits as well—most notably dramatic improvements in standards of housing, nutrition, health, and education. And the life of subsistence farming was often brutal. The point is, rather, that far-reaching changes in the economic bases of society led to new social problems, and that these problems in turn spurred the development of the welfare state.

The American Welfare State in the Late Twentieth Century

The American welfare state, although less developed than those of most western European nations, encompasses a broad array of programs that benefit almost every citizen in some way. These programs include education, housing assistance, social insurance (such as pensions, unemployment insurance, and workers' compensation), health care, public assistance (means-tested cash aid for the poor), and programs for veterans. Together, federal, state, and local governments in the United States spent about $1.4 trillion on social programs in 1993, constituting 65 percent of all government spending.[6]

The major programs of the American welfare state can be divided into three general areas: education, social insurance, and means-tested programs for the poor. Education alone accounts for almost one-fourth of all government social spending (figure 1.1). But education is a unique aspect of the welfare state in two ways. First, unlike most social programs, which are funded primarily at the federal level, education is overwhelmingly paid for by state and local governments; while our national government pays for 75 percent of noneducational social programs, state and local governments pay for almost 95 percent of government educational spending.[7] Second, education differs from most other welfare-state programs in that its benefits go disproportionately to more economically privileged Americans. Funding for primary and secondary education is generally higher in more affluent states and communities, and publicly funded higher education tends to benefit the middle class. As one scholar of welfare-state development points out, public higher education represents a transfer of resources from the parents of the less affluent to the children of the more affluent.[8]

Outside of education, the remaining government social programs can

Figure 1.1   Social Welfare Spending in the United States (all levels of government)

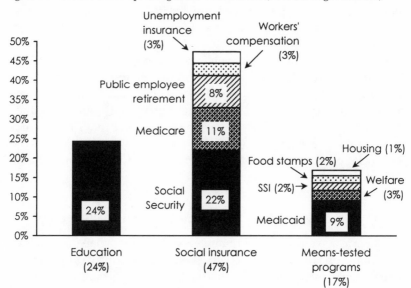

Source: U.S. Bureau of the Census, *Statistical Abstract: 1997*, p. 373.

Note: Programs shown total 89% of all government social spending. Not shown are medical research and hospital support (5%), veterans programs (3%), and miscellaneous other programs (3%). Welfare includes AFDC and General Assistance.

be divided into social insurance programs, which provide benefits to those who have made previous contributions through earmarked taxes, and means-tested programs, which offer benefits only to the poor. The social insurance programs, which include Social Security, Medicare, the public employee retirement program, workers' compensation, and unemployment insurance, account for 47 percent of all social spending.

The welfare state is often associated with aid to the poor. But as figure 1.1 shows, five-sixths of all social spending is for universal programs like old-age pensions and education that also benefit the middle class and the well-off; only 17 percent of government social spending is directed toward means-tested programs that specifically target the poor. Among these means-tested programs, "welfare" has by far the highest public profile. TANF/AFDC offers aid to poor families with dependent children, about 90 percent of which are headed by single mothers,[9] while General Assistance is a program of last resort for poor adults without dependent children. GA is both funded and administered by state governments, and while benefit levels and eligibility criteria vary from state to state, General Assistance typically provides only the most minimal support to its beneficiaries. Together these two programs constitute only 2.6 percent of government social spending and about 1.7 percent of all government spending. Food stamps, a quasi-welfare program that benefits a somewhat larger group of poor Americans, and SSI, which offers assistance to the aged, blind, and disabled poor, each account for just under 2 percent of social spending.

In addition to these cash and near-cash benefit programs, the Earned Income Tax Credit (EITC) also provides cash to poor Americans. Unlike General Assistance, SSI, or TANF, however, the EITC works entirely through the federal income tax structure. Low-income families with children receive a tax "refund" through the EITC that may exceed the total amount of federal income tax that they owe. Even families with earnings too low to owe any federal income tax can receive a "refundable tax credit" through the EITC. (Note that while the EITC can benefit low-income workers who owe no federal income tax, these workers often pay state income tax in addition to Social Security and Medicare payroll taxes.) Because the EITC operates through the tax system and because it often serves simply to reduce taxes owed, it has not been portrayed as a "welfare" program. Whether separating the EITC from more straightforward cash-transfer programs makes sense or not, the fact is that neither the American government nor the American public considers the EITC a form of welfare.

As figure 1.1 reveals, most means-tested social spending does not provide cash assistance or cash-like aid such as food stamps. Rather, most targeted spending for the poor provides in-kind benefits in the form of medical care (Medicaid) or housing assistance. Medicaid alone costs state and federal governments $125 billion a year and accounts for 9 percent of all social spending (and over half of all means-tested social spending), while housing programs in the form of public housing and rental assistance comprise an additional 1.4 percent of social welfare expenditures.

The Growth and Decline of "Welfare"

Of all the programs of the welfare state, "welfare" generates the greatest controversy and receives the most sustained attention from politicians, the press, and the public. Social Security and Medicare occasionally attract interest, especially when new concerns about these programs' continued viability are raised. But over the past thirty years, welfare has never been out of the political spotlight for long. TANF/AFDC and state-run General Assistance are the quintessential "welfare" programs, since they provide cash benefits to the working-age, able-bodied poor.

In dollar terms, however, General Assistance is a minuscule program. Only $3.3 billion was spent on General Assistance in 1994, compared to the $26 billion spent on AFDC.[10] AFDC also served many more people than did General Assistance programs. In 1994, more than 14 million people were receiving AFDC in any given month, while only 1.1 million were receiving General Assistance.[11] Measured in terms of either dollars or numbers of recipients, TANF/AFDC is clearly America's most significant "welfare" program.

The AFDC program (originally called Aid to Dependent Children, or ADC) was an element of Franklin Roosevelt's New Deal. Established during the depression as part of the Social Security Act of 1935, ADC represented the first federal commitment of cash support for poor children, and by 1939 ADC was providing grants to about 700,000 children of single mothers.[12] Although an important improvement over the previously existing state-run mothers' pensions programs, ADC provided limited benefits and spotty coverage; in 1940 the average ADC family received only $32 per month (about $360 in today's dollars) and only one out of every three eligible children was receiving benefits.[13] In the original formulation, states were required to pay for two-thirds of the cost of their ADC programs, with the federal government covering the remaining third. (In contrast, the federal government picked up half the cost of the Social Security Act's program of assistance for the aged and blind.) In addition, states were allowed to set their own eligibility criteria, a freedom that was often used to exclude black mothers and "unworthy" (i.e., divorced or never married) white mothers. Over the next decades, restrictions were eased and the federal government accepted a larger share of the cost.

By the early 1960s the ADC program had expanded considerably from its small beginnings. Benefits slowly grew and the benefit formula was changed to include a grant for the mother as well as the dependent children (accordingly, the program was renamed Aid to Families with Dependent Children, or AFDC, in 1962). In today's dollars, average monthly payments increased from $360 in 1940 to $581 in 1960, a 60 percent rise in real purchasing power.[14] During this period, the number of families on the rolls also grew, from 370,000 families in 1940 to 800,000 in 1960.[15] Note that it was not welfare alone that expanded during this period. Social insurance programs grew even faster. In 1945 only 1.3 million people were receiving Social Security benefits, compared to 14.8 million in 1960.[16]

But the greatest expansion in both public assistance and social insurance was yet to come. The fastest growth in AFDC came between 1965 and 1975. During this period, the proportion of all American families

Figure 1.2   AFDC Enrollment and Average Benefit Payments, 1950–1995

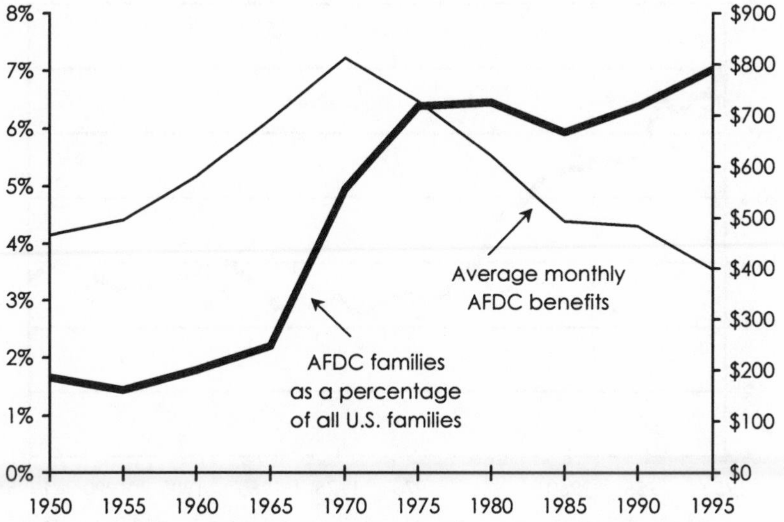

Sources: Statistical Abstract of the United States, various years; U.S. House of Representatives, 1996 Green Book.

Note: Average benefit payments are in constant 1997 dollars.

receiving AFDC tripled, from 2.2 percent in 1965 to 6.4 percent in 1975 (figure 1.2). Naturally, the growing numbers of families on AFDC required growing numbers of state and federal dollars. Adjusted for inflation, spending for AFDC increased from $10 billion in 1965 to $27 billion in 1975.[17] But AFDC spending stopped growing in 1976 and then started to decline. By 1995, inflation-adjusted expenditures for benefit payments had declined by 15 percent from 1975, while the number of families receiving AFDC increased by 37 percent over this period.[18] Compared to 1975, we are now spending less money (in terms of real purchasing power) and spreading it more thinly to cover considerably more poor people. The consequence, of course, is that average AFDC benefits have fallen dramatically. As figure 1.2 shows, after peaking around 1970, the average monthly AFDC benefit had lost over half its purchasing power by 1995. Average annual benefits in 1995 amounted to less than $5,000 per family per year.

Welfare and the War on Poverty

The period of greatest expansion in the AFDC program coincided with the advent of Lyndon Johnson's "War on Poverty." In his first State of the Union address in January 1964, Johnson proclaimed, "This

Figure 1.3   Percentage of Americans in Poverty, 1950–1995

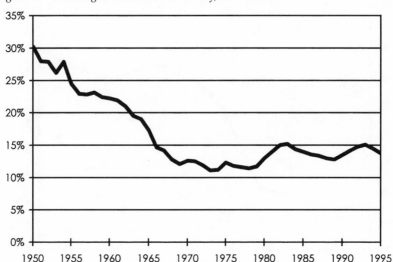

Sources: Murray, *Losing Ground,* p. 245; U.S. Bureau of the Census, *Statistical Abstract: 1997,* p. 475.

administration today, here and now, declares unconditional war on poverty in America." The struggle would not be easy, Johnson said, but "we shall not rest until that war is won." [19] The war on poverty has not been won, of course. But despite the scaling back of AFDC, more progress against poverty has been made than is often supposed. Figure 1.3 shows the percentage of Americans with incomes below the official government poverty line from 1950 to 1995. Due largely to the tremendous economic growth of the postwar years and the expansion of Social Security, the poverty rate fell by nearly half, from 30 percent in 1950 to 17 percent in 1965. It continued to decline, to about 11 percent in the mid-1970s, and then it crept back up. In 1995, 14 percent of Americans were poor. This figure is somewhat better than the 19 percent poverty rate in 1964, when the War on Poverty was announced, but it is not a dramatic improvement.

The apparent lack of progress against poverty over the past thirty years, as indicated in figure 1.3, is due in part to the slowdown in economic growth over the past decades. But the official poverty rate does not fully reflect the conditions of America's least well-off for a number of reasons. First, ironically enough, public assistance is not designed to move people out of poverty. AFDC benefits varied dramatically from state to state (as does TANF), but in no state did AFDC pay enough to lift a family above the poverty line (this has been true as well for TANF). General Assistance programs cover even less of the "poverty deficit," that is, the difference between an individual's or family's income and the income they would need to rise above the poverty line.

Since most antipoverty programs fail to provide sufficient benefits to lift recipients out of poverty, they cannot, by design, lower the official poverty rate. Beneficiaries are less poor than they would be without government cash assistance, but they remain poor nevertheless. Furthermore, only cash benefits are counted as income in determining whether a family falls below the government poverty line. As we saw earlier, most means-tested assistance is not in the form of cash aid. But a family with earnings and/or public assistance payments that total less than the poverty threshold will be considered poor no matter how great the benefits the family receives from food stamps, public housing, Medicaid, or other in-kind antipoverty programs. Thus, however much they may improve the quality of life for their beneficiaries, these programs will not lift them above the poverty line.

To assess the true condition of poorer Americans, we need to consider not only their cash income, but also the value of the other benefits they receive. Christopher Jencks has calculated adjusted poverty rates that reflect these noncash benefits. For example, if the average out-of-pocket medical expenditures for a poor family *not* receiving Medicaid is $500 a year, then Jencks assigns a value of $500 to Medicaid benefits. Using this procedure for all noncash benefits, he finds that the adjusted poverty rates show considerably greater progress against poverty than the official "income only" poverty rates. For example, the official poverty statistics show a decline of 24 percent between 1965 and 1980, while the adjusted poverty rate declined by 44 percent.[20] While the War on Poverty failed to reach its lofty (and perhaps unrealistic) goals, there is little question that the economic condition of America's least well-off is better now than it was thirty years ago. There is also, however, little question that much remains to be done and that new obstacles, such as the globalization of labor markets and the decline of industrial employment, make further progress against poverty even harder to achieve.

Welfare Reform and the End of AFDC

For sixty years, AFDC provided cash assistance to poor families. But President Clinton and the 104th Congress eliminated the AFDC program in 1996, replacing it with Temporary Assistance for Needy Families (TANF). Although Clinton had come into office promising to "end welfare as we know it," his priorities lay elsewhere. But Clinton's hand was forced when the Republicans gained control of Congress in the 1994 midterm election. Facing his own reelection campaign in 1996, Clinton signed into law the most sweeping welfare reforms since the establishment of ADC in the 1930s. The most important aspects of the 1996 welfare act (which is discussed at greater length in chapter 8) are the introduction of time limits on welfare receipt, the imposition of work requirements on welfare recipients, and the grant of substantial freedom to states in administration of the program. States may impose their own restrictions on welfare receipt and may shift spending from cash assistance to other forms of support such as child care for welfare recipients entering training programs or for former welfare recipients who have taken jobs.

In the twelve months following passage of the 1996 welfare reforms, welfare caseloads fell by 12 percent.[21] This decline in the number of people receiving welfare was trumpeted as evidence of the success of welfare reform, but it appears that large numbers of former recipients have been unable to find regular paid employment after leaving welfare.[22] Furthermore, this period was characterized by an extremely strong economy and the lowest levels of unemployment in many decades.[23] We would therefore have expected some decline in welfare use as a consequence of economic conditions alone, and former welfare recipients' difficulty in finding work is all the more worrisome given the favorable economic climate. Many states are still in the process of reshaping their welfare systems in response to the new opportunities and incentives of the 1996 welfare act, and no doubt they will continue to do so for some time, especially if an economic downturn increases the need for support among those least able to fend for themselves. In short, a clear evaluation of the impact of the 1996 welfare reforms will not be possible until we can assess the performance of the reformulated state welfare policies under the more challenging conditions of economic adversity.

The American Welfare State in Comparative Perspective

Cross-national studies of welfare-state development typically identify the United States as a "reluctant welfare state" or a "welfare state laggard." Compared with other affluent industrial nations, the United States does indeed devote less of its resources to government social spending. Among the world's developed nations, only Japan spends less of its gross national product on social programs, and the Scandinavian countries, which tend to be the biggest welfare-state spenders,

Figure 1.4   Government Social Spending as a Percentage of GNP

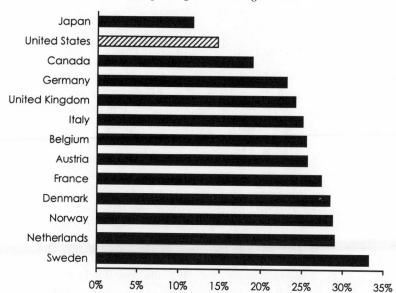

Source: Organization for Economic Cooperation and Development, *New Orientations in Social Policy,* pp. 59–60.

devote twice as much of their GNP to government social programs as does the United States (figure 1.4).

The United States not only spends a smaller portion of its assets on social programs than most other developed nations, it also lacks many of the benefits found elsewhere. Most conspicuously, the United States lacks government-supported universal health care, a benefit taken for granted by the citizens of virtually every other affluent democracy. Government programs for families and children are also less developed in America. For example, virtually every European welfare state (except the United Kingdom) provides subsidized child care for preschool children in poor families, while such subsidies remain extremely limited in the United States.[24] Paid maternity benefits are also common in Europe but absent in the United States. Mothers get at least three months of government benefits at the same rate as their previous salary in Belgium, Germany, Greece, France, Portugal, Holland, and Luxembourg, while Swedish mothers (or fathers) receive twelve months of benefits at 90 percent of their previous earnings.[25] Perhaps most importantly, social programs in the United States are less effective at raising people out of poverty than are programs in other developed countries. For example, one study found that child poverty in the United States was only reduced from 22.3 percent to 20.4 percent as a consequence of government programs.[26]

Public Opinion and Public Policy

Most efforts to account for our comparatively underdeveloped welfare state focus on political structure. Some scholars point to the importance of labor-based political parties in the development of the European welfare states and the lack of such a party in the United States.[27] A related literature focuses on the importance of strong industrial labor unions, which America also lacks.[28] A third school identifies state structure as a key factor in explaining different patterns of welfare-state development.[29] From this perspective the dispersed political power of the American federal system and the resulting weakness of our national bureaucracies help to explain why the welfare state did not grow as quickly or develop as completely in America as it did in more centralized European states.

But political structures are not the only differences between countries that might be relevant to the development of the welfare state. Nations also differ in the values or ideologies held by their citizens. This fourth perspective has been labeled the "cultural" or "national values" approach to the cross-national study of the welfare state, and analyses using this approach have often focused on the prominence of liberal individualism in American political culture. Following in the tradition of Louis Hartz, these scholars view American culture as dominated by the nineteenth-century liberalism rooted in the thinking of Thomas Hobbes and John Locke. Americans, from this point of view, distrust government and value individual rights and private property above other social goods.[30]

While few contest that social and political structures influence government policy, the importance of public attitudes is less widely accepted. However, evidence does support the contention that public attitudes shape government policy in important ways.[31] An influential study by Benjamin Page and Robert Shapiro found that over a forty-five-year period, changes in public opinion often preceded changes in government policy across a range of substantive issues.[32] Page and Shapiro compared the direction of changes in responses to public opinion surveys between two points in time with changes (or lack of changes) in public policy during a period beginning with first survey and ending one year after the second survey. They found that, when policy changed during the period under examination, it changed in the same direction

as public opinion 66 percent of the time. Moreover, when public attitudes changed by 20 percentage points or more on a particular issue,
government policy changed in the same direction over 90 percent of the
time. (The authors considered the possibility that changes in government policy explain changes in public attitudes rather than the other
way around but concluded that this is a less important or less frequent
phenomenon than the influence of public opinion on policy.)

Another approach to ascertaining whether public attitudes shape
government policy looks not over time but across states, examining
how attitudes vary from place to place. One study gathered data from
over 66,000 respondents from forty-seven U.S. states.[33] The authors constructed a "liberaiism" score for each state, based on its residents' responses when asked whether they considered themselves liberal, moderate, or conservative. After taking into account state differences in
income, education, and level of urbanization, they found that states
with more liberal citizens tended to have more liberal government policies. This relationship was observed across a wide range of issues,
including educational expenditures, criminal justice policy, tax policy,
and state ratification of the federal Equal Rights Amendment. Most
important for our purposes, they also found that more liberal states had
more generous eligibility levels for AFDC and Medicaid, and higher
average benefits levels in these programs, than did states with more
conservative residents.

If public opinion influences government policy, we might expect to
find that Americans are less enthusiastic supporters of the welfare state
than are the citizens of countries that devote more of their resources to
social programs. Indeed, compared with western Europeans, Americans express far more limited support for government responsibility for
social welfare. In one survey, for example, only 34 percent of Americans
said it is an "essential responsibility" of the government to see to it that
everyone who wants a job can have one, compared with 55 percent of
Britons, 60 percent of Germans, and 79 percent of Italians (table 1.1).
Similarly, 42 percent of Americans said that it is an essential government responsibility to provide good medical care, compared with
63 percent of Germans, 74 percent of Britons, and 79 percent of Italians. Americans were also the least likely to view looking after old
people and providing adequate housing as essential government responsibilities, in comparison with the citizens of these other countries.
(Austrians, Swedes, Finns, and Netherlanders were asked the same
questions. On all four questions, Americans were the least supportive
of government responsibility of all eight countries.)[34]

Table 1.1 Attitudes toward Government Responsibility in the United States, Germany, Italy, and Britain

	U.S.	Germany	Italy	Britain
How much responsibility does the government have for . . .				
Seeing to it that everyone who wants a job can have one?				
Essential responsibility	34%	60%	79%	55%
Important responsibility	37	34	15	31
Some responsibility	24	6	5	13
No responsibility	4	1	1	2
Providing good medical care?				
Essential responsibility	42	63	79	74
Important responsibility	36	32	16	21
Some responsibility	20	6	4	5
No responsibility	3	0	1	0
Looking after old people?				
Essential responsibility	41	51	69	58
Important responsibility	40	42	23	31
Some responsibility	18	6	8	11
No responsibility	1	1	1	1
Providing adequate housing?				
Essential responsibility	25	39	69	61
Important responsibility	38	46	22	27
Some responsibility	32	14	7	12
No responsibility	5	1	1	1

Source: Smith, "The Welfare State in Cross-National Perspective," p. 417.

Notes: Question wording—"Now we would like to know how you feel about some of the particular issues and problems that people often talk about these days. . . . Tell me how much responsibility you think the government has for dealing with the problem. Is it something that you feel is (1) essential for government to do, (2) something that government has an important responsibility to do, (3) some responsibility to do, or (4) no responsibility at all to do?" Because of rounding, sums of percentages may not equal 100. Results exclude respondents saying "don't know" or providing no answer.

These data appear to support the popular impression that Americans are uniquely hostile toward, or at least uniquely unsupportive of, government responsibility for social welfare. An ethos of individual self-reliance does run strong in our political culture, and we are clearly less eager to assign government the responsibility for our well-being than are citizens of other economically developed countries. Yet a closer look at table 1.1 shows that even in the United States, notions of self-responsibility may not run so deep as to preclude support for the welfare state. While Americans do not express the same level of support for government responsibility that Europeans do, they nevertheless believe that government has an important role in these areas. For example, fully 71 percent of Americans think that it is either an "essential" or an "important" responsibility of government to see to it that everyone who wants a job has one. While this is lower than the percentage of Europeans who express this opinion, it still indicates very strong support for government social responsibility. Similarly, 78 percent of Americans think that providing good medical care is an "essential" or "important" government responsibility, while 81 percent think the government should look after old people, and 63 percent think the government should provide adequate housing.

Public Support for Social Spending in the United States

Rather than a confirmation of American individualism, the results shown in table 1.1 are better understood as an indication of the surprisingly strong support for government social responsibility that exists in this land of "rugged individualism." In fact, Americans not only support most of the welfare-state programs that currently exist, but they also think that in most areas the government is not doing enough to help its citizens.

Table 1.2 shows Americans' preferences for increasing or decreasing spending in a variety of social welfare domains.[35] In almost every area, majorities believe that spending should be increased, while only small numbers of Americans think spending should be decreased from current levels. Strong support for the welfare state is clearly evident with regard to the elderly, health care, education, and child care. In none of these areas does more than 13 percent of the public express a desire to cut back from current levels of spending, and in most cases between half and three-quarters of Americans think spending should be increased. Experts on public opinion have long recognized Americans' broad support for government social programs.[36] Yet the perception remains widespread that the American welfare state lacks popular appeal. As Fay Cook and Edith Barrett note, it is widely—but erroneously—believed that the American welfare state suffers from a "legitimacy deficit" among the American people.[37]

The public's desire to spend more for the elderly, health care, education, and child care is at variance with the image of Americans as opponents of the welfare state. But spending on these programs represents government efforts that benefit large numbers of Americans from all social classes. Perhaps the current or expected personal benefits from these programs help to overcome the public's general inclination

Table 1.2 Spending Preferences for Various Social Welfare Programs

	Cut Spending	Increase Spending	Difference
The elderly			
Care for the elderly[a]	1%	75%	+74%
Social Security[b]	7	47	+40
Senior citizens[c]	10	51	+41
Health care			
Health[d]	13	65	+52
Improving and protecting the nation's health[d]	9	67	+58
Medicare[e]	4	63	+59
Medicaid[e]	9	49	+40
Education			
Education[d]	5	73	+68
Improving the nation's education system[d]	6	72	+66
Public school systems[b]	6	65	+59
Financial aid for college students[b]	13	42	+29
Child care			
Child care[f]	10	56	+46
Child care for poor children[g]	6	61	+55
The poor			
Fighting poverty[c]	11	71	+60
Poor people[h]	7	55	+48
Assistance to the poor[d]	15	59	+44
Solving the problem of the homeless[h]	6	73	+67
The unemployed			
Retraining programs for displaced workers[b]	10	52	+42
Unemployment insurance[e]	18	24	+ 6
Unemployed people[c]	36	22	−14
Food aid			
Food programs for low income families[i]	9	56	+47
Food stamps[j]	43	9	−34
Welfare			
Welfare[d]	63	14	−49
People on welfare[c]	71	10	−61

Notes: All questions in this table ask whether "government spending" or "federal government spending" for the stated program should be increased, decreased, or kept the same, or whether current spending is too high, too low, or about right. Results are based on national telephone surveys and exclude respondents saying "don't know" or providing no answer.

[a] National Election Study, 1988.
[b] Times Mirror poll, December 1, 1994.
[c] NBC/*Wall Street Journal* poll, April 21, 1995.
[d] General Social Survey, 1994.
[e] ABC/*Washington Post* poll, February 1986.
[f] National Election Study, 1994.
[g] General Social Survey, 1990.
[h] National Election Study, 1992.
[i] Gallup poll, May 10, 1991.
[j] *Time*/CNN poll, December 7, 1994.

against government social spending. If so, we might expect support to evaporate when we turn from these universal components of the welfare state to government efforts to help the poor. As table 1.2 demonstrates, however, this does not seem to be the case. When asked about spending for the poor, the public again expresses a desire for more, not less, government activity. Over 70 percent of Americans say we are spending too little on "fighting poverty," while a similar number think spending for the homeless needs to be increased. Smaller numbers— but still majorities—think we are spending too little on "poor people," on "assistance to the poor," and on "child care for poor children." And as was true for education, health care, child care, and the elderly, very few Americans believe spending for the poor should be reduced from current levels.

If we limited our attention to these five areas of social welfare, we might well come to view the American public as strong supporters of the welfare state, demanding more activity and higher levels of spending from their government. This impression is not inaccurate, but it is incomplete. As table 1.2 shows, public attitudes toward spending for the unemployed and for food aid are more ambivalent, while attitudes toward spending for welfare are strongly negative. With regard to unemployment, a majority want spending increased for retraining programs for displaced workers, but the public is divided on whether spending should be increased or decreased for unemployment insurance. Spending for "unemployed people" is the least favored of these three options, but this is an ambiguous referent that could include not only popular efforts like retraining programs, but also such broadly unpopular programs as food stamps and welfare (which, after all, go largely, although not exclusively, to the unemployed).[38]

As table 1.2 shows, food stamps, and even more so welfare, stand out as conspicuous exceptions to the high levels of public support for most welfare-state programs. Only 9 percent of Americans think spending for food stamps should be increased, while 43 percent think spending should be cut. And welfare is even more unpopular than food stamps; 60 percent to 70 percent of those polled think we are spending too much for welfare (or for "people on welfare"), and most of the rest prefer to keep welfare spending where it is rather than increase it.

Why Is Welfare Different?

As tables 1.1 and 1.2 illustrate, Americans are of two minds when it comes to the welfare state. In most areas, they think government has important responsibilities to provide social benefits to its citizens: not only do most Americans support most aspects of government social provision, they also think spending should be increased. But welfare, and to a lesser extent food stamps, are glaring exceptions to this pattern. What explains this sharp contrast between the public's broad support for the welfare state and its emphatic rejection of welfare itself?

A number of suggestions have been made to explain the patterns of public support or opposition to government social programs. Some have argued, for example, that Americans harbor a general ideological opposition to government responsibility but are nonetheless fond of specific existing programs of the welfare state.[39] From this perspective the public is inconsistent, or at least ambivalent, in applying its general principles to specific cases. General questions are thought to evoke ideological responses that are likely to be unsupportive of the welfare state, while questions about specific programs elicit more favorable responses based on practical rather than ideological concerns. Negative responses to "welfare," from this perspective, reflect a general ideological opposition to government responsibility, whereas evaluations of particular programs such as Social Security, Medicare, or Medicaid reflect (generally positive) program-specific perceptions and attitudes.

The idea that the broad individualist orientations of American political culture run counter to the welfare state is sound. But the pattern of responses revealed in table 1.2 is inconsistent with the notion that broad questions elicit more negative reactions than questions about specific existing programs. For example, the broad question about government spending to "care for the elderly" receives even greater support than the specific question about Social Security. Similarly, the broad question about "fighting poverty" elicits a very high level of support, but food stamps, the only clearly defined existing antipoverty program in the table, is quite unpopular with the American public.

The pattern of public support for the welfare state exhibited in table 1.2, therefore, cannot be explained by a tendency to oppose government help in general but support specific existing programs. Four alternative explanations for the exceptional unpopularity of welfare will be explored in chapters 2 and 3: first, that welfare violates Americans' individualist orientations in a way that other social programs do not; second, that self-interest leads middle-class Americans to support universal social programs but oppose means-tested programs that benefit only the poor; third, that opposition to welfare stems from skepticism about the true need of welfare recipients; and finally, that negative attitudes toward blacks underlie white Americans' opposition to welfare.

2

Individualism, Self-Interest, and Opposition to Welfare

A s we saw in chapter 1, Americans distinguish between welfare, which they want to cut, and virtually every other aspect of the welfare state, which they think should be expanded. In this chapter I consider the roles of individualism and self-interest in explaining Americans' dislike of welfare. It is often claimed that Americans' firm belief in individual effort and responsibility accounts for their opposition to welfare. As we will see below, Americans *are* attracted to individualist notions of self-responsibility. But the conviction that individuals *should* support themselves is tempered by the recognition that sometimes they cannot, and in such cases, Americans overwhelmingly believe that government needs to step in. In principle, at least, Americans claim to support a wide range of government assistance programs for the needy, including cash support for working-age adults (shown below in table 2.3). American individualism is not absolute. Instead, it is a "bounded individualism" that does not preclude government help for the less fortunate, even when that help takes the form of welfare.

In principle, then, Americans support welfare; but in practice, as we saw above, they want welfare spending cut. With this contrast in mind, I next consider the possibility that middle-class and well-off Americans want to cut welfare spending because they do not like paying taxes for programs that benefit only the poor. What I find is that well-off Americans *are* more likely to want welfare spending cut, but this desire is not motivated by self-interest; rather, it reflects the different experiences with and perceptions of welfare that characterize Americans of different social classes.

Individualism and Opposition to Welfare

Americans are widely viewed as individualistic opponents of the welfare state. Compared with the more socially minded Europeans, Americans are thought to place a higher value on self-reliance and individual initiative and to recoil from the idea of government responsibility for individuals' well-being. Commentators across the political spectrum have attributed Americans' opposition to welfare to this individualistic orientation.[1] For example, in their popular study of the American welfare state, Theodore Marmor, Jerry Mashaw, and Phillip Harvey write, "[C]ommitment to individual and family autonomy, market allocation of most goods and services, and limited and decentralized governance . . . tell us much about why we have the welfare state arrangements we do and about the probable direction of future developments. These commitments bound the feasible set of policy alternatives."[2]

Individualism refers to a belief in the primary importance of the individual rather than the community, but within this broad outline, many forms of individualism can be distinguished. The term "individualism" was first adopted by opponents of the French Revolution who feared that concern with the rights of individuals would lead to the unraveling of society. In *Reflections on the Revolution in France*, Edmund Burke expressed his apprehension that "the commonwealth itself would, in a few generations, crumble away, be disconnected into the dust and powder of individuality, and at length dispersed to all the winds of heaven."[3] For Burke and others who feared the passing of the old regime, individualism was an unwelcome and foreboding specter. But proponents of the new liberal state, in America and elsewhere, embraced individualism as a corrective to the rigid social hierarchies and ascriptive norms of European society.

In his study of individualism, Steven Lukes identifies a number of philosophical varieties and includes the following among the central components of individualism: belief in the intrinsic value and dignity of individual human beings, belief in the autonomy of individuals from social pressures and norms, belief in the value of privacy and the right of individuals to be left alone to pursue their own ambitions, and belief in the ability of people to develop themselves in their own unique ways.[4] Each of these ideas has a place in American political culture, yet none captures the dominant chord of American individualism, which concerns its economic rather than philosophical implications. In America, according to Lukes, individualism came to refer to "equal individual rights, limited government, *laissez-faire*, natural justice and equal opportunity, and individual freedom."[5]

It was this American individualism of individual rights and limited government that Alexis de Tocqueville described in his classic study, *Democracy in America*. A French aristocrat and civil servant, Tocqueville journeyed to America in the 1830s to study the most democratic and egalitarian society of his time. Although there was much that he admired about American society, Tocqueville also expressed deep concerns about the impact of individualism on Americans' social and political life. He portrayed the Americans of his day as isolated individuals, only weakly connected to any larger political community, and acknowledging responsibility only for themselves:

> Individualism is a calm and considered feeling which disposes each citizen to isolate himself from the mass of his fellows and withdraw into the circle of family and friends; with this little society formed to his taste, he gladly leaves the greater society to look after itself. . . .
> The inhabitants of democracies . . . readily fall back upon themselves and think of themselves in isolation. . . . It is therefore always an effort for such men to tear themselves away from their private affairs and pay attention to those of the community.[6]

The isolation and self-sufficiency that Tocqueville described led, he believed, to the conviction that each individual was responsible for himself or herself alone. "Such folk owe no man anything and hardly expect anything from anybody. They form the habit of thinking of themselves in isolation and imagine that their whole destiny is in their own hands."[7]

While Tocqueville was sympathetic toward the American experiment with democracy, he was also critical of Americans' embrace of individualism, fearing that the exaltation of the individual could lead to the degeneration of society:

> If the citizens continue to shut themselves up more and more narrowly in the little circle of petty domestic interests and keep themselves constantly busy therein, there is a danger that they may in the end become practically out of reach of those great and powerful public emotions which do indeed perturb peoples but which also make them grow and refresh them. . . . The prospect really does frighten me that they may finally become so engrossed in a cowardly love of immediate pleasures that their interest in their own future and in that of their descendants may vanish, and that they will prefer tamely to follow the course of their destiny rather than make a sudden energetic effort necessary to set things right.[8]

Tocqueville's was not the only voice critical of American individualism, but even those who criticized American society often did so in the name of individualism. Ralph Waldo Emerson envisioned an America even more radically individualist than that described by Tocqueville. "The union," Emerson wrote, "is only perfect when all the uniters are isolated. . . . Each man, if he attempts to join himself to others, is on all sides cramped and diminished."[9] The self-sufficiency advocated by the New England Transcendentalists was one alternative American doctrine rooted in individualism. The romantic individualism of Walt Whitman and the antigovernment and antibusiness ideology of the Populists were other oppositional visions of America that reflected the premises and values of individualism.

Americans' long-standing attraction to individualism remains strong. Whatever else they may emphasize, studies of American political culture almost always acknowledge the prominence of individualism in our society.[10] Many explanations have been offered for Americans' individualistic orientation. Some have pointed to the frontier as fostering individualism.[11] Others have offered America's Protestant heritage or the desire of the early republic to compete with Europe as explanations for our concern with individual effort and achievement.[12] And still others have noted that the lack of a feudal past allowed Americans to institute a minimal and decentralized government without fearing the restoration of the *ancien régime*.[13] Whatever the reasons for Americans' attraction to the ethic of individual effort and responsibility, these values are still expressed clearly in Americans' political thinking. Surveys of public attitudes show that Americans are firmly committed to the belief that people are responsible for their own well-being.

When asked to choose between individual responsibility and government aid, Americans invariably respond that individuals should be responsible for themselves. As table 2.1 shows, the American public almost unanimously believe that "people should take advantage of every opportunity to improve themselves rather than expect help from the government" (96 percent of Americans agree with this sentiment). And when asked whether "government is responsible for the well-being of all its citizens and has an obligation to take care of them" or "people are responsible for their own well-being and have an obligation to take care of themselves," 74 percent of Americans place the responsibility on individuals rather than government. In fact, Americans are so committed to the doctrine of individual effort and responsibility that four out of five believe that "trying to get ahead on one's own efforts" is "extremely" or "very" important "in making someone a true American."

From the early days of the republic, individualism has been a cen-

Table 2.1 Beliefs about Individual Responsibility

	Percentage Agree
People should take advantage of every opportunity to improve themselves rather than expect help from the government.[a]	96
How important do you think trying to get ahead on one's own efforts is in making someone a true American?	
Extremely important	35
Very important	45
Somewhat important	14
Not at all important[b]	5
Government is responsible for the well-being of all its citizens and has an obligation to take care of them.	26
or	
People are responsible for their own well-being and have an obligation to take care of themselves.[c]	74
The government should just let each person get ahead on their own.	47
or	
The government should see to it that every person has a job and a good standard of living.	29
or	
Both equally.[b]	25

Notes: Results are based on national telephone surveys and exclude respondents saying "don't know" or providing no answer.

[a] National Election Study pilot survey, 1989.

[b] National Election Study preelection survey, 1992.

[c] *Los Angeles Times* poll, April 1985.

tral element of American political culture. Our popular literature is full of self-made men who ask little of their society (and often give little in return). From the industrial entrepreneurs glorified in nineteenth-century magazines to the cowboy heroes of western films and fiction, America has romanticized the individual.[14] Our culture celebrates the virtues of individual achievement and nurtures an individualist orientation in our political life, expressed, at least rhetorically, in the public's mistrust of government and commitment to self-reliance.

As we saw above, most Americans want to cut spending for welfare, and this opposition to welfare contrasts not only with widespread support for education, health care, and aid for the elderly, but also with positive responses to other questions about help for the poor. Perhaps welfare is singled out for censure because it uniquely violates Americans' strong commitment to individualism. To some extent, of course, any government assistance to the poor (or indeed the nonpoor as well) is a violation of individualistic norms. But welfare might be distinguished by the nature or degree to which it conflicts with the individualist orientations of the American public.

This "culture of individualism" explanation for opposition to welfare is consistent with some of the attitudinal patterns we saw in chapter 1. For example, the strong support for spending for the elderly may reflect the fact that this population group is not expected to be working and therefore constitutes an exception to the norm of individualistic self-reliance. And the public's strong support for education spending may reflect the fact that education is the means by which individuals achieve self-sufficiency. Government assistance in this domain can therefore be seen as an "investment in individualism." Health care may also represent an exception to the individualistic norm both because the sick, by virtue of their condition, often cannot fulfill the individualistic expectation of self-support and because most Americans recognize that without health insurance, few people with substantial health problems would have the means to pay for their care. In this case too, government spending may represent an "investment" in individuals that (it is hoped) enables them once again to fulfill the desired norm of self-sufficiency.

Is welfare then the object of opprobrium because it violates the individualistic ethos without any promise of furthering self-sufficiency down the road? Or is welfare too thought of as an "investment in individualism"—a transitional program that helps recipients get back on their feet and become self-supporting? Welfare may be just this kind of transitional program for many of those who receive benefits, but the public clearly views welfare more as a "trap" than as an avenue toward self-reliance. Studies of AFDC beneficiaries found that about 40 percent of new AFDC recipients were off the welfare rolls within one year and about 60 percent were off within two years of the time they began receiving welfare.[15] Many of these welfare recipients, however, did return to the welfare rolls. When we add up all the time spent on AFDC during the nine years after the birth of a first child, we find that about one-third of women who received AFDC used it for less than two years, another third for three to five years out of the first nine, and the remainder for six years or more. Only about 6 percent of AFDC recipients spent all of these first nine years on welfare.[16]

Whether these figures indicate that welfare is used briefly to return people to self-sufficiency or that welfare is more of a long-term alternative to self-support is hard to say; for some recipients it is one and for some the other. What is clear, however, is that welfare has been viewed by the public as a long-term substitute for economic self-reliance. When a 1995 survey asked whether "most people on welfare are using welfare for a short period of time and will get off it eventually" or "most people on welfare are so dependent on welfare that they will never get off it," only 15 percent said most use welfare for a short time; 79 percent said most welfare recipients will never get off welfare.[17] The extent to which these perceptions will change as a result of the time limits imposed by the 1996 welfare reform legislation remains to be seen. Changes in perceptions will depend, of course, on how time limits are actually implemented at the state level (and especially on how strictly limits are applied and how large a portion of the welfare caseload is exempted).

Are Americans, then, principled opponents of welfare? Do they reject it because, unlike education, health care, or aid for the elderly, giving money to working-age poor people violates the norm of individual responsibility? Individualism does have important implications for Americans' welfare views, but it does not appear that this commitment is strong enough to preclude support for welfare. As we saw in chapter 1, Americans are not enthusiastic about *welfare spending*, but it appears that this lack of enthusiasm is not based on an individualist objection to the *principle* of welfare. That is, despite their desire to cut welfare spending, most Americans believe that the government must help the poor and that this help should include cash assistance.

Table 2.2 shows that between 80 and 90 percent of Americans support government help for the poor, believe that the government must be involved in combating poverty, and favor the government helping people who are unable to support themselves, and about 70 percent say the government has a responsibility to take care of the poor and to guarantee every citizen enough to eat and a place to sleep. But while Americans are clearly committed to government efforts to aid the poor, such aid can take many forms. Giving money or other benefits directly to poor people is not the most favored method of dealing with poverty. When asked whether it is better to spend money trying to eliminate the causes of poverty or give money to poor people so they can get on their feet, 73 percent of respondents prefer to address the causes of poverty.[18] But eliminating the causes of poverty is a long-term project, and most Americans are not optimistic about our ability to accomplish this goal. Seventy-five percent of Americans believe that, even if the government were willing to spend whatever is necessary to eliminate poverty in the

Table 2.2 Principled Support for Government Help for the Poor

	Percentage Agree
Favor the government helping people who are unable to support themselves.[a]	88
There must be substantial government involvement to handle the problem of poverty. *or* The problem of poverty can be handled mainly by volunteer efforts.[b]	85 15
In principle, favor federal government actions on behalf of the poor.[b]	80
The government has a responsibility to take care of the poor.[c]	71
The government should guarantee every citizen enough to eat and a place to sleep.[d]	69
It is the responsibility of the government to take care of people who can't take care of themselves.[e]	66

Note: Results are based on national telephone surveys and exclude respondents saying "don't know" or providing no answer.

[a] *Los Angeles Times* poll, February 1985.

[b] *Los Angeles Times* poll, April 1985.

[c] CNN poll, March 1992.

[d] Times Mirror poll, July 1994.

[e] CBS/*New York Times* poll, August 1996.

United States, "the government doesn't know enough about how to do that," and 92 percent believe that poverty will always be a major problem for our society.[19]

While eliminating the causes of poverty is clearly the most attractive solution, what should be done for those who are unable to escape poverty now? As table 2.3 shows, in principle at least, most Americans do support monetary assistance directly to poor people. Between 70 and 80 percent of respondents agree that the government should help people who cannot support themselves by giving them enough money to meet their minimum needs. And when asked to choose among four alternative models of welfare, 77 percent of Americans expressed a preference for a "tax-supported relief program for all those who have a clear need for assistance."[20]

But if Americans support even monetary aid directly to poor people, then what lies behind their desire to cut welfare spending? Is this

Table 2.3 Principled Support for Welfare

	Percentage Agree
When people can't support themselves, the government should help by giving them enough money to meet their basic needs.[a]	78
The government has a basic responsibility to help families who have no means of support by giving them enough money to meet their minimum needs.[b]	71
Welfare, including aid to the aged, the blind, and the disabled, should be supported by voluntary private contributions, not by government funds or taxes.	5
or	
Welfare should be a tax-supported relief program, but only for those who, because of age or disability, cannot fend for themselves. It should be limited to as few recipients as possible and it should provide only bare necessities.	17
or	
Welfare should be a tax-supported relief program for all those who have a clear need for assistance. Qualifications should be fairly stringent. However, a decent level of living should be provided for those who do qualify.	55
or	
Welfare programs should be tax-supported, and they should provide *all* who need it a decent level of living and enough supporting services to allow them to achieve their full potentials.[c]	22

Note: Results are based on national telephone surveys and exclude respondents saying "don't know" or providing no answer.

[a] National Race and Politics Study, February–November 1991.

[b] National Election Study pilot survey, 1989.

[c] Research Institute in Social Welfare survey, October 1972–March 1973.

abstract support only a superficial nod toward aiding the poor, which dissolves once the prospect of paying for these benefits is raised? Does a self-interested desire to lower taxes dominate the more generous inclination to support government help for the needy?

Self-Interest and Opposition to Welfare

As a motive for political behavior, self-interest has always held a central place in liberal democratic theory. To theorists like Hobbes and Locke, the very existence of government results from the impossibility of reconciling competing interests in the hypothesized "state of nature." So too did the framers of our own government view *homo politicus* as motivated by the pursuit of self-interest. In *The Federalist Papers*, Alexander Hamilton admonishes his readers to remember that "men are ambitious, vindictive, and rapacious," and instructs them that government is necessary only "[b]ecause the passions of men will not conform to the dictates of reason and justice without constraint."[21]

The concern of the founders, however, was not primarily with the "irrational" passions of men, but with the conflicts that necessarily arise from their rational pursuit of self-interest. They saw the central task of government as the regulation of these competing interests:

> Those who hold and those who are without property have ever formed distinct interests in society. Those who are creditors, and those who are debtors, fall under a like discrimination. A landed interest, a manufacturing interest, a mercantile interest, a moneyed interest, with many lesser interests, grow up of necessity in civilized nations, and divide them into different classes, actuated by different sentiments and views. The regulation of these various and interfering interests forms the principal task of modern legislation. . . .[22]

The view that political actors are driven by the desire to maximize their own individual interests remains the dominant understanding today. As one popular textbook puts it (echoing Harold Lasswell's famous book title), "Politics is deciding 'who gets what, when, and how.' It is an activity by which people try to get more of whatever there is to get— money, prestige, jobs, respect, sex, even power itself."[23]

However true the self-interest model of political behavior may be for political elites, there is good reason to doubt that calculations of individual self-interest underlie the political preferences of the mass public. On the contrary, the empirical evidence suggests that for most people, most of the time, politics is not about the pursuit of individual gain, and that policy preferences reflect considerations of self-interest only weakly, if at all. In their review of survey-based studies of self-interest effects, Jack Citrin and Donald Philip Green conclude that calculations of personal costs and benefits play only a limited role in shaping political preferences among members of the American public.[24] Citrin and Green find, for example, that support for government-funded health insurance is just as high among those who already have private health insurance as among those who do not; that whites' attitudes toward school busing are unrelated to whether they have school-age children, reside in a district threatened by a busing plan, or send their children to all-white public schools; and that men and women do not differ significantly in support for "women's issues" such as the Equal Rights Amendment, sex-based affirmative action, or abortion.

Although it appears that most people, most of the time, do not base their political preferences on calculations of individual self-interest, some circumstances and some issues are more conducive to self-interested considerations than others. When the effect of a policy is clear and certain, and when it has the potential to make a significant impact on an individual's well-being, self-interest is likely to play a larger role in shaping political preferences. Thus, support for property tax reduction in the form of California's Proposition 13 was substantially higher among homeowners than among renters, and among homeowners, approval was related to the amount of tax savings that survey respondents anticipated receiving from the passage of the tax-cutting proposition.[25]

Are public attitudes toward welfare another exception to the general absence of self-interest effects? Academics, politicians, and journalists alike seem to think so. In their seminal 1960 study of public opinion and voting behavior, the authors of *The American Voter* wrote that "primitive self-interest" alone could best explain variation in Americans' social welfare views,[26] and this opinion is echoed in a spate of more recent studies that also view self-interest as an important explanation for Americans' opposition to welfare.[27]

The self-interest thesis suggests that middle-class taxpayers will tend to oppose means-tested welfare programs that benefit only the poor. This belief takes different forms in the various debates over the politics of the welfare state. For example, those who argue for universal social programs rather than programs targeted specifically at the poor often invoke this presumed middle-class self-interest in claiming a greater political popularity for universal programs. A similar presumption of middle-class self-interest is found in claims that an expanding economy leads to greater public support for welfare, while hard times generate opposition as struggling middle-class families put their own interests ahead of the needs of the worse-off. Finally, surveys show that the middle class and the well-to-do are more likely to oppose welfare than are the poor, and this difference is often attributed to the different economic interests of poor and nonpoor Americans. As we will see, however, each of these claims rests on faulty assumptions or inadequate investigation of the relationship between welfare attitudes and economic self-interest. Contrary to the strongly held beliefs of many political analysts, the evidence indicates that calculations of individual economic self-interest play little role in shaping Americans' welfare policy preferences and cannot account for the public's desire to cut back on welfare spending.

Are Universal Programs More Popular Than Means-Tested Programs?

Strong public support for universal programs such as Social Security and Medicare, combined with opposition to means-tested programs like food stamps and "welfare," has led many observers to conclude that middle-class self-interest explains the differing levels of support for different aspects of the welfare state. Theda Skocpol, for example, argues that "Americans will accept taxes that they perceive as contributions toward public programs in which there is a direct stake for themselves, their families, and their friends, not just 'the poor.' "[28] Skocpol identifies nineteenth-century poor houses, early twentieth-century mothers' pensions, and the Great Society programs of the 1960s as examples of means-tested programs that failed politically. In each case, Skocpol argues, programs that began with high hopes could not sustain their political support and were either starved for funds or abandoned entirely.

In contrast, Skocpol cites Civil War pensions and Social Security as universal programs that sustained strong public support. But as Robert Greenstein points out, an assessment of the popularity of means-tested versus universal social programs must compare otherwise similar programs.[29] Skocpol's universal programs—Civil War pensions and Social Security—both serve the elderly, an especially sympathetic group since they are not expected to work. In contrast, the means-tested programs that Skocpol discusses all serve more "morally ambiguous" clientele. Greenstein compares the fate of similar universal and means-tested programs during the Reagan administrations. He notes, for example, that the universal Social Security program was cut in 1981 and 1983. In contrast, the means-tested program for the elderly, Supplemental Security Income (SSI), was expanded during the early 1980s. Other means-tested programs such as Medicaid and food stamps were cut in 1981 and 1982, but expansions to these programs between 1983 and 1989 left them in better fiscal shape than when Reagan first took office. Greenstein restricts his study to one president's time in office. But since Reagan was particularly hostile to means-tested programs, the durability of these programs under his administration serves to challenge the contention that means-tested programs are more politically vulnerable than universal programs.

Of course many factors influence the political fate of a social program in addition to its popularity with the public, and trying to gauge public support by examining the funding history of a program is a risky business. What do survey data have to say about the willingness of middle-class Americans to pay for programs that benefit only the poor?

Most Americans consider themselves "middle class," and the self-interest thesis would therefore lead us to expect that the public would be more supportive of government help for the middle class than of government help for the poor.[30] The most straightforward test of this thesis fails utterly. When asked to make an explicit choice, most Americans indicate a preference for government efforts on behalf of the poor, not the middle class. For example, when asked whether it is more important for the government to spend money to help poor people or more important for the government to spend money to help middle-income people, 54 percent of respondents sided with poor people and only 19 percent with the middle class (23 percent said both or neither).[31] And contrary to the perception that the public now views government as the agent of redistribution of funds from the embattled middle class to the coddled poor, only 26 percent of Americans agreed that "the government should worry more about the problems of middle class people and less about the problems of poor people," while 69 percent disagreed.[32]

When asked in the abstract to choose between the needs of the poor and their apparent self-interest as members of the middle class, most Americans prefer to see government devote its resources to helping the poor. But if support for government help for the poor and the middle class is not posed as an either/or choice, does the public then reveal a preference for assistance to the middle class? That is, if the question is posed such that expressing a desire for government help for the middle class need not imply a lack of concern for the poor, do most Americans then reveal stronger support for social programs oriented toward the middle class? Once again, the self-interest thesis comes up short. In one question, for example, 78 percent of respondents agreed that "government should play an active role in improving health care, housing and education for middle income families."[33] High support, to be sure, but an even higher 81 percent agreed that "government should play an active role in improving health care, housing and education for low income families."

When asked about general priorities for government spending or government efforts to improve the lives of Americans, the public displays no evidence of a self-interested preference for help for the middle class. The same pattern is repeated when Americans are asked about specific existing programs that are targeted at the poor or that provide benefits to the middle class as well. For example, Social Security and SSI both provide cash support for the elderly and the disabled, but Social Security is a universal program while only the poor are eligible for SSI. Contrary to the self-interest hypothesis, SSI receives just as strong support as Social Security. In one survey respondents were asked whether spending should be increased or decreased for Social Security and for SSI (which was described as "income assistance given to low-income elderly, blind, or disabled people"). In each case 57 percent of respondents said spending should be increased and only 3 percent said spending should be decreased.[34] The high level of support for SSI is especially impressive because, unlike Social Security, SSI is not a contributory program and therefore does not carry the implication that recipients have earned their benefits.

Another set of parallel programs consists of Medicare, available to all Americans eligible for Social Security, and Medicaid, which provides medical benefits only to the poor. Surveys show that Medicare receives somewhat more support from the public, but Medicaid nonetheless garners strong public support even among middle-class respondents, few of whom would expect to benefit from the program themselves.[35] In one recent survey, respondents were asked whether they favored or opposed cutbacks in various programs in order to help balance the federal budget. To ensure that respondents understood the difference between Medicare and Medicaid, the survey described Medicare as "the health insurance program for the elderly," and Medicaid as "the government health insurance program for the poor." Eighty-eight percent opposed cutbacks in the non means-tested Medicare program, while 73 percent opposed cuts in Medicaid.[36]

The higher levels of support for Medicare could be due to the perceived self-interest of middle-class respondents. On the other hand, only 20 percent of the respondents to this survey support cuts in Medicaid—a program from which few of them will receive any direct benefit—even when proposed cuts are cast as an effort to balance the federal budget. Furthermore, there are other differences between the two programs that might help to explain the higher level of support for Medicare. First, like Social Security, eligibility for Medicare is determined by previous contributions through a payroll tax. Thus Medicare benefits may be perceived as earned in a way that Medicaid benefits are not. Second, Medicare's primary beneficiaries are the elderly, a particularly sympathetic group, while Medicaid is open to poor people of all ages. The greater support for Medicare, then may be due (in part, at least) not to middle-class self-interest but to these other differences between the two programs.

We also see from the same survey that public support differs greatly for the two means-tested programs, food stamps and Medicaid. Although both were clearly described to respondents as programs for the poor, a slim plurality supported cutbacks in the food stamp program (48 percent supported cutbacks, 45 percent opposed them), while the public overwhelmingly opposed cutbacks in Medicaid. Clearly then, the self-interest of middle-class taxpayers is not a compelling explanation for the opposition to food stamps evident in this survey. After all, these same taxpayers appear happy to pay for the means-tested Medicaid program from which they would no more expect to benefit. With regard to both general questions about government help for the middle class and the poor, and specific questions about Social Security versus SSI, and Medicare versus Medicaid, we find at most a small deficit in support for means-tested programs compared to similar universal programs. There is, thus, little evidence to support an account of welfare politics that rests on the perceived economic self-interest of the middle class.

Does Support for Welfare Decline during Hard Times?

It is widely presumed that hard times strain the public's generosity of spirit for their fellow citizens. Most people, after all, place their own family's welfare above that of strangers. When the economy is growing, it is believed, many citizens are willing to share some of their economic gains with those less fortunate than themselves. But when times turn bad, these same citizens are thought to adopt a more Darwinian orientation: their generosity toward the poor is replaced by concern with the well-being of their own families, and their willingness to pay taxes to provide welfare for the poor dissipates. Lester Thurow, for example, writes, "The middle class is altruistic but not willing to sacrifice. In periods of great economic progress when their incomes are rising rapidly, they are willing to share some of their income and jobs with those less fortunately situated than themselves, but . . . in a period of falling real incomes, the middle class wants back the income that they have been devoting to social welfare spending . . . ."[37]

This theory of economic adversity is often cast in terms of the economic downturn of the mid-1970s. Following the oil shock of 1973, the American economy took a sharp turn for the worse. Both unemployment and inflation increased and family incomes stagnated. After growing at an annual rate of about 3 percent during the 1960s, per capita economic output increased at a rate of only 1.3 percent during the first half of the 1970s.[38] Around the same time, government spending on welfare, which had been growing quickly throughout the 1960s, leveled off. After tripling between 1965 and 1975, AFDC spending (adjusted for inflation) peaked in 1976 and has been declining since.[39] Many assume that these events are related and that changing public attitudes provide the link. Michael Katz, for example, the distinguished historian of the American welfare state, writes, "The energy crisis of 1973 ushered in an era of stagflation in which public psychology shifted away from its relatively relaxed attitudes toward the expansion of social welfare. Increasingly worried about downward mobility and their children's future, many Americans returned to an older psychology of scarcity. As they examined the sources of their distress, looking both for villains and ways to cut public spending, ordinary Americans and their elected representatives focused on welfare and its beneficiaries. . . ."[40] While often applied to the economic downturn of the 1970s, the same logic applies to any period of economic decline. Referring to the early 1980s, William Julius Wilson writes, "As the economic situation worsened, Ronald Reagan was able to convince many working- and middle-class Americans that the decline in their living standards was attributable to expensive and wasteful programs for the poor. . . ."[41]

Do economic troubles really lead the public to support cutbacks in spending for the poor? Consistent measures of public preferences toward welfare spending go back to 1972, so we can assess both the claim that the economic problems of the mid-1970s led to greater public opposition to welfare spending and the more general claim that "hard times lead to hard hearts." Figure 2.1 shows annual change in per capita gross domestic product and public preferences for increasing or decreasing welfare spending. The relationship between these two trends is striking in two ways. First, except for the mid- to late 1980s, there is a remarkably strong and consistent relationship between economic conditions and public attitudes.[42] And second, this relationship is exactly the opposite of the one so widely believed to exist.

When the economy soured between 1973 and 1974, the public became *less*—not *more*—opposed to welfare spending, and when the economy improved briefly in the late 1970s, public opposition to welfare spending increased. Similarly, the economic slide between 1978 and 1982 was accompanied (with some delay) by decreasing opposition to welfare spending, while the improving economy of the early 1990s saw a return

Figure 2.1 National Economic Conditions and Opposition to Welfare Spending, 1972–1994

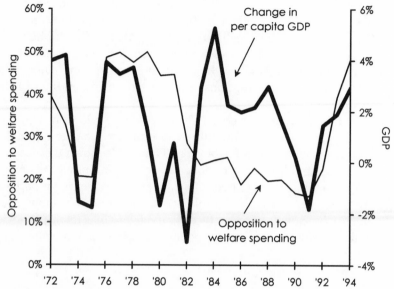

Sources: Welfare spending data for 1972, 1979, 1981 and 1984 from Roper polls of 10/71, 12/78, 12/80 and 12/83; for 1992, CBS/*New York Times* poll of 5/92; for all other years, General Social Survey (February–April of each year). GDP data for 1972–1992 from U.S. Bureau of the Census, *Statistical Abstract: 1993*, p. 445; for 1993, Census Gopher (gopher.census.gov or http://www.census.gov); for 1994, Bureau of Economic Analysis, personal communication.

Notes: Question wording for opposition to welfare spending—"We are faced with many problems in this country, none of which can be solved easily or inexpensively. I'm going to name some of these problems, and for each one I'd like you to tell me whether you think we're spending too much money on it, too little money, or about the right amount. . . . Welfare." Chart shows for each year the percentage saying "too much" minus the percentage saying "too little." For GDP—Annual change in real per capita gross domestic product.

to more conservative views on welfare spending. Far from displaying a self-interested stinginess, the American public clearly responds to periods of national economic difficulties with more generous attitudes toward welfare.

Only one period in the past twenty-five years does not fit this pattern. Between 1982 and 1988 the economy grew strongly, averaging almost 3 percent annual growth.[43] But as figure 2.1 shows, public attitudes toward welfare spending remained unexpectedly liberal during this period, failing to respond to the improved economic performance. One possibility that would explain both the exception of the mid-1980s and the general relationship between the nation's economy and the public's attitudes toward welfare is that opposition to welfare spending is rooted less in economic self-interest than in perceptions that welfare recipients are not really trying to get ahead. The public's tendency to prefer higher levels of welfare spending in economic slowdowns and lower levels when the economy is prospering could be a response to changing perceptions of how needy or deserving of help poor people are.

To test this alternative theory (which we will explore in depth in chapter 3) we can examine the impact of economic change on public views about responsibility for poverty. Figure 2.2 shows the public's responses to the following question: "In your opinion, what is more often to blame if people are poor—lack of effort on their own part, or circumstances beyond their control?" As the figure shows, public beliefs about the causes of poverty do vary over time in response to economic conditions. When the economy prospers the public tends to

Figure 2.2   National Economic Conditions and Blame for Poverty, 1981–1994

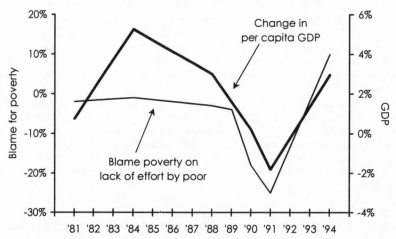

Sources: "Blame for poverty"—CBS/*New York Times* polls of 3/82, 12/90, 12/94; Gallup polls of 12/84, 7/88, 8/89; *Los Angeles Times* poll of 1/92. GDP data for 1981–1991, U.S. Bureau of the Census, *Statistical Abstract: 1993*, p. 445; for 1994, Bureau of Economic Analysis, personal communication.

Notes: Question wording for "Blame for poverty"—"In your opinion, which is more to blame if people are poor—lack of effort on their own part, or circumstances beyond their control?" Chart shows for each year the percentage saying "lack of effort" minus the percentage saying "circumstances." "GDP" axis shows annual change in real per capita gross domestic product.

blame the poor for not trying hard enough; when the economy stalls, poverty is more likely to be attributed to circumstances beyond the control of the poor. In fact, changes in responses to this survey question almost perfectly track changes in the economy, with the exception again of the mid-1980s, when public attitudes were less conservative than the strong economy would have led us to expect.

The pattern across both of these measures of welfare attitudes is consistent. Far from hardening hearts, bad times lead the public to express greater support for welfare spending and a stronger belief that poverty is due to circumstance beyond the control of the poor. This pattern is consistent with the notion that public attitudes toward welfare are driven by perceptions of need or deservingness, not the economic self-interest of middle-class taxpayers. Also consistent across these two measures, however, is the exception of the mid-1980s when public attitudes were more sympathetic toward the poor than measures of economic performance would predict. But economically, the mid-1980s were characterized both by dramatic improvements in overall economic growth (following the recession of 1982) and by increasing inequality.[44] As a consequence, the prosperity that middle- and upper-class Americans experienced during this period was not shared by the poor. If the public was aware that the rising economic tide was not lifting the boats of those at the bottom of the income distribution, then their "unexpectedly" sympathetic attitudes toward the poor would make sense.

Survey data show that the public was indeed well aware that the economic gains of the mid-1980s were not shared equally by all. In a 1984 survey whose results are depicted in figure 2.3, 71 percent of respondents thought the well-to-do were better off financially than they had been a year before, but only 35 percent thought this was true for the middle class, and only 15 percent thought the poor had improved their economic situation (indeed, 43 percent thought the economic situation of the poor had declined). Respondents were also positive about their own economic fortunes and the economic future of the nation as a whole, but most respondents correctly perceived that the poor were being largely excluded from the economic recovery.[45]

As I have suggested, the more generous attitudes toward the poor that Americans express during economic downturns could result from a genuine concern for others. But greater support for welfare during hard times might also arise from a concern for one's own future well-being. National economic difficulties might make even middle-class families fear the possibility of becoming poor themselves, and their

Figure 2.3   Perceived Economic Well-Being of Different Groups, 1984

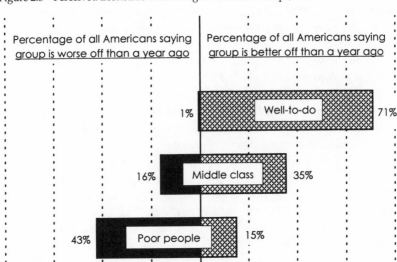

Source: Mutz and Mondak, "Dimensions of Sociotropic Behavior."

Note: Question wording—"Would you say that [the well-to-do/the middle class/poor people] are better off, worse off, or about the same financially compared with a year ago?"

more generous views on welfare spending could be a way of covering their bets. In bad times, even many middle-class families may be living "one paycheck away from poverty"; if they should need government help due to illness, unemployment, or some other unfortunate development, they want it to be there.

Such thinking may play a part in explaining the shift toward more liberal views on welfare spending during periods of poor economic performance. But we have already seen evidence suggesting that the greater public sympathy for the poor evident in these times is not a reflection of self-interested calculations. For it is not only spending preferences that change in response to economic cycles, but perceptions of poor people as well. Yet perhaps these more sympathetic views of the poor combine with a self-interested fear of joining their ranks. If so, then economic downturns should elicit greater support for welfare among those most insecure about their economic future. Even in times of economic insecurity and negative economic growth, Americans with the highest incomes are in little danger of finding themselves in need of welfare. And even if such fears are present for some of these high-earning Americans, they are surely not as widespread or as strongly

Figure 2.4   Opposition to Welfare Spending by Family Income, 1972–1994

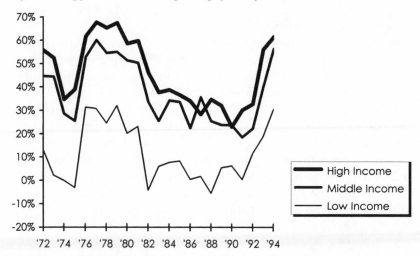

Sources: For 1972, 1979, 1981 and 1984, Roper polls of 10/71, 12/78, 12/80 and 12/83; for 1992, CBS/*New York Times* poll of 5/92; for all other years, General Social Survey (February–April of each year).

Note: Question wording—"We are faced with many problems in this country, none of which can be solved easily or inexpensively. I'm going to name some of these problems, and for each one I'd like you to tell me whether you think we're spending too much money on it, too little money, or about the right amount. . . . Welfare." Chart shows for each income group for each year the percentage saying "too much" minus the percentage saying "too little."

felt as they might be among those of more moderate means. Thus the self-interest hypothesis predicts that those with the lowest incomes should respond most clearly to national economic adversity, while high-income Americans should be less likely to shift their views on welfare spending in a liberal direction.

Figure 2.4 shows the welfare spending preferences of Americans with family incomes in the lowest, middle, and highest third of all incomes for each year. Those with low incomes are consistently the most supportive of welfare—an observation that we will explore in some depth below. But the patterns of change in welfare support are virtually identical for each income group, with opposition to welfare rising in good times and falling in bad. This similar patterning of welfare attitudes over time reflects the broader tendency for policy attitudes to move in parallel among different subgroups of the public. For example, after examining public views on dozens of different issues, Benjamin Page and Robert Shapiro conclude that, "[f]or the most part, the preferences of the many small publics that make up the general public stay in tandem—moving in parallel or standing still together."[46]

Regression analyses confirm that welfare spending preferences among each of the three income groups respond similarly to changes in economic conditions. For the bottom third of the income distribution, each percentage point increase in economic growth leads to a 1.9 percentage point increase in opposition to welfare.[47] In contrast, a percentage point increase in economic growth leads to a 2.0 point increase in opposition to welfare among the middle-income group and a 1.7 point increase among those with the highest incomes. In short, the impact of national economic conditions is nearly as strong among the income group least likely to worry about ever needing welfare as it is among those who are most likely to envision needing welfare themselves some day.

Does Self-Interest Lead to Different Views of Welfare among the Middle Class and the Poor?

We have already seen that middle-class self-interest is not a plausible explanation for differences in public support for different social programs or for changes in support for welfare over time. We now examine the role of self-interest in explaining class differences in attitudes toward welfare: do middle- or high-income Americans oppose welfare more than the poor? And if so, do they do so out of self-interest? As figure 2.5 shows, the least well-off are clearly the most supportive of welfare. Of the poorest Americans—those with family incomes of less than $10,000—only 30 percent feel that welfare spending should be cut, while 37 percent would like to see welfare spending increased. As family income rises, the desire to cut welfare spending grows sharply until income reaches about $40,000, above which welfare spending preferences remain fairly constant, with about 60 percent preferring to cut welfare. The less popular preference for increasing welfare spending follows the opposite pattern, declining from 37 percent among the lowest income group to 16 percent among those with family incomes between $30,000 and $40,000, and then remaining fairly constant as family income increases. (This pattern of support for welfare spending among different income groups is not a result of differences in race, sex, age, education, or geographical region. As shown in appendix table A.1, when these other characteristics are taken into account, the pattern shown in figure 2.5 remains virtually unchanged.)

Figure 2.5   Welfare Spending Preferences by Income Level

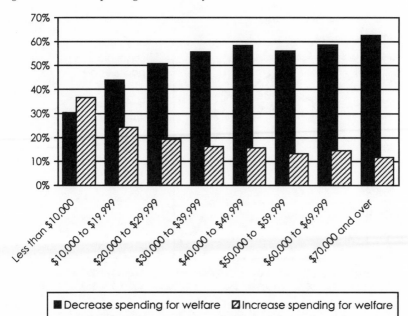

Source: General Social Survey, 1972–1994. *N* = 17,807.

Note: Question wording—"We are faced with many problems in this country, none of which can be solved easily or inexpensively. I'm going to name some of these problems, and for each one I'd like you to tell me whether you think we're spending too much money on it, too little money, or about the right amount. . . . Welfare." Family income from each year has been converted into 1995 dollars.

Economic self-interest is clearly one possible explanation for the lower support for welfare among the better-off. Those with moderate to high family incomes are less likely to be welfare recipients themselves, less likely to have friends or family receiving welfare payments, and less likely to think that they might need welfare in the future. If the differing interests of the poor and the middle class explain the pattern of declining support for welfare seen in figure 2.5, then we should observe a similar pattern of declining support for other means-tested programs (but no such decline for universal social programs). The left panel of figure 2.6 shows that income is indeed unrelated to support for universal programs: spending preferences for Medicare and Social Security remain roughly constant as family income increases. The right panel of figure 2.6 shows the expected decline in support for welfare as income increases, but it also shows that this pattern is not repeated for

Figure 2.6   Support for Universal and Means-Tested Programs by Income Level

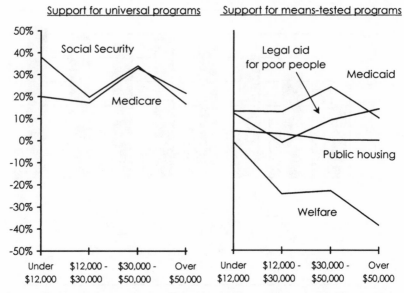

Source: Washington Post survey, sponsored by the Harvard School of Public Health and the Henry J. Kaiser Family Foundation, July–September 1995. $N = 1,970$.

Note: Question wording—"A number of spending reductions have been proposed in order to balance the federal budget and avoid raising taxes. Would you favor or oppose making major spending reductions in each of the following federal programs?" Chart shows percentage of each income group opposing cuts in program minus percentage favoring cuts.

other means-tested programs; there is no significant relationship between income level and support for Medicaid, for legal aid for poor people, or for public housing. For these programs, support among the well-off (who stand to benefit least) is just as strong as support among the lowest income group (who have the most to gain from these programs).

The well-off are the strongest opponents of welfare and the poor its strongest supporters. But the same high-income Americans who oppose welfare do not oppose other means-tested antipoverty programs, which suggests that their opposition to welfare must stem from sources other than their economic self-interest. Perhaps these different preferences with regard to welfare spending reflect not different interests between the poor and nonpoor but different experiences. Most Americans with middle to high incomes have never received welfare and have rather limited experiences with poverty. Of those with family incomes over $30,000, for example, fewer than 7 percent have ever received money from AFDC, General Assistance, SSI, or food stamps.[48] Thus, differences in welfare attitudes among different income groups could result from different perceptions of poverty and welfare.

The most extensive survey to measure Americans' perceptions of poverty and welfare was conducted by the *Los Angeles Times* in 1985.[49] This survey reveals both similarities and differences in how the poor and the nonpoor perceive poverty and welfare. As table 2.4 shows, the poor and the nonpoor agree that most poor people are hardworking and prefer to earn their own living rather than rely on welfare: only 4 percent more nonpoor than poor think that "most poor people are lazy," and only 7 percent more nonpoor think that "most poor people would prefer to stay on welfare."[50] The poor and the nonpoor also share similar views of who has the greatest responsibility for helping the poor, dividing responsibility roughly equally among the government, poor people and their families, and churches and charities.

The largest gaps in perceptions between the poor and the nonpoor concern the conditions faced by the poor and the impact of welfare. The nonpoor are much more likely to think that jobs are available for anyone who wants to work (a 26 percentage point gap between the poor and nonpoor), and they are also more likely to think that job training is the way to fight poverty (a 19 percentage point gap). The nonpoor are also more pessimistic about the future prospects of poor Americans, with 80 percent believing that most poor people will probably remain poor (compared with 58 percent of the poor who hold this belief).

With regard to welfare, the poor and nonpoor also part ways. The nonpoor are much more likely to say that welfare makes poor people dependent and encourages them to remain poor (79 percent of the nonpoor hold this view compared with 58 percent of the poor). Finally, the nonpoor are more opposed to fighting poverty by giving money to poor people. Only 28 percent of the nonpoor believe that it is better to give poor people money to get back on their feet than to try to eliminate the causes of poverty. In contrast, 45 percent of the poor think that giving poor people money is better than trying to eliminate the causes of poverty.

The views of poverty and welfare shown in table 2.4 suggest that the greater opposition to welfare spending among the better-off arises, at least in part, from differing perceptions of the nature of poverty and the impact of welfare on the poor. The nonpoor are more likely than the poor to see poverty as a permanent state and to see welfare as less helpful in moving people out of poverty. In particular, the perceptions that

Table 2.4 Perceptions of Poverty and Welfare among the Poor and the Nonpoor

	Percentage Agree		
	Poor	Nonpoor	Difference
Similar perceptions among poor and nonpoor			
Most poor people are lazy.	23	27	+4
Most poor people prefer to stay on welfare.	22	29	+7*
or			
Most poor people would rather earn their own living.	78	71	−7*
Who has the greatest responsibility for helping the poor?			
The government	35	36	+1
The poor and their families	34	35	+1
Churches and charities	29	26	−3
Different perceptions among poor and nonpoor			
There are jobs available for anyone who is willing to work.	34	60	+26***
The best thing to do about poverty is give poor people job training.	58	77	+19***
Most poor people have been poor for a long time and will probably remain that way.	58	80	+22***
Welfare benefits make poor people dependent and encourage them to remain poor.	58	79	+21***
or			
Welfare benefits give poor people a chance to stand on their own two feet and get started again.	42	21	−21***
It's better to try to eliminate the causes of poverty.	55	72	+17***
or			
It's better to give money to poor people so they can get on their feet.	45	28	−17***

Source: Los Angeles Times poll, April 1985. Ns for poor range from 264 to 343, for nonpoor from 1,725 to 1,953. Results exclude respondents saying "don't know" or providing no answer.

*$p < .05$; ***$p < .001$.

most poor people will remain poor for a long time and that welfare has become a "trap" that makes the poor dependent distinguish the perceptions of the nonpoor and the poor.

Unfortunately, the *Los Angeles Times* survey containing the questions shown in table 2.4 did not ask respondents their preferences with regard to welfare spending. Consequently, we must turn elsewhere to test the hypothesis that opposition to welfare among higher-income Americans results from their different experiences with poverty and welfare and their different views about the extent to which welfare serves to "trap" the poor. For this analysis I make use of a 1994 survey sponsored jointly by CBS News and the *New York Times*.[51] While this survey has fewer questions about poverty and welfare than the *Los Angeles Times* survey examined above, it did ask respondents whether they themselves, or any member of their family, had ever received "food stamps or other welfare benefits" and whether they thought welfare spending should be increased, decreased, or kept about the same.

As expected, the CBS/*New York Times* survey shows that those with higher incomes are more opposed to welfare than are lower-income Americans. Overall, 59 percent of respondents with family incomes above $50,000 think welfare spending should be cut compared with 42 percent of those with incomes under $15,000. But of the high-income respondents who had received welfare themselves or have family members who had been on welfare, only 29 percent think spending for welfare should be cut. It would appear that the experience of having walked a mile in a welfare recipient's shoes (or of having had a family member on welfare) does dampen the desire to cut welfare spending, even among financially secure respondents with over $50,000 in family income.[52]

Past experience with welfare is clearly an important influence on welfare spending preferences. But to what extent do differences in welfare experience explain the greater tendency of the better-off to oppose welfare? To answer this question, we can examine the impact of family income on welfare spending preferences by itself, and then again after taking into account whether a respondent has ever received welfare. By statistically controlling for welfare receipt, we can assess the extent to which the impact of family income is due to a lack of experience with welfare and poverty among the better-off. If the apparent impact of family income declines once welfare receipt is controlled for, we can conclude that part of the reason for the greater opposition to welfare among the well-off arises from differences in history of welfare use for respondents with different family incomes.

A linear probability model of opposition to welfare spending using the CBS/*New York Times* survey shows that the impact of family income does decline, and quite substantially, when we take past experience with welfare into account. Using income alone to predict opposition to welfare spending, we find a 19 percentage point difference between those in the lowest and highest income categories (see appendix table A.2 for details). When experience with welfare is held constant however, the predicted impact of family income declines from 19 percentage points to only 8 percentage points, indicating that over half of the impact of family income on welfare policy preferences can be accounted for by the difference in experience with welfare between high-income and low-income respondents.

High- and low-income Americans differ both in their experience (or lack of experience) with welfare and in their perceptions of the impact of government assistance on welfare recipients. Although the 1994 CBS/*New York Times* survey did not ask explicitly about perceptions that welfare "traps" the poor, the survey did contain a question about whether the government should impose a time limit on welfare use by mothers with young children. If higher-income respondents oppose welfare because they think it saps the work ethic of recipients, they should be more likely to favor time limits, even for young mothers. When we take into account both respondents' history of welfare receipt and whether or not they support time limits for welfare mothers with young children, the impact of family income on opposition to welfare declines further; in this case only 6 percentage points separate the highest and lowest income groups.

In sum, while we cannot account fully for the greater tendency of higher-income respondents to oppose welfare, the bulk of this difference appears to be due to the lack of experience with welfare common among those with higher family incomes and differing perceptions of welfare and its impact on the poor. As the findings in table 2.4 show, income is not related to different perceptions of whether poor people are lazy or whether the government has a responsibility to help the poor. But income is related to beliefs about the impact of welfare itself, especially whether welfare serves to help the poor get back on their feet or undermines their desire to support themselves.

The fear among the well-off that help for the poor undermines their commitment to work is as old as public assistance itself. The doctrine of "less eligibility"—that poor relief must always amount to less than the lowest wage of the least skilled worker—was incorporated into the Elizabethan poor laws precisely to maintain poor people's incentive to work.[53] Welfare is a cash program, which can provide an alternative to paid work. In-kind programs like Medicaid, legal aid, or public housing, however, can supplement employment earnings but cannot replace them. Thus higher-income Americans' greater concern with work disincentives of welfare might lead them to oppose cash assistance to the poor but support spending for other antipoverty programs.

Of course, professing to believe that other people are "trapped" by welfare could be a cynical justification for a self-interested resentment toward paying taxes to help others. For some well-off Americans this is surely the case. But on the whole, higher-income Americans who say that welfare traps the poor and who want to see welfare spending cut do not object to other means-tested programs. This suggests that their negative perceptions of welfare are genuine and do not represent simply an effort to put a more acceptable face on an unwillingness to help those who are worse off.

The available survey questions give us only a rough sense of the attitudinal differences between poor and nonpoor Americans. But our concern at the moment is with the plausibility of self-interest as the explanation for the greater opposition to welfare among the middle and upper classes. Here the evidence is clear. Consistent with what we saw in comparing support for different welfare-state programs, and in changes in support for welfare over time, we find that variation in support for welfare among individuals from different economic strata cannot, for the most part, be attributed to the effects of economic self-interest.

3

Racial Attitudes, the Undeserving Poor, and Opposition to Welfare

Individualism does not lead Americans to reject welfare on principle, nor does self-interest lead them to object to welfare spending. But Americans do object to welfare spending, despite the strong support they express both for universal social programs and for other forms of spending for the poor. In this chapter I focus on two additional explanations for opposition to welfare, both of which concern perceptions of welfare recipients rather than the nature of welfare programs. In particular, we will see first that the public is strongly suspicious of the true need of welfare recipients and second, that white Americans view blacks as lacking commitment to the work ethic. Furthermore, both of these beliefs are strongly related to opposition to welfare: Americans who hold these popular views are strong opponents of welfare spending, while those who reject these beliefs think spending for welfare should be increased.

Before we examine the public's attitudes toward welfare recipients, however, we will look briefly at yet another alternative explanation for the public's opposition to welfare spending. As we saw in chapter 2, Americans simultaneously support welfare in principle but prefer to cut welfare spending. This contrast could be explained by the belief that welfare programs are simply too costly, either because too much money is wasted by inefficient bureaucracies or because benefit levels are too high.

As with other areas of government spending, the public does perceive high levels of waste and inefficiency in welfare. Sixty-nine percent of respondents to one national survey agreed that "when something is run by the government it is usually inefficient and wasteful," and respondents' average estimate of the percentage of welfare spending devoted to administrative costs is 53 percent.[1] (Actual administrative costs of antipoverty programs range from about 6 percent to 20 percent, depending on the program.)[2]

One might expect perceptions of inefficiency to dampen the public's willingness to spend money for welfare, but this does not seem to be the case. Another survey, for example, asked whether "most of the money we pay for welfare goes to the bureaucrats instead of going to the people who need help."[3] Almost two-thirds of the respondents agreed with this statement, but those who agreed were only marginally more likely to favor welfare spending cuts. Of those who agreed, 48 percent wanted welfare spending cut; of those who disagreed, 45 percent wanted to cut welfare spending. Apparently perceived waste or inefficiency is simply not a salient consideration in Americans' thinking about welfare.

If the perception of waste and inefficiency is not behind the desire to cut spending, perhaps Americans think that welfare programs are too generous. The belief that we are spending too much money on welfare could stem from the perception that welfare, food stamps, and similar programs go beyond providing for minimum needs. Surveys show, however, that three out of four Americans believe that "poor people can hardly get by on what the government gives them,"[4] and half agree that "one of the main troubles with welfare is that it doesn't give most people enough to get along on."[5] Another indication that the general preference for decreased welfare spending does not reflect a desire for across-the-board cuts in benefit levels is that only 16 percent of the respondents to one survey thought that "cutting the amount of money given to all people on welfare" is a good idea.[6]

The Undeserving Poor

Perceptions of waste do not explain the desire to cut welfare spending, nor do Americans blame excessive welfare costs on extravagant benefit levels. A much more popular view is that the cost of welfare is inflated by bloated welfare rolls filled with undeserving recipients. The perception that many current welfare recipients should not be receiving welfare is widespread. As table 3.1 shows, only 31 percent of Americans believe that most welfare recipients who can work try to find jobs. On the other hand, two out of three Americans say that most people who receive welfare benefits are taking advantage of the system, and only one in three believes that most welfare recipients are genuinely in need of help.

Americans are not shy about expressing their strong opposition to the use of welfare by people who could be supporting themselves. In a survey of Indiana residents, respondents were asked whether welfare

Table 3.1 Perceived Need of Welfare Recipients

	Percentage Agree
Most people on welfare who can work try to find jobs so they can support themselves.[a]	31
In your view, are most people who receive welfare payments genuinely in need of help or are they taking advantage of the system?	
Taking advantage of the system	66
Genuinely in need of help[b]	34
Most able-bodied people on welfare prefer to sit home and collect benefits even if they can work.	59
or	
Most able-bodied people on welfare really want to work but can't because of circumstances.[c]	41
Do you think that most people who receive money from welfare could get along without it if they tried, or do you think most of them really need help?	
Most could get along without it	61
Most really need help[d]	39

Note: Results are based on national telephone surveys and exclude respondents saying "don't know" or providing no answer.
[a] Kluegel and Smith, *Beliefs about Inequality*, p. 153.
[b] *Time*/CNN poll, December 1994.
[c] ABC News poll, January 1995.
[d] NBC/*Wall Street Journal* poll, April 1995.

benefits should be indexed to the cost of living.[7] Although they were asked only whether they supported or opposed this idea, many respondents spontaneously expressed to the interviewers their feelings about welfare, and many of these feelings involved criticism of welfare recipients who did not really need government help. For example, an eighty-six-year-old widower said, "I worked 'til I was seventy-six and there were people who are younger and stronger and more able to work than I and [they are] on food stamps." A fifty-nine-year-old high school dropout was even more emphatic, telling the interviewer, "As far as welfare, I think it's for the birds and I don't like it for the reason that some of them don't need to be on welfare and they take their coupons and trade them and go buy beer and whisky. I think it should be thoroughly investigated."

The notion that welfare recipients should be "thoroughly investigated" was also shared by a thirty-four-year-old man, who had this to say: "I know people here in Indiana who are too blankity blank [sic] lazy to get off their butts. If they searched their cases a little bit then I would agree [that benefits should be indexed to the cost of living], but they don't. I know it's not just in Indiana. Anybody can get a nickel who tries to get a nickel. I know people who can work, but as long as they can get free money and food what's the use of working."

Although a certain amount of cynicism about the true need for welfare is to be expected, the belief that most welfare recipients do not really need it—a belief that surveys show is held by the majority of the American public—is quite remarkable. As we have seen, Americans do not oppose welfare in principle; if the need is genuine, Americans believe the government has a responsibility to help. But while Americans' commitment to individualism is not so great as to preclude support for welfare, Americans do expect the recipients of government benefits—like everyone else—to share that commitment to individual responsibility.

Americans are clear and strong in objecting to the use of welfare by people who do not really need it. Fully 74 percent of the public agrees that "criteria for getting on welfare are not tough enough."[8] But this objection does not stem from a lack of sympathy for the poor, or from an unwillingness to pay the costs, for we have seen that most Americans think government spending to help the poor should be increased.[9] Nor does it stem from an individualistic rejection of the idea of welfare, since large majorities of Americans think the government should be giving aid—even direct monetary assistance—to those in need. Americans' individualistic ideology, rather than resulting in a principled rejection of welfare as such, provides a basis for judging the moral worthiness of welfare recipients. Americans support government aid for those who are trying—but nevertheless failing—to make it on their own. But the "undeserving poor," who choose to rely on welfare when they could be supporting themselves, receive little sympathy.

This combination of support for welfare in principle and cynicism toward current welfare recipients was also expressed by many of the Indiana respondents. One young woman was equally clear in approving of welfare in principle but objecting to its abuse by those not really in need: "There is too much welfare fraud out there, too many people taking advantage of it who don't need it and too many people who need it who can't get it because the other people out there are using it who don't need it." Another respondent also contrasted the abuse of welfare by those who do not really need it with the unmet needs of those who should be getting government help: "There are too many people on welfare," this seventy-two-year-old man told the interviewer, "and those who need it aren't on it. There are too many getting it who don't deserve it and there should be more supervision in the program." The same combination of support for welfare but concern over its abuse was conveyed by a young woman who said simply, "I have mixed feelings about [indexing benefits]. I think people abuse welfare, [but indexing] would be a great idea for the needy."

As we have seen, Americans' widely shared commitment to individualism does not result in a principled objection to welfare. Most of the programs of the welfare state are very popular with the American public, and a large majority of Americans agree that government should provide monetary assistance to those who are unable to support themselves. But the perception of welfare abuse is widespread. Indeed, as the survey evidence presented above suggests, it would be hard to exaggerate the level of cynicism toward welfare recipients held by the American public. This perception of welfare recipients' dishonesty and freeloading is at the core of Americans' conviction that welfare spending should be cut.

The impact of perceptions of abuse by welfare recipients can be seen in figure 3.1. This figure shows the different levels of opposition to welfare spending for survey respondents with differing attitudes toward the true need of welfare recipients. Among those who strongly agree that "most welfare recipients could get by without it if they really tried," 59 percent think welfare spending should be cut, and only 18 percent want to increase spending for welfare. At the other end of the spectrum, among those (few) Americans who strongly disagree that "most welfare recipients could get by without it if they really tried," only 22 percent think welfare spending should be cut while 43 percent want to increase spending for welfare. As expected, the stronger the belief that the welfare rolls are filled with the undeserving, the greater the desire to cut spending for welfare. In chapter 4 I will subject this relationship between perceptions of deservingness and opposition to welfare spending to a more rigorous statistical test, but for now I note that welfare spending preferences differ markedly for Americans with different views on whether most people on welfare really need the help they are getting.

Cynicism and suspicion toward the recipients of government benefits help to explain some of the patterns of support and opposition to welfare-state programs examined in chapter 1. For example, table 1.2 shows that Americans are even more disposed toward cutting spending for "people on welfare" than they are toward cutting spending for

Figure 3.1 Welfare Spending Preferences and Beliefs about the Deservingness of Welfare Recipients

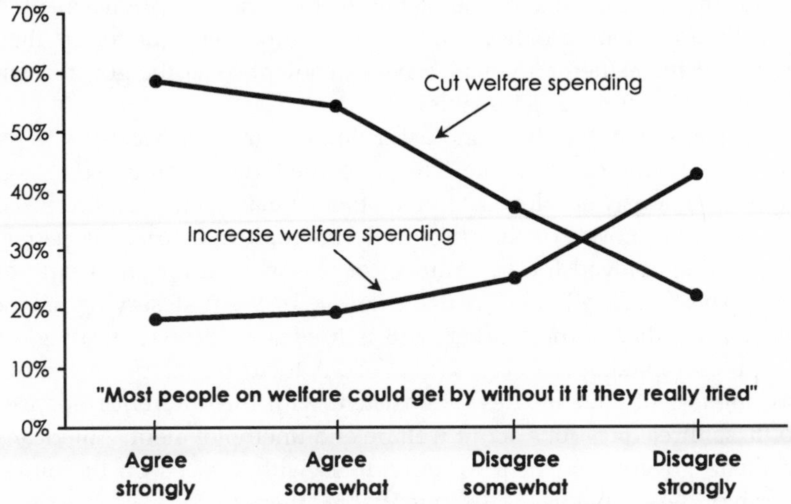

Source: National Race and Politics Study, 1991. *N* = 1,182.

"welfare" per se (71 percent versus 63 percent). While it might seem these two questions amount to the same thing, it appears that a more negative response is elicited when attention is focused on *the people* who benefit from welfare, rather than the program itself.

A similar pattern is found among the three questions in table 1.2 related to spending for unemployment. The public clearly supports increased spending for "retraining programs for displaced workers," is ambivalent about spending for "unemployment insurance," and prefers to cut spending for "unemployed people." Each of these three apparently similar references to unemployment carries different implications of the causes of unemployment and therefore of the extent to which the unemployed are deserving of help. The reference to retraining programs is explicit: these workers were "displaced" from their previous jobs, the blame for their unemployment being clearly assigned to circumstances outside of their control. Furthermore, the money is to be spent for training programs that will enable them to reenter the labor force and support themselves once again. Clearly these are deserving Americans.

Spending for unemployment insurance represents an intermediate case. Unemployment insurance, as most survey respondents probably know, is available only to former workers, and only for a set period of time. The ambiguity in this case concerns the reasons for their unemployment: were these workers laid off through no fault of their own? Or do they share some of the blame for their current predicament?[10] Equally important, are they actively looking for a new job, or are they living off their unemployment benefits, content to let the government pay their rent as long as possible?

Questions about motives and deservingness are even greater with regard to "unemployed people." To some, the term "unemployed" suggests "previously employed," but to others it may conjure up images of the never-employed or the chronically unemployed. After all, people can be unemployed for any number of reasons and for any length of time. The "welfare loafer" is one example of the undeserving unemployed; another is the worker who is fired for stealing, cheating, or simply not making the necessary effort. A focus on the perceived deservingness of beneficiaries is consistent with the different responses to these three questions about welfare and unemployment: Americans evaluate government help to individuals with a focus on the moral worth or deservingness of the potential recipient.

The contrast between Americans' strong desire to help the poor and their equally strong desire to cut back on welfare spending springs from the distinction between two kinds of poor people: between those who are trying to help themselves and those who are not, between those who share a commitment to individual responsibility and those who prefer to rely on the government for support—in short, between the deserving poor and the undeserving poor.

The distinction between the deserving poor and the undeserving poor has long been central to Americans' understanding of the causes of, and appropriate responses to, poverty. Long before the emergence of the welfare state, Americans distinguished between those among the poor who deserved help and those who did not. In 1834 the Reverend Charles Burroughs explained, "In speaking of poverty, let us never forget that there is a distinction between this and pauperism. The former is an unavoidable evil, to which many are brought from necessity. . . . It is the result, not of our faults, but of our misfortunes. . . . Pauperism is the consequence of wilful error, of shameful indolence, of vicious habits. It is a misery of human creation, the pernicious work of man, the lamentable consequence of bad principles and morals."[11] In his study of public orientations toward the poor, Michael Katz describes America's historical preoccupation with distinguishing between different classes of poor people. "Public officials in the early nineteenth century attempted to distinguish between the able-bodied and the impotent poor; a few decades later, officials transmuted these categories into the moral distinction between the worthy and the unworthy, or the deserving and the undeserving poor. . . . Contemporary politicians, moralists, and editorial writers still frequently refer to the deserving and the undeserving poor. . . . These terms serve to isolate one group of poor people from the rest, to stigmatize them." [12]

Given the long history of distinguishing between the deserving and the undeserving poor, it is not surprising that most Americans are sensitive to the misuse of welfare by those who could get along without it. What is remarkable, though, is that so many Americans believe that the *majority* of welfare recipients could get along fine without it. Among welfare recipients at least, the undeserving poor are seen as constituting a very large group indeed. In the next section I explore one of the factors that helps to explain the cynical outlook the American public holds toward those on welfare: their race.

Racial Attitudes and Opposition to Welfare

Once we shift our focus from the public's views of welfare as a program to the public's beliefs about welfare recipients, the racialized nature of American poverty comes to the fore. Although political elites typically use race-neutral language in discussing poverty and welfare, it is now widely believed that welfare is a "race-coded" topic that evokes racial imagery and attitudes even when racial minorities are not explicitly mentioned. In discussing the recent debates over welfare reform, for example, the *Minneapolis/St. Paul Star Tribune* writes, "[R]ace coursed just beneath the surface of the welfare debate, and 'welfare' and 'urban' have often been used as political code words that really mean 'minority.' " The *Star Tribune* goes on to quote John Powell of the University of Minnesota Law School as saying, "A lot of this discussion is racism in drag. . . . When you talk about welfare, vouchers, urban strategies, crime, poverty, you're really talking about race." [13]

Since the mid-1960s, poverty and race have been closely linked in the public mind. Where "the poor" once conjured up images of southern European or Irish immigrants, or of white dust-bowl farmers, urban blacks now dominate our perceptions of poverty. The most salient contemporary images of the poor—the homeless beggar, the welfare queen, the teenage ghetto gang member, the heroin addict shooting up in an abandoned building—are strongly associated with minorities in both the mass media and the public imagination. Although most city dwellers are neither poor nor black, discussions of "urban policy" or "how to help America's cities" are taken to mean "what should we do about poor black neighborhoods" and the crime and poverty with which they are associated.

In part, the connection between "poor" and "black" exists simply because African Americans account for a disproportionate number of poor people in the United States. Only one in ten white Americans falls below the official government poverty line, but three out of ten blacks are poor.[14] Still, blacks are a small segment of the American population, and even though they are disproportionately poor, they comprise only a minority (currently about 27 percent) of all poor people.[15]

When we are trying to understand popular opposition to welfare, however, public perceptions are more important than demographic realities. Surveys show that Americans substantially overestimate the percentage of blacks among the poor. When one survey asked, "What percent of all the poor people in this country would you say are black?" the median response was 50 percent.[16] Another survey simply asked, "Of all the people who are poor in this country, are more of them black or are more of them white?" Fifty-five percent of the respondents chose black, compared with 24 percent who chose white (with 31 percent volunteering "about equal").[17] In chapter 5 we will examine the causes of these misperceptions; for now we simply note that the public's exaggerated perception of the degree to which African Americans make up the poor magnifies the role of racial attitudes in shaping antipoverty policy preferences.

As a first step in assessing the impact of racial attitudes on welfare views, I examine the preference for increasing or decreasing welfare spending among Americans with different perceptions of blacks. To the extent that racial perceptions shape welfare policy preferences, we would expect to find that those who view blacks most sympathetically are the most supportive of welfare, while Americans with the most negative views of blacks are most opposed to welfare. In 1990 and again in 1994, the General Social Survey asked whether blacks tend to be hardworking or tend to be lazy, allowing respondents to choose any point along a seven-point scale. Forty-four percent of respondents placed blacks on the "lazy" half of this scale, while only 20 percent chose the "hardworking" half. Further, respondents with different perceptions of blacks' commitment to the work ethic expressed very different attitudes toward welfare. As figure 3.2 shows, among those who most strongly viewed blacks as hardworking (at point 1 on the scale) only 35 percent wanted to decrease welfare spending, while 47 percent thought spending for welfare should be increased. At the other end of

Figure 3.2   Welfare Spending Preferences and Perceptions of Blacks' Work Ethic

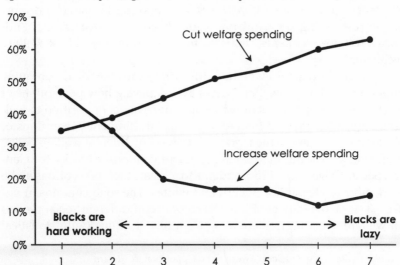

Source: General Social Survey, 1990 and 1994 combined, N = 1,293.

Note: Question wording—"I'm going to show you a seven-point scale on which the characteristics of people in a group can be rated. . . . A score of 1 means that you think almost all of the people in that group tend to be "hard-working." A score of 7 means that you think almost everyone in the group tends to be "lazy." A score of 4 means you think that the group is not towards one end or another, and of course you may choose any number in between. . . ."

the scale, however, 63 percent of respondents who viewed blacks as lazy preferred to cut welfare spending, while only 15 percent thought welfare spending should be increased.

Of course, blacks are not the only racial minority that Americans might associate with poverty. Average incomes for both Hispanics and Native Americans are far below those of non-Hispanic whites, and although Asian Americans as a whole are well-off financially, some Asian subgroups (e.g., Cambodians and Laotians) are economically disadvantaged.[18] In parts of the country where members of these groups are concentrated, the public may associate poverty as much with these other minority groups as with African Americans. Nevertheless, for the country as a whole, it remains overwhelmingly true that blacks are the minority group that the public most associates with poverty and welfare. This is reflected, for example, in a survey question about the racial composition of welfare recipients. When respondents were asked whether more people on welfare are white or nonwhite, only 35 percent chose white. When they were then asked whether most nonwhite welfare recipients are black, Hispanic, Asian, or American Indian, fully 68 percent chose black (with 18 percent choosing Hispanic and most of the rest saying they did not know).[19] For most Americans, "minority welfare recipients" appears to mean primarily "black welfare recipients."

We might also assess whether attitudes toward blacks are uniquely important in shaping welfare views by comparing how perceptions of blacks and perceptions of other social groups affect opposition to welfare. Figure 3.2 showed that Americans with different perceptions of blacks' commitment to the work ethic have very different welfare policy preferences. In addition to asking about perceptions of blacks, the General Social Survey asked respondents to indicate their perceptions of the work ethic of Hispanics, Asians, and whites. The solid columns in figure 3.3 show the impact of these perceptions of different social groups on welfare spending preferences, taken one at a time (with statistical

Figure 3.3   Stereotypes of Social Groups and Opposition to Welfare

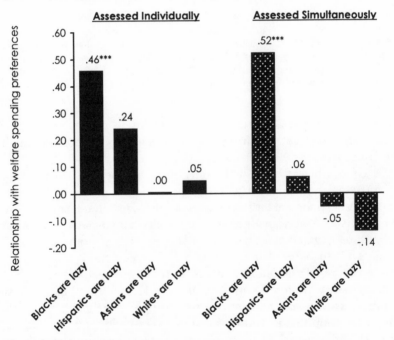

Source: General Social Survey, 1994, N = 579 to 631.

Note: Figure shows the regression coefficients for each stereotype as a predictor of welfare spending preferences while holding constant age, sex, education, family income, and region of residence. See appendix table A.3 for details and full regression results.

***$p < .001$.

controls for respondents' age, sex, education, income, and region). Respondents' beliefs about blacks' commitment to the work ethic is the strongest predictor of welfare attitudes. Beliefs about Hispanics do show some relationship with welfare spending preferences (although much weaker and statistically nonsignificant), while beliefs about the work ethic of Asians and whites are virtually unrelated to preferences for increasing, maintaining, or decreasing spending for welfare.

While the solid columns in figure 3.3 show the impact of each group stereotype taken individually, the spotted columns show the unique impact of each stereotype when perceptions of the other social groups are simultaneously taken into account. Using this approach, we can estimate the impact of a particular group stereotype for people who have similar views on the work ethic of each of the other groups in question. This shows even more clearly the special importance of perceptions of blacks. If we hold constant respondents' beliefs about the work ethic of Hispanics, Asians, and whites, their perceptions of blacks continue to have a strong influence on welfare policy preferences. But when we hold constant beliefs about blacks, respondents' views of Hispanics, Asians, and whites show no significant relationship to their preferences for welfare spending.

It appears that not only do Americans perceive blacks as numerically the most important minority group among welfare recipients, but Americans' attitudes toward welfare are far more strongly influenced by perceptions of blacks than by perceptions of other racial or ethnic groups. As the country's Hispanic population continues to grow, attitudes toward welfare and poverty may become as strongly associated with perceptions of Hispanics as they are now with perceptions of blacks.[20] For the present, however, perceptions of blacks continue to play the dominant role in shaping the public's attitudes toward welfare. A full understanding of Americans' welfare views would need to consider attitudes toward a variety of minority groups. Because no study can hope to illuminate every aspect of any complex social issue, however, I will concentrate on attitudes toward African Americans in examining the role of racial and ethnic minorities in shaping the public's thinking about welfare, recognizing that my story must remain somewhat incomplete in this (as in many other) respects.

If welfare and poverty have indeed become "racialized," as many believe and as the relationships shown in figures 3.2 and 3.3 appear to confirm, why, exactly, is this so? One possibility is that race-based opposition to welfare derives from a general dislike of blacks. Alternatively, race-based opposition might stem from a more policy-oriented rejection of *government* efforts to assist blacks. Or opposition might reflect specific racial stereotypes, like the perception of blacks as lazy that is reflected in figure 3.2. To better understand the nature of race-based opposition to welfare, we need to examine the variety of racial attitudes that might play a part in generating such opposition.

Varieties of Racial Attitudes

Racial attitudes encompass a wide range of feelings, beliefs, policy preferences, and behavioral inclinations.[21] To assess the impact of the various dimensions of racial attitudes on Americans' welfare views, I make use of the 1986 National Election Study (NES) survey.[22] Although more recent surveys are available, the 1986 NES contains the most comprehensive array of racial-attitude items from any single national survey, including the more recent National Election Study surveys. From the many questions about blacks contained in the 1986 NES, ten items were chosen that represent a broad array of racial attitudes (shown in figure 3.4). Specifically excluded, however, are questions that tap both racial attitudes and attitudes toward welfare or toward government social spending more generally. For example, questions about "federal spending on programs that assist blacks" or the belief that "most blacks who receive money from welfare programs could get along without it if they tried" are excluded. Answers to these questions are indeed related to respondents' preferences for increasing or decreasing welfare spending, but the reason for this relationship is ambiguous: it could be due to respondents' feelings about government spending or welfare recipients more generally, rather than to the specifically racial components of these questions. By excluding these questions, we lessen the possibility that any relationships found between racial attitudes and welfare views arise not from the racial attitudes themselves but from the confounding of these two different factors in the racial-attitude measures.[23]

The following analyses of racial attitudes are limited to white respondents from the 1986 NES. African Americans are excluded from these analyses for two reasons. First, racial attitudes clearly play different roles in shaping policy preferences among blacks and among nonblacks, and the 1986 NES contains too few African American respondents for reliable analysis.[24] Furthermore, African Americans are considerably more supportive of welfare than are nonblacks: combining six recent years of General Social Survey data (to obtain sufficient numbers of black respondents), we find that 53 percent of white Americans want to cut back welfare spending (and only 17 percent want to increase it), while only 33 percent of blacks want to decrease welfare spending, and 38 percent want to increase it.[25] Clearly, we cannot fully

Figure 3.4   Survey Measures of Attitudes toward Blacks

A. "Blacks lack work ethic"
  (1) It's really a matter of some people not trying hard enough; if blacks would only try harder they could be just as well off as whites.

  (2) Generations of slavery and discrimination have created conditions that make it difficult for blacks to work their way out of the lower class. (scoring reversed)

B. "Blacks are innately inferior"
  (3) Blacks come from a less able race and this explains why blacks are not as well off as whites in America.

  (4) The differences are brought about by God; God made the races different as part of his divine plan.

C. Negative feelings toward blacks
  (5) Respondents' feelings toward blacks on a 100-point "feeling thermometer" where "ratings between 50 degrees and 100 degrees mean that you feel favorable and warm toward [blacks] . . . and ratings between 0 degrees and 50 degrees mean that you don't feel favorable toward [blacks]." (scoring reversed)

D. "Helping blacks is not government's job"
  (6) Some people feel that if black people are not getting fair treatment in jobs, the government in Washington ought to see to it that they do. Others feel that this is not the federal government's business. . . . How do you feel?

  (7) Do you think the government in Washington should see to it that white and black children go to the same schools, or stay out of this area as it is not the government's business?

E. Opposition to affirmative action
  (8) Some people say that because of past discrimination blacks should be given preference in hiring and promotion. Others say that such preference in hiring and promotion is wrong because it gives blacks advantages they haven't earned. What about your opinion . . . ?

  (9) Some people say that because of past discrimination it is sometimes necessary for colleges and universities to reserve openings for black students. Others oppose quotas because they say quotas give blacks advantages they haven't earned. What about your opinion . . . ?

F. "Civil rights leaders push too fast"
  (10) Do you think that civil rights leaders are trying to push too fast, are going too slowly, or are they moving at about the right speed?

Source: National Election Study, 1986.

understand the American public's attitudes toward welfare without attending to the preferences and beliefs of blacks as well as nonblacks. But the more limited purpose of assessing the role of racial attitudes in shaping opposition to welfare is well served by focusing on nonblack respondents only.

To facilitate analysis and interpretation, I combined the ten racial-attitude items shown in figure 3.4 into multi-item indices (see appendix for details). Based on theoretical and empirical considerations, the ten individual survey questions were reduced to six different racial-attitude measures (labeled A through F in figure 3.4), each of which has different implications for our understanding of the racialized nature of welfare views.

The first index shown in figure 3.4 reflects respondents' perceptions of the causes of racial inequality. A series of questions is introduced in the survey as follows: "In past studies we have asked people why they think white people seem to get more of the good things in life in America—such as better jobs and more money—than black people do. These are some of the reasons given by both blacks and whites. Please tell me whether you agree or disagree with each reason as to why white people seem to get more of the good things in life . . . ."

The first two reasons offered reflect respondents' attribution of the cause of racial inequality either to lack of effort by blacks or to slavery and discrimination. Most white respondents agree with at least one of these two explanations for racial inequality, and some agree with both. But, as one would expect, those who think blacks' lack of effort is to blame are less likely to agree that slavery and discrimination are important factors, compared with whites who reject lack of effort as an explanation. Together these two questions tap what social psychologists call the internal/external attributional dimension: lack of effort identifies the cause of racial inequality as an internal (or "dispositional") characteristic of African Americans, while slavery and discrimination locates the causes of racial inequality in external (or "situational") conditions.[26] Although these two questions are less direct than the "hardworking versus lazy" scale examined in figure 3.2, they tap the same underlying beliefs about blacks' commitment to (or lack of commitment to) the work ethic. (Unfortunately, the 1986 NES lacks a more straightforward question reflecting perceptions of blacks as lazy.)

Another explanation for racial inequality stems from the belief that blacks, as a race, are innately inferior to whites. While notions of innate or biological inferiority are much less popular now than they were during their peak in the late nineteenth century,[27] there are still a minority of whites willing to acknowledge such beliefs to survey interviewers. (Because the idea of innate racial inferiority is socially unacceptable in many circles, the number of whites who hold these beliefs is undoubtedly larger than the number that are willing to express them on surveys.) On the 1986 NES survey, 6 percent of white respondents agreed that blacks come from a less able race, and 15 percent agreed that differences between blacks and whites are brought about by God as part of his divine plan.[28]

In contrast to these more cognitively based explanations for racial inequality, the third measure of racial attitudes in figure 3.4 reflects respondents' feelings toward blacks. This survey question asks respondents to indicate how warm or cold they feel toward blacks using a 100-point "feeling thermometer," in which "ratings between 0 degrees and 50 degrees mean that you don't feel favorable toward the person [or group] and don't care too much for that person [or group]" and "ratings between 50 degrees and 100 degrees mean that you feel favorable and warm toward that person [or group]." This measure, then, should reveal the extent to which opposition to welfare is rooted in whites' general negative affect toward blacks.

The next two sets of racial-attitude measures tap respondents' support for government and business policies to assist blacks. The first of these (labeled "helping blacks is not government's job") indicates the extent to which race-based opposition to welfare is rooted in a reluctance to use government to combat racial inequality. The second of these policy-focused measures ("opposition to affirmative action") indicates attitudes toward preferential treatment for blacks in hiring and in college admissions and reflects the extent to which white opposition to welfare grows out of a rejection of efforts to use racially targeted social policy to compensate for racial discrimination.

Finally, the last racial-attitude measure asks whether civil rights leaders have been trying to push too fast. This question is designed to assess the extent to which whites feel threatened by black progress or angered by black leaders. To the extent that this question emerges as a particularly powerful predictor of opposition to welfare, we can conclude that whites oppose welfare because they view it as part of a larger set of unwelcome accommodations to blacks' demands. Scores on this question, as on the other five measures of racial attitudes shown in figure 3.4, range from zero to one, with higher scores indicating more negative views of blacks (see the appendix for details of index construction and reliability).

To assess respondents' attitudes toward welfare, I use two questions from the 1986 NES survey. Since the survey did not ask about spending preferences for welfare per se, I use instead a question about whether spending for food stamps should be increased, decreased, or kept the same. This measure is attractive because it reflects respondents' policy views toward a means-tested benefit program. Yet the food stamp program is not a paradigmatic example of "welfare" since it provides not cash but a cash-like scrip that can be used only to purchase approved foodstuffs. Because food stamps can be sold or traded, however, they are more like cash than are other in-kind benefits such as medical care or housing. Thus food stamps can be considered a "quasi-welfare" program that shares many of the characteristics of cash welfare, including fairly low support among the public (although not as low as "welfare" itself; see table 1.2).

The second measure of respondents' welfare attitudes gauges feelings toward welfare recipients with the same 100-point "feeling thermometer" used to assess feelings toward blacks. Although this measure is not policy oriented, it does refer directly to "welfare" and therefore compensates somewhat for the less direct measure of spending preferences that refers to food stamps instead. In addition to these two separate measures of welfare attitudes, I also examine the impact of racial views on an index that combines attitudes toward spending for food stamps with feelings toward welfare recipients. All three of these measures are scored from zero to 100, with high scores indicating greater opposition to welfare.

To assess the relative importance of the various dimensions of racial attitudes in shaping whites' welfare views, I include the six racial-attitude measures shown in figure 3.4 in a series of multiple regression analyses predicting each of the three welfare attitude indicators in turn. As table 3.2 shows, only four of the six dimensions of racial attitudes are significantly related to welfare views. Neither the belief that blacks are innately inferior to whites nor the thermometer measure of feelings toward blacks shows a statistically significant relationship to any of the three welfare attitude measures. Of the other four measures of racial views, the belief that blacks lack a commitment to the work ethic is the most powerful predictor of all three welfare measures (and, as appendix table A.4 indicates, this holds true for standardized as well as unstandardized regression coefficients).

The desire to cut spending for food stamps is associated not only with the perception that blacks lack a strong work ethic but also with opposition to affirmative action, with the belief that civil rights leaders are pushing too fast, and somewhat less strongly, with the belief that helping blacks is not the government's job. In contrast to these findings, the

Table 3.2 Racial Attitudes and Opposition to Welfare

	Cut Spending for Food Stamps	Negative Feelings toward Welfare Recipients	Combined Index
"Blacks lack work ethic"	20.1**	14.3***	17.2***
"Blacks are innately inferior"	−4.3	5.1	−0.2
Negative feelings toward blacks	0.7	8.7	3.1
"Helping blacks is not government's job"	11.2*	1.4	4.1
Opposition to affirmative action	14.8*	8.5	10.4*
"Civil rights leaders push too fast"	14.2*	4.3	11.7**

Source: National Election Study, 1986. Ns = 357 to 381.

Notes: Table shows unstandardized regression coefficients. Dependent variables are scored from 0 to 100, with high scores indicating negative attitudes toward food stamps or welfare recipients. Predictors are scored from 0 to 1, with high scores indicating negative attitudes toward blacks. See figure 3.4 and appendix for details. Analyses include white respondents only.

$*p < .05; **p < .01; ***p < .001$.

only dimension of racial attitudes that is significantly related to white respondents' feelings toward welfare recipients is the belief that blacks lack a commitment to the work ethic; none of the other five racial-attitude measures significantly predicts this aspect of welfare views. Finally, the combined index of attitudes toward welfare is most strongly related to perceptions of blacks' work ethic, and less strongly, although still significantly, related to both opposition to affirmative action and the belief that civil rights leaders are pushing too fast. In sum, while welfare attitudes are associated with a number of different aspects of racial views, the perception that blacks are lazy is consistently the most powerful predictor of white Americans' opposition to welfare.

Racial Stereotypes and Welfare Policy Preferences

The relationships between racial attitudes and opposition to welfare shown in table 3.2 echo what we saw in figure 3.2: the belief that blacks lack commitment to the work ethic appears to play an important role in generating opposition to welfare among white Americans. This finding has a number of important implications for our understanding of race and welfare. First, to the extent that opposition to welfare is race based, it does not primarily reflect a general dislike of blacks, such as that measured by the "feeling thermometer," nor, for the most part, does it stem from the belief that helping blacks is simply not the government's job. Opposition to affirmative action and negative reactions to black leaders or black progress do show some connection with whites' welfare views, but the most important race-based source of opposition to welfare is the perception that blacks' economic problems stem from their own lack of effort.

As we will see in chapter 6, the belief that African Americans lack commitment to the work ethic reflects a centuries-old stereotype of blacks as lazy, shiftless, and unambitious. While the nature, causes, and consequences of stereotypes will be examined later, it is important to note that stereotypes differ from other racial attitudes in important ways. First, although stereotypes often contain affective elements, they are rooted in cognitive constructs embodying *beliefs* about members of a social group.[29] Stereotypes can be positive (e.g., Asians are good at math), negative (e.g., blacks are lazy), or neutral (e.g., Latinos like spicy food), but they always involve factual claims about group members (which may or may not be true). Hostility toward, or dislike of, a group may be one *reason* for adopting a negative stereotype, just as negative beliefs about a group may lead to hostility or dislike. Nevertheless, it is important to distinguish an individual's affective orientations toward a group from the beliefs about that group that he or she may hold.[30]

Stereotypes sometimes develop out of individuals' own experiences with group members. Most stereotypes, however, are beliefs shared within a given society that are learned not from personal experience but from the culture at large as they are passed on from one generation to the next. This is clearly true of the stereotype of blacks as lazy. Long before the birth of the welfare state, the defenders of slavery argued that blacks were unfit for freedom because they were too lackadaisical to survive on their own. This stereotype has been traced by social psychologists through generations of white Americans. Although some evidence suggests that it is not as widespread as it once was, the belief that blacks lack a commitment to the work ethic remains both a popular perception among whites and (as we have seen) an important influence on their political attitudes.

The two sources of opposition to welfare discussed in this chapter—the perception that most welfare recipients are not truly needy and the belief that blacks are lazy—are parallel judgments about the character of distinct but overlapping groups. In chapter 5 we will look in more detail at the racialization of poverty and welfare in America, and in chapter 6 we will explore the nature and history of racial stereotypes. But first we need to subject these findings about the impact of racial attitudes and perceptions of the true need of welfare recipients to a more rigorous analysis. In the next chapter I will use more sophisticated statistical techniques to disentangle the racial and nonracial sources of opposition to welfare, while taking into account the variety of other demographic characteristics and political views that shape public attitudes toward welfare.

4

Assessing Alternative Explanations: Statistical Models of Welfare Attitudes

The previous chapters explored four alternative explanations for Americans' opposition to welfare: individualism, economic self-interest, perceptions that welfare recipients are undeserving, and racial attitudes. In the analyses below, these four explanations (along with other possible influences) are assessed in combination, using data from a single large-scale national survey. Combining the various factors that influence Americans' welfare views into a single comprehensive statistical model has two important advantages. First, the different factors that have an impact on welfare attitudes do not operate in isolation. With a comprehensive model we can take account of the relationships *among* these factors as well as the impact of each factor on opposition to welfare. Second, by drawing on data from a single survey and combining the different influences on welfare views into a single model we can assess the relative importance of each factor in shaping Americans' welfare policy preferences.

As we will see below, a variety of political attitudes and demographic characteristics have some effect on opposition to welfare, but two factors stand out as the most significant. The beliefs that blacks are lazy and that welfare recipients are undeserving are by far the strongest influences on white Americans' welfare views. In addition, the stereotype of blacks as lazy is doubly important because it influences the perception that welfare recipients are undeserving. Finally, a survey-based experiment reveals that perceptions of black welfare recipients are far more important than perceptions of white welfare recipients, not only in generating opposition to welfare but also in shaping a wide range of perceptions and policy preferences toward poverty and welfare.

Survey Data and Measures

The survey data analyzed in this chapter come from the 1991 National Race and Politics Study (NRPS), a nationwide random-digit telephone survey conducted by the Survey Research Center at the University of California, Berkeley.[1] The NRPS is one of a series of innovative surveys conducted by the Survey Research Center and directed by Paul Sniderman, all of which make use of randomized experiments to measure public attitudes in new ways. (Further details on the NRPS can be found in Paul Sniderman and Edward Carmines's *Reaching Beyond Race* and in *Perception and Prejudice,* edited by Jon Hurwitz and Mark Peffley.[2]) Like the analysis of racial attitudes in chapter 3, the analyses in this chapter are restricted to nonblack respondents only.

Respondents' welfare attitudes and the various demographic and attitudinal predictors of those attitudes are measured by one or more questions from the NRPS. Each of the survey measures is described below, and the complete question text and response categories, as well as the details of scale construction and reliability for analyses in this chapter, can be found in the appendix.

Opposition to Welfare Spending

Respondents' opposition to welfare spending is assessed by a question that asks, "Suppose you had a say in making up the federal budget, would you prefer to see more spent, less spent, or the same amount of money spent on welfare as it has been?" A desire to increase welfare spending is scored zero, maintain spending is scored 50, and cut welfare spending is scored 100.

Individualism

As discussed in chapter 2, individualism can take many forms. But the variety of individualism most prominent in American culture and most relevant to the study of welfare attitudes involves the preference for limited government and concern with individual initiative and responsibility. In the analyses below, this preference is measured by a survey question that asks how strongly respondents agree or disagree that "the government in Washington tries to do too many things that should be left up to individuals and private businesses." Like the other predictors included in these analyses, this question is scored from 0 to 1 (with higher scores indicating stronger individualist orientations).

Family Income

In chapter 2, we saw that family income is related to opposition to welfare and that this relationship appears to be due largely to factors other than economic self-interest. In particular, we found that Americans with higher incomes are more opposed to welfare because they are less likely to have used welfare themselves (or had family members who had been welfare recipients) and are more likely to view welfare as a "trap" than as a means to help poor people get back on their feet again. The NRPS lacks questions about either actual welfare use or perceptions that welfare is a long-term substitute for self-support. I therefore include family income in the models of welfare attitudes, recognizing that its impact on welfare policy preferences largely reflects these differences in experience with and beliefs about welfare.

Perception of Welfare Recipients as Undeserving

The third source of opposition to welfare discussed earlier concerns the perception that most welfare recipients could get along without welfare and hence do not deserve government assistance. To measure this belief, two survey questions from the NRPS are combined. The first asks whether "most people on welfare could get by without it if they really tried" and the second, whether "most people on welfare would rather be working than taking money from the government." Naturally, respondents who agreed with the first of these statements tended to disagree with the second. In combining these questions the response categories were recoded so that respondents who agreed strongly with the first question and disagreed strongly with the second received the highest scores on the index measuring perceptions that welfare recipients are undeserving (see appendix).

Perception of Blacks as Lazy

As we saw in chapter 3, a number of different dimensions of racial attitudes are related to white Americans' views on welfare. In the analysis in this chapter, I focus on the dimension that proved to be the most important in generating opposition to welfare: the perception that blacks lack commitment to the work ethic. Perceptions of blacks as lazy are assessed by the difference in the scores respondents give to two items from a series of personal characteristics applied to African Americans. The series is introduced as follows: "Now I'll read a few words that people sometimes use to describe blacks. Of course, no word fits absolutely everybody, but, as I read each one, please tell me using a number from zero to ten how well you think it describes blacks as a group. If you think it's a very good description of most blacks, give it a ten. If you feel a word is a very inaccurate description of most blacks, give it a zero." Respondents' scores for "hardworking" are subtracted from their scores for "lazy." Consequently, the highest scores for the combined index of perceptions of blacks as lazy are assigned to those respondents with the highest scores on the "lazy" question and the lowest scores on the "hardworking" question.

Party Identification

In addition to measures of the four explanations for opposition to welfare discussed above, a number of other possible influences on welfare policy preferences are included in the model. The first of these concerns respondents' identification with the Democratic or Republican parties. As decades of research has demonstrated, political parties are an important influence on Americans' voting behavior and political attitudes, helping individuals to understand political issues and determine where they stand on the policy debates of the day.[3] Parties provide "informational shortcuts" for voters and citizens. The candidates' party affiliation is all the information many voters have in elections for lower offices, and in most cases this information is enough to permit voters to identify the candidate that most closely shares their political views. Parties similarly provide informational cues on political issues. For people who think of themselves as Republicans (or Democrats), knowing what the Republican (or Democratic) leadership thinks about welfare may influence their own position. Individuals' political party identification may also reflect the party identification and political thinking of their friends and neighbors. Republicans tend to spend time with other Republicans, and Democrats with other Democrats. Since most political conversations take place with politically like-minded people, social networks may reinforce voters' tendencies to share the views of the political party with which they identify.[4]

The modern welfare state was born under Franklin Roosevelt, a Democratic president, and expanded under Lyndon Johnson, another Democrat. Even as the Democrats have tried in recent years to distance their party from its strong identification with (at least some aspects of) the welfare state, the Democrats remain much more strongly identified with government social programs than do the Republicans. Not surprisingly, then, previous research shows that Republicans express greater opposition to welfare than Democrats.[5] Consequently, the analyses in this chapter will take into account respondents' identification with the Democratic or Republican parties.

Liberal/Conservative Ideology

Another possible influence that will be included in this chapter's statistical models concerns an individual's general liberal or conservative orientation. "Liberal" and "conservative" can mean many different things (and do mean different things to different people). Nevertheless, one element of conservatism, as the term is used today, is an opposition to government activism in general and to government spending to redress social ills in particular. Self-identified conservatives are consequently more likely to oppose welfare than are liberals,[6] and survey measures asking whether, "generally speaking," respondents consider themselves liberal, moderate, or conservative are included in the statistical models below.

Age, Sex, Region, Education, and Marital Status

In addition to family income and the various attitudinal measures discussed above, a number of demographic characteristics might be thought to play a role in shaping Americans' welfare views. First, respondents' age might influence their welfare spending preferences, either because older respondents differ in their political attitudes and orientations (e.g., older Americans are more likely to identify as Democrats but are also more likely to express individualist outlooks) or because they differ in their perceived self-interest. Welfare is associated with young families, and older Americans should therefore be less likely to see welfare as a program from which they might directly benefit (and indeed the most prominent welfare program, TANF/AFDC, is limited to families with dependent children).

We might also expect men to oppose welfare more strongly than women. First, since AFDC is targeted to women, men should be less likely to see themselves as potential welfare beneficiaries. Second, past research on sex differences in political attitudes has found that women tend to be more supportive of government social programs and generally express more "compassionate" views on issues from the death penalty to care for the elderly to foreign policy.[7]

Another demographic characteristic that might affect welfare views is region of residence, in particular whether respondents live in the South or elsewhere in the United States. We include a measure of southern residence in the analyses both because the South is traditionally the most politically conservative region of the country and because southern whites remain more racially conservative than whites living outside the South.[8] To assess the impact of racial attitudes on welfare preferences accurately we must therefore take into account the regional differences in whites' racial views. Respondents' education and marital status are also included in the analyses below. Each of these characteristics might be thought to influence welfare views themselves, and each might also play a role in accounting for *other* relevant characteristics such as family income or political orientations.

The Logic of Statistical Controls and Causal Modeling

As explained above, the goal of this chapter is to evaluate the relative importance of these various influences on Americans' welfare spending preferences by examining them simultaneously in a single statistical model. But to assess the contribution of each of these different predictors of welfare spending preferences, we must recognize that each of them can influence welfare views not only directly but also through its influence on the other predictors in the model. Age can have a direct influence on respondents' preferences for increasing or decreasing welfare spending, but it can also influence such preferences through its impact on other political orientations. For example, older Americans might oppose welfare spending because they are more committed individualists than are younger Americans. In this case, some of the influence of age on welfare attitudes is channeled through attitudes toward individualism. A complete understanding of the sources of opposition to welfare would recognize both the total impact of age and the *way* in which age comes to influence attitudes toward welfare.

To assess the total effect of each predictor on welfare attitudes as well as the paths through which that predictor exerts its influence, we must estimate both the direct and indirect impact of each predictor using a multistage regression model. This technique is somewhat more complex than the more common single-equation model, but it provides both an estimate of the total impact of each influence on welfare views and an understanding of *how* that influence operates. (In contrast, single-equation models only provide estimates of the direct impact of each predictor, ignoring indirect influence altogether.)

Figure 4.1   Multistage Causal Model of Opposition to Welfare Spending

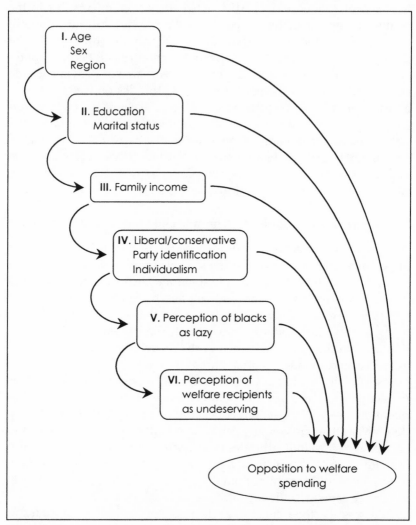

Note: To avoid an overly complex figure, I have omitted the arrows showing variables' direct influence on subsequent stages other than the immediately subsequent stage (e.g., the arrows indicating the direct influence of stage I variables on stages III through VI). Thus variables from each causal stage can influence variables in all subsequent causal stages both directly and indirectly.

Figure 4.1 shows the multistage causal model that undergirds the analyses in this chapter. The eleven predictors of welfare spending preferences are divided into six different causal levels, depending on the causal relationships thought to exist among the different predictors. In the first level are those factors that are most "causally remote" from respondents' welfare views, consisting of respondents' age, sex, and region of residence. As the arrows in figure 4.1 indicate, these characteristics might influence welfare spending preferences both directly and through their influence on the other predictors in the model. The relationships among predictors that are combined into a single causal stage (such as age, sex, and region) are ignored in these analyses, either because the relationships are too weak to be of any consequence (e.g., the impact of age on region of residence) or because the relationships among the predictors are ambiguous. Ambiguous relationships occur, for example, among liberal/conservative ideologies, party identification, and commitment to individualism (all contained in level IV of figure 4.1). Each of these broad political orientations both influences and is influenced by the other two. It is therefore impossible to grant any one of these factors priority over the others, and they are instead assigned to the same causal level.

Unavoidably, models of the type shown in figure 4.1 are an approximation of a more complex reality. We hope that the causal assumptions imbedded in the model reflect the predominant directions of influence among the predictor variables, but we know that some of the complexities of these relationships will be missed. For example, we know that marital status has a strong influence on family income; single people have lower family incomes than those who are married, even among people of the same age and sex. Consequently, marital status is placed causally prior to family income in the model. Nevertheless, we also know that income *can* influence marital status, since men with lower incomes and unsteady work histories are less likely to marry. As long as most of the association between marital status and income reflects the influence of the former on the latter, our model will serve as a useful approximation, and the resulting coefficients will represent a useful, if imperfect, estimate of the true impact of each of these influences on welfare attitudes.

Two additional causal ambiguities in the model of opposition to welfare spending deserve comment. First, respondents' party identification and their liberal or conservative orientation are considered to be causally prior to whether they perceive blacks as lazy. This placement reflects the belief that both partisanship and ideological orientation are fundamental aspects of political identity that remain highly stable over time and are only minimally affected by perceptions of blacks' commitment to the work ethic.[9] On the other hand, it would be surprising if whites' racial attitudes did not have some impact on their party identification or their self-described ideological orientation, and many believe that racial issues have played a central role in the declining fortunes of the Democratic Party over the past few decades.[10]

Given the ambiguity surrounding the causal connection between racial attitudes on the one hand and partisanship and ideology on the other, the ordering of these measures in the model of opposition to welfare provides a conservative estimate of the influence of racial attitudes on welfare views. That is, the model's estimate of the impact of beliefs about blacks' commitment to the work ethic represents a minimum assessment; to the extent that racial attitudes influence welfare views through their effect on respondents' partisanship and ideology, this model understates the total impact of racial attitudes.

The second causally ambiguous relationship among the predictors shown in figure 4.1 involves racial attitudes and perceptions of welfare recipients. The model indicates that beliefs about blacks' commitment to the work ethic are causally prior to attitudes toward welfare recipients. This placement reflects the notion that general beliefs about blacks influence people's views of subgroups of black Americans, such as those receiving welfare. In addition, perceptions of the deservingness of welfare recipients may be more open to short-term fluctuations (as the longitudinal analyses in chapter 2 indicate), in comparison to the more stable attribution of characteristics to different racial groups. Nevertheless, the perception that welfare recipients (of whatever race) are undeserving may negatively affect respondents' views about blacks as a group, and inasmuch as this is true, this model will overestimate the independent effect of racial attitudes and underestimate the impact of perceptions of welfare recipients as undeserving. Again, such ambiguities are unavoidable in any attempt to disentangle the influences of multiple factors (and these ambiguities, it should be stressed, are only ignored, not resolved, in traditional single-equation models of political attitudes). Fortunately, we will be able to address the ambiguous relationship between racial attitudes and nonracial views of welfare recipients with evidence of another kind altogether, the randomized "welfare mother experiment" described below.

Recognizing that the causal relationships shown in figure 4.1 constitute only a plausible simplification of the influences on whites' opposition to welfare, the impact of each predictor in the model can be calculated by estimating separate multiple regression equations for each causal level. Each equation includes the predictors for one of the six causal levels, along with all the predictors from causally prior levels as well. This series of regressions (the complete results of which are found in the appendix) provides the estimates for the total impact of each hypothesized influence on respondents' opposition to welfare spending. These equations also provide the necessary information to separate the part of a given predictor's total impact that is channeled through the causally subsequent predictors in the model from the part that affects welfare spending preferences directly. Using this approach, the estimate for any predictor's direct influence reflects that part of its relationship with opposition to welfare spending that is unaccounted for by the causally subsequent predictors included in the model. Note, however, that some of this "direct" influence may in fact be channeled through other causally intervening variables that were not included in the NRPS. (At times it may be possible to use other sources of survey data to better explain the "direct" influence of a particular predictor, as is done below in the case of respondents' age.)

Predicting Opposition to Welfare

The results of the model described above are found in table 4.1 (and summarized in figure 4.2, found later in this section). The three columns of table 4.1 show the direct, indirect, and total effects of each predictor on nonblack respondents' opposition to welfare spending. The coefficients in table 4.1 represent the amount of change on the 100-point spending preferences measure associated with the full range of values on each predictor variable. For example, the coefficient of 13.9 for the total effect of income indicates that, among respondents with the same age, sex, region, education, and marital status, those with the highest incomes (over $70,000) score 13.9 points higher in opposition to welfare than those with the lowest incomes (under $10,000). The first two columns in table 4.1 show that, of these 13.9 points, only 0.9 can be accounted for by the causally subsequent variables in levels IV, V, and VI, and the remaining 13.0 points represent the "direct" impact of income on opposition to welfare.

The first three causal levels of the welfare attitudes model contain the six demographic predictors: age, sex, region, education, marital status, and family income. As indicated by the asterisks in column three of

Table 4.1 Predictors of Opposition to Welfare Spending

	Direct Effect	Indirect Effect	Total Effect
I. Age	18.6	−2.2	16.4**
Sex	0.8	−2.4	−1.6
Region	−4.3	5.4	1.1
II. Education	0.1	−7.8	−7.7
Marital status	5.5	5.0	10.5***
III. Family income	13.0	0.9	13.9**
IV. Liberal/conservative ideology	12.9	5.1	18.0***
Party identification	11.0	3.0	14.0***
Individualism	10.4	5.1	15.5***
V. Perception of blacks as lazy	23.7	16.3	40.0***
VI. Perception of welfare recipients as undeserving	41.7	0.0	41.7***

Source: National Race and Politics Study, 1991. $N = 996$.

Notes: Table shows unstandardized regression coefficients. Dependent variable is scored 0, 50, or 100 for increase, maintain, or decrease welfare spending. All predictors are scored from 0 to 1, with high scores for female, southerner, married, conservative, and Republican. Analyses include nonblack respondents only. See appendix table A.5 for details.

*$p < .05$; **$p < .01$; ***$p < .001$.

table 4.1, only three of these six predictors have statistically significant impacts on opposition to welfare (see page 241, note 50 for an explanation of statistical significance). Of the six demographic predictors, respondents' age has the largest impact on opposition to welfare spending. Holding sex and region constant, the oldest respondents score 16.4 points higher in opposition to welfare than the youngest. The impact of age on welfare spending preferences is not accounted for by the other variables in the model, as indicated by the negligible coefficient for the indirect effect of age.[11]

Since age has a substantial impact on opposition to welfare and we cannot account for that impact using questions from the NRPS, I turn to the 1986 General Social Survey (GSS) to explain why older Americans are more opposed to welfare than young Americans. In an analysis parallel to that conducted for income in chapter 2, I first calculated the impact of age on opposition to welfare spending and then examined a number of variables that might account for this impact when entered as statistical controls in a regression equation. Using the same coding scheme employed for table 4.1, I found that the GSS produced a coefficient of 14.6 for the total effect of age as a predictor of opposition to welfare spending (full results are reported in appendix table A.9). After examining a number of possible explanations, I found that most of this impact can be accounted for by the perception that welfare leads to family breakup and encourages single motherhood. Two questions from the GSS address this issue. The first asks whether or not welfare encourages young women to have babies before marriage and the second, whether welfare discourages young women who get pregnant from marrying the father of the child. When these two questions are added to the regression of age on welfare spending preferences, the impact of age declines from 14.6 to only 4.5. Thus most of the impact of age on welfare spending preferences can be attributed to the greater fear among older Americans that welfare fosters out-of-wedlock births among young women.

Marital status is the second important predictor of opposition to welfare. Table 4.1 shows that married respondents score 10.5 units higher on the 100-point scale of opposition to welfare, in comparison to unmarried respondents of the same age, sex, region, and education. About half of the influence of marital status is indirect and is therefore accounted for by the more causally proximate variables in the model. The full series of regression models provided in the appendix reveals that married respondents are more likely to oppose welfare partly because they have higher family incomes than the unmarried (explaining 42 percent of the indirect impact of marital status) and partly because married people have somewhat more conservative political orientations than their unmarried peers (explaining an additional 28 percent of the indirect impact of marriage).

Income is the third demographic predictor that is significantly related to opposition to welfare spending. As the last column in table 4.1 shows, the full range of income (from less than $10,000 to over $70,000) is associated with a 13.9 point difference in welfare spending preferences. As with age, virtually none of the impact of income is accounted for by the more causally proximate variables in the model, but as we saw in chapter 2, this impact can be explained largely by differences between better- and worse-off Americans in experience (or lack of experience) with welfare and perceptions that welfare has become a long-term trap for its recipients rather than an avenue out of poverty.

The fourth causal level of the welfare attitudes model contains three broad political orientations, each of which has a significant impact on opposition to welfare. Strong conservatives are 18 points higher in opposition to welfare than are strong liberals with the same demographic characteristics (i.e., age, sex, region, education, marital status, and income). Similarly, respondents who strongly identify with the Republican Party are 14 points higher in opposition to welfare than are demographically similar Democrats. Finally, individualists—who agree strongly that the government has encroached on the proper domain of individuals and business—are 15.5 points higher in opposition to welfare than are those who disagree strongly with this notion. Each of these three political orientations primarily influences opposition to welfare spending directly. Still, between one-fifth and one-third of the total impact of these variables is accounted for by perceptions of blacks as lazy and perceptions of welfare recipients as undeserving.

Causal levels five and six contain what are clearly the most important predictors of welfare policy preferences. Respondents who think that blacks are lazy and those who think welfare recipients are undeserving express dramatically higher levels of opposition to welfare. Among respondents with the same demographic characteristics, ideology, party identification, and attitudes toward individualism, those who hold the most extreme views of blacks as lazy score 40 points higher in opposition to welfare than those who view blacks as hardworking. Moreover, those who feel most strongly that welfare recipients could get along without it are almost 42 points higher in opposition to welfare than otherwise similar respondents who think most people on welfare would rather be working if they could. Each of these predictors is over twice as strong as the next most powerful predictor of opposition to welfare (liberal/conservative ideology). Most of the impact of racial views on opposition to welfare is direct, but a substantial portion (about 41 percent) is accounted for by the tendency of those who view blacks as lazy to also view welfare recipients as undeserving. Since perceptions of deservingness constitutes the last causal stage in the model, the impact on opposition to welfare is necessarily direct only.

The results in table 4.1 are summarized in figure 4.2, which illustrates graphically the direct, indirect, and total effect of each of the significant predictors and underlines again the importance of racial views and perceptions of welfare recipients as undeserving. These findings add strong support to our earlier analyses suggesting that racial attitudes and perceptions of deservingness are central elements in generating public opposition to welfare. This model of welfare attitudes also

Figure 4.2   Predictors of Opposition to Welfare Spending

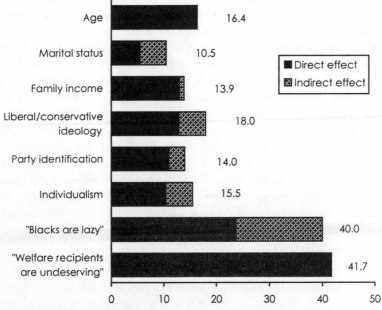

Source: National Race and Politics Study, 1991.

Notes: Figure shows regression analysis of welfare spending preferences (only statistically significant predictors are shown). See table 4.1 and appendix for details.

confirms that individualist beliefs play a role in generating opposition to welfare, although individualism is clearly less important than racial attitudes or perceptions of deservingness. Finally, among the attitude measures, conservative ideology and identification with the Republican Party both contribute toward opposition to welfare.

These analyses also show that demographic characteristics influence respondents' welfare views. Age, marital status, and family income all have significant impacts on opposition to welfare spending. While it is easy to see how the impact of each of these characteristics might reflect economic self-interest, the supplementary analyses in this chapter and in chapter 2 suggest that it is the attitudes and experiences associated with age, marital status, and income that explain most of their impact on opposition to welfare. As we saw above, the greater opposition of the elderly is due in large measure to their greater concern with the impact of welfare on the family. Greater opposition among the married is due in part to their more conservative outlooks and higher incomes.

And most of the impact of income itself, as we saw in chapter 2, can be accounted for by the lack of experience with welfare among higher-income Americans and the perception among the better-off that welfare too often becomes a long-term trap for the poor.

To the extent that these analyses of welfare spending preferences overlap with previous work conducted by other scholars, the results are consistent. For example, Fay Cook and Edith Barrett present a multi-level latent-variable model of spending preferences for AFDC. Cook and Barrett do not include measures of racial attitudes in their analyses, but in those cases where their predictors parallel the predictors used in the models above, the results are similar.[12] Taking a different approach, Jim Kluegel and Elliot Smith present a single-equation model of welfare attitudes using a wide array of predictors. Kluegel and Smith do include racial attitudes in their model and find it to be among the strongest predictors of welfare views, but their theoretical interests lie elsewhere and racial attitudes do not figure prominently in their subsequent discussion or analysis.[13]

Determinants of Racial Attitudes and Perceptions of Welfare Recipients as Undeserving

The multistage analysis of welfare attitudes shows that the two most important sources of opposition to welfare are the perceptions that blacks are lazy and that welfare recipients are undeserving. The next step in analyzing the sources of Americans' opposition to welfare is to take a "step back" from this analysis and examine the determinants of these two factors. The analyses in table 4.2 use the same set of predictor variables but this time examine their impact, not on welfare spending preferences, but on perceptions that welfare recipients are undeserving and blacks are lazy. For brevity's sake, table 4.2 reports only the total effect of each predictor, but the full regression results are provided in appendix tables A.6 and A.7.

We see first that age is a significant influence on both perceptions of welfare recipients and racial attitudes, but with opposite effects. Older respondents are less likely to view welfare recipients as undeserving but more likely to think that blacks are lazy. The first of these findings underscores the observation made earlier that older Americans are more opposed to welfare spending because they think welfare breaks up families, not because they think people on welfare are undeserving. The more negative views of blacks expressed by older respondents may reflect the generational differences that have emerged over the past

Table 4.2 Predictors of the Perceptions That Welfare Recipients Are Undeserving and Blacks Are Lazy (total effects only)

	Welfare Recipients Are Undeserving	Blacks Are Lazy
I. Age	−11.0**	7.5**
Sex	−1.0	0.3
Region	6.4***	5.4***
II. Education	−20.4***	−15.0***
Marital status	3.3	1.7
III. Family income	−0.5	−1.7
IV. Liberal/conservative ideology	9.0**	5.4*
Party identification	5.8**	2.8
Individualism	11.6***	1.4
V. Perception of blacks as lazy	39.1***	

Source: National Race and Politics Study, 1991. N = 996.

Notes: Table shows unstandardized regression coefficients. Dependent variable is scored 0, 50, or 100 for increase, maintain, or decrease welfare spending. All predictors are scored from 0 to 1, with high scores for female, southerner, married, conservative, and Republican. Analyses include nonblack respondents only. See appendix tables A.6 and A.7 for details.

*p < .05; **p < .01; ***p < .001.

half-century as younger cohorts of whites have adopted more liberal racial attitudes than their older peers.[14]

Region has a smaller but consistent effect on these two sets of beliefs. Although the differences are not great, residents of the South hold more negative views of both welfare recipients and blacks. Education is only weakly (and nonsignificantly) related to welfare spending preferences, but it is a strong predictor of both perceptions of welfare recipients and racial attitudes. Respondents with the highest education (some graduate education) score about 20 points lower in perceiving welfare recipients as undeserving and 15 points lower in perceiving blacks as lazy, compared with those at the lowest educational level (eighth grade or lower).

The three general political orientations—liberal/conservative ideology, party identification, and individualism—all shape perceptions of welfare recipients, but only ideology is significantly related to the belief that blacks are lazy. Finally, we see once again the importance of racial attitudes in explaining welfare views: the belief that blacks are lazy is the strongest predictor of the perception that welfare recipients are undeserving, with a coefficient (39.1) almost twice as strong as that of the next most powerful predictor (education). Considering the analyses in tables 4.1 and 4.2 together, racial attitudes stand out as a key factor in understanding white Americans' opposition to welfare. Not only is the perception of blacks as lazy the second most powerful predictor of welfare spending preferences, but it is the most important influence on the perception that welfare recipients are undeserving (which is itself the most powerful predictor of welfare spending preferences).

But before we accept that racial attitudes are central to Americans' opposition to welfare, there is one complicating factor we need to consider. As discussed in chapter 3, poor people in this country are disproportionately black, and more important for our purposes, Americans *perceive* the poor to be disproportionately black. As a consequence, it is difficult to disentangle Americans' perceptions of blacks from their perceptions of poor people in general. For example, respondents' evaluation of blacks as lazy may simply reflect their beliefs that poor people in general tend to be lazy and that blacks tend to be poor. The question arises, then, to what extent are the racial views that so strongly influence welfare attitudes tied specifically to respondents' beliefs about blacks, as opposed to their broader beliefs about poor people of all races? We cannot be confident that we have uncovered the operation of racial attitudes until we have succeeded in disentangling these two overlapping sets of beliefs.

The most common technique for statistically isolating one set of beliefs from another is to include them both in a multiple regression model like those used in this chapter. In this case, however, we run into a problem. To successfully "partial out" perceptions of the poor from similar perceptions of blacks, we need to ask identical (or nearly identical) questions about these two different target groups. However, we cannot simply ask respondents to evaluate both blacks and poor people using the same questions. Because social norms of equality apply to racial issues, respondents may feel pressured to provide the same responses to questions about blacks and about whites.[15] For example, if white respondents acknowledge their belief that black welfare recipients are lazy, they face a pressure to say that white welfare recipients are lazy as well, if asked in a subsequent question. Alternatively, if they first indicate that whites on welfare would prefer to be working, they might feel pressured to respond that African American welfare recipients would rather be working too. To avoid this kind of consistency pressure, I use a survey-based experiment from the NRPS that yields independent and "uncontaminated" measures of respondents' attitudes toward poor blacks and poor whites.

Using a Survey Experiment to Assess Racial Attitudes

To gauge white respondents' true views of poor blacks and poor whites with identical questions, I analyze the results of an experimental manipulation in the NRPS in which half the respondents are asked only about blacks and the other half are asked otherwise identical questions about whites. Because each respondent is asked about only one racial group, consistency pressures are absent. Thus, rather than compare two questions (or sets of questions) asked of the same group of respondents, I compare the answers given by two different groups of respondents. Key to this experiment (as to all true experiments) is the fact that respondents are *randomly* assigned the "black" or "white" versions of these questions. With a large enough sample (like that found in public opinion surveys) random assignment of respondents to different experimental groups ensures that the different groups will be nearly identical in every way, including the attitudes of interest. Consequently, we can treat the two experimental groups as equally representative of the larger population of Americans from which they are drawn. Thus, although we have not asked any single respondent about both poor blacks and poor whites, we can nevertheless assess attitudes toward both groups with confidence.

This technique combines the advantages of the randomized experiment with those of the sample survey.[16] By randomly assigning respondents to different question "treatments" we ensure that differences in responses result from differences in the questions asked, and since the random assignment is uncorrelated with respondents' characteristics we need not worry that differences in responses to poor blacks and poor whites are confounded with other factors such as education, region, or political attitudes. By embedding this experiment within a large-scale national survey, we also retain the ability to generalize to the American population at large, an ability that is severely limited in the typical small-scale experiment.

By means of this "survey experiment" we can reveal something of the thought process respondents use in evaluating welfare: when white Americans assess welfare in general, or identify their preferences with regard to welfare spending, are they thinking more about black welfare recipients, white welfare recipients, or both equally? In the "welfare mother" experiment from the NRPS, respondents are asked their impressions of a welfare recipient described as either a black or white woman in her early thirties, who has a ten-year-old child and has been on welfare for the past year.[17] Respondents are first asked how likely it is that the woman described will try hard to find a job and second, how likely it is that she will have more children in order to get a bigger welfare check. Half of the respondents are randomly assigned to the "black version" of the question and the other half, to the "white version." For this analysis, the responses to the questions about jobs and children are combined into an index of negative welfare mother stereotypes,[18] with those saying it is very unlikely that the welfare mother will look for a job and very likely that she will have more children receiving the highest scores.

If respondents are thinking more about black welfare mothers when they offer their overall views of welfare, then we would expect the black version of the welfare mother experiment to be a better predictor of opposition to welfare than the white version. Because the two versions of these questions are identical except for the race of the hypothetical welfare mother, and because respondents were randomly assigned to one version of the questions or the other, we can feel certain that, if the two versions do differ in their ability to predict whites' welfare views, this difference reflects the influence of respondents' racial attitudes.

To assess the relative importance of black and white welfare mother stereotypes in explaining opposition to welfare spending, I repeat the regression analyses of table 4.1 using responses to the black and white versions of the welfare mother experiment in place of the measures of blacks as lazy and welfare recipients as undeserving. Because different groups of respondents were asked the black and white versions of the welfare mother questions, separate analyses are conducted for each group. However, to ensure that any differences found in comparing these results arise from the race of the hypothetical welfare mother, and not from chance variations between the two randomized groups, the relationships among the *other* variables in the analysis are set equal across the two treatment groups.[19]

The predictors in causal levels I through IV of table 4.3 are the same as those in the earlier analyses in tables 4.1 and 4.2. Consequently, the coefficients for these predictors of opposition to welfare spending in table 4.3 are very similar to what we found in the analysis of welfare spending preferences in table 4.1.[20] Of primary interest in table 4.3 are the coefficients in level V, which indicate the impact of the black and white welfare mother stereotypes on respondents' opposition to welfare. The analysis shows that, as suspected, beliefs about black welfare mothers are more important in generating opposition to welfare

Table 4.3 Predictors of Opposition to Welfare Spending: The Welfare Mother Experiment

	White Welfare Mother	Black Welfare Mother
I. Age	15.1**	15.1**
Sex	−0.3	−0.3
Region	4.7	4.7
II. Education	−9.0	−9.0
Marital status	8.4**	8.4**
III. Family income	12.3**	12.3**
IV. Liberal/conservative ideology	15.1**	15.1**
Party identification	11.9**	11.9**
Individualism	11.4**	11.4**
V. Negative views of welfare mother	15.9**	30.0***

Source: National Race and Politics Study, 1991. $N = 879$.

Notes: This table reports total effects only (using unstandardized regression coefficients) from two separate series of regression analyses, one series for those respondents who were randomly assigned questions about a black welfare mother and a separate series for respondents randomly assigned questions about a white welfare mother. Dependent variable is scored 0, 50, or 100 for increase, maintain, or decrease welfare spending. All predictors are scored from 0 to 1, with high scores for female, southerner, married, conservative, and Republican. Analyses include nonblack respondents only. See appendix table A.8 for details.

$^*p < .05; ^{**}p < .01; ^{***}p < .001.$

spending than are beliefs about white welfare mothers. Using identically worded questions, we find that stereotypes of black welfare recipients are almost twice as strong in predicting opposition to welfare as are stereotypes of white welfare recipients. Nonblack respondents with the most negative views of black welfare recipients are 30 points higher in opposition to welfare than are those with the most positive views of black welfare mothers. In comparison, the difference between respondents with the most negative and most positive views of white welfare mothers is only 15.9 points. Despite the fact that blacks constitute only 36 percent of all welfare recipients, they clearly dominate the American public's thinking about welfare.[21]

Welfare Mother Stereotypes and Other Welfare Attitudes

If racial attitudes truly pervade the public's thinking about poverty and welfare, then the same logic that applies to welfare spending prefer-

Figure 4.3   Correlations between Welfare Attitudes and Stereotypes of Black or White
Welfare Mothers

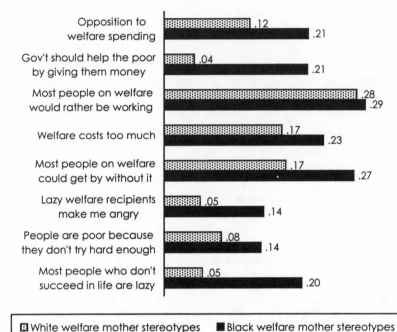

Source: National Race and Politics Study, 1991. N = 502 to 1,002 (some questions were
asked of a random subsample of respondents).

ences should apply to other aspects of welfare attitudes. That is, compared with their perceptions of white welfare mothers, respondents'
perceptions of black welfare mothers should be more strongly related
to most of their attitudes, perceptions, and policy preferences with regard to welfare. Figure 4.3 shows that this is exactly the case. Black welfare mother stereotypes have consistently stronger correlations than do
white welfare mother stereotypes with a wide range of welfare attitude
measures. On one of these eight questions, black welfare mother stereotypes barely edge out white welfare mother stereotypes as a predictor,
but on most of the questions the difference is substantial. Indeed, in
some cases the association with welfare attitudes is four or five times as
large for the black version of the welfare mother questions as it is for
the white version.

African Americans are a minority of both poor people and welfare
recipients, and political elites usually talk about welfare in race-neutral

terms. Yet images of blacks have come to dominate the public's thinking about poverty and welfare, generating negative perceptions of welfare recipients and fostering demands for cuts in welfare spending. Why does race play such a central role in the public's attitudes toward welfare? To answer this question we need to explore what is so often missing from analyses of survey data: the cultural and historical context that gives rise to contemporary attitudes. As we will see in chapter 5, poor Americans have been disproportionately black for centuries, but the current racialized image of poverty emerged only in the 1960s. By looking at historical changes in public images of the poor, we can better understand the current dominance of racial attitudes in the public's thinking about poverty.

5

The News Media and the Racialization
of Poverty

As we have seen, racial attitudes play a central role in generating opposition to welfare spending among white Americans and in shaping whites' views on many aspects of poverty and welfare. In this chapter I investigate the historical process by which race has come to dominate the public's thinking about the poor.

It might seem that this question is barely worth asking. After all, it is a simple fact that poor people in this country are disproportionately black. Yet African Americans constitute a small percentage of all Americans, and even though they are more likely to be poor than are whites, they nevertheless constitute a minority of both poor people (of whom 27 percent are black) and welfare recipients (of whom 36 percent are black).[1] As we saw in chapter 3, however, the public exaggerates the extent to which African Americans compose the poor. On average, Americans believe that blacks make up not 27 percent, but 50 percent of all poor people. In the following pages I explore the shifting images of the poor that have held sway during different periods of American history. I argue that the exaggerated link between blacks and the poor that now exists in the public's imagination developed only in the 1960s, and that it developed in response to a series of rather dramatic social changes and events. But I also argue that the racialization of poverty images in this period reflected a preexisting stereotype of blacks as lazy. As media discourse on poverty and welfare became more negative in the mid-1960s, the complexion of the poor grew darker.

African Americans: The Once Invisible Poor

The American public now associates poverty and welfare with blacks. But this was not always the case. Although African Americans have always been disproportionately poor, black poverty was ignored by white society throughout most of American history. The "scientific" study of poverty in America began around the end of the nineteenth century. During this period social reformers and poverty experts made the first systematic efforts to describe and analyze America's poor.[2] Racial distinctions were common in these works, but such distinctions usually referred to the various white European "races" such as the Irish, Italians, and Poles; this early poverty literature had little or nothing to say about blacks. The classic work from this era is Robert Hunter's book *Poverty*, published in 1904.[3] Hunter drew from the existing statistical and ethnographic accounts of poverty to paint a picture of the American poor at the turn of the century. Although Hunter spent considerable time discussing the work habits, nutritional needs, and intelligence of the Italians, Irish, Poles, Hungarians, Germans, and Jews, African Americans escaped his attention altogether.[4]

During the 1920s, African American migration from the rural South to northern cities began to accelerate. These growing black communities, and especially the emergence of Harlem as a highly visible urban black neighborhood, brought some attention to African American poverty. According to one study, white America's "revolutionary recognition" of black life and culture in the 1920s was evident in the popular white-oriented periodicals of the day. During this period popular mass-circulation magazines printed numerous stories on Negro life and culture.[5] But this increased attention focused more on blacks as symbols of the Jazz Age and on Harlem as a place of "laughing, swaying, and dancing."[6] White Americans remained profoundly uninformed and unconcerned about black poverty.

The Great Depression, of course, brought the topic of poverty to the forefront of public attention. But as the American economy faltered, and poverty and unemployment increased, white writers and commentators remained oblivious to the sufferings of the black poor. For example, I. M. Rubinow's *Quest for Security*, published in the middle of the depression and often cited in subsequent literature on poverty, made no mention of blacks.[7] Although poverty remained a pressing concern during the 1940s, the bombing of Pearl Harbor and America's subsequent entrance into World War II naturally focused public concern elsewhere.

During the postwar period, the country's attention turned to rebuilding the domestic economy and fighting communism both at home and abroad. Poverty seemed like a distant problem during the postwar years. The economy grew dramatically after the war, and living standards rose quickly. By one estimate, poverty in the United States declined from 48 percent in 1935, to 27 percent in 1950, to 21 percent in 1960.[8] Along with economic growth came lifestyle changes. By 1960, 86 percent of American homes had televisions, automobile ownership had increased as the population shifted toward suburbs, and middle-class Americans had become homeowners on a scale never seen before.[9] Few people worried about those being left behind during America's postwar growth. In the 1950s Americans—and American journalists— were busy celebrating "The American Century"; *Time*, *Newsweek* and *U.S. News and World Report* each published an average of just sixteen stories about poverty *for the entire decade*.[10]

Poverty was "rediscovered," however, in the 1960s. Stimulated first by the publication of John Kenneth Galbraith's *The Affluent Society* (in 1958) and then by Michael Harrington's *The Other America* (in 1962), the American public and policy makers alike began once more to notice the poor. John Kennedy is said to have been shaken by the grinding poverty he saw in West Virginia during the 1960 presidential campaign, where a lack of both education and job opportunities had trapped genera- tions of poor whites in the primitive conditions of rural poverty.[11] And early in his presidency Kennedy launched a number of antipoverty pro- grams focusing on juvenile delinquency, education and training pro- grams, and federal assistance for depressed regions of the country. But the poverty programs of the early 1960s, and the popular images of the poor that went along with them, were just as pale in complexion as those of the turn of the century. Attention to poor blacks was still quite limited both in the mass media and, apparently, among Kennedy ad- ministration staffers.[12] If there was a dominant image of poverty at this time, it was the white rural poor of the Appalachian coal fields.

Background Conditions for the Racialization of Poverty

Popular images of poverty changed dramatically, however, in the mid-1960s. After centuries of obscurity, at least as far as white America was concerned, poor blacks came to dominate public thinking about pov- erty. Two social changes set the stage for the "racialization" of popular images of the poor. The first was the widespread migration of rural southern blacks to northern cities. At the turn of the twentieth century, over 90 percent of African Americans lived in the South, and three-quarters of all blacks resided in rural areas.[13] Blacks had been leav- ing the South at a slow rate for decades, but black migration from the South grew tremendously during the 1940s and 1950s. The average black out-migration from the South between 1910 and 1939 was only

55,000 people per year. But during the 1940s it increased to 160,000 per year, during the 1950s it declined slightly (to 146,000 per year), and between 1960 and 1966 it fell to 102,000 per year.[14] As a consequence of this migration, African Americans, who accounted for only 2 percent of all northerners in 1910, comprised 7 percent by 1960, and, perhaps more importantly, made up 12 percent of the population in urban areas.[15]

As a result of migration, the population of northern, urban blacks grew steadily during the 1940s and 1950s and continued to grow, though at a slower rate, in the 1960s. But as we will see below, the racialization of public images of the poor occurred fairly suddenly and dramatically between 1965 and 1967. Clearly there is no simple connection between the growth of African American communities in northern cities and public perceptions of the poor as black. Nevertheless, the growth of the black population in the North was one link in a chain of events that led to the dramatic changes in how Americans thought about poverty.

A second change that paved the way for the racialization of poverty images was the changing racial composition of AFDC, the nation's most conspicuous program to aid the poor. As established in the Social Security Act of 1935, the ADC program (as it was then called) was structured in such a way as to permit states to limit the number of black recipients. Individual states were allowed considerable discretion to determine both the formal rules governing ADC eligibility and the application of those rules. At the insistence of southern legislators, the clause mandating that ADC provide "a reasonable subsistence compatible with health and decency" was removed from the Social Security Act, thereby allowing states with large black populations to provide extremely low benefits.[16] In 1940 the national average ADC payment was about $13.00 per month per child; in contrast, black children in Arkansas were receiving only $3.52 per month while those in South Carolina were getting just over $4 per month.[17] Other southern states also established very low benefit levels, with payments for black children averaging between five and eight dollars per month.[18]

In addition to imposing low benefit levels for black families, states excluded many black mothers from ADC by the discretionary application of "suitable home" policies.[19] These policies gave caseworkers wide latitude to deny ADC benefits to families with children born out of wedlock or to mothers thought to be engaged in illicit relationships. Furthermore, despite the fact that ADC was envisioned as a program to assist single mothers so that they could devote their time to raising their children rather than working for a wage, some southern states provided only seasonal benefits to blacks, eliminating assistance when additional labor was needed in the fields during harvest time.[20]

As a result of these various policies, African Americans were disproportionately excluded from ADC. In 1936 only 13.5 percent of ADC recipients were African American, despite blacks' much higher representation among poor single mothers.[21] Over the next three decades, however, the proportion of blacks among ADC recipients rose steadily (figure 5.1). This increase resulted from a variety of influences, both legislative and economic. For example, the establishment of Social Security survivors' benefits in 1939 removed proportionately more white than black widows from the ADC rolls, thereby increasing the percentage of blacks among those remaining.[22] In addition, an increase in the federal matching-grant contribution to the ADC program from one-third to one-half of total state ADC expenditures encouraged some states to expand their coverage or to begin participating in the ADC program for the first time.[23]

As figure 5.1 shows, the percentage of African Americans among ADC/AFDC recipients increased steadily from about 14 percent in 1936 to about 46 percent in 1973; thereafter the proportion of blacks declined slowly until it reached about 36 percent in 1995. Between the mid-1960s and early 1970s, then, African Americans made up a very substantial minority of AFDC recipients. Consequently, as the welfare rolls began

Figure 5.1   Percentage African American among ADC/AFDC Recipients, 1936–1995

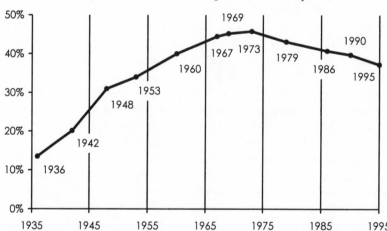

Sources: For 1936–53 and 1967–79, Turner, *Federal/State Aid to Dependent Children;* for 1960, Piven and Cloward, *Regulating the Poor;* for 1986–95, U.S. House of Representatives, 1998 Green Book.

to expand in the late 1960s (figure 1.2), the public's attention was drawn disproportionately to poor blacks. Yet the pattern of growth in the proportion of African American welfare recipients shown in figure 5.1 also makes clear that the sudden shift in images of poverty during the 1960s cannot be attributed to any sudden change in the makeup of the welfare population. The proportion of blacks among AFDC participants had been growing steadily for decades. Like black migration to the North, the changing racial composition of the welfare rolls constituted a background condition that contributed to the changes in public perceptions of the poor, but it did not serve as a precipitating cause of those changes. After all, the proportion of blacks among welfare recipients was almost as high in 1960 as it was in 1967, yet public concern in 1960 was still focused on poor whites, in particular, the poor rural whites of Appalachia.

Precipitating Events in the Racialization of Poverty

Gradual demographic changes in residential patterns and welfare receipt by African Americans laid the groundwork for the changes to come in how Americans viewed the poor. But the more immediate precipitating events were the shift in focus within the civil rights movement from the fight for legal equality to the battle for economic equality and the urban riots that rocked the country during the summers of 1964 through 1968.

In the 1950s, African Americans living in the South attended segregated schools, rode segregated buses, and used segregated bathrooms. Blacks could not drink from "white" water fountains, eat in "white" restaurants, or sleep in "white" hotels. African Americans had little voice in government and little hope for fair treatment from the white police or the white judiciary. In the North, legal segregation of the races was less common, but racial discrimination by individuals, governments, and other institutions maintained high levels of both residential and school segregation.[24]

Some progress toward racial equality did occur in the immediate postwar years. Fair- employment laws were adopted in twelve states and thirty cities by 1953; median black family income rose from 41 percent of white family income in 1940 to 57 percent by 1952; and school enrollment among blacks increased from 68 percent in 1940 to 75 percent by 1950, only four percentage points lower than white school enrollment.[25] But the South in particular remained steadfast in its resistance to racial equality and its commitment to the *de jure* separatism of

Jim Crow. Black protests against racial injustice had been sporadic in the early decades of the twentieth century and had largely died out during World War II. But in the mid-1950s, the modern civil rights movement began a concerted and sustained effort to force an end to the injustice and indignities of racial segregation. In December 1955, Rosa Parks, a black seamstress, was jailed for refusing to vacate her seat on a segregated bus. Ms. Parks' quiet protest began the Montgomery Bus Boycott, led by a previously unknown young black minister named Martin Luther King Jr. The eventual success of the year-long bus boycott led to a decade of demonstrations, protests, and sit-ins throughout the South, all pressing the demand for legal equality and an end to racial segregation.

The struggles of the early civil rights movement were for equal rights, black enfranchisement, and an end to legal segregation. These efforts produced their most significant successes with the passage of the Civil Rights Act of 1964 and the Voting Rights Act of 1965. The Civil Rights Act prohibited segregation in public accommodations and banned discrimination by trade unions and schools, and by employers involved in interstate commerce or doing business with the federal government. It also called for the desegregation of public schools and outlawed some of the voting procedures used to impede African Americans. The Voting Rights Act, passed the following year, banned literacy tests and established federal government oversight of registration and voting in jurisdictions with low voter turnout (primarily southern counties with high proportions of blacks). As a consequence of these and other legal measures, nationwide voter registration rates among African Americans increased from only 29 percent in 1962 to 67 percent in 1970.[26]

In the second half of the 1960s, civil rights leaders shifted their attention from legal inequality to economic inequality. Although the battle for black enfranchisement in the South had a long way to go, the first large urban uprisings during the summer of 1964 and the greater number of ghetto riots during the summers to follow shifted both the geographical and programmatic focus of the struggle for racial equality.

Of course, racial economic inequality was hardly a new concern to civil rights leaders. In 1963 the National Urban League had called for a "crash program of special effort to close the gap between the conditions of Negro and white citizens" and released a ten-point "Marshall Plan for the American Negro." In the same year, Martin Luther King issued a similarly conceived "G.I. Bill of Rights for the Disadvantaged."[27] But these early efforts were almost wholly overshadowed by the struggle for basic civil rights in the South.

In 1966, however, Martin Luther King and the Southern Christian Leadership Conference (SCLC) focused their attention on the plight of the black urban poor of the northern ghettos. With help from the AFL-CIO and the United Auto Workers, King and the SCLC organized demonstrations and rent strikes in Chicago to dramatize the dire economic conditions facing so many urban blacks. King called for a variety of measures aimed at improving the lot of Chicago's black population: integrating the *de facto* segregated public schools, reallocating public services to better serve minority populations, building low-rent public housing units, and removing public funds from banks that refused to make loans to blacks.[28]

For all his efforts, King achieved little in Chicago. Mayor Richard Daley claimed his administration was already making the necessary efforts to improve life for low-income blacks; the more moderate local civil rights organizations resented King's intrusion and the attention he received; and black militants called King a sell-out for compromising with the white political powers. But the concern with northern urban blacks' economic problems exemplified by the Chicago Freedom Movement and the 1968 Poor People's March on Washington (led, after King's assassination, by Ralph Abernathy) helped to focus public attention on the problem of black poverty.[29]

At least as important as the shifting focus of civil rights leaders were the ghetto riots themselves. Poor blacks, for so long invisible to most of white America, made their presence known in the most dramatic way possible. During the summer of 1964 riots broke out in Harlem, Rochester, Chicago, Philadelphia, and New Jersey. Five lives were lost and property damage was estimated at $6 million.[30] Civil rights leaders tried to respond to these disturbances, but much of their attention, and the rest of the country's as well, was still focused on the South. The Voting Rights Act had been passed, but much work remained in actually registering black voters. Mississippi, in particular, had been staunchly resisting blacks' efforts to vote.

To press for voting rights in Mississippi, the leading civil rights organizations united to mobilize local blacks and out-of-state volunteers for the Freedom Summer of 1964. Nine hundred volunteers, many of them white college students from the country's elite universities, joined the effort to register Mississippi's blacks. White Mississippi responded with violence. Twenty-seven black churches were burned that summer in Mississippi, and thirty blacks were murdered between January and August of 1964. But the nation's attention was grabbed by the murder of three young civil rights workers—James Chaney, Andrew Goodman, and Michael Schwerner—the first a black Mississippian, the other two white New Yorkers. The three disappeared while returning from an investigation of the burned-out Mt. Zion Methodist Church in Neshoba County, Mississippi. Only after a six-week search by the FBI were their bodies found, buried in an earthen dam.[31]

Despite the riots, news coverage of race relations during the summer of 1964 was dominated by the events in Mississippi. But in the next few years, ghetto uprisings and the militant voices of Malcolm X, Stokeley Carmichael, and the Black Panthers would become increasingly central fixtures in the struggle for racial equality. In August 1965, the Los Angeles neighborhood of Watts exploded. A six-day riot left 34 people dead (all but three of them black), 900 injured, and nearly 4,000 arrested, and caused $30 million in property damage.[32] The Watts riots were followed that summer by more disturbances in Chicago and in Springfield, Massachusetts. The summers of 1966 and 1967 saw even more rioting, as blacks took to the streets in dozens of American cities. In 1967 alone, rioting led to at least 90 deaths, more than 4,000 injuries, and nearly 17,000 arrests.[33]

There is no doubt that the rioting of the mid-1960s marked a dramatic chapter in American race relations. But the impact of the riots on white Americans' attitudes toward blacks remains subject to debate. Some see the urban riots of the 1960s as ushering in a new era of antiblack racism. Donald Kinder and Lynn Sanders, for example, point out that blacks and whites reacted very differently to the riots, which blacks tended to see as expressions of legitimate grievances, and whites, as senseless violence.[34] Yet survey-based studies reveal little that could be interpreted as a negative shift in whites' racial attitudes during this period. On the contrary, the many survey questions on racial attitudes that span the period of the mid-1960s show either no change or a liberal shift in whites' attitudes.[35] As one in-depth study of the Watts riots concluded, "The very sharp polarization that did occur immediately over blacks' tactics, and particularly over the rioting, apparently did not generalize into more negative or resistant white attitudes toward blacks and their progress. Indeed, if anything, whites' support for blacks' progress seemed, in the long run, to have increased somewhat."[36]

The ghetto riots of the mid-1960s were played out before a rapt television audience, and blacks and whites often drew different conclusions from the upheavals they witnessed. But even if the riots had little lasting impact on white Americans' racial views, there is no question that the ghetto revolts of 1964–67 helped bring the black urban poor to the forefront of American social problems.

Portrayals of Poverty in the News Media

It is clear that the black poor were ignored by white Americans throughout most of our history, including the first two-thirds of the twentieth century, and it is equally clear that blacks now figure prominently in public perceptions of the poor. But did Americans' images of the poor really change dramatically between the early and late 1960s as the historical narrative I have outlined would suggest? Unfortunately, pollsters did not think to ask about perceptions of the racial composition of the poor until recently. But we can examine changes in the way the poor have been portrayed in the mass media. While we cannot assume that media portrayals necessarily reflect popular beliefs, changing images of the poor in the news can tell us how news professionals thought about the poor at different times, as well as what sorts of images of poverty the public was being exposed to through the mass media. Since we have good reason to think that media portrayals have a strong impact on public perceptions (see chapter 6), news images provide at least some evidence of how the American public viewed the poor. At the very least, media coverage will tell us something about the aspects of poverty (or the subgroups of the poor) that played a prominent role in public discussion of these issues during different periods.

To assess changes in news media portrayals of poverty over the past forty-five years, I examined three weekly newsmagazines, *Time*, *Newsweek*, and *U.S. News and World Report*. I chose these magazines because they are widely read, are national in coverage and distribution, and have been published continuously for many decades. They also contain large numbers of pictures, an especially important consideration in studying the racial portrayal of the poor. To the extent that our interest lies in the perceptions of the racial composition of the poor that magazine readers are likely to form, the pictures of poor people are more influential than the textual information these magazines contain. First, the typical reader of these magazines looks at most, if not all, of the pictures but reads far fewer of the stories. Thus, even a subscriber who does not bother to read a particular story on poverty is quite likely to see the pictures of poor people that it contains.[37] Second, while specific information about the racial makeup of the poor is found periodically in these newsmagazines, such information is quite rare. Between

1960 and 1990, fewer than 5 percent of poverty-related stories had any concrete information on the racial composition of the poor or any sub-groups of the poor, such as AFDC recipients or public housing ten-ants.[38] Finally, research on the impact of news stories and the process by which readers (or TV viewers) assimilate information suggests that people are more likely to remember pictures than words and more likely to form impressions based on examples of specific individuals than on abstract statistical information.[39]

To assess media portrayals of poverty, I first identified every poverty-related story in these three magazines published from 1950 through 1992. Using the *Readers' Guide to Periodical Literature*, I developed a set of core topics, including "poor," "poverty," "welfare," and "relief." For each year, stories indexed under these topics as well as cross-references to related topics were collected. In all, 1,256 stories were found under 73 different index topics.[40] Note that the stories selected for this analysis were only those that focused directly on poverty or related topics. Many stories with a primary focus on race relations, civil rights, urban riots, or other racial topics also included discussions of poverty, but in these contexts readers would expect to find coverage of black poverty in particular and might not draw conclusions about the nature of American poverty in general. By excluding race-related sto-ries, however, this analysis provides a conservative estimate of the ex-tent to which African Americans populate media images of the poor.

Newsmagazine coverage of poverty varied dramatically across this time period. The thick line in figure 5.2 shows the average number of stories on poverty for these newsmagazines for each year from 1950 through 1992. The lack of interest in poverty during the 1950s is appar-ent; in five of these ten years only a single story on poverty appeared in each magazine, and in no year did more than three stories on poverty appear. Equally clear from figure 5.2 is the first brief spike in media coverage of poverty in response to the Kennedy administration's efforts in 1961 and the much more dramatic growth in media attention to pov-erty beginning in 1964. The increase in poverty stories in the 1960s was clearly a response to the political initiatives of the Kennedy and John-son administrations rather than a reaction to any growth in the severity of poverty in America. Indeed, as the thin line in figure 5.2 shows, the poverty rate was declining during this period and continued to decline, more or less steadily, until 1973.

To determine the racial content of newsmagazine coverage of pov-erty, I identified each poor person pictured in each of these stories as black, nonblack, or undeterminable. In all, 6,117 poor individuals were

Figure 5.2 Number of Poverty Stories in Newsmagazines and U.S. Poverty Rate, 1950–1992

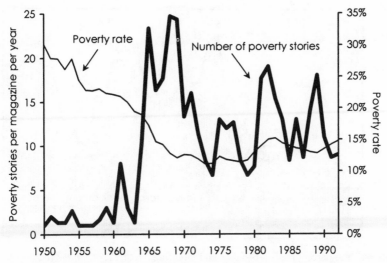

Sources: Poverty rate—Murray, *Losing Ground*, p. 245; U.S. Bureau of the Census, *Statistical Abstract: 1995*, p. 480. Poverty stories—*Time, Newsweek*, and *U.S. News and World Report*.

depicted in the 1,256 poverty stories, and of these race could be determined for 4,388, or 72 percent (poor people for whom race could not be determined are excluded from the results reported below).[41] The three magazines differed in the number of poverty stories published during this period, with *U.S. News and World Report* running 549 stories, *Newsweek*, 391, and *Time*, 316. The percentage of blacks among pictures of the poor was similar at each magazine, however, ranging from 52 percent in *U.S. News and World Report* to 57 percent in *Time*.[42] Combining the coverage of poverty from the three magazines, over half (53.4 percent) of all poor people pictured during these four and a half decades were African American. In reality, the average percentage of African Americans among the poor during this period was 29.3 percent.[43]

Magazine portrayals overrepresent African Americans in pictures of the poor, but the degree of overrepresentation of blacks has not been constant throughout this period. The thick line in figure 5.3 shows the variation in the percentage of African Americans pictured in poverty stories in *Time, Newsweek*, and *U.S. News and World Report* from 1950 through 1992. (Adjacent years with small numbers of poverty stories are combined to smooth out the random fluctuations that result when the percentage of blacks is calculated from a small number of pictures.) Images of poverty in these magazines did change quite dramatically in

Figure 5.3   Percent African American in Newsmagazine Pictures of the Poor, 1950–1992 (compared with true percent black)

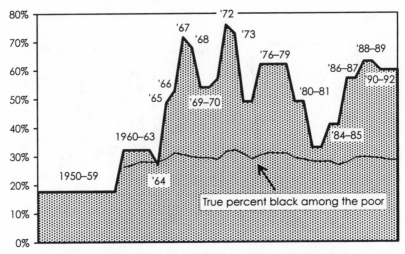

Sources: True percent black—Baugher and Lamison-White, *Poverty in the United States: 1995,* pp. C2–C4. Magazine pictures—*Time, Newsweek,* and *U.S. News and World Report.*

the mid-1960s. From the beginning of this study through 1964, poor people were portrayed as predominantly white. But starting in 1965 the complexion of the poor turned decidedly darker. From only 27 percent in 1964, the proportion of African Americans in pictures of the poor increased to 49 percent and 53 percent in 1965 and 1966, and then to 72 percent in 1967. Nor has the portrayal of the poor returned to its previous predominantly white orientation. Although there have been important declines and fluctuations in the extent to which blacks have been overrepresented in pictures of poverty (which we will explore shortly), African Americans have generally dominated news media images of the poor since the late 1960s. From 1967 through 1992, blacks averaged 57 percent of the poor people pictured in these three magazines—about twice the true proportion of blacks among the nation's poor.

Early Newsmagazine Coverage of Poverty: 1950–1964

Newsmagazines in the 1950s contained few stories on poverty and few pictures of blacks in the stories that were published. Between 1950 and 1959, only 18 percent of the poor people pictured in these magazines were African American. The increased attention to poverty in the early 1960s was accompanied by some increase in the proportion of blacks depicted among the poor, but this racialization of poverty images was quite modest compared with what was to come.

Newsmagazine coverage of poverty was generally rather sparse between 1960 and 1963. The exception was 1961, when a total of twenty-four poverty-related stories appeared in the three magazines (more than in 1960, 1962, and 1963 combined). Much of the press attention to poverty in 1961 was in response to the Kennedy administration's anti-poverty initiatives, with coverage focusing on a new housing bill, the revival of the depression-era food stamp program, and federal aid for distressed areas. These policy-focused stories were illustrated almost exclusively with pictures of poor whites.

A second theme in media coverage of poverty during 1960–63 was welfare abuse and efforts to reduce it. Some of these stories focused on Senator Robert Byrd's 1962 investigation into welfare fraud in Washington D.C., which uncovered welfare recipients who spent their benefits on alcohol or who were secretly living with boyfriends that welfare investigators found hiding in closets or bathrooms. Pictures of poor blacks and poor whites were both found in these strongly antiwelfare stories.

Finally, five of the forty-one stories published from 1960 through 1963 focused on the controversial "crackdown" on welfare by Joseph Mitchell, the city manager of Newburgh, New York. Mitchell claimed that recent black migrants from the South were swelling Newburgh's public assistance rolls. In response he instituted a thirteen-point program aimed at removing as many people from welfare as possible. Not surprisingly, coverage of Newburgh was illustrated with pictures of blacks (although Newsweek did point out that in fact 60 percent of relief recipients in Newburgh were white).

Newsmagazine coverage of poverty in the early 1960s presaged later coverage in two ways. First, stories on new policy initiatives tended to be both neutral in tone and dominated by images of whites. This was the case with the Kennedy administration's programs during 1961, and it was repeated in coverage of the Johnson administration's War on Poverty three years later. In contrast, the more critical stories about existing programs, such as reports on the Byrd committee's investigation of welfare abuse, were more likely to contain pictures of blacks. Once again, this pattern is repeated in the later 1960s, as largely negative "field reports" from the War on Poverty programs start to appear in the media.

News coverage of poverty expanded dramatically beginning in 1964 and reached its height between 1965 and 1969. Without question the impetus for this growth in coverage was the Johnson administration's War on Poverty, announced in January 1964. Almost four-fifths of all poverty-related stories published in 1964 dealt explicitly with the War on Poverty, as did a majority of the poverty-related articles appearing in 1965 and 1966. By 1967, stories about urban problems and urban re-development had become an important component of poverty cover-age, but stories on welfare, jobs programs, and other aspects of the War on Poverty continued to account for most of the poverty-related news coverage.

For our purposes, the most significant aspects of news stories on pov-erty in 1964 were the strong focus on the War on Poverty and the con-tinued portrayal of the poor as predominantly white. A good example of this overall tendency is the most substantial poverty story of the year, a twelve-page cover story called "Poverty, U.S.A." that *Newsweek* ran on February 17.[44] The cover of the magazine showed a white girl, perhaps eight or ten years old, looking out at the reader from a rustic shack, her hair disheveled and her face covered with dirt. As this picture sug-gests, the story had a strong focus on Appalachia, but it profiled a va-riety of poor people from around the country. Yet of the fifty-four poor people pictured in this story, only fourteen were black.[45] Significantly, the poor white people who appeared in this story resided in both urban and rural areas; there were, for example, six photos of poor whites from Appalachia as well as photos of a thirty-seven-year-old "Main Street wino" from Los Angeles, an unemployed father of five from Detroit, and an "old lady alone with poverty" in San Francisco.

This story was typical of War on Poverty coverage during 1964 in its substantial focus on rural poverty, its emphasis on images of poor whites, and its generally neutral tone toward the Johnson administra-tion's antipoverty efforts. Like this story, most of the early coverage of the War on Poverty consisted of descriptions of antipoverty pro-grams, profiles of Johnson's "poverty warriors," and accounts of pov-erty in America, most often illustrated with examples of individual poor people. Clearly, the expansion of news coverage that accompanied the War on Poverty did not coincide with the racialization of poverty images. At its inception at least, the War on Poverty was not portrayed by the news media as a program for blacks.

The Racialization of Poverty in the News: 1965–1967

The year 1965 saw another large jump in media attention to poverty and a clear turning point in the racialization of poverty images in the news. The percentage of blacks among pictures of the poor jumped from 27 percent in 1964 to 49 percent in 1965. One factor that clearly does *not* explain the larger number of poor African Americans in the news during this period is true change in the proportion of blacks among the poor. As the thin line in figure 5.3 shows, the true percentage of blacks among the poor increased only marginally between the early and late 1960s (from 27 percent to 30 percent), while the percentage of blacks found in newsmagazine portrayals of the poor more than doubled during this period.

The most conspicuous change in the coverage of poverty between 1964 and 1965 is the tone of stories covering welfare and the War on Poverty. Whereas coverage in 1964 focused on the initiation of the War on Poverty and general descriptions of the American poor, stories in 1965 were much more critical examinations of the government's anti-poverty efforts. Three lines of criticism were prominent: First, many stories questioned Sargent Shriver's leadership of the antipoverty effort, focusing on mismanagement, confusion, and waste in the Office of Economic Opportunity. Second, considerable attention was devoted to local disputes between city government and community groups over control of War on Poverty resources. Finally, substantial coverage focused on difficulties within the Job Corps program, one of the first War on Poverty programs to get off the ground. General stories on the War on Poverty and stories about problems in the Job Corps accounted for most of the poor people pictured in early 1965. Fifty percent of the poor pictured in War on Poverty stories during this period were black, as were 55 percent of those in stories on the Job Corps.

We saw above that media coverage from the early 1960s tended to use pictures of poor blacks to illustrate stories about waste, inefficiency, or abuse of welfare, and pictures of poor whites in stories with more neutral descriptions of antipoverty programs. This pattern is repeated in 1964 and 1965 as coverage of the War on Poverty becomes more critical and portrayals of the poor become "more black." This association of African Americans with negative stories on poverty is clearest in coverage of the Job Corps. The most visible of the War on Poverty's numerous job training programs, the Job Corps consisted of dozens of residential centers in both urban and rural locations at which young men (and less often, young women) were to learn discipline along with basic job skills.

News coverage of the Job Corps program focused on problems such as poor screening of participants, inadequate facilities, and high drop-out rates. But the most sensational objections concerned the behavior of Job Corps members and the aversion to Job Corps centers by nearby towns. For example, a long story in *U.S. News and World Report* published in July 1965 (and illustrated with about equal numbers of blacks and nonblacks) reported charges of "rowdyism" at Job Corps centers, including a dormitory riot in Tongue Point, Oregon, "in which lead pipes were hurled" and the alcohol-related expulsion of eight girls from a St. Petersburg, Florida, center. "Another worry," the story indicated, was the "antagonism between Corpsmen and nearby townsmen." People in Astoria, Oregon, for example, "complained about hearing obscene language at the movie theater," while residents of Marion, Illinois, were upset about a disturbance at a roller skating rink that occurred when some Job Corps members showed up with liquor. Although these incidents were not explicitly linked to black Job Corps participants, the pictures of blacks in Job Corps stories (comprising 55 percent of all Job Corps members pictured) was much higher than the proportion of African Americans pictured in the more neutral stories about the War on Poverty from the previous year.[46]

As we will see, the pattern of associating negative poverty coverage with pictures of blacks persists over the years and is too widespread and consistent to be explained as the product of any particular antipoverty program or subgroup of the poor. But the sharp increase in the percentage of African Americans pictured in poverty stories in 1965 can also be attributed to the increasing involvement of civil rights leaders in the antipoverty effort. Neither the civil rights movement nor civil rights leaders were mentioned in any of the thirty-two poverty stories published in 1964, but during the first half of 1965 almost one-quarter (23 percent) of the poverty-related stories made some mention of black leaders. Most of these stories dealt with the battles for control over War on Poverty funds, especially, but not only, those channeled through the community action programs. Although the involvement of black community leaders was a minor element in news coverage of poverty from this period, it undoubtedly helped to shift the media's attention away from the previous years' focus on poor whites.

Coverage of poverty during the second half of 1965 was similar to that of early 1965 with two exceptions. First, the Watts riots, which began on August 11, intensified the growing awareness of black poverty in this country. Perhaps surprisingly, neither the Watts riots themselves nor the problems of inner-city blacks figured prominently in poverty coverage during the second half of 1965. Nevertheless, 26 percent of poverty stories from the latter half of 1965 did make at least a brief

Figure 5.4 Subject Matter of Newsmagazine Poverty Stories, 1964–1967

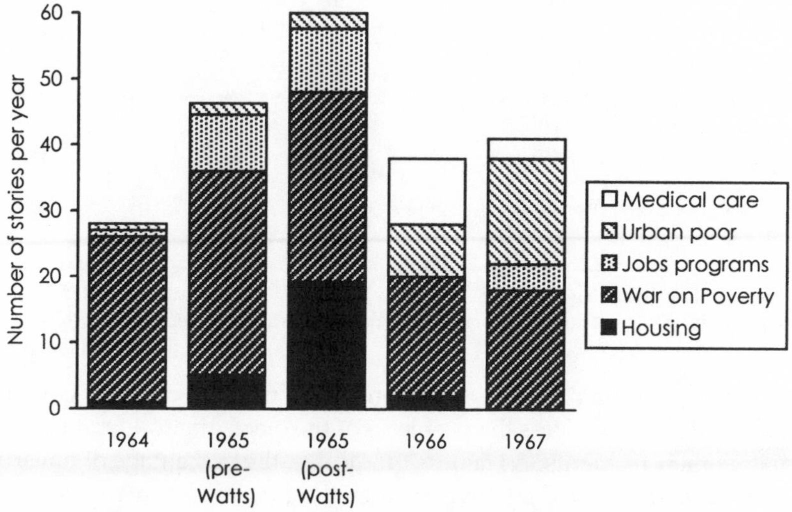

Source: Time, Newsweek, and U.S. News and World Report.

mention of the riots. The most common focus of poverty coverage during this period continued to be the War on Poverty. In addition, a number of stories covered the establishment of the Department of Housing and Urban Development (HUD) (but none of the eight stories on HUD and housing programs during this period contained pictures of poor people).

To more fully delineate changes in media coverage of poverty during the crucial years of 1964 through 1967, figure 5.4 shows the main subjects of newsmagazine poverty stories (with 1965 broken into two periods to compare pre-Watts and post-Watts coverage). In every year during the mid-1960s, the War on Poverty was the single most common poverty subject in these magazines, accounting for 45 percent of all poverty stories over these four years. As figure 5.4 shows, coverage of urban poverty did increase in 1966 and 1967 to the point where almost as many stories in 1967 were written on problems of the urban poor as on the War on Poverty. Thus part of the racialization of poverty during this period clearly concerns the growing focus on America's cities.

There is little evidence of an immediate change in media coverage of poverty after Watts. But coverage did change in response to the greater number of riots in the summers of 1966 and 1967. At least as important as the riots themselves were the reactions to those riots, particularly

Table 5.1 Racial Content of Newsmagazine Stories on Poverty, 1964–1967

	1964	1965	1966	1967
Percentage black in pictures of poor people	27	49	53	72
Percentage black in pictures of poor people, excluding stories on urban poverty	27	48	54	58
Percentage of stories mentioning blacks	29	51	55	64
Percentage of stories mentioning riots or civil rights	0	26	31	38

Note: Based on an analysis of all poverty-related stories in *Time, Newsweek,* and *U.S. News and World Report* published between January 1, 1964, and December 31, 1967.

civil rights leaders' greater focus on urban poverty and the government's efforts to address the problems of the black ghettos, or at least to placate their residents. As table 5.1 indicates, the percentage of poverty stories that mentioned ghetto riots or civil rights leaders increased from 26 percent in 1965, to 31 percent in 1966, and 38 percent in 1967. (As table 5.1 also shows, the changing pictorial representation of the poor was paralleled by a growing tendency to mention African Americans within the text of poverty-related stories.)

How are we to understand the changing focus of poverty coverage over this four-year period and the concomitant racialization of poverty images? One possibility is that a series of events (e.g., riots, new government programs) led news organizations to focus on new aspects of poverty or new subgroups of the poor and that these subgroups happened to be disproportionately black. This explanation is almost surely true to some degree. For example, pictures of the poor in stories on urban poverty from 1964 through 1967 were 95 percent black. Consequently, the increase in urban poverty stories accounts for some part of the racialization of poverty coverage during this period. On the other hand, even if we exclude urban poverty stories, the percentage of blacks in pictures of the poor grew dramatically over these four years; as table 5.1 shows, of those stories that were not focused on urban poverty, the percentage of blacks among pictures of the poor more than doubled, growing from 27 percent in 1964 to 58 percent in 1967.

While growing attention to urban poverty did contribute to the changing racial portrayal of the poor between 1965 and 1967, it cannot explain the sharp increase in the percentage of blacks in poverty pictures between 1964 and 1965. Coverage during both of these years was dominated by stories on the War on Poverty, with no particular emphasis on urban problems in either year. Furthermore, the jump in percent black had already occurred before the Watts riots in August 1965; indeed, newsmagazine poverty stories included just as high a percentage of blacks in the first half of 1965 as they did in the months following Watts.

A second possibility is that the mainstream (white-dominated) news media were more likely to associate negative poverty stories with blacks and neutral or positive stories with whites. I have already suggested that this tendency can be observed in the coverage of poverty from 1960 through 1963, and the same phenomenon might explain the sharp increase in pictures of poor blacks between 1964 and the earlier (pre-Watts) months of 1965. Negative views of blacks were more common in the 1960s than they are today, and it would be surprising if these attitudes were not shared, at least to some degree, by the white news professionals who shaped the coverage of poverty.[47] Notions about blacks' "cultural foreignness," especially with regard to the mainstream values of individual initiative and hard work, might well have led newsmagazine writers, editors, and photographers to associate African Americans with negative coverage of poverty.

Of course, the racial patterns within poverty coverage in 1960–63 and 1964–65 are slender threads on which to hang so important a claim. A wealth of other evidence, however, points in the same direction. In particular, we can make use of the full breadth of newsmagazine coverage between 1950 and 1992 to examine both the differences in the racial portrayals of different subgroups of the poor, and changes over time in racial images of the poor as media coverage responds to changing social conditions. In both cases, we find that positive coverage of poverty— coverage that focuses on either more sympathetic subgroups of the poor or periods in which the poor as a whole were viewed more sympathetically—was more likely to include pictures of poor whites than was the negative coverage of poverty associated with less sympathetic groups and less sympathetic times.

Changing Racial Portrayals of the Poor: 1968–1992

Poverty took on a black face in newsmagazines during the tumultuous years of the mid-1960s. But as urban riots subsided and the country's attention turned toward Vietnam, Watergate, and the economic problems of the 1970s, the racial portrayal of the poor in news coverage did not return to the predominantly white images of the 1950s and early 1960s. Instead, as figure 5.3 indicates, the racial representation of the poor in media images of poverty fluctuated considerably, with very high proportions of African Americans in 1972 and 1973 and dramatic "whitening" of poverty images during the economic recessions of 1974–75 and 1982–83. To understand variations over time in the racial portrayal of poverty, I examine next these three extremes in the racial images of the poor.

Images of Blacks and the "Welfare Mess": 1972–1973

Coverage of poverty during 1972 and 1973 focused primarily on perceived problems with welfare and efforts at welfare reform. Almost half of the poverty coverage in these two years focused directly on welfare or related antipoverty programs, while the next most frequent poverty topic (housing) accounted for only 20 percent of newsmagazine reporting on poverty. As we saw in chapter 1, the percentage of all Americans receiving welfare increased dramatically from about 2 percent in the mid-1960s to about 6 percent in the mid-1970s, while aggregate spending on welfare more than doubled, from .24 percent of GNP in 1965 to .60 percent in 1975.[48] The growth of welfare spending during this period resulted from a number of factors, including higher benefit levels in many states and the court-mandated elimination of residency requirements and "man in the house" rules. The most important components of welfare growth, however, were the jump in the percentage of eligible families that applied for aid and the rise in the percentage of families that were enrolled from among those who did apply.[49]

By the early 1970s, the expansion of welfare had come to be viewed as an urgent national problem that demanded action. Newsmagazine stories during 1972 and 1973 almost invariably referred to this situation as the "welfare mess" and published story after story focusing on mismanagement in state welfare bureaucracies or abuse of welfare by people who could be supporting themselves (or welfare cheating by people who in fact were supporting themselves and collecting welfare at the same time). Of course, newsmagazines did not simply take it upon themselves to turn a critical eye toward welfare; they were reporting on the political events of the time. Numerous welfare reform proposals were debated in Congress during this period; welfare was an important issue in the 1972 presidential election, with both Richard Nixon and George McGovern offering plans to fix the "welfare mess"; and in 1973 President Nixon closed down the Office of Economic

Opportunity, the central administrative arm of President Johnson's War on Poverty.

The racial composition of the welfare population hardly changed between the late 1960s and the early 1970s (figure 5.1), but the images of the poor in newsmagazine stories changed dramatically. Fifty-two percent of poor people pictured in poverty and welfare stories from 1969 and 1970 were African American, but in 1972 and 1973 blacks comprised 70 percent of the poor people pictured in stories indexed under poverty and 75 percent of those pictured in stories on welfare. Nor was the heavy representation of blacks limited to stories on poverty and welfare per se. Virtually all poverty-related coverage during these two years—whatever the topic—was illustrated with pictures of blacks. During 1972 and 1973, African Americans composed 76 percent of the poor people pictured in stories on all other poverty-related topics, including housing, urban problems, employment programs, old age, unemployment, and legal aid. Overall, the sustained negative coverage of welfare during 1972–73 was accompanied by the highest proportions of blacks in newsmagazine images of the poor of any point during the entire forty-three-year period examined.

Blacks and Whites in Poverty: 1974–1975

The mid-1970s marked the first severe economic downturn since the tremendous period of sustained growth that began in the early 1960s. Of particular concern during 1974 and 1975 was unemployment, which had risen from under 5 percent in 1970 to 8.5 percent in 1975.[50] In contrast to the very heavily black coverage of poverty in 1972–73, only 49 percent of the poor people pictured in stories published during 1974 and 1975 were black (slightly below average for the entire 1968–1992 period). General stories on poverty and welfare were still common during these years, accounting for 27 percent of all poverty coverage. Not surprisingly, however, given the economic conditions of the time, unemployment and government efforts to combat it emerged as an important focus of poverty-related news coverage, accounting for 24 percent of all poverty stories in 1974–75 (compared with only 3 percent in 1972–73). In addition, 14 percent of poverty stories focused on hunger (also up from 3 percent in 1972–73).

Unlike stories about poverty published in 1972 and 1973, poverty coverage in 1974–75 varied dramatically in racial complexion depending on the topic of the story. General stories on poverty and welfare continued to contain primarily pictures of blacks. Sixty-nine percent of poor people in these stories were African American, a figure hardly changed from the 73 percent black in such stories from 1972 and 1973. But poverty stories that focused on unemployment policy were illustrated predominantly with whites. The poverty-related coverage of unemployment in 1974 and 1975 dealt largely with government jobs programs and other efforts to "put America back to work," and only 37 percent of poor people pictured in these stories were black. Stories on hunger pictured somewhat larger numbers of blacks (50 percent), while the few stories on homelessness from 1974 and 1975 pictured no African Americans at all.

As the focus of media coverage of poverty shifts in response to changing conditions and events, we would expect to find changes in the racial portrayals of the poor. In this case, the negative stories on welfare from 1972 and 1973 contained many more pictures of blacks than the sympathetic stories on unemployment published during 1974 and 1975. To some extent this shift is warranted, since the percentage of blacks among welfare recipients in the early 1970s was higher than the percentage of blacks in jobs programs during the mid-1970s. In other words, African Americans may be associated with the less sympathetic topics of poverty coverage simply because they are more likely to be found among subgroups of the poor that arouse less sympathy. During the 1970s, blacks did in fact compose a larger percentage of welfare recipients than of government jobs programs participants or of the poor in general. Nevertheless, the size of these differences is not sufficient to account for the dramatically larger differences in the racial *portrayals* of these different groups.

In the early 1970s, African Americans comprised about 32 percent of all poor Americans and about 43 percent of AFDC recipients (figs. 5.3 and 5.1, respectively). In contrast, during the mid-1970s, blacks accounted for about 30 percent of the participants in the Comprehensive Employment and Training Act (or CETA) program, which was the largest and most politically prominent jobs program during this period.[51] Since blacks comprised 37 percent of the poor people pictured in unemployment-related coverage during 1974–75, they were actually overrepresented in these sympathetic news stories. Nevertheless, these stories were much more accurate in their racial portrayals than were the unsympathetic stories on welfare from the previous years. That is, African Americans comprised a minority of both welfare recipients and CETA participants, but newsmagazines only slightly exaggerated their representation in jobs programs (37 percent in magazine pictures versus 30 percent in reality during 1974–75) and dramatically exaggerated their numbers among those on welfare (75 percent in magazine pictures versus 43 percent in reality during 1972–73).

While sympathy was extended to unemployed Americans and support was broad for jobs programs such as CETA, welfare continued to be attacked during the mid-1970s, as it had been in the 1972–73 period. *Time* magazine declared in 1975 that "practically everyone feels that welfare has become a hydra—sustaining many who do not deserve help, breeding incredible bureaucracy and inefficiency, and entangling the nation in ideological clashes over just how much aid should go to whom."[52] There were a few sympathetic stories during 1974–75 that drew a connection between national economic difficulties (principally unemployment) and the conditions facing welfare recipients. But most coverage of welfare continued to stress its spiraling costs and the burden of caring for the poor when government was being squeezed for funds due to the state of the economy. Welfare stories continued to stress abuse by welfare recipients who could be supporting themselves and the supposed resentment of the middle class toward paying for "welfare loafers." And unlike the unemployment-related stories, stories on welfare were filled primarily with black faces: during 1974–75, fully 76 percent of the poor people pictured in welfare stories were African American.

In sum, the newsmagazine coverage of poverty and welfare from the affluent period of the early 1970s was overwhelmingly negative in tone and dominated by pictures of African Americans. The economy faltered during 1974 and 1975, however, and in these years news coverage of poverty was decidedly more mixed in tone. Negative stories about welfare were still plentiful, and these stories still tended to be illustrated with pictures of blacks. But more positive coverage of the problems of the unemployed were also common, and in these stories the faces of the poor were predominantly white. These patterns of news coverage from the 1970s are consistent with the patterns we observed in the 1960s: negative coverage of poverty tends to be associated with African Americans while positive coverage is illustrated with pictures of whites. As we will see next, this pattern also extends to the unusually sympathetic stories on poverty published during the "Reagan recession" of the early 1980s.

Sympathetic Coverage of White Poverty: 1982–1983

The recession of the early 1980s brought America's worst economic performance in decades. Per capita gross domestic product fell over 3 percent between 1981 and 1982, unemployment rose to almost 11 percent, and the poverty rate increased from about 11 percent in 1979 to over 15 percent in 1983.[53] Coincident with this economic downturn were the Reagan administration's domestic spending cutbacks and rhetorical attacks on government antipoverty programs.

The rather dire conditions of America's poor, and the political controversy that erupted in response to President Reagan's efforts to "trim the safety net," led to a substantial increase in the amount of news coverage of poverty. After publishing only 43 stories on poverty in 1979 and 1980, the three weekly newsmagazines published 103 poverty stories in 1982 and 1983. Reflecting the nature of the times, news coverage of poverty during the early 1980s was concentrated on the growing problems of poverty and unemployment and on debates over the proper response of government to these conditions. About 39 percent of poverty-related newsmagazine stories in 1982–83 focused on poverty or government antipoverty programs, with another 28 percent on unemployment or efforts to combat it. In addition, smaller numbers of stories concerned homelessness, housing programs, and legal aid (each constituting 6 percent to 8 percent of poverty coverage).

This period of widespread public concern with poverty also saw the lowest percentage of blacks in magazine portrayals of the poor of any time since the early 1960s. Overall, only 33 percent of poor people pictured in poverty-related stories during 1982 and 1983 were black. But unlike coverage during the recession of 1974–75, news coverage in 1982–83 often drew a connection between national economic conditions and the problems of the poor. Moreover, poor whites in news coverage during the early 1980s were more likely to be found in general stories on poverty and welfare than in stories on unemployment.

The two most common themes of poverty stories during this period concerned the growth of poverty and the debates over government cutbacks. Although a few of these stories sought to convince readers that "The Safety Net Remains" (as a *Time* magazine story from February 1982 was titled), most of this coverage was highly critical of the Reagan administration's efforts to trim government programs for the poor. A good example is *Newsweek's* prominent story titled "The Hard-Luck Christmas of '82," which proclaimed, "With 12 million unemployed and 2 million homeless, private charity cannot make up for federal cutbacks."[54] This story went on to describe the desperate condition of poor families living in camp tents or in automobiles, portraying them as the noble victims "who are paying the price of America's failure of nerve in the war on poverty." Reflecting the general lack of black faces in these sympathetic poverty stories, "The Hard-Luck Christmas of '82" included only 17 African Americans among the 90 poor people pictured.[55] As a whole, blacks made up only 30 percent of the poor people pictured in general stories on poverty and antipoverty programs in 1982–83.

A less common, but important, theme in poverty stories from this period concerned the "newly poor," that is, formerly middle-class Americans who fell into poverty during the recession of the early 1980s. Typical of this coverage is a (white) family of four profiled in a *U.S. News and World Report* story from August 1982.[56] This story describes how the Telehowski family was "plunged into the ranks of the newly poor" when the father lost his job as a machinist with an auto-parts company. No longer able to afford a car or even an apartment, the Telehowskis reluctantly applied for welfare and became squatters in an abandoned house in inner-city Detroit. The story about the Telehowskis, with their two small children and their determined struggle to support themselves, indicates the extraordinary sympathy that the "newly poor" received in news coverage from the early 1980s. *Newsweek* went even farther in proclaiming the virtues of the newly poor, writing, "The only aspect of American life that has been uplifted by the continuing recession: a much better class of poor person, better educated, accustomed to working, with strong family ties."[57]

It is not surprising, of course, that poverty is portrayed in a more sympathetic light during economic hard times. What is noteworthy, however, is that along with shifts in the tone of news reporting on the poor come shifts in the racial mix of the poor people in news stories. As figure 5.3 shows, the true proportion of blacks among America's poor did not change appreciably between the early 1970s and the early 1980s (or indeed, at any time during the past thirty-five years). But the racial portrayals of the poor in newsmagazines did shift dramatically as media attention turned from highly critical coverage of welfare during 1972–73 to highly sympathetic stories on poverty during the recession of the early 1980s. Some of the racial shift in poverty images is attributable to the different proportions of blacks among different subgroups of the poor. But the fairly small demographic differences can neither explain nor justify the much larger differences between the racial images associated with the sympathetic portrayals of the "deserving poor" in the early 1980s and the unsympathetic portraits of the "undeserving poor" in the early 1970s.

Racial Portrayals of Subgroups of the Poor

The news media's tendency to use pictures of poor blacks in unsympathetic poverty stories and pictures of poor whites in sympathetic

Table 5.2 Percentage African American in Newsmagazine Pictures of the Poor, 1950–1992

Topic	Number of Stories	Number of Poor People Pictured	Percentage African American
Underclass	6	36	100
Urban problems, urban renewal	91	97	84
Poor people, poverty	182	707	59
Unemployment	102	268	59
Legal aid	30	22	56
Welfare, antipoverty programs	399	965	54
Housing, homeless	272	508	52
Children	45	121	51
Employment programs	45	181	50
Education	22	95	43
Medical care	43	36	28
Hunger	52	176	25
Old-age assistance	28	12	0

Notes: An additional 79 stories (not shown above) were indexed under miscellaneous other topics; 133 stories (11% of all poverty stories) were indexed under more than one topic. The database includes all stories on poverty and related topics published in *Time, Newsweek,* and *U.S. News and World Report* between January 1, 1950, and December 31, 1992. A breakdown of detailed subject categories can be obtained from the author.

stories can also be observed among the various topics in poverty coverage over the entire 1950–1992 period. Table 5.2 shows the percentage of African Americans in pictures of poor people for thirteen different aggregated subject categories.[58] The story topics shown in table 5.2 relate to members of the poverty population that receive varying levels of public support or censure. For example, surveys show greater sympathy for the poor in general than for welfare recipients, and a stronger desire to help poor children or the elderly than poor working-age adults.[59] And despite the negative coverage that the Job Corps received in stories from the mid-1960s, we would generally expect more sympathetic responses to stories about poor people in employment programs than to stories about nonworking poor adults.

Of the thirteen topics shown in table 5.2, seven fall into a fairly narrow range in which African Americans comprise between 50 percent and 60 percent of all poor people pictured. These include "sympathetic" topics, such as poor children (51 percent black) and employment programs (50 percent), and "unsympathetic" topics, such as public welfare (54 percent). Of those topics that do differ substantially in percent African American, however, fewer blacks are shown in stories on the more sympathetic topics of education (43 percent black), medical care

(28 percent), and hunger (25 percent), while stories about the elderly poor—one of the most sympathetic subgroups of poor people—are illustrated exclusively with pictures of poor whites. In contrast, only African Americans are found in stories on the underclass, perhaps the least sympathetic topic in table 5.2. Although the underclass lacks any consistent definition in either popular or academic discourse,[60] it is most often associated with intergenerational poverty, chronic unemployment, out-of-wedlock births, crime, drugs, and "welfare dependency as a way of life."[61] In fact, blacks do compose a large proportion of the American underclass, the exact proportion depending on how the underclass is defined. But even those definitions that result in the highest percentages of African Americans consider the underclass to include at least 40 percent nonblacks, in contrast to the magazine portrait of the underclass as 100 percent black.[62]

With regard to topic of story, then, we find the same tendency that we found in examining changes in media coverage of poverty over time. In both cases, pictures of African Americans are disproportionately used to illustrate the most negative aspects of poverty and the least sympathetic subgroups of the poor.

TV News Coverage of Poverty

The three newsmagazines examined here have a combined circulation of over ten million copies, and 20 percent of American adults claim to be regular readers of "news magazines such as *Time, U.S. News and World Report,* or *Newsweek.*"[63] In addition, these magazines influence how other journalists see the world. In one study, for example, magazine and newspaper journalists were asked what news sources they read most regularly.[64] Among these journalists, *Time* and *Newsweek* were the first- and second-most frequently cited news sources and were far more popular than the *New York Times,* the *Wall Street Journal,* or the *Washington Post.*

Despite the broad reach of these weekly magazines, and their role as "background material" for other journalists, there can be little doubt that television is the dominant news source for most Americans. In recent surveys, about 70 percent of the American public identifies television as the source of "most of your news about what's going on in the world today."[65] If the racial content of TV news coverage of poverty were to differ substantially from that found in newsmagazines, our confidence in the analysis of newsmagazines would be severely limited.

Unfortunately, the analyses of newsmagazine coverage reported

above cannot be replicated with television news. First, tapes of television news broadcasts are unavailable for shows aired before the middle
of 1968. This alone would preclude the use of television news to examine the critical period of the mid-1960s. In addition, television news
stories on poverty typically picture far larger numbers of poor people
but provide much less information about the poor individuals pictured
than do newsmagazine stories. Still, we can to some degree determine
whether newsmagazine coverage of poverty is unique to that medium
by comparing patterns of news coverage on television with those found
in newsmagazines for the period in which both sources are available.

   The first question we might ask is simply whether the ups and downs
of news attention to poverty found in newsmagazines is repeated in
television news coverage. To examine this relationship, I searched the
Vanderbilt Television News Index and Abstracts for all stories on poverty
and related topics broadcast on the ABC, NBC, and CBS nightly news
between 1969 and 1992.[66] In all, there were 3,387 such stories during this
twenty-four-year period, ranging from a high of 570 stories in 1969 to a
low of only 14 stories in 1980. Similarly, during the same period the
three newsmagazines published the largest number of poverty stories
in 1969 (73 stories) and the fewest in 1979 (20 stories) (the second-
smallest number of poverty stories in newsmagazines was found in
1980). Over the entire period, there is a clear correspondence between
the number of stories on poverty appearing in any year in television
news and newsmagazines: the correlation between the number of stories per year in TV and newsmagazines is .57. Some of the poverty coverage in newsmagazines and on network television is a product of a
news organization's decision to draw attention to some specific aspect of poverty. However, the substantial correlation between the ebbs
and flows of stories about the poor in these two media suggest that
the quantity of poverty coverage in any time period is largely determined by "real world" events such as economic conditions and political
initiatives.

   The second, and more important, question concerning the similarities
between television and newsmagazine coverage of poverty concerns
the racial representation of the poor. Measuring the racial representation of poverty in television news requires the painstaking examination
of hours of television news stories. Because it was impossible to code
the full twenty-four years of television news, I chose three historical
periods: 1968, the earliest year for which TV news shows are available
and a year in which magazines portrayed the poor as predominantly
black; 1982–83, a time when magazine images of poverty contained the

Figure 5.5   Racial Portrayal of Poverty in Newsmagazines and Television News

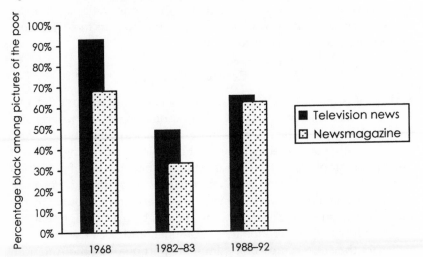

Source: *Time, Newsweek,* and *U.S. News and World Report,* and ABC, NBC, and CBS nightly news shows. Ns for the magazines are 275, 226, and 556 poor people, and Ns for television are 84, 669, and 1,100 poor people, for the three time periods respectively.

lowest proportion of blacks for the entire period studied; and 1988–92, a more recent period that also contained a high proportion of blacks in newsmagazine stories on poverty.

Figure 5.5 shows the percentage of blacks among pictures of the poor for these three periods. We see first that the overrepresentation of African Americans in poverty stories that generally characterized newsmagazine coverage after 1964 was also true for television news. In fact, in each of the three periods examined, television news exaggerated the percentage of blacks among the poor to an even greater extent than did the newsmagazines. Equally important, the changing patterns of racial representation found in the newsmagazines is reflected in television news as well. In both media, 1968 contained extremely high proportions of blacks among pictures of the poor; 1982–83, the smallest proportions; and 1988–92, proportions somewhere in the middle. Of course, a more complete analysis of poverty coverage in these two media might reveal some important differences. But the data examined suggest that the patterns of coverage found in newsmagazines are not idiosyncratic to that particular medium. Television news also substantially exaggerates the extent to which blacks compose the poor, and as with newsmagazine coverage, the complexion of poverty in TV news shifts over time as events draw attention to more sympathetic and less sympathetic subgroups of the poor. In short, it appears that the distorted coverage of poverty found in newsmagazines reflects a broader set of dynamics that also shape images of the poor in the even more important medium of television news.

Conclusions

Perhaps it is unreasonable to expect a "sociologically accurate" depiction of poverty in news stories. Certainly some aspects of poverty and some subgroups of the poor are more newsworthy than others. And news departments, after all, are in the business of selling news. If news photographers seek out the most sensational images of poverty to attract readers or viewers we should hardly be surprised. For most Americans, the most powerful images of poverty are undoubtedly the black urban ghettos. These concentrations of poverty represent the worst failures of our economic, educational, and social welfare systems. Yet they also represent a minuscule portion of all the American poor. Only 6 percent of all poor Americans are blacks living in urban ghettos.[67]

Furthermore, and most significantly, racial distortions in the portrayal of poverty are not limited to stories on the urban underclass. The overrepresentation of blacks among the poor is found in coverage of most poverty topics and appears during most of the past three decades. Yet just as importantly, black faces are *unlikely* to be found in media stories on the most sympathetic subgroups of the poor, just as they are comparatively absent from media coverage of poverty during times of heightened sympathy for the poor.

Journalists are professional observers and chroniclers of our social world. But they are also residents of that world and are exposed to the same stereotypes and misperceptions that characterize society at large. As we will see in chapter 6, the stereotype of the lazy black has been a staple of our culture for centuries and its reflection in contemporary news coverage of poverty is only one current manifestation of this long-held belief.

6

Media Distortions: Causes and Consequences

News portrayals of the poor have changed dramatically over the past forty years, with the most important shift in poverty coverage involving the transition from images of whites in the 1950s and early 1960s to images of African Americans in the mid-1960s. But even after the dramatic "racialization" of poverty between 1965 and 1967, the racial character of poverty coverage fluctuated, with larger proportions of blacks appearing during periods of negative poverty stories and smaller proportions during periods when press coverage of the poor was more sympathetic.

In this chapter, I examine the causes and consequences of the media distortions documented in chapter 5. The media, I argue, are instrumental in shaping our understanding of the social world we inhabit. As Walter Lippmann noted eighty years ago, we necessarily rely on the accounts of others to form our beliefs about our world. "Our opinions," he wrote, "cover a bigger space, a longer reach of time, a greater number of things, than we can directly observe. They have, therefore, to be pieced together out of what others have reported."[1] Already in Lippmann's time, and more so in our own, "reports about the world" come primarily through the mass media.

Do Media Images Shape Public Perceptions of the Poor?

News coverage itself constitutes an important "artifact" of American political culture. But news coverage has a special significance as a cultural product because we know that it not only reflects, but also influences, public concerns and beliefs. The news brings to our attention the many aspects of society that lie beyond our individual experience—not only the activities of political leaders and popular celebrities, but the myriad images that convey secondhand the nature of the world that surrounds us.

Numerous studies have demonstrated the power of the media to shape public perceptions and political preferences. Some of these studies trace changes over time in media content, comparing it with public responses to survey questions, while others present study participants with various television or print stories and then examine the impact on their social and political knowledge, attitudes, and policy preferences (these latter studies typically disguise the manipulated news stories by including them in a news show along with other stories). Media content has thus been shown to affect the importance viewers attach to different political issues, their standards for making political evaluations, their beliefs about the causes of national problems, their positions on political issues, and their perceptions of political candidates.[2]

Based on this body of research, we would expect the media's coverage of poverty and welfare to influence the public's beliefs and attitudes about the poor. The most direct evidence of this influence comes from a study conducted at the University of Michigan by Ruth Hamill and her colleagues.[3] Hamill randomly assigned some of her subjects to read a short article from a popular magazine. The article contained a vivid and fairly unflattering description of a mother of three living in New York City who had been on welfare for the last thirteen years. After these study participants read the article, they were asked about their reactions to the article itself and also about their beliefs concerning welfare recipients in general (for example, whether most welfare recipients work hard to improve their situations). The other randomly chosen group of subjects was asked the same questions about welfare recipients but was not given the magazine article to read. Hamill found that those subjects who had first read the unflattering article about a single welfare mother expressed significantly more negative views about welfare recipients in general than did subjects who had not read the article.

Hamill's experiment shows that a single magazine story about a single welfare mother can influence readers' views about welfare recipients in general. But in this study, subjects' beliefs about welfare were assessed immediately after they read the unflattering description of a welfare mother, and we have no way of knowing how long the influence of this article may have persisted. Still, in the "real world," Americans encounter not one, but a constant stream of stories about welfare and poverty; even if the impact of an individual story fades over time, the cumulative effect may be much larger than that produced by the single story Hamill's subjects were exposed to. In any case, this study shows that negative news accounts of individual welfare recipients do have a direct and measurable impact on readers' beliefs about welfare recipients in general.

Another aspect of Hamill's study is also of interest. In addition to presenting her subjects with the article describing a New York mother on welfare, she provided some subjects with statistics about the average length of stay on welfare for women in New York. Some (randomly selected) subjects were told that the average stay on welfare was fifteen years (roughly consistent with the mother in the news story), while others were told the average stay on welfare was only two years (consistent with the true condition at the time of the study). Remarkably, this aggregate information had no impact on subjects' beliefs about welfare recipients in general. The vivid description of a single welfare mother shifted subjects' beliefs about welfare recipients in a negative direction, and the size of this shift was as large for subjects who were led to believe that this mother's stay on welfare was much longer than average as it was for subjects who were led to believe that it was typical.

Hamill's experiment not only shows the potential power of the media to shape the public's beliefs about the poor, but it also suggests that these beliefs may be influenced more by the specific examples found in news stories than by the statistics on poverty that accompany them. This conclusion is consistent with a number of other experiments that also show that specific examples exert a more powerful influence over readers' perceptions than does aggregate information. For example, studies examining opinions on the importance of seatbelts, the mandatory imposition of computer courses at a college, and the replacement of coin telephones with card telephones all found that specific examples had a stronger or more lasting impact on subjects' beliefs than did more informative, but less "reader-friendly," aggregate statistics.[4]

For most people, it appears, beliefs are more likely to change in response to concrete stories or specific examples than in response to aggregate information. This "sensitivity to examples" underlines the importance of the specific individuals that news stories on poverty choose to focus on. In understanding the role of race in the public perceptions of poverty, the power of examples to shape perceptions suggests that what matters most is the race of the specific poor people pictured in news stories, not the aggregate statistics about the racial composition of the poor that occasionally accompany those stories.

The importance of pictures in the news is confirmed by other studies that indicate that visual elements of the news are highly salient to viewers. For example, in an article titled "Seeing is Remembering," Doris Graber reported her findings that people were more likely to remember what they saw in a television news story than what they heard.[5] Graber exposed viewers to a range of TV news stories and found that her subjects were over twice as likely to remember visual themes as they were to remember story themes that were presented verbally. She attributed this difference to the simplicity and immediacy of the pictures, concluding that "the mass of visual detail can be absorbed at a mere glance. Words, by contrast, must be processed sequentially and often represent complex, abstract information."[6]

Not only do past studies indicate that visual elements in the news are comparatively important to viewers, but they also show that the race of the individuals pictured is a salient visual cue. For example, Shanto Iyengar and Donald Kinder presented subjects with television news stories about unemployment in which the unemployed individual pictured was either black or white. Following the unemployment story (which was included as part of a larger compilation of news stories), subjects were asked to name the three most important problems facing the nation. Of those white viewers who were randomly assigned to view the story about an unemployed white person, 71 percent said that unemployment was among the three most important national problems. Of those whites who saw a story about an unemployed African American, however, only 53 percent felt that unemployment was a pressing national concern.[7]

Similar studies on other topics have also found that the race of "everyday individuals" in TV news stories has a significant impact on the attitudes and beliefs of viewers. In another experiment conducted by Shanto Iyengar, viewers were shown virtually identical stories about either a poor black person or a poor white person and were later asked to suggest ways to reduce poverty. Those who had been randomly assigned to watch a story about a poor black person were more likely to suggest that poor people need to work harder or acquire more job skills, while those who had seen a story about a poor white person were more likely to suggest societal solutions such as creating more unskilled jobs or lowering interest rates.[8]

Unfortunately, we lack direct evidence that the proportion of African Americans pictured in news stories on poverty shapes the public's perceptions of the racial composition of the poor. Nevertheless, the substantial existing research on the influence of the news media strongly suggests that this is the case. Researchers have shown that the mass media can exert a powerful influence on public perceptions and attitudes, that concrete examples are more powerful influences on readers' beliefs than is aggregate information, that the content of news pictures is more likely to be remembered than the content of news stories, and that the race of people pictured in news stories is a salient and influential aspect of the story for many viewers.

While past research on the influence of the news suggests that pictures of poor people in news stories shape public perceptions—and misperceptions—of the poor, another indication that the media shape beliefs in this way stems from the implausibility of the alternative hypotheses. If the media are not the dominant influence on public perceptions of the poor, then these perceptions must be shaped by either personal encounters with poor people or conversations about poverty with friends and acquaintances. Conversations with others might indeed be an important influence, but this begs the question of how an individual's conversation partners arrived at *their* perceptions. On the other hand, if personal encounters with poor people explain the public's perceptions, then variation in individuals' perceptions should correspond with variations in the racial mix of the poor people they encounter in everyday life.

Although the personal encounter thesis is plausible, survey data show that the racial makeup of the poor in an individual's state appears to have almost no impact on his or her perceptions of the country's poor as a whole. For example, residents of Michigan and Pennsylvania, where African Americans make up 31 percent of the poor, believe that 50 percent of America's poor are black.[9] In Washington and Oregon, blacks constitute only 6 percent of the poor, yet residents of these states believe that the American poor are 47 percent black. Finally, blacks make up only *1 percent* of the poor in Idaho, Montana, Wyoming, North Dakota, South Dakota, and Utah, yet survey respondents from these states think that blacks account for 47 percent of all poor people in this country. Thus, despite the large state-by-state differences in the percentage of blacks among the poor, personal experience appears to have little impact on public perceptions of the racial composition of the poor. Most tellingly, even in places where poor blacks are virtually absent, whites perceive the nation's poor as a whole to be made up largely of African Americans.

Not only do we find little variation in racial perceptions of the poor across states, but we also find little variation across other population groups. Although one might expect those with more education to hold more accurate understandings of current social conditions, differences in racial perceptions of the poor are fairly small and not systematically related to demographic characteristics. When asked whether most poor people are white or black, for example, 47 percent of respondents who lack a high school degree chose black, compared with 59 percent of high school graduates, 57 percent of those with some college education, and 48 percent of college graduates. Nor do perceptions differ for blacks and whites. Fifty-two percent of blacks and 55 percent of whites said that most poor people are black.[10]

It is interesting to note that white Americans not only exaggerate the proportion of blacks among the poor, but they also exaggerate the proportion of blacks among the American population as a whole. When a *Washington Post* survey asked respondents to guess what percentage of the U.S. population is African American, the average response among whites was 23 percent, almost twice the true rate of 12 percent. (Black respondents expressed similar perceptions, with an average guess that 25 percent of the population is African American.[11]) As was the case for perceptions of the poor, perceptions of the racial composition of the American population as a whole appear to have little to do with the racial mix of people in an individual's environment. Whites living in the District of Columbia or in one of the seven states in which African Americans comprise over 20 percent of the population guessed that 25 percent of all Americans are black. But whites living in the nine states in which African Americans constitute less than 1 *percent* of the population had similar perceptions, guessing that blacks account for 23 percent of the American population.[12]

Like their perceptions of the black poor, whites' perceptions of black Americans in general appear to reflect media images rather than "real life" encounters with people of different races. Studies show that the representation of African Americans in both fictional television and television news has grown to the point where blacks are now overrepresented in both contexts. Lorelei Williams studied prime-time drama and situation comedies on network television during 1997 and found that blacks comprised 25 percent of all characters and 27 percent of major characters on these shows.[13] Williams also found that blacks were overrepresented on network television news, although to a somewhat lesser extent; 17 percent of the news subjects on the TV news shows she examined were black.

It would seem that Americans' misperceptions of the racial composition of both the public as a whole and poor people in particular reflect the nature of the media images that surround us. Previous research focusing on an array of issues has shown that the media can have a significant impact on public opinion. And judging by the similarity in public perceptions across states, it appears that differences in personal exposure to people of different races has little impact on perceptions about the population as a whole. People do draw on other sources of information and imagery about the social world, but it would be hard to deny that the news media are a centrally important source in a society as large and "media-centric" as our own. When news reports offer misleading images, it is inevitable that public perceptions and reality will diverge.

Consequences of Public Perceptions of the Race of the Poor

To understand how different racial images of the poor shape attitudes toward welfare, we can compare the views of those Americans who think most welfare recipients are black with the views of those who think most welfare recipients are white. In a 1994 CBS/New York Times survey, 55 percent of the respondents said that most people on welfare are black, and these respondents hold consistently more negative views about welfare recipients' true needs and their commitment to the work ethic than do respondents who think that most welfare recipients are white. As table 6.1 shows, among respondents who think most welfare recipients are black, 63 percent said that "lack of effort on their own part" is most often to blame when people are on welfare, while only 26 percent blamed "circumstances beyond their control." But among respondents who thought most welfare recipients are white, 50 percent blamed circumstances and only 40 percent attributed the problem to a lack of effort. Those who saw most welfare recipients as black also expressed substantially more negative views about welfare recipients when asked whether most people on welfare really want to work and whether most people on welfare really need it (table 6.1). These differences between respondents with different perceptions of the racial composition of the poor are not caused by differences between these two groups in other characteristics. When regression analysis is used to control for respondents' age, sex, education, family income, and liberal/conservative ideologies, the differences shown in table 6.1 diminish only slightly (see appendix table A.10 for full regression results).

Both media portrayals and public perceptions exaggerate the degree to which African Americans compose the poor. Although we lack direct

Table 6.1 Perceptions of Welfare Recipients

	Think Most Welfare Recipients Are Black	Think Most Welfare Recipients Are White
In your opinion, what is more to blame when people are on welfare?		
Lack of effort on their own part	63%	40%
Circumstances beyond their control	26	50
Do most people on welfare want to work?		
Yes	31	55
No	69	45
Do most people on welfare really need it?		
Yes	36	50
No	64	50

Source: CBS/*New York Times* poll, December 1994. N = 371 to 674.

Notes: Respondents were asked, "Of all the people who are on welfare in this country, are more of them black or are more of them white?" Respondents volunteering "about equal" are not shown in the table. All differences between respondents who think most welfare recipients are black and those who think most welfare recipients are white are significant at $p < .001$. These differences diminish only slightly and remain highly significant when controls are added for age, sex, education, family income, and liberal/conservative ideology (see appendix table A.10). Results exclude respondents saying "don't know" or providing no answer.

evidence that media distortions are the cause of the public's misperceptions, substantial indirect evidence suggests that this is likely. Whatever the cause, it is clear that misperceptions of the racial character of American poverty have important consequences for how people view welfare recipients. Even taking into account differences in education, income, liberal/conservative orientations, and other factors, Americans who mistakenly believe that most welfare recipients are black are substantially more likely to view welfare recipients as "the undeserving poor."

Explaining Racial Misrepresentations

In his classic study of newsmagazines and network television news, Herbert Gans identified availability and suitability as the most significant determinants of news content.[14] By "availability," Gans meant the accessibility of potential news to a journalist facing a variety of logistical constraints and time pressures, while "suitability" concerns a story's importance and interest to the audience and its fit within the framework of the news medium (whether newspaper, magazine, or television news).

Gans argued that availability is a product of both the news organization and the social world in which it operates. For example, economically and politically powerful individuals and organizations use their resources to make themselves more accessible to journalists, and the location of news bureaus in large cities lends an urban slant to the national news. Thus news "availability" reflects the social structure that exists outside of news organizations as well as decisions made within those organizations.

With regard to the pictorial representation of poverty, the availability of different subgroups of the poor may shape the images captured by news photographers. Because news bureaus and the photographers they employ tend to be found in and around large cities, it should not be surprising that the poverty images produced by these organizations are dominated by the urban poor. And if African Americans make up a larger share of the urban poor than of the country's poor in general, then the "availability" of poor blacks to news photographers might contribute to their overrepresentation in magazine and television news.

This "geographic" explanation for the overrepresentation of blacks in poverty news sounds plausible, but census data show that it is clearly wrong, at least in this form. Within the nation's ten largest metropolitan areas, blacks constitute 32.1 percent of the poverty population, only marginally higher than the 27 percent of all poor Americans who are black.[15] Thus the poverty population that urban-based photographers have ready access to does not differ substantially in its racial composition from the American poor as a whole.

Another version of the "geographic" explanation may hold more promise in accounting for the overrepresentation of blacks in newsmagazine pictures of poverty. When an urban-based photographer receives an assignment for pictures of poor people, he or she is likely to look in those neighborhoods in which poor people are most concentrated. It is simply more efficient to look for poor people in neighborhoods with high poverty rates than to seek out the relatively few poor people in more economically heterogeneous neighborhoods.

To the extent that photographers look for poor people in poor neighborhoods, the racial mix of their photographs will reflect not the racial composition of poverty in the entire metropolitan area, but the composition of poverty in poor neighborhoods within the metropolitan area. Because poor blacks are more geographically concentrated than poor

whites,[16] neighborhoods with high poverty rates are likely to be disproportionately black compared with the poverty population as a whole.
In other words, poor whites tend to be "spread around" in both poor
and nonpoor neighborhoods, while poor African Americans are more
likely to live in neighborhoods with high poverty rates.

To gauge the extent to which the geographic concentration of African
American poverty might lead to the misrepresentation of the poor in
newsmagazines, I again examined the ten largest metropolitan areas,
this time looking at the racial composition of only those poor people
living in poor neighborhoods. In his studies of urban poverty, William
Julius Wilson identifies as "poverty areas" census tracts in which at
least 20 percent of the population is poor.[17] Using this criterion, about
half (51 percent) of the poor people in these ten cities live in "poverty areas," and blacks constitute 47 percent of the poor people living
in these neighborhoods—substantially higher than the percentage of
blacks among all poor people in these ten metropolitan areas. If photographers were even more selective in the neighborhoods they chose, they
would encounter poverty populations with even higher percentages of
African Americans. For example, in what Wilson calls "high poverty
areas" (census tracts with poverty rates of at least 30 percent), blacks
comprise 53 percent of the poor in these ten cities. And if photographers were to visit "extreme poverty areas" (with poverty rates of at
least 40 percent), they would find that 61 percent of these poor are
black.

Thus, in the ten largest metropolitan areas as a whole, about 32 percent of poor people are black, but in the very poorest neighborhoods of
these cities, blacks comprise over 60 percent the poor. For photographers working under deadline, the easier availability of poor African
Americans might skew the images of poverty that appear in the national news. Although Gans focused on the forces that shape the substantive text of the news, the production of news pictures follows the
same logic. Social structures outside of the newsroom influence the
availability of news content. Because poor blacks are disproportionately available to news photographers, they may be disproportionately
represented in the resulting news product.

But the disproportionate availability of poor African Americans cannot explain all of the racial distortions in media images of poverty. First,
only the poorest neighborhoods contain the extremely large proportions of poor blacks found in news stories on poverty during most of
the past three decades. And by focusing exclusively on these neighborhoods, photographers would have to ignore the vast majority of urban

poor, not to mention the millions of poor people living in smaller cities or rural areas. Only 9 percent of the nation's poor live in "extreme poverty areas" as defined above, and as we saw, once the definition of poverty areas is broadened to include a larger percentage of the poor, the proportion of blacks declines significantly.[18]

Furthermore, the residential concentration of black poverty can at best explain the racial mix of photographs that a newsmagazine photo editor has available to choose from. Because a photo editor typically has a vastly larger number of pictures available than will be used for publication, the racial composition of the photographs that ultimately appear in the magazine will reflect the selection criteria of the photo editor. A photographer will typically produce anywhere from four hundred to four thousand photographs for a single newsmagazine story.[19] Thus even if photographers submit, on average, three pictures of poor African Americans for every two pictures of poor whites, magazine photo editors have the ability to determine the racial mix of the few pictures that find their way into print.

The third and most important limitation of availability as an explanation for media portrayals of the poor is that the racial distortions in the media's images of poverty vary dramatically over time. As we saw in the previous chapter, the proportion of African Americans in newsmagazine pictures of the poor grew from only 27 percent in 1964 to 72 percent in 1967. Nor was this the only significant racial change in the portrayal of the poor. Images of poverty have shifted up and down over the past decades. In 1967–68 and 1972–73, about 70 percent of the pictures of poor people in newsmagazines were of blacks. In contrast, less than 50 percent of the poor in newsmagazine photographs were black in 1974–75, and only 33 percent were black in 1982–83.

The substantial shifts over time in the racial content of media coverage of poverty clearly do not reflect changes in the "availability" of the black poor. Poor blacks did not suddenly become easier for photographers to find after 1964, nor did they somehow become more elusive during the mid-1970s or the early 1980s, when their appearances in newsmagazines (and on television news) declined. The shifting racial images in the media show that judgments of "suitability" rather than (or in addition to) accessibility shape the pictorial representation of poverty in the national news.

Judgments of suitability enter into both the selection of news stories and the content of those stories (and of the pictures used to illustrate them). Perhaps the most fundamental aspect of suitability with regard to story content concerns the veracity of the news story. Accuracy and

objectivity remain primary goals among news professionals,[20] yet as
Gans argued, journalists cannot assess a story's accuracy and objectivity
without drawing on their own set of "reality judgments." Such judgments constitute the background understanding of society on which a
news story is built, and journalists' efforts to accurately portray the subject matter of their stories depend not only on the specific information
newly gathered for a particular story, but also on this background understanding. While journalists' understandings of society derive in part
from their professional work, they inevitably share in varying degrees
the popular understandings, and misunderstandings, held by the larger
society in which they live.

To better understand the production of media images of the poor, I
interviewed the photo editors at *Time, Newsweek,* and *U.S. News and
World Report* who are responsible for poverty stories in these magazines. Newsmagazine stories on American poverty appear primarily in
either the "National News" section, which tends to contain hard news
stories such as government poverty or unemployment statistics, or the
"Society" section, which contains softer news like stories on runaways,
welfare hotels, and so on (the exact titles of these sections differ somewhat among the magazines). At each magazine, I spoke with the senior
photo editors in charge of these two sections.[21]

Most of the photo editors I spoke with expressed a concern that their
selection of photographs should faithfully reflect the subject of the story
and that the photographs of poor people should provide a fair portrayal
of the demographics of poverty in the United States.[22] Given the concern for accuracy professed by most of the photo editors I talked with,
it is important to know whether these news professionals subscribe to
the same stereotypes of the poor as the rest of the American public. To
assess whether newsmagazine photo editors share the public's perceptions of the poor, I asked each of the editors I contacted the same question that the public was asked in the 1991 National Race and Politics
Study: What percent of all the poor people in this country would you
say are black? As a group, these photo editors did share the public's
misperceptions regarding the racial composition of the poor, but not to
the same degree. On average, the six photo editors I spoke with estimated that 42 percent of America's poor people are black, less than
the public's estimate of 50 percent, but still higher than the true figure
of 27 percent. (Averaging the responses of the photo editors I spoke
with may be somewhat misleading; the three editors responsible for the
"national news" sections of the magazines, in which the majority of
poverty coverage appears, had more accurate perceptions of the racial

composition of the poor than did the editors responsible for the "Society" sections, where poverty stories appear less often. Consequently, the "effective" perceptions of the editors that choose photographs for poverty stories may be lower than this 42 percent average suggests.)

While the misperceptions of poverty held by the photo editors I spoke with are significant in themselves, even more significant is the substantial discrepancy between these editors' perceptions and the images appearing in their stories. I interviewed the editors at the three newsmagazines in the fall of 1993. Although I lack data on newsmagazine stories during 1993, blacks made up about 62 percent of pictures of the poor during the preceding five-year period (from 1988 through 1992, with a slight increase across these five years). Thus it appears that the images that these photo editors chose deviated substantially from their own stated perceptions of the racial composition of America's poor.

One explanation for the deviation between photo editors' perceptions of poverty and the nature of the images they select might be that news coverage concentrates on subgroups of the poor that contain larger numbers of blacks. By this reasoning, the overrepresentation of African Americans in pictures of the poor reflects the fact that not all poor people are equally "newsworthy." In particular, the subgroups of the poor that news professionals (and presumably their audiences) find most interesting and important may contain higher proportions of African Americans than the poor as a whole. After all, news coverage of poverty is only occasionally about the poor as an undifferentiated category; more often it focuses on particular subgroups of the poor and particular aspects of poverty.

As an explanation for the high proportions of African Americans found in poverty stories, this account has two problems. First, although the subgroups of the poor that figure most prominently in news stories do contain somewhat higher proportions of blacks than the poor as a whole, the difference is much too small to account for the imbalance of racial images found in news stories. And second, the overrepresentation of African Americans in newsmagazine coverage of poverty is not limited to stories on particular subgroups, but is just as prevalent in general stories on poverty or poor people overall.

Table 6.2 shows the topics of newsmagazine stories on poverty during the most recent five-year period examined (1998 through 1992). The largest numbers of poverty-related stories during this period focused on housing programs, homelessness, poor children, and public assistance (there were also a substantial number of stories about poverty

Table 6.2 Percentage African American in Newsmagazine Pictures of the Poor, 1988–1992

Topic	Number of Stories	Number of Poor People Pictured	Percentage African American
Underclass	6	36	100
Poor people, poverty	33	147	69
Housing programs	49	65	66
Education	4	17	65
Homelessness	47	138	63
Children	24	70	60
Public assistance	25	97	57
Employment programs	9	52	40
Medicaid	7	6	17
All poverty-related stories	182	560	62

Notes: Sums of column entries exceed totals shown because stories may be indexed under more than one topic. An additional 14 stories (not shown above) were indexed under miscellaneous other topics; 36 stories (17% of all stories) were indexed under more than one topic. Includes all stories on poverty and related topics published in *Time, Newsweek,* and *U.S. News and World Report* between January 1, 1988, and December 31, 1992. For details on subject categories, see Gilens, "Race and Poverty in America."

and poor people in general). In fact, each of these specific poverty subgroups contained somewhat higher proportions of African Americans than did the poor as a whole. Overall, blacks comprised 29 percent of America's poor during these five years, but they made up 40 percent of people receiving government housing benefits, 39 percent to 41 percent of the homeless, 34 percent of poor children, and 33 percent of people receiving means-tested government assistance.[23] Yet even taking the somewhat higher proportions of African Americans in these poverty subgroups into account, newsmagazine portrayals substantially overrepresented blacks in every one of these subgroups. As table 6.2 shows, 66 percent of the pictures of the poor in stories on housing programs were of blacks, as were 63 percent of the pictures in stories on homelessness. Similarly, pictures of poor children were 60 percent black, and blacks comprised 57 percent of the pictures of poor people in stories about public assistance.

The extent to which these pictures exaggerate the presence of blacks among the poor can be better assessed by calculating a "weighted" proportion of African Americans among the poor that takes into account the amount of attention devoted to each subgroup of poor people. If the press disproportionately writes about poor children or the homeless, then the percentage of blacks among these subgroups of the poor would receive more weight in the overall calculation. Applying this approach to the nine categories of coverage shown in table 6.2 yields a weighted percentage black among the poor of approximately 36 percent.[24] Thus the true overall proportion of blacks among the poor during this period was 29 percent, the true proportion of blacks among the mix of subgroups of the poor found in the three newsmagazines was 36 percent, and the proportion of blacks found in *pictures* of the poor in the three newsmagazines was 62 percent. In short, the greater "newsworthiness" of specific aspects of poverty cannot account for much of the discrepancy between the reality of American poverty and the highly racialized images found in the news.

The analysis of the various poverty subgroups in table 6.2 shows that, among those poverty subgroups that received the greatest attention from newsmagazines, the true proportion of African Americans was far lower than that shown in the images of these groups in the news. But table 6.2 also shows that this overrepresentation of blacks among the poor is even more pronounced in general stories about poor people as a whole. As the second line of the table indicates, fully 69 percent of the 147 poor people pictured in these general poverty stories were black.

Thus, the "subgroup newsworthiness hypothesis" does not appear to be a viable explanation for the racial misrepresentation of the poor in the news. A less charitable explanation for the high proportions of blacks in newsmagazine poverty stories is that photo editors' professed concern with accuracy reflects an effort to portray their work in the best possible light, rather than their honest evaluation of how they actually make choices among photographs. News images may diverge from reality—and from news editors' own perceptions of that reality—because their desire to accurately reflect social conditions is weaker than their desire to attract readers' attention. Photo editors may (rightly or wrongly) feel that a picture of a poor black person is more compelling to their readers than a picture of a poor white.

News professionals may cater to the perceived stereotypes of their readers by choosing images that they think will be most easily recognized as poor people or will be most likely to tap readers' emotional connections with the topic of poverty. Such a process need not entail a conscious effort to misrepresent the racial complexion of the poor. It is just as likely to result from a lack of conscious attention to the racial imagery that accompanies stories on poverty. As editors choose from among hundreds of photographs available for a particular story, they may be drawn to some pictures over others for reasons that they are neither fully aware of nor fully able to articulate. Among these reasons may well be the race of those pictured.

This account of the shaping of news images as a *subconscious* process is bolstered by the fact that none of the photo editors I talked with had any clear idea about the racial breakdown of the photos of poor people that appeared in their magazines. When told that newsmagazine pictures of the poor over the previous five years were about 62 percent black, many expressed considerable surprise. If the racial composition of the poor in the news results largely from a subconscious process, this process is likely to reflect not only editors' subconscious impressions of their readers' expectations, but also editors' own subconscious beliefs about poor people. Given the opportunity to consciously reflect on the racial composition of the poor, these editors conjectured that most poor Americans are nonblack; but it may be that, in the everyday process of choosing news photographs, the unexamined, subconscious impressions guiding their ideas of "what the poor should look like" reflect a sense that blacks compose a majority of America's poor. In other words, editors' conscious judgments may differ from the "seat of the pants" intuitions that actually guide their selection of photographs. Social psychologists have demonstrated that even people who explicitly reject specific stereotypes often use those same stereotypes subconsciously in evaluating members of the relevant social group.[25] Thus, photo editors who consciously reject the stereotype of the poor as black may nevertheless subconsciously employ just that stereotype in selecting pictures to illustrate American poverty.

The "subconscious stereotypes" explanation for racially biased news images of poverty can also help explain another apparent discrepancy between the views of media professionals and the content of the news. Both popular perceptions and empirical research indicate that the professionals who work in news organizations tend to be liberal in their personal political orientations. For example, surveys show that, compared with the public as a whole, journalists are considerably more likely to vote for Democrats, to identify as liberals, and to hold liberal views on social issues, including racial policies.[26] My own interviews with newsmagazine photo editors were consistent with this research. For example, I asked each a question from the 1991 National Race and Politics Study: "Whose fault would you say it is that blacks are worse off than whites—would you say that white people are mostly to blame, that blacks themselves are mostly to blame, or would you say that they both share the blame equally?" Most of the editors I talked to said that white people are mostly to blame for racial inequality—a view that, according to the national survey, is held by less than 15 percent of the American public.[27]

Despite the liberal political attitudes of news professionals and the liberal racial views expressed by the photo editors I interviewed, we have seen that news coverage of poverty not only exaggerates the percentage of blacks among the poor but consistently portrays poor blacks more negatively than poor whites. The previous chapter's analysis of changes in racial imagery over time found that images of poor blacks are most numerous during periods when poverty coverage is most critical of the poor and least numerous during periods when coverage of poverty takes on a more sympathetic tone. In addition, we saw that pictures of blacks were least likely to be found in stories on the most sympathetic subgroups of the poor. The analysis of the full 1950–1992 period in chapter 5 found the fewest pictures of African Americans in stories on old age assistance, hunger, medical care, and education, while the analysis of 1988–92 above found the lowest percentages of poor blacks in stories on Medicaid and employment programs.

Further analysis of the racial content of poverty coverage during 1988 through 1992 shows that the newsmagazines studied not only portrayed poor blacks less favorably than poor whites, but that these negative representations of poor blacks were also more distorted than the representations of the nonblack poor.[28] Children and the elderly are the most sympathetic age groups among the poor, and the underrepresentation (or overrepresentation) of these groups in the media might therefore lessen (or heighten) sympathy for the poor among the public.[29] Magazine portrayals of poor children are fairly accurate: in reality, 47 percent of poor African Americans are under 18 years old, compared with 52 percent of those shown in newsmagazine poverty stories. Similarly, 37 percent of the nonblack poor are under 18, compared with 35 percent of those in newsmagazines. Unlike children, the elderly poor represent a relatively small proportion of all poor Americans. But the elderly poor also differ from children in being substantially underrepresented in newsmagazine stories on poverty. Government statistics indicate that 12 percent of the nonblack poor and 8 percent of poor blacks are over 64 years old. In contrast, only 5 percent of the nonblack poor in newsmagazines were over 64 years old, and a minuscule 1 percent of poor African Americans in newsmagazine stories on poverty were over 64.[30] For both racial groups, the elderly—which constitute a very sympathetic age group among the poor—are underrepresented in newsmagazine coverage of poverty, but this neglect of the elderly poor is more pronounced in news portrayals of poor blacks than in portrayals of the nonblack poor.

The working poor also constitute a sympathetic subgroup of the poor, and this subgroup too is underrepresented in newsmagazines. Once again, we find that newsmagazine images of poor African Americans are both more negative and less accurate than images of poor nonblacks. In reality, poor blacks are somewhat less likely to work than are poor whites, but the difference is modest: 42 percent of poor blacks work compared with 54 percent of the nonblack poor.[31] Among poor people pictured in newsmagazine poverty stories, however, only half as many blacks as nonblacks were identified as working (12 percent of blacks compared with 27 percent of nonblacks). With regard to both work status and age, newsmagazines portrayed both the black and the nonblack poor in a more negative light than is warranted, but in both cases the images of poor blacks were more negative (and less accurate) than those of poor whites.

Despite journalists' liberal reputation in general and their liberal views on racial issues in particular, poverty stories in the national news media consistently portray poor blacks more negatively than poor whites. As one of the photo editors I interviewed suggested, only some kind of "subtle racism" can explain the consistent pattern of negative racial imagery that accompanies news media stories on poverty. Most journalists appear to consciously reject the stereotype of blacks as lazy. But in the everyday practice of their craft, and especially in their choice of photographs to illustrate stories on poverty, these same journalists portray poor blacks as more blameworthy than poor whites. Photo editors' conscious beliefs notwithstanding, media images of the poor reflect the cultural stereotypes of blacks as lazy and poor blacks as more responsible for their plight than are poor whites.

Subconscious Stereotypes

It might seem overly speculative to suggest that journalists (or other people) hold subconscious stereotypes that they consciously reject. Yet psychologists, using a variety of ingenious methods, have show that this is indeed quite common.[32] The psychological notion of subconscious or "implicit" stereotyping rests on the idea that people hold a variety of beliefs and perceptions that influence their behavior but of which they are normally unaware. When people act purposefully and reflectively, their conscious beliefs and perceptions guide their actions, but when they act "on impulse" their subconscious stereotypes can influence their decisions.

One of the techniques psychologists have used to measure implicit stereotypes is subconscious "priming" of experimental participants to think about blacks; this is done in such a way that the participants are unaware that they have been exposed to a racial prime. For example, in one influential study, Patricia Devine used a tachistoscope, a device that flashes words on a screen so briefly that observers cannot consciously make out what words have been presented.[33] Devine randomly divided her subjects (all of them white) into two groups; one group was shown words associated with blacks (words like "Negroes," "Blacks," and "Africa") and the other was shown neutral words unrelated to race (for example, "number," "said," and "sentences"). She then presented both groups with a description of a hypothetical individual named Donald who was engaging in a number of behaviors that might or might not be judged to be hostile (such as refusing to pay his rent until his apartment was repainted). Donald's race was not indicated in the description, and Devine expected that the subjects exposed to race-related primes would apply their own stereotypes of blacks when interpreting Donald's behavior, while subjects exposed to race-neutral primes would not. After reading the description of Donald's actions, the subjects were asked to evaluate how hostile they thought he was.

Devine found that subjects who were subconsciously exposed to the black-related words judged Donald's behavior to be more hostile than did those exposed to the non race-related primes. This difference emerged despite the fact that subjects were unable to tell what words they had been exposed to via the tachistoscope. Devine interpreted this finding as showing that racial stereotypes (in this case the stereotype of blacks as hostile) can be activated in a person's subconscious, without the person holding these stereotypes being aware. By being made to think subconsciously about blacks, the white subjects applied their existing negative stereotypes in evaluating the ambiguous behavior of the hypothetical "Donald." Those subjects exposed to the non race-related primes, however, did not interpret Donald's actions in the context of race and consequently saw his ambiguous behavior as less hostile.

As important as the subconscious activation of stereotypes is, another aspect of Devine's experiment is even more significant for our purposes. When Devine separated her subjects into those who scored high on a survey-type measure of racial prejudice and those who scored low, she found that both groups were equally affected by the racial priming. That is, by making blacks salient to her subjects on a subconscious level, Devine caused both the ostensibly "high-prejudice" and the ostensibly "low-prejudice" subjects to apply negative stereotypes of blacks to their evaluations of Donald's behavior. In contrast, when simply asked to list their (conscious) thoughts in response to black

Americans, high-prejudice subjects were much more likely than their low-prejudice counterparts to include themes like "hostile," "violent," or "aggressive." When thinking consciously about blacks, the low-prejudice subjects rejected the stereotype of blacks as hostile, but when reacting subconsciously, they drew upon this stereotype nonetheless.

Devine and other "implicit stereotyping" researchers theorize that most people in our culture are exposed to a set of stereotypes about blacks (and other social groups) that they internalize to varying degrees. Because these stereotypes are internalized, those who consciously reject them must make a deliberate effort to disregard these stereotypes in their everyday lives. When people are acting subconsciously, however, these "rejected" stereotypes can still influence people's perceptions and behaviors. The profound implication of this research is that good will toward blacks and a conscious rejection of negative stereotypes are not enough to guarantee that the insidious beliefs about African Americans that are part of our culture will not influence behavior. To "rise above" negative stereotypes we must become conscious of their operation and purposefully act to defuse their influence over our judgments. Of course, not everyone holds the same subconscious stereotypes of blacks, or of any other group.[34] But studies of implicit stereotyping suggest that negative stereotypes of blacks (and others) can influence the subconscious behavior of even those who explicitly reject these stereotypes.

The research on implicit stereotyping suggests that photo editors who consciously reject the stereotype of blacks as lazy may still react subconsciously on the basis of this stereotype. To overcome the influence of subconscious stereotypes, news professionals, like other Americans, must consciously "monitor" their reactions to racially charged stimuli. When choosing images to accompany stories on poverty, journalists must pay explicit attention both to the overall racial representation of the poor and to the specific conditions under which pictures of poor blacks are used. Although we have no direct evidence that photo editors or television news producers hold negative subconscious stereotypes of blacks, we also have no reason to think they differ in this regard from other racial liberals for whom psychologists have found this to be true.

During the 1960s, the prominence of African Americans in America's social and political life increased dramatically. Significant obstacles still impede the complete acceptance of blacks into the institutions that govern our society. But in the 1960s, the claims of African Americans to full and equal citizenship first gained widespread (although hardly universal) acceptance among both governing elites and the white public. The increased attention to blacks in general was reflected in the increased numbers of black faces in news coverage of poverty from this period. But this new attention to the black poor did not represent the efforts of liberal news professionals to draw sympathetic attention to this previously ignored group. On the contrary, African Americans became prominent in news stories on poverty only when those stories turned a critical eye to the problems and controversies related to the War on Poverty. Far from painting a sympathetic portrait of poor blacks, the "newly racialized" poverty coverage of the mid-1960s, like the coverage of poverty during the decades that followed, tended to associate African Americans with the most negative aspects of poverty and the most unsympathetic subgroups of the poor.

Subconscious stereotypes represent the most plausible explanation for the discrepancy between the racial liberalism of news professionals and the negative images of blacks that are found in news coverage of poverty. Yet in the end, the explanations for these negative images are less important than the images themselves. Whether or not any individual news professional harbors subconscious stereotypes of blacks, the content of poverty stories both reflects and reinforces such stereotypes. When magazine readers or television viewers see blacks depicted more often as the undeserving poor and whites as the deserving poor, they are likely to form their own stereotypes about race and poverty. And just as news professionals may be unconscious of the stereotypes that shape the content of their coverage, so magazine readers and television viewers may be unaware of the stereotypes that they acquire based on the way poverty is portrayed in the news.

7

Racial Stereotypes and Public Responses to Poverty

ontrary to what one might expect from journalists' liberal reputation, there was no "honeymoon" period in the mid-1960s when the newly discovered black poor were portrayed positively in the media. As we saw in chapter 5, poor blacks became prominent in poverty coverage only as that coverage turned negative in response to the perceived failings of the War on Poverty programs. The stereotype of blacks as lazy is evident not only in the newly racialized images of poverty from the mid-1960s but in the fluctuating coverage of the poor during the ensuing decades. As we have seen, poor whites have been more likely to appear as illustrations of the deserving poor— the elderly, the working poor, and those struggling against adverse economic conditions—while poor blacks have appeared more often in unsympathetic stories on welfare abuse or the underclass. But the stereotype of blacks as lazy long predates the current association of race and poverty. Indeed, this stereotype has been an enduring element of American culture for centuries.

Slavery and Racial Stereotypes

The history of black/white relations in America has been profoundly shaped by slavery, and the image of blacks as lazy owes much to the nature of this "peculiar institution." Many white slave owners appear to have had genuine misgivings about the institution of slavery— Thomas Jefferson being the most prominent example—and the appropriate stereotypes of blacks could go a long way toward assuaging their guilt. More importantly, perhaps, the desire to maintain the slave system created material incentives for whites to view blacks in particular derogatory ways. Negative stereotypes of blacks were used in arguing that slavery was necessary to keep blacks in check, or even that slavery was in blacks' own best interest. Because blacks lacked the intelligence, maturity, or industriousness needed to survive in society, some argued, slavery was a benefit to both blacks and whites. As Ronald Takaki notes in his study of racial attitudes in nineteenth-century America, blacks were often viewed as children who depended on whites to provide for their needs: "[W]hile slave masters fondly praised their bondsmen for their affection and dependency, they also complained about their laziness, and repeatedly noted how black laborers had to be supervised or they would not work. Blacks were like children in their inability to plan and to calculate: They would not 'lay up in summer for the wants of winter' and 'accumulate in youth for the exigencies of age.' "[1]

Nor did the example of free blacks in the North serve to undermine this image. Freedom for blacks, it was argued, "only conferred on [them] the privilege of being more idle."[2] In the 1830s a professor at William and Mary College explained, "In the free black, the principle of idleness and dissipation triumphs over that of accumulation and the desire to better our condition . . . and he . . . prefers sinking down into the listless, inglorious repose of the brute creation, to rising to that energetic activity which can only be generated amid . . . civilized society."[3]

Ironically, the greater the misgivings and ambivalence whites felt, the greater the need for stereotypes of blacks that could justify slavery. As antislavery sentiment grew in the North, negative stereotypes of blacks became even more important to slavery's defenders. Only by portraying blacks in the most negative light could the injustice of slavery be made palatable. In essence, slave owners needed a Sambo; they needed to believe that blacks were lazy, ignorant, happy-go-lucky, and childlike in order to justify slavery.

While slavery fostered negative racial stereotypes among whites, it also created incentives for blacks to display many of these same behaviors. The appearance of ignorance, for example, could be used to deflect whites' suspicions or answer their accusations. Fear of punishment was often slaves' only incentive to work hard. Lacking any positive reward for hard work, slaves appeared to be lazy, doing only enough to get by. Furthermore, hard work could carry negative consequences. By working hard on a given day, slaves might generate a new expectation among their overseers that they would then be required to meet on a regular basis. Finally, the refusal to work hard served as a form of resistance to white slave masters. Takaki points out that the same behavior could be perceived very differently by masters and slaves: "Lying, stealing, laziness, immaturity, ignorance, and even affection all contained within them an aggressive quality: They constituted in effect resistance to efficiency, discipline, work, and productivity. Where the master perceived laziness, the slave saw refusal to be exploited. Thus the same action held different meanings, depending on whether one was master or slave."[4]

The social conditions of slavery, then, created an incentive structure that discouraged hard work and initiative and led whites to perceive slaves as lazy. The stereotype of blacks as lazy was so firmly entrenched that even a leading abolitionist, William Lloyd Garrison, felt it necessary to concede that "it would be absurd to pretend that as a class they [blacks] maintain a high character . . . [or] to deny that intemperance, indolence, and crime prevail among them to a mournful extent."[5] Slavery thus laid the foundations for the stereotype of blacks as lazy that continues to shape not only white Americans' racial views, but their welfare policy attitudes as well.

The Stereotype of the Lazy Black in the Twentieth Century

Slavery may have been responsible for establishing the stereotype of blacks as lazy, but this stereotype did not disappear with the end of slavery. Seventy years after the abolition of slavery, Daniel Katz and Kenneth Braly surveyed Princeton undergraduates about their perceptions of various ethnic groups.[6] Students were given a list of eighty-four traits and were asked to select the five that were "most characteristic" of the group in question. In characterizing blacks, 75 percent chose "lazy" as among these five traits; it was second in popularity after "superstitious" and twice as popular as the next most frequently chosen trait, "happy-go-lucky." In contrast, the students chose "lazy" as a characteristic of only one of the nine other ethnic groups in the survey (Italians), and only 12 percent chose "lazy" as one of the five most characteristic traits of this group.[7] Although the Princeton students who participated in this study were not typical Americans, the survey results suggest that the stereotype of blacks as lazy was still a central element of whites' racial attitudes in 1933.

Katz and Braly broke new ground in the study of ethnic stereotypes, and their procedure has been replicated twice with Princeton undergraduates, in 1951 and again in 1967.[8] In both replications the proportion of students characterizing blacks as lazy declined (as did the level of agreement among students about the traits associated with blacks).

Nevertheless, "lazy" remained among the most popular traits used to describe blacks. In 1951, 31 percent of the students surveyed placed "lazy" on their list of five traits for blacks, a dramatic decline from the 75 percent found in 1933. By 1967, only 26 percent placed "lazy" among the five most characteristic traits (table 7.1). But "lazy" remained among the more common traits used in describing blacks in both of these later studies. In the original study "lazy" was the second most widely chosen trait, while in 1951 "lazy" had fallen only to third, and in 1967 this trait was tied for third with "pleasure loving."

The once-strong consensus among Princeton students that blacks are lazy has clearly declined over the decades as these students' stated perceptions of blacks have become more positive. Much of this decline is surely due to genuine changes in white students' perceptions of black Americans. But part of the decline can likely be accounted for by the emergence of social norms against the expression of antiblack attitudes or beliefs. In addition, some of the change in the responses of Princeton students may have resulted from changes in the social and economic composition of the Princeton student body. Whatever the reasons, by

Table 7.1 Princeton Students' Stereotypes of Blacks, 1933–1967

	Percentage Choosing Trait		
	1933	1951	1967
Superstitious	84	41	13
Lazy	75	31	26
Happy-go-lucky	38	17	27
Ignorant	38	24	11
Musical	26	33	47
Ostentatious	26	11	25
Very religious	24	17	8
Stupid	22	10	4
Physically dirty	17	—	3
Naive	14	—	4
Slovenly	13	—	5
Unreliable	12	—	6
Pleasure loving	—	19	26
Sensitive	—	—	17
Gregarious	—	—	17
Talkative	—	—	14
Imitative	—	—	13

Source: Karlins, Coffman, and Walters, "On the Fading of Social Stereotypes."

Note: Table shows the percentage of students choosing each trait as among the five traits "most typical" of blacks.

the late 1960s fewer Princeton students were willing to label blacks as lazy. Yet this racial stereotype was far from abandoned. The trio of Princeton studies shows that blacks continued to be characterized as less committed to the work ethic than other groups. The trait "lazy," for example, which was chosen as characteristic only of blacks and Italians in 1933, was applied to blacks alone in the 1951 and 1967 studies. Furthermore, "industrious," which was not chosen as characteristic of blacks at any time period, appeared in students' descriptions of Chinese, Germans, Irish, Japanese, Jews, and "Americans" at all three periods.

Recent survey data also indicate that the stereotype of blacks as lazy remains credible for many Americans. In a national survey conducted in 1996, respondents were asked to place blacks as a group on a seven-point scale with "lazy" at one end and "hardworking" at the other.[9] Thirty-nine percent of whites placed blacks on the lazy side of the scale, and only 15 percent placed blacks on the hardworking side. When asked the same question about whites, only 13 percent of white respondents placed whites as a group on the lazy side of the scale, while 41 percent placed them on the hardworking side. The stereotype of blacks as lazy has clearly endured. Large numbers of white Americans still believe that blacks lack commitment to the work ethic, a failing that few whites attribute to their own racial group.

The "Kernel of Truth" Hypothesis

Why has the view of blacks as lazy persisted through centuries of American history? One possible explanation for any stereotype is simply that the stereotype reflects an essential truth, though perhaps in an exaggerated form. Although stereotypes are sometimes conceived of as necessarily false beliefs about social groups, many social psychologists have come to view stereotypes as neither necessarily true nor necessarily false. Donald Campbell, for example, argues against focusing on the "truth content" of stereotypes.[10] Campbell notes that social groups do differ in many important ways, and that these differences naturally serve as the basis for group stereotypes. The presumption that stereotypes are apt to contain important truths can be found in Walter Lippmann's early writing on the subject as well. Although Lippmann recognized the pernicious nature of stereotypes, he also saw them as an inevitable part of social life, and he believed that a stereotype that has stood the test of time is likely to be true in some essential way: "The myth is, then, not necessarily false. It might happen to be true. It may happen to be partly true. If it has affected human conduct a long time, it is almost certain to contain much that is profoundly and importantly true."[11] Lippmann's faith in "the test of time" now appears naive. As we will see shortly, stereotypes can persist for many reasons even in the face of contrary evidence, and the longevity of a stereotype appears to be more a consequence of its attractiveness to those who hold it than of any truth that it might contain.

The empirical data available offer no evidence that there is a "kernel of truth" to the belief that blacks are less committed to the work ethic than are whites. Both in the attitudes they express in surveys, and in their behavior with regard to work, black Americans display the same commitment to work as their white counterparts. In 1987 the General Social Survey included a black oversample, which permitted more exact comparisons of blacks' and whites' attitudes. In this survey 74 percent of whites and 79 percent of blacks said that they would continue to work even if they were to get enough money to live comfortably for the rest of their lives. And when asked to rank the importance of five job characteristics, 51 percent of whites and 56 percent of blacks ranked "working hours are short, lots of free time" last of the five (the other features were high income, no danger of being fired, chances for advancement, and work important and gives a feeling of accomplishment). Based on the attitudes they express on surveys, African Americans are no less committed to the work ethic than are whites.

When we turn from attitudes to actual behavior, we find that by some measures blacks are slightly less attached to work than whites, while by other measures they are slightly more attached. For example, overall labor force participation is marginally lower for blacks than it is for whites. In 1996, 64 percent of all black adults were either working or actively looking for work, compared with 67 percent of white adults.[12] Among blacks and whites who are working, however, blacks are slightly more likely than whites to be working full-time. Of all civilian workers, 15 percent of blacks and 19 percent of whites worked part-time in 1996.[13] These are, of course, crude measures of commitment to the work ethic, and they do not take into account the different social and economic circumstances faced by black and white Americans. These statistics nevertheless offer at least some insight into the attitudes and behaviors of blacks and whites with respect to work. Yet if the stereotype of blacks as lazy does not contain some "essential truth," why has it proved so enduring?

The Nature and Function of Stereotypes

Stereotypes endure because they are useful in a variety of ways to those who hold them. As generalizations about people (or objects) based on category membership, stereotypes systematize and simplify the social world; they reduce the infinite variety of individual people and experiences to a more manageable array of *types* of people and experiences.[14] Stereotypes can vary in the extent to which they are "categorical" (implying that every member of the category shares some trait) or "qualified" (implying that members of the category tend to share the relevant trait to a greater degree than nonmembers).[15] But in either case, stereotypes help to ease our encounter with a complex reality by organizing people or things into meaningful categories (meaningful, at least, from the point of view of those who hold the stereotypes).

Although stereotypes are undeniably useful in helping us manage the "blooming buzzing confusion" of our social world, they necessarily distort that world as well. First, and most obviously, when we judge individuals by the social categories they inhabit we necessarily *misjudge* them to some degree. Even if our stereotypes are accurate characterizations of social groups (which they often are not), the individuals that compose those groups invariably display a range of attributes, and stereotypes often bias our perceptions of those whom we stereotype. Indeed, the very process of dividing the world into categories appears to lead to the exaggeration of differences among the categories and the neglect of differences within them. This tendency has been observed across a remarkably wide range of settings and subject matter. For example, in a classic experiment by Henri Tajfel and A. L. Wilkes, subjects were asked to judge the length of eight lines of varying size.[16] For a random half of the subjects, the four shorter lines were labeled "A" and the four longer ones "B." These subjects significantly exaggerated the difference in length between the "A" lines and the "B" lines, and they exaggerated as well the similarity in the length of lines within each of the two groups. The other subjects were presented with the same set of eight lines but without the labels "A" and "B." These subjects did not misjudge the lines as the first group had done.

When people rather than lines are classified, the categories often carry connotations of good and bad. In particular, we expect ingroups to be evaluated more favorably than outgroups, and experimental evidence shows this to be the case even in regard to the most trivial of group memberships. For example, Michael Billig and Henri Tajfel divided subjects into two groups and asked each subject to evaluate paintings that supposedly had been done by members of the groups.[17] The groups were formed by flipping a coin, and subjects were aware of the purely random nature of group membership. Yet even under these conditions, subjects exhibited ingroup bias, rating paintings by members of their own group as more creative, appealing, and interesting than those of the other group.

The ingroup bias in artistic judgments displayed by Billig and Tajfel's subjects shows that, even in the absence of any concrete motivation to favor one's own group, mere group membership tends to affect how people view group insiders and outsiders. The power of this tendency is underlined in Billig and Tajfel's experiment by the fact that, even when subjects knew that the only basis for group membership was the toss of a coin, they still expressed ingroup favoritism in their judgments. While these biased judgments of artistic merit are of little consequence in themselves, the ingroup biases of real-world social groups have profound implications. On a wide variety of dimensions, people display biased evaluations of individuals based on group membership. For example, in what Thomas Pettigrew has labeled the "ultimate attribution error," people tend to attribute undesirable behavior of outgroup members to "internal" or dispositional traits but tend to attribute undesirable behavior of ingroup members to characteristics of the situation.[18] For example, Georgette Wang and Jack McKillip found that subjects who were given descriptions of a (hypothetical) car accident were more likely to blame the driver for the accident when he was said to be from a different ethnic group than when he was described as a member of the subject's own ethnic group.[19]

Because our identities are shaped by the social groups with which we identify, ingroup biases help to create positive social identities and enhance self-esteem. When we judge members of our own group more favorably than outgroup members, we enhance our perception of our own self-worth as a member of a group with valued characteristics.

Although stereotypes are useful for the individuals who hold them, most stereotypes are acquired rather than created "from scratch" by their holders. Stereotypes of social groups are shared constructs that are learned from socializing agents such as parents, schools, and the media. As a consequence, people may hold quite detailed (and wholly erroneous) stereotypes of social groups that they have never come in contact with.[20] And because stereotypes are social constructs, more powerful social groups may be able to "impose" their preferred stereotypes on less powerful groups. In a variation on the Marxist concept of "false consciousness," subordinate social groups may come to share the negative stereotypes that more powerful groups hold of them.[21] Thus the pattern of ingroup favoritism exists alongside another pattern: low-status social groups are more likely to hold both negative self-stereotypes and positive other-group stereotypes than are high-status groups.[22]

Stereotypes can serve not only psychic needs (for example, by enhancing self-esteem through ingroup bias) but material interests as well. In particular, social psychologists view stereotypes as one means by which a (usually more powerful) group can justify its treatment of, or advantage over, an outgroup. The stereotype of blacks as lazy was already discussed as a justification for slavery, and the same stereotype now serves to justify the continued social and economic inequalities between blacks and whites. Similarly, stereotypes of immigrants are used to justify cutbacks in the government benefits available to legal immigrants (to say nothing of the policies toward illegal immigration promoted on the basis of such stereotypes). In a similar fashion, stereotypes are common during wartime as a way to incite and mobilize the population against an external enemy. Negative stereotypes of Germans and Japanese were used to rally the country during World War II and justify the internment of U.S. citizens of Japanese ancestry.

Although stereotypes often reflect the material interests of those who subscribe to them, the influence of such interests may be unrecognized or unacknowledged. For example, while the institution of slavery served the material interests of southern whites, few white slaveholders would have been willing to acknowledge that self-interest lay behind their views of blacks. Because those who hold a stereotype believe it to be true, and the truth of a stereotype is seen by its adherents as the necessary and sufficient condition for holding it, the influence of self-interest on a stereotype is unlikely ever to be recognized by those who hold it. Indeed, for any given individual, the motives for holding a particular stereotype may be impossible to discern; after all, the fact that a stereotype serves the interests of its holder does not mean that the stereotype is a result of those interests. Nevertheless, it is clear that, in the aggregate, stereotypes evolve and are maintained in part because they serve the material interests of the groups that adhere to them, most often the dominant groups of a society.

In addition to serving the psychic needs of individuals and the material interests of specific groups, stereotypes can also legitimate the social system as a whole. Psychologists have shown that people have a strong desire to believe the world is a just place and that individuals usually get what they deserve. Certainly this faith in the basic fairness of our economic system has been a prominent element of how we Americans view our country. By this logic, personal economic prosperity is itself a mark of virtue, and failure an indication of deficiencies.

In a series of influential experiments, Melvin Lerner showed that people respond to the suffering of others by derogating the victim, even when that suffering is clearly undeserved.[23] Similarly, Lerner showed that people respond to undeserved good fortune by raising their esteem for the beneficiary of good luck. In one study, for example, subjects were assigned to watch one of two kinds of "learning sessions" in which a "learner" (in reality a confederate of the experimenter) would attempt to memorize pairs of words. In the first situation, the learner would be rewarded with money for each correct response; in the second, she would receive an electric shock for every wrong answer. (No actual shocks were administered. A buzzer was used to simulate the administration of an electric shock and the learner merely acted as if she were being shocked.) The experimental subjects (i.e., the observers of the learning sessions) were told that whether the learner was assigned to the "reward" condition or the "punishment" condition would be determined at random.

Lerner found that subjects who had watched the learner receive what they believed to be electric shocks rated the learner more negatively (e.g., as less intelligent, less friendly, and less mature) than did subjects who watched the learner being rewarded for her correct answers. These differences arose despite the fact that the same person acted as the learner in both conditions, and the subjects in both conditions had identical (and minimal) contact with the learner.

In a similar experiment focused on the impact of "unearned rewards," Lerner asked subjects to listen to two people working together on a joint task, and then to evaluate how much each of them had contributed to the task. Subjects were told that, due to funding limitations, only one of the two workers would be paid for his participation in the task, and that the worker to be paid would be chosen at random after the task was completed.

In fact the subjects were played a tape recording of two confederates identified as "Tom" and "Bill" working on the task. After listening to the work session, but before being asked to evaluate the workers' contributions, a random half of the subjects were told that Tom was chosen to be paid and the other half, that Bill was the lucky worker. The results of the study showed that, after listening to the identical tape, subjects who were informed that Tom was to be paid for his effort rated Tom's contributions more highly, while those told that Bill was the one to be paid thought Bill contributed more to the task. Despite the subjects' awareness that the decision to pay Tom or Bill was purely random (and decided after the task was completed), their perceptions of the relative contribution of the two workers reflected a desire to believe that the one who was rewarded with pay was the more "worthy" of the two.

Lerner's "just world" experiments are so compelling because the advantaged or disadvantaged position of the people being judged was determined at random. Subjects lacked any basis from which to conclude that the "learner" who was rewarded rather than shocked, or the "worker" who was paid rather than not, was in any way deserving of his or her fate. Nevertheless, his subjects sought to ease their own discomfort with unearned reward or undeserved pain by devaluing those who were unjustly disadvantaged and holding in higher esteem those upon whom fate had smiled.

The real-world socioeconomic incarnation of the "belief in a just world" is the notion that success must have been earned by those who enjoy it while poverty reflects the failings of the poor. Of course, few people think that economic outcomes depend solely on merit; most recognize that luck, unearned advantages, and unfair disadvantages also play a part in determining who is rich and who is poor.[24] But in accounting for economic success, most Americans rank highly such personal characteristics as "hard work and initiative" and "personal drive," while they consider "lack of thrift" or "lack of effort by the poor" to be the most important determinants of poverty.[25] In short, Americans express considerable faith in the "openness" of our economic system. For example, in one survey, 70 percent agreed that "America is the land of opportunity where anyone who works hard can get ahead."[26] The logical implication of this "belief in a just (economic) world" is that economic success is a mark of virtue, and economic failure an indication of personal shortcomings. Furthermore, this syllogism is applied not only to individuals, but to social groups as well. Thus blacks' economic disadvantage is itself taken as an indication that as a group they are less industrious than whites.

The belief that economic success can serve as an indicator of social groups' talents, efforts, or ambition may be incorrect, but it is not irrational, nor need it rest on animosity toward those who fail to prosper. Whether our economic system is open and fair enough to permit this deduction is an empirical question. If Americans believe—rightly or wrongly—that this is the case, then the conclusions they draw about the characteristics of social groups may be logically justified (even if they are empirically wrong). This is not to say, of course, that the perception of fairness *cannot* reflect an animosity toward those at the bottom of the social order or a desire to justify one's own privileged position. Only that such a belief *need not* reflect these "ulterior" motives.

In sum, the stereotype of blacks as lazy can serve many functions for the white Americans who hold it. This stereotype can boost whites' self-esteem by identifying them as the more industrious or able racial group, it can justify existing social and economic inequalities between blacks and whites, and it can help to maintain the comforting belief that the world is basically just.

Stereotypes, Ill Will toward Blacks, and White Americans' Policy Preferences

Among survey analysts, a debate has raged for two decades about the extent to which white Americans remain prejudiced against blacks. At the core of this debate lie two empirical observations. First, the number of white Americans expressing opposition to the principle of racial equality has declined precipitously. For example, the percentage of whites saying that black and white children should go to the same schools increased from 32 percent in 1942 to 95 percent in 1995.[27] But at the same time, large numbers of whites—often majorities—express opposition to the policies designed to advance equality between blacks and whites (policies such as affirmative action or school busing). So a critical question is, To what extent does whites' opposition to policies designed to promote racial equality stem from some form of racial animosity or prejudice?

To answer this question, we first need a definition of "prejudice." Among the many understandings of prejudice offered over the years, we find: "an affective, categorical mode of mental functioning involving rigid prejudgment and misjudgment of human groups"; "an antipathy based on a faulty and inflexible generalization"; and "thinking ill of others without sufficient warrant."[28] As these understandings suggest, prejudice is related to, but distinct from stereotyping. Stereotyping draws our attention to the cognitive content of inter-group orientations, while prejudice involves the affective component as well. Often these two elements exist together, in part because they are mutually reinforcing. Socially acquired antipathies toward other groups may lead to the

adoption of negative stereotypes; on the other hand, negative stereotypes reinforce negative affect toward the relevant outgroups. Yet theo-
ries of prejudice often stress its emotional or irrational nature and its
roots in childhood socialization—characteristics that may or may not
be shared with stereotypes.[29] I will use the term "prejudice" to refer to
attitudes that embody a general dislike of or hostility toward another
social group.

Do white Americans' opposition to racial policies such as affirmative
action or school busing reflect prejudice in the sense described above,
and if not, to what should we attribute this opposition? Three perspectives on this question have been offered, each with very different
understandings of whites' racial policy preferences. One perspective,
most closely identified with David Sears and Donald Kinder, argues
that a new form of racism emerged in the 1960s.[30] In their view, unlike
"old fashioned racism," contemporary racism eschews notions of ge-
netic inferiority. Yet like its earlier incarnations, contemporary racism
is seen as reflecting a fundamental antipathy or dislike of African
Americans. Sears, Kinder, and their colleagues construe contemporary
racism as an amalgam of antiblack affect and traditional American values such as individualism, and they view this constellation of attitudes
as the most important source of whites' opposition to policies designed
to benefit blacks.

In contrast to the "new racism" school of thought, Lawrence Bobo
argues that white opposition to programs that aim to redress racial
inequalities stems in large part from the competition between racial
groups over concrete resources.[31] From this "realistic group conflict"
perspective, whites' racial policy views are shaped less by an emotional
or "irrational" antipathy toward blacks, and more from a calculation
that specific policies will benefit black Americans at the expense of
whites. The group conflict model understands changes in whites' racial
attitudes as an effort to maintain a racial advantage in the distribution
of scarce resources under changing historical circumstances.

Finally, Paul Sniderman and his colleagues offer a third perspective
on this debate. Sniderman argues that whites' objections to policies
such as school busing or affirmative action stem less from antiblack sentiments or from conflicts over scarce resources than from nonracial values such as a preference for limited government or a belief in individual
effort and reward. From this point of view, what whites object to in
affirmative action is not that blacks are the beneficiaries, but that an
inappropriate criterion (an individual's race) is employed in determining the allocation of valued goods. [32]

None of the authors involved in this debate denies the continued existence of antiblack prejudice. Clearly, many white Americans still harbor ill will toward blacks. When asked by survey interviewers, small but significant proportions of white Americans express blatantly prejudicial attitudes, and surely many more hold these views but will not acknowledge them. For example, on a 1996 survey, 13 percent of white respondents expressed support for laws against marriages between blacks and whites, a sentiment that would be hard to explain on any basis other than antipathy toward blacks.[33] Still, these three perspectives do differ greatly in the relative importance they assign to racial prejudice, and in the other factors that they identify as important in explaining white Americans' racial policy preferences.

My focus in this book has not been on racial policy, but on welfare, a race-neutral program that provides benefits to poor people of all racial and ethnic groups. Yet the same question arises in regard to welfare as in regard to racial policy: to what extent does racial prejudice explain whites' opposition to welfare, and to what extent should this opposition be attributed to other racial attitudes or to nonracial considerations? The analyses in chapter 4 showed that both racial views and nonracial considerations influence white Americans' welfare policy preferences. Respondents' liberal/conservative orientation, their party identification, their attitudes toward individualism, and their views on whether welfare recipients are deserving all had some impact on their preference for increasing or decreasing welfare spending. But we also saw that racial attitudes play an important role in shaping white Americans' welfare policy preferences. The perception that blacks are lazy emerged as the strongest determinant of whites' beliefs about welfare recipients, and it was a powerful influence on their preferences with regard to welfare spending. Despite welfare's formally race-neutral structure, beliefs about blacks are central in shaping white Americans' views of welfare.

If opposition to welfare is shaped by whites' racial views, how exactly should we understand the nature of these views? We saw in chapter 3 that the specific dimension of racial attitudes most important in shaping opposition to welfare is the stereotype of blacks as lazy. In contrast, the question that most directly reflects racial prejudice—whites' general feelings toward blacks—was only weakly related to opposition to welfare. Yet the possibility remains (as Sears and others have suggested) that the poor predictive power of questions that tap affective orientations toward blacks may stem either from whites' reluctance to express racial hostility to survey interviewers or from the poor quality of the survey measures that have been developed to assess such orientations.[34]

Complicating our task even more, racial stereotypes themselves can embody both group interest and prejudice. As discussed above, stereotypes persist, in part, because they help to justify the concrete advantages that some social groups hold over others. And prejudiced whites would naturally find negative racial stereotypes attractive since such stereotypes reconfirm their holders' feelings that blacks are unworthy. But stereotypes cannot be reduced to either group interest or prejudice. While for some whites the stereotype of blacks as lazy reflects their racial prejudice or their concern with maintaining white economic advantage, other whites may acquire the same stereotype through socialization or may adopt it in response to the perception that economic opportunity is widespread and that blacks' economic struggles—like the struggles of other economically disadvantaged groups—indicate a lack of effort or initiative. To understand the racial component of antiwelfare attitudes, we need to know whether the stereotype of blacks as lazy primarily reflects whites' racial prejudice, results from whites' desire to maintain the concrete advantages they enjoy over blacks, or indicates purely cognitive beliefs about the work ethic of black Americans.

One way to assess the underlying "meaning" of the lazy-black stereotype is to compare its influence on whites' welfare views with the influence of other perceptions of blacks. If whites' belief that blacks are lazy is primarily a reflection of a more general prejudice or antipathy toward blacks, then the content of this particular stereotype should be fairly unimportant. In that case, other negative stereotypes of blacks that similarly reflect whites' underlying antipathy would serve just as well (or nearly as well) as predictors of white opposition to welfare. On the other hand, if the cognitive content of this particular stereotype *is* important, then we would expect other stereotypes of blacks (for example, as violent or unintelligent) to be much less strongly related to whites' welfare policy preferences.[35]

Paul Sniderman and Thomas Piazza used just this approach in their analysis of racially targeted government assistance.[36] They found that whites' attitudes toward government help for blacks was strongly related to their beliefs about blacks' effort and responsibility but quite weakly related to other beliefs such as whether blacks tend to be violent or whether they have less inborn ability than whites. Sniderman and Piazza concluded that the large variability in the impact of different racial views indicates that white opposition to race-targeted government assistance is not rooted in a broad antiblack prejudice, but in the specific perception that blacks are not trying hard enough.

To assess whether the impact of the lazy-black stereotype on whites' welfare attitudes reflects a more general prejudice toward blacks, I make use of the 1992 National Election Study, which included identical measure of three racial stereotypes, asking respondents to indicate whether "blacks in general" tend to be lazy as opposed to hardworking, unintelligent as opposed to intelligent, and violent as opposed to peaceful (in each case, respondents were asked to indicate their perceptions by using a seven-point scale). Figure 7.1 shows that these three stereotypes differ substantially in their influence on whites' welfare views. When each stereotype is considered individually, the perception that blacks are lazy has a far stronger impact on welfare spending preferences than either the perception that blacks are unintelligent or that blacks are violent (with regression coefficients of .49, .29, and .22, respectively—see appendix table A.11 for details).

We can further assess the influence of these three different stereotypes on whites' welfare views by statistically "partialling out" the unique component of each stereotype (shown in the dotted bars in figure 7.1).

Figure 7.1   Alternative Racial Stereotypes and Opposition to Welfare

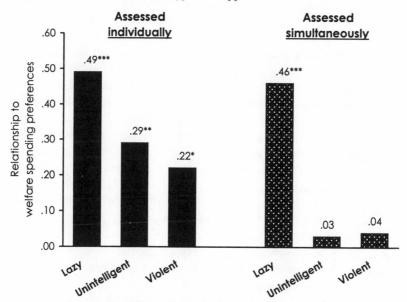

Source: National Election Study, 1992 (white respondents only). N = 1,527 to 1,550.

Note: Figure shows the regression coefficients for each stereotype as a predictor of welfare spending preferences while holding constant age, sex, education, family income, and region of residence. See appendix table A.11 for details and full regression results.

*p < .05; **p < .01; ***p < .001.

This approach shows that, even for whites who hold the same perceptions of blacks' intelligence and inclination toward violence, perceptions of blacks' laziness remain strongly associated with welfare spending preferences (the regression coefficient is reduced only from .49 to .46). In contrast, when we statistically hold constant perceptions of blacks' laziness, the other two stereotypes have no independent influence on welfare spending preferences whatsoever (with nonsignificant regression coefficients of only .03 and .04).

Clearly then, these different stereotypes are not interchangeable; when whites express their views about whether blacks are lazy or hardworking they are not simply revealing a general antipathy (or a general sympathy) toward blacks. Instead whites' perceptions that blacks lack commitment to the work ethic represents a specific racial judgment that cannot be reduced to a broad negative orientation toward blacks. While prejudice surely plays some part in generating negative stereotypes of blacks, these different stereotypes also reflect unique cognitive constructs that have different origins and different consequences for white Americans' political views.

Another way we can evaluate the different potential "meanings" of the lazy-black stereotype is by looking at the implications of these alternative understandings for whites' policy views. If white opposition to welfare reflects a general antipathy toward blacks, then any program perceived to benefit primarily African Americans will be unlikely to gain wide support among the white public. But if many of the white Americans who believe blacks are lazy do not also harbor a more general dislike of or ill will toward blacks, then the vulnerability of antipoverty programs to race-based opposition should vary, depending on the degree to which they evoke the relevant negative racial stereotype. Those antipoverty programs (like welfare) that are thought to undermine the work ethic, or reward those who are too lazy or undisciplined to support themselves, should be most vulnerable to racial politics, while programs viewed as enhancing self-sufficiency—even if strongly identified with African Americans—should sustain more support among the white public.

Of existing government antipoverty programs, welfare and food stamps are clearly associated with blacks and consistently receive the lowest levels of public support. But there are other programs that are just as strongly associated with racial minorities that receive much greater support from the public. For example, in one survey 67 percent of white respondents indicated that they believed the majority of food stamp recipients are racial minorities while 80 percent of white respondents believed this to be true for public housing.[37] Yet public housing programs are far more popular than food stamps: only 36 percent of Americans object to cutting food stamps to balance the federal budget, but 59 percent oppose cuts in public housing for this purpose.[38] Furthermore, survey data show that some of the most popular antipoverty programs are among those most strongly associated with minorities. Both Head Start and job training programs receive overwhelming support from the public, with majorities saying we should increase spending in both these areas.[39] Yet 59 percent of whites believe that most children enrolled in Head Start classes are minorities, and 68 percent think that minorities account for most of those in job training programs.[40]

Programs that are seen as enhancing the ability of poor people to support themselves, rather than rewarding the lazy with government "handouts," do not evoke the same negative racial imagery. Unlike welfare, public housing is a supplement to, not a substitute for, self-support (after all, even public housing tenants must pay rent for their apartments). And Head Start and job training programs are intended to help individuals succeed on their own. Because these programs are seen as helping people help themselves, not rewarding them for their failure to work, they are less vulnerable to the politics of racial stereotyping.

Even race-targeted programs in which benefits are limited to African Americans can receive support from a majority of white Americans. For example, in a recent survey, 66 percent of white Americans expressed support for "educational programs to assist minorities in competing for college," while 69 percent favored "government financing for job training for minorities to help them get ahead in industries where they are underrepresented."[41] Both of these programs are designed to "help minorities help themselves." Similar levels of support have been found for other "opportunity enhancing" programs targeted toward blacks. For example, in a 1990 survey, 70 percent of whites favored "providing special college scholarships for black children who maintain good grades," and 68 percent of whites favored "spending more money for schools in black neighborhoods, especially for pre-school and early education programs."[42]

If race-based opposition to welfare among whites were driven primarily by ill will toward blacks, we would hardly expect to find so many white Americans supporting both racially identified and explicitly race-targeted programs that benefit blacks.[43] This is not to say, of course, that ill will toward blacks is absent from American society or that it plays no role in explaining white Americans' opposition to welfare. Far too many white Americans still express an odious prejudice toward blacks. Yet these views cannot plausibly be said to reflect the

outlook of most white Americans: not only do most whites fail to claim
these views in surveys, they also express support for programs that are
inconsistent with such views.

Racial prejudice, understood as a general antipathy toward or dislike
of blacks, surely plays some role in generating opposition to welfare
among white Americans. But the contrast between the broad nature of
this opposition and the broad support among whites for some race-
targeted and racially identified programs that assist blacks strongly
suggests that other explanations for opposition to welfare must be
found. When we turn to the group-conflict model, we see that it too
is largely inconsistent with the patterns of whites' policy views discussed above. The group-conflict model suggests that white opposition
to welfare stems from an unwillingness to help blacks improve their
economic position, especially when that improvement would come at
the expense of whites. But the race-associated and race-targeted programs that whites do support promise to do much more to help blacks
than welfare or food stamps might. Certainly this seems true if we accept the view of welfare as a trap that keeps people down rather than
as temporary assistance that allows them to get back on their feet (and
as table 2.4 shows, the overwhelming majority of nonpoor Americans
do view welfare in this way). It is hard to see how whites' defense
of their group interests would lead them to oppose welfare and food
stamps (which most believe benefit primarily minorities) but support
job training and public housing (which even larger numbers of whites
think benefit primarily minorities).[44]

Furthermore, some of the race-targeted programs that do receive
support from the majority of white Americans explicitly or implicitly
aim to help (deserving) blacks *in competition with whites*. As indicated
above, 66 percent of whites approve of "educational programs to assist
minorities in competing for college" and 69 percent support "job training for minorities to help them get ahead in industries where they
are underrepresented." Both of these popular race-targeted programs
promise to help blacks to excel in ways that would appear to threaten
white interests. The key to their popularity clearly does not reside in
their lack of threat to the group interests of whites; it appears to lie
instead in the fact that they benefit those who are trying to support
themselves.

The belief that black Americans lack commitment to the work ethic is
central to whites' opposition to welfare. But it appears that this race-
based opposition does not primarily reflect either a general racial animosity or an effort to defend whites' concrete group interests. Rather,

the racial component of white opposition to welfare seems to reflect the most important nonracial basis of welfare opposition: the perception that recipients are undeserving. Despite the decline of the stereotype of blacks as lazy over the course of the twentieth century, we have seen that this stereotype endures. When asked to rate both blacks and whites in terms of their tendency to be lazy or hardworking, 58 percent of whites rate blacks as the lazier of the two groups, 37 percent say blacks and whites are equal in this regard, and a scant 5 percent say whites are lazier than blacks.[45] The cynicism that white Americans express toward welfare recipients is fed by their belief that blacks lack a commitment to work, in combination with their exaggerated impressions of the extent to which African Americans populate the country's welfare rolls.

The stereotype of blacks as lazy has a long history in American culture and is implicated in both media portrayals and public attitudes toward poverty and government antipoverty policy. It is beyond the scope of this book, and perhaps impossible, to distinguish with certainty the alternative sources of this stereotype and their changing importance over time. But the evidence offered here does suggest that however important racial prejudice and group interest may have been in generating this stereotype, these are not now the primary factors that sustain it. No doubt to some degree, and for some white Americans, the belief that blacks are lazy does reflect a general antipathy toward blacks, and for others it appeals to their determination to maintain whites' economic advantages. But for many white Americans, the stereotype of blacks as lazy grows out of the belief that the American economic system is essentially fair, and that blacks remain mired in poverty despite the ample opportunities available to them. These perceptions in turn are fed by media distortions that neglect the "deserving poor" in general and portray poor blacks in a particularly unsympathetic light.

Would a better-informed citizenry be less cynical about the motives of welfare recipients or the character of African Americans? Although questions based on counterfactual assumptions are always difficult to answer, we do know that Americans with more accurate perceptions of the racial composition of the welfare population are substantially less cynical about the needs and motives of welfare recipients (table 6.1), and that such perceptions are strongly related to opposition toward welfare (tables 4.1 to 4.3). But only if substantial changes occur in the media's coverage of poverty will we be able to tell with any certainty whether the views held by today's less knowledgeable Americans will change.

8

Beyond the Attitude Survey: Public Opinion and Antipoverty Policy

My aim in this book has been to elucidate Americans' political attitudes, and more specifically, to identify the nature and sources of public opposition to welfare. Political attitudes are of interest for their own sake: understanding how Americans think and feel about political issues contributes to our broader understanding of the society we live in and the nature of our fellow citizens. But in a democracy, public attitudes also matter because citizens' preferences can influence government policy. As discussed in chapter 1, researchers have found substantial congruence between public attitudes as expressed on surveys and public policy. Within the United States, for example, states with more conservative populations adopt more conservative policies, and for the country as a whole, changes in public preferences are more often than not followed by congruent changes in government policy. Of course many factors other than public opinion also shape government decision making, and popular desires are only partially reflected in public policy. Nevertheless, across a range of issues, from military spending to anticrime policy to the welfare state, the activities of government appear to correspond in some substantial measure to the public's preferences.

Although my principal concern is the public's beliefs, attitudes, and policy preferences, I turn in this chapter to an examination of government policies as an alternative source of information about the nature of opposition to welfare in America. I look first at the variation in welfare policy among the different states, noting the relationship between states' racial characteristics and the generosity of their welfare programs. I then turn to welfare reform and ask whether the attitudes toward welfare discussed in earlier chapters are reflected in the substance of welfare reform and the public's reaction to it. Finally, I take a closer look at Americans' expressed desire to do more to help the poor. Using both survey data and other kinds of evidence, I assess whether Americans' generous responses to survey questions should be taken seriously, or viewed as simply the result of survey respondents' desire to present themselves as caring people.

Racial Context and State-Level Welfare Policy

The American welfare state includes programs that span the range from fully federal in nature (like Social Security) to fully state-run and financed (like General Assistance). Between these two poles are a variety of federal/state programs in which both regulations and funding are shared between the states and the federal government. In particular, individual states have considerable latitude in designing and administering many antipoverty programs, and we can take advantage of the resulting variability across states to assess whether the attitudinal dynamics revealed by surveys are reflected in the policy options that state governments adopt.

The survey analysis presented in previous chapters showed that negative racial attitudes, and in particular, cynicism toward the work ethic of poor blacks, is at the core of popular opposition to welfare. If this is the case, then we would expect the predominantly white electorate to be least enthusiastic about state welfare spending in states with high proportions of blacks among the poor, and most supportive in states with the smallest numbers of poor blacks. Further, if these varying levels of public support influence state government policy, then we should find the most generous welfare policies in states with the lowest proportions of blacks among the poor and the least generous policies in states with the highest proportions of poor blacks. Because we lack survey data on state-level policy preferences, we will have to examine this hypothesized dynamic by comparing states' racial demography with the welfare policies they adopt.

AFDC provides an excellent basis for judging whether a state's welfare policy is influenced by the racial composition of the poor people in that state. Although many of the regulations affecting this program originated with the federal government, states were allowed to set their own eligibility and benefit levels, and these levels differed widely across states. In 1996, for example, average AFDC benefits ranged from only $120 per month in Mississippi to $555 per month in California.[1] (Alaska and Hawaii, with their unusually high living costs, provided even higher average AFDC benefits of $721 and $649, respectively.)

Numerous studies have sought to explain the differences across

states in AFDC policies and benefit levels. Like studies of public attitudes toward welfare, most of these have ignored race. But those that
have included some measure of the racial mix of a state's poverty population have consistently found race to be a significant influence on state-
level AFDC policy, even when other state characteristics such as income and education levels are taken into consideration. Larry Orr, for
example, estimated that a state with an all-white AFDC caseload would
offer almost $2000 more per year in AFDC benefits than a state with
an all-black AFDC caseload.[2] Because Orr controlled statistically for
states' average income and for region of the country, he argued that the
low benefit levels found in states with more blacks on welfare did not
simply reflect either a lesser ability of those states to pay for benefits or
a bias against welfare in southern states with large numbers of poor
blacks.

Gerald Wright also examined differences in average AFDC benefits
across states.[3] As predictors, Wright used the proportion of blacks
among each state's population and a measure of the scope of each state's
civil rights laws. The first of these measures serves as a proxy for the
extent to which welfare benefits in each state would flow to African
Americans, and the second a proxy for the racial liberalism or conservatism of the state. Like Orr, Wright also took into account differences
in states' average income levels, as well as a host of other state characteristics such as average educational attainment and levels of urbanization and industrialization. Wright found strong associations between
his measures of racial environment and AFDC benefit levels: states with
the smallest proportions of blacks and those with the most progressive
civil rights laws offered the highest average AFDC benefits.

Evidence from attitude surveys showing the importance of racial
considerations in shaping opposition to welfare are corroborated by the
patterns of race and AFDC spending examined above. Our confidence
in these results would be strengthened, however, if we found that racial
demography not only affects state policy for those programs that surveys suggest should be affected, but also that racial demography is *unrelated* to programs that surveys suggest should *not* be affected.

Whereas welfare is viewed as providing benefits largely to the undeserving poor, attitudes toward unemployment insurance are more
mixed (table 1.2). More importantly, racial stereotypes, which strongly
influence attitudes toward welfare, are almost wholly unrelated to attitudes toward assistance for the unemployed. The left panel of figure 8.1 shows the strong association between welfare spending preferences and the belief that "if blacks would only try harder they could be
just as well off as whites." Among white Americans who agree strongly

Figure 8.1   Desire to Cut Welfare or Unemployment by Perceptions of Blacks' Work Ethic

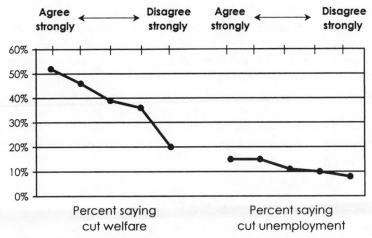

"If blacks would only try harder they could be just as well off as whites"

Source: National Election Study, 1992. N = 2,154 for welfare and 2,184 for unemployment.
Note: See appendix table A.12 for details.

with this sentiment, over 50 percent think welfare spending should be cut compared to only 20 percent among those who disagree strongly. In contrast, few white Americans think spending for unemployment should be cut, irrespective of their beliefs about blacks' commitment to the work ethic. As the right panel of figure 8.1 shows, only 15 percent of whites who agree strongly that blacks just need to try harder want to cut spending for unemployment, compared with about 8 percent of those who disagree strongly with this perception of blacks. Regression analyses confirm that beliefs about blacks' commitment to the work ethic is a far stronger predictor of preferences for spending on welfare than of preferences for spending on unemployment; the analogous regression coefficients are 19.1 for welfare spending and 5.6 for unemployment (see appendix table A.12 for details).

Based on attitude surveys, we would expect to find that a state's racial demography would have a strong relationship to its AFDC policies but a weaker relationship to its choices regarding unemployment insurance. Christopher Howard conducted parallel analyses of state AFDC and unemployment spending and found exactly this pattern.[4] Howard took into account state levels of income, education, and urbanization, and he also controlled statistically for the extent of the problem to which each policy is addressed (i.e., in his analysis of AFDC, he controlled for the state poverty rate, and in his analysis of unemployment benefits, for the state unemployment rate.) Howard found that states with higher proportions of blacks in their population had significantly lower AFDC benefit levels, but similar unemployment benefit levels, compared with states with fewer blacks.[5]

The racial patterning of AFDC benefits across the states not only corroborates the claim that "race matters" in discussing Americans' responses to poverty, but also shows that racial considerations go beyond influencing the public's policy preferences and actually shape government decision making as well. Furthermore, the *lack* of an association between racial demography and state unemployment benefit levels provides important confirmation that the constellation of attitudes that surveys reveal find their expression in the social policy choices made by state governments.

Welfare Reform

Differences in social welfare policies across states provide one "handle" on the relationship between public attitudes toward welfare and government policy. Examining how welfare has changed over time and how these changes relate to public opinion is another way to help illuminate the findings from attitude surveys.

When ADC was established in the 1930s, most married women with children did not work outside the home, and policy makers expressly intended to provide a means by which poor single mothers could also remain home with their children. But women's roles changed over the following decades, and more and more married women from all social classes entered the workforce. This trend accelerated after 1960, as even married women with young children began to work in the paid labor force. In 1960, 19 percent of married women with children under six years old were working. By 1970 the proportion had grown to 30 percent, and by 1990 almost 60 percent of married women with children under six years old were working.[6] As politicians and the public came to view paid work as an acceptable alternative for married women with children, dependence on welfare by single mothers began to be viewed as less desirable than self-support.

As middle-class women's participation in the paid labor force grew, expectations for welfare mothers changed. In addition, the desire to move single mothers off welfare and into jobs was fed by changes in the demographics of single parenthood. In 1960, only 4 percent of single mothers had never been married and almost 26 percent were widows.[7] Widows cannot be blamed for their situation, but women who bear children out of wedlock are viewed with much less sympathy (the "moral status" of the divorced or separated might occupy some ambiguous middle ground, depending on why the marriage dissolved). Over the years the proportion of single mothers who are widows has decreased while the proportion of single mothers who have never married has grown. Today 36 percent of single mothers have never married, and only 4 percent are widows.[8]

These two factors—Americans' changing attitudes toward women and work on the one hand, and the declining "moral stature" of single mothers in general, and AFDC recipients in particular—combined to convince many Americans that most able-bodied single mothers on welfare should be working, at least once their children reach school age. These social and cultural changes dramatically changed how welfare was understood. Rather than serving as a means to allow poor single mothers to *avoid* the need to work for pay, welfare became viewed as a temporary expedient to tide women over until they could again support themselves. During the 1960s, policy makers increasingly came to view AFDC as harboring too many women who should be working for a living. Thus began a decades-long effort to reduce the welfare rolls by moving welfare mothers into the paid labor force.

The first fledgling "welfare-to-work" reforms were passed under President Kennedy in 1962. These early efforts offered federal funding for local welfare departments to provide social services to AFDC recipients in the hope of moving them off the welfare rolls.[9] Kennedy's welfare reform efforts involved little money, however, and had a greater symbolic than practical significance. More substantial welfare reform took place under the Johnson administration. Although Johnson's 1964 War on Poverty reshaped the face of the American welfare state, the thrust of the War on Poverty was to provide alternatives to, rather than reforms of, welfare. The Job Corps, community action programs, legal aid, and Head Start were programmatically and administratively separate from AFDC, which was not reformed as part of the War on Poverty. In 1967, however, Johnson did sign welfare reform legislation. These amendments to the AFDC laws reflected the same set of concerns and the same kinds of responses that have characterized welfare reform efforts under virtually every president since Johnson. Like most later welfare reforms, the 1967 amendments reflected a mix of punitive and supportive policies designed to satisfy as broad a political spectrum as possible (and also like most later welfare reforms, neither liberals nor conservatives were particularly happy with the legislation).

Among the most important changes in welfare regulations resulting from the 1967 welfare amendments was the institution of the so-called thirty-and-a-third rule. Until this time, any income that welfare recipients reported was deducted from their welfare check, creating, in essence, a 100 percent tax on earnings and constituting a strong disincentive to work for those already on welfare. The thirty-and-a-third rule allowed welfare recipients to keep the first $30 per month of earnings, plus one-third of their remaining pay. As expected, this change resulted in an increase in the proportion of welfare recipients who worked, but it also led to an increase in the welfare caseload as women who were previously ineligible for AFDC due to income from low-wage jobs now became eligible.

In addition to adding the thirty-and-a-third rule, the 1967 welfare reforms established the Work Incentive Program (or WIN), which funded day care and job training for AFDC recipients. Through this mix of supportive services and financial inducements, policy makers hoped to entice welfare mothers to take paying jobs and eventually to become fully self-supporting. But in addition to these "carrots" designed to reduce the welfare rolls, the 1967 amendments also included the "stick" of mandatory work requirements. All AFDC recipients except those with children under six years old were expected to work or to enroll in job training or "work readiness" programs. However, a variety of exemptions allowed most AFDC recipients to escape this work requirement. For example, states could exempt recipients from work requirements if work was deemed "inimical to the welfare of the family," a vague condition that surely applied in some way to just about all single mothers on welfare.[10] Because training programs cost states additional money, at least in the short run, most states were happy to take full advantage of the opportunities to exempt their welfare recipients from these new requirements.

Taken as a whole, the changes to AFDC enacted in 1967 contained most of the elements that would reappear in various configurations in the repeated efforts at welfare reform over the next thirty years. Work requirements, monetary work incentives, job training or work readiness programs, and funding for day care, transportation, and other needs to facilitate work would all be part of the continuing effort to move poor single women off government assistance and into the workforce.

President Nixon took office in 1969 and soon announced his own plan to reform welfare. Nixon's Family Assistance Plan (or FAP) reflected the "guaranteed income" approach to welfare that had won favor with both conservative free-market economists and liberal policy makers. Under the Family Assistance Plan, AFDC and its cumbersome eligibility criteria would be eliminated. Instead, every family in the country would be guaranteed a minimum basic income set by the federal government. The FAP would also have expanded funding for day care for poor families and enlarged the federal commitment to public service jobs for welfare recipients. While liberals generally approved of these aspects of the FAP, Nixon's proposal also contained stricter work requirements than those under the existing AFDC regulations. Furthermore, the new benefit level for government support would have been below that prevailing in most states (but above the existing benefit levels in many southern states). The Family Assistance Plan was passed by the House of Representatives but became bogged down in the Senate Finance Committee, where it was attacked by conservatives who opposed the expansion of federal assistance to the poor and by liberals who objected to the work requirements and low benefit levels. With few friends but plenty of enemies, the Family Assistance Plan died, and Nixon turned his attention elsewhere.

President Carter offered the next attempt at welfare reform. Like Nixon, Carter proposed to provide a national minimum income to all American families. His proposal would have consolidated AFDC, food stamps, and SSI and would have established work incentives and public service jobs to help recipients become self-supporting. Like the FAP, President Carter's proposed reforms fell victim to the combined attacks of liberals and conservatives, and it died in the Senate in 1978.

Next to tackle welfare reform was Ronald Reagan. Reagan came into office with a determination to act quickly to implement his agenda of trimming the welfare state and enlarging the military. The Reagan administration's first welfare reforms were contained in the Omnibus Budget Reconciliation Act of 1981. OBRA, as it was called, eliminated the thirty-and-a-third rule, thereby reinstating the effective 100 percent tax on welfare recipients' earnings, and it cut the existing exemptions for work-related expenses (such as child care and transportation), making paid employment an even less attractive option for those on welfare.

These changes in AFDC regulations in the early Reagan years left welfare recipients substantially worse off than they had been, especially when we consider the simultaneous cutbacks in unemployment insurance, food stamps, Medicaid, vocational education, public service employment, and child nutrition passed by Congress at the president's behest. While many of these programs did recover after Reagan's initial assault, AFDC benefit levels and eligibility criteria remained at historically low levels, despite the severe recession of the early 1980s.

As assessed by overall measures of economic performance, the recession of 1982 was followed by an economic boom that lasted for much of the 1980s. Yet the benefits of that economic recovery did not seem to "trickle down" to the poor. Rather than raising all boats, the economic tide of the 1980s brought enormous benefits to the well-off but only modest benefits to poor and middle-income Americans. Income inequality increased faster during the 1980s than at any other point in postwar history,[11] and by the late 1980s a bipartisan consensus had emerged that changes in welfare were needed to cope with the persistently high rate of poverty. After much debate, Congress and the Reagan administration agreed on a set of reforms that contained many of the same elements of previous welfare reform proposals.

Like earlier welfare reform efforts, Reagan's Family Support Act of 1988 tried to move people off welfare through a combination of work requirements and new benefits to facilitate the transition to paid employment. The law required that states enroll 15 percent of AFDC recipients in job training or "basic skills" programs and it provided increased funds for medical care and child care for women leaving welfare or participating in job training. Unlike many earlier efforts at welfare reform, the Family Support Act was passed by Congress and signed into law. Nevertheless, the initial goals were modest, and the money appropriated was far too little to meet even these modest goals. Further, the Family Support Act was passed just as the economic expansion of the 1980s was coming to an end. The downturn in the economy reduced states' tax revenues and, under these more financially constrained circumstances, few states were willing to allocate the funds necessary to make the newly established job training programs work. In consequence, the Family Support Act showed little success in helping welfare recipients become self-supporting.

This history of half-hearted and failed efforts at welfare reform attests to both the political and financial difficulties of remaking welfare and also the continuing popular desire to decrease the welfare rolls and facilitate the transition to self-support. President Clinton made welfare reform one of his campaign issues in 1992, and he came into office promising to "end welfare as we know it." Once in office, Clinton chose to address other concerns, but after vetoing two Republican welfare reform bills, and facing his own reelection campaign in 1996, Clinton signed a far-reaching set of changes to the country's welfare laws in the form of the "Personal Responsibility and Work Opportunity Reconciliation Act." The themes and goals of this welfare reform act were familiar: moving people off welfare and into work by a combination of work requirements, job training, and additional funding for child care and other social services. In addition to instituting these familiar reforms, the 1996 legislation altered welfare in three significant ways.

First, Clinton's 1996 welfare reform act abolished AFDC as an entitlement program and replaced it with Temporary Assistance for Needy Families (TANF). Under AFDC, the states had set eligibility and benefit levels and the federal government contributed between 50 percent and 80 percent of the cost, depending on economic conditions within each state. Under this formulation, states spent more money on welfare than they might have otherwise since they were required to pay only half or less of the tab. Furthermore, once eligibility criteria were set, any state resident meeting those criteria would be entitled to receive AFDC benefits. Under TANF, states are given a "block grant" or fixed sum of money to spend on cash assistance and social services for the poor (with financial incentives to place a substantial percentage of welfare recipients into job training or public service jobs, or to move them off welfare entirely). The new formula for welfare spending has only minimal provisions to increase federal spending if the number of needy families grows, and states that want to raise their own spending levels no longer benefit from federal matching funds.

In addition to putting in place new spending formulations, the 1996 welfare legislation placed time limits on welfare receipt. Under the 1996 law, states cannot use federal funds from TANF block grants to provide aid to any adult who has received welfare for more than five years (although other federal, state, or local funds can be used for this purpose). Under the new legislation, states can exempt up to 20 percent of their welfare caseloads from this time limit, but they can also shorten the time limit should they so desire.

The third major change in the 1996 welfare reform act lies in the much wider discretion allowed to states to formulate their own welfare policies. Within the guidelines provided, states can decide what kind of education, job training, or public service work to require of TANF recipients. States can also choose to deny welfare to unwed parents under age 18, withhold welfare benefits for additional children born to women already receiving welfare, and limit the welfare benefits given to those who have moved from other states to the amount they would have received from their former state. (This flexibility broadened and institutionalized the system of "waivers" that had been authorized under the 1988 Family Support Act and had been expanded under presidents Bush and Clinton.)

The impact of the 1996 welfare law will be difficult to gauge for a number of reasons. First, the reforms have already been "reformed." For example, many of the benefits for legal immigrants eliminated by the 1996 act have been reinstated, and pressure to further amend the 1996 regulations will arise as states struggle to meet the various caseload-reduction and welfare-to-work targets necessary to avoid financial sanctions.[12] In addition, states are still reformulating their welfare policies in response to the 1996 legislation and are likely to continue to do so for some years to come. Finally, the impact of Clinton's welfare reform is difficult to judge because the period since its passage has been blessed with a booming economy and historically low unemployment. As a result, scholars have been unsure how much to attribute the recent decline in welfare caseloads and increase in labor force participation to the legislative changes enacted in 1996.[13]

Public Opinion and Welfare Reform

Americans' views on welfare reform reflect the constellation of attitudes toward poverty and welfare we examined in earlier chapters. We saw that the American public expresses strong support for the welfare state broadly conceived and claims a desire to do more to help the poor; at the same time, however, the public says that spending on welfare itself should be cut. These simultaneous desires, I argued, grow out of a genuine concern for the needy coupled with a cynicism toward the true needs and motives of welfare recipients and a conviction that many of those receiving welfare should be supporting themselves instead.

Consistent with their view that most welfare recipients lack a commitment to the work ethic, Americans strongly support both work requirements and time limits for welfare recipients. But most Americans do not adopt a punitive attitude toward welfare reform. Along with work requirements and time limits, most also support an array of education and job training benefits, as well as social services such as transportation and child care, to make self-support a more viable option for those currently on welfare. And when pressed about the conditions under which work requirements and time limits should be imposed, most Americans are willing to carve out a variety of exemptions. Americans may be cynical toward those on welfare, but their survey responses suggest that they are surprisingly tender-hearted in their preferences with regard to welfare reform.

Work Requirements

Americans' views on welfare reform coincide quite well with the kinds of changes that have been proposed and (less often) implemented over the years. Chief among these is work requirements, which have been a part of every welfare reform effort since the Johnson administration.

Surveys show that Americans strongly support the idea of work requirements for those on welfare (table 8.1).[14] In one survey, for example, 92 percent of respondents said "the government should create work programs for people on welfare and require people to participate," and in another, 97 percent said we should "require welfare recipients to work in exchange for their benefits."

Although the public overwhelmingly supports work requirements in the abstract, many Americans are willing to make exceptions in particular circumstances. For example, the nearly unanimous support for work requirements declines to 71 percent in the case of "single parents with drug or alcohol problems," and to 63 percent in the case of "any family the government cannot find a job and provide child care for." A similar number of Americans (60 percent) continue to favor work requirements for welfare recipients "that cannot find a job where jobs are hard to find," while only 37 percent would apply work requirements to people with "a significant physical or mental disability" (table 8.1).

A common concern in establishing work requirements for welfare recipients involves families with young children. When asked in the abstract, almost three out of four respondents agree that welfare mothers with young children should be required to work (table 8.1).[15] But as one might expect, the conviction that welfare mothers should be working rather than caring for their children is strongest with regard to older children, and it weakens as the age of the children in question declines. In one survey, for example, fully 68 percent of the respondents said they would exempt a welfare mother from work requirements if she had a child under three months old. Fifty-seven percent would extend this exemption to mothers with children under one year old, 40 percent to those with kids under three, and only 22 percent to all mothers with children under five years old. The "tipping point" in this survey seems to be somewhere between ages one and three. For children less than one year old, most respondents favored exemptions from work requirements, but the majority of respondents felt that welfare mothers with children over three years old should be working. (Roughly the same tipping point is found in another survey, also shown in table 8.1.)

Finally, when push comes to shove, those favoring work requirements must face the situation where a welfare recipient either refuses to work or simply cannot find or keep a job. When confronted with this situation, most Americans believe that at least a minimal level of government aid should nevertheless be continued, at least if the well-being of children is involved. When one recent survey asked, "What if a welfare recipient has a young child at home to support and either won't

Table 8.1 Public Support for Work Requirements for Welfare Recipients

	Percentage Supporting Work Requirements
General support for work requirements	
Do you think the government should create work programs for people on welfare and require people to participate in the programs, or not?[a]	92
Do you favor or oppose this proposal: Require welfare recipients to work in exchange for their benefits.[b]	97
Exceptions to work requirements	
Work requirements should apply to . . .	
Single parents with drug or alcohol problems.	71
Any family the government cannot find a job and provide child care for.	63
Any family that cannot find a job where jobs are hard to find.	60
Any family where the parent has a significant physical or mental disability.[c]	37
Work requirements for families with young children	
Do you think that women with young children who receive welfare should be required to work or should they stay at home and take care of their young children?[d]	74
Work requirements should apply to . . .	
Single parents with children under one year of age.	43
Single parents with children under three years of age.[c]	61

	Percentage Agree
A single mother who is on welfare should be excused from having to go to work if she has a child at home who is . . .	
Younger than 5 years old.	22
Younger than 3 years old.	40
Younger than 1 year old.	57
Younger than 3 months old.	68
A single mother on welfare should have to go to work regardless of whether she has a young child at home.[e]	32

Note: Results are based on national telephone surveys and exclude respondents saying "don't know" or providing no answer.

[a] CBS/*New York Times* poll, April 1, 1995.

[b] NBC/*Wall Street Journal* poll, April 21, 1995.

[c] *U.S. News and World Report* poll, November 30, 1993.

[d] CBS/*New York Times* poll, December 11, 1995.

[e] Associated Press poll, January 24, 1997.

work or simply can't hold a job?" 61 percent of respondents said the government should provide enough aid to keep the family fed and sheltered, while 39 percent felt their benefits should be cut off entirely.[16] Given Americans' cynicism toward welfare recipients, the high levels of support for work requirements is not surprising. What is less expected, however, is that most Americans are willing to make exceptions to such requirements in the case of mothers of young children, and a substantial minority consider problems with drugs or alcohol or difficulty in finding a job to be legitimate reasons to exempt recipients from work requirements. As is true with most areas of public opinion, Americans' attitudes toward welfare reform appear more nuanced as we look closer and ask more penetrating questions. Despite their negative beliefs about welfare recipients as a group, Americans consider the specific circumstances of different welfare recipients, rather than applying broad generalizations to all people on welfare.

Social Services

If the threat of withholding welfare payments constitutes the "stick" intended to prod welfare recipients into self-support, the "carrot" consists of the education and social services that make work feasible. Past welfare reform initiatives have all paid at least rhetorical respect to the need to help welfare mothers into the labor force, and like work requirements, this effort too is consistent with the public's thinking about poverty and welfare.

Table 8.2 shows the strong public support for education, job training, and child care to help welfare recipients become self-supporting. For example, 96 percent of Americans favor "providing job training to welfare recipients," and the same proportion say that "the government should provide more job training, education, and childcare for poor people." This support not only demonstrates the public's desire to assist welfare recipients rather than simply push them off welfare, but it also reflects Americans' abiding faith in individuals' abilities to improve their situation if given the necessary tools. Surveys show that Americans believe education, ambition, and hard work are the essential elements necessary to "getting ahead in life," and that they are far more important than natural ability, knowing the right people, having well-educated parents, or coming from a wealthy family.[17]

In addition to supporting education and job training, most Americans also favor government help to welfare recipients in the form of child care and transportation to work (with support for child care being

Table 8.2 Public Support for Education and Social Services for Welfare Recipients

	Percentage Supporting Program
Education and job training	
Do you favor or oppose providing job training to welfare recipients?[a]	96
Do you think the government should provide more job training, education, and child care for poor people?[b]	96
If people lose their welfare benefits and cannot find work, would you favor a job training program to help them?[c]	96
Child care and transportation	
Do you favor or oppose providing child care for poor mothers who leave welfare for work?[a]	94
The government should provide child care to low-income mothers who are on welfare who take jobs or are in job training.[d]	87
Do you favor or oppose having government help pay for child care and transportation for welfare recipients who work or are in job training or education courses?[e]	81
To help welfare recipients get off welfare and become self-supporting, the government should pay the costs of commuting to a job or job training classes.[f]	67

Note: Results are based on national telephone surveys and exclude respondents saying "don't know" or providing no answer.

[a] NBC/*Wall Street Journal* poll, April 1995.
[b] The Joint Center for Political and Economic Studies poll, July 1992.
[c] CBS/*New York Times* poll, August 1996.
[d] Henry J. Kaiser Foundation/Harvard School of Public Health poll, December 1994.
[e] *U.S. News and World Report* poll, November 1993.
[f] CNN/*USA Today* poll, April 1994.

somewhat more popular). As with education and job training, Americans almost unanimously approve of government-provided child care for welfare mothers who take jobs or enroll in job training. The two relevant survey questions in table 8.2 find 87 percent and 94 percent of respondents supporting government-provided child care for women moving off welfare into the workforce. When asked about child care *and* transportation, a slightly lower 81 percent express support, while the one question in table 8.2 that asks about transportation alone (rather than in combination with child care) found somewhat lower support. Nevertheless, even in this case fully two-thirds of respondents said the government should pay the costs of commuting to a job or to job training classes "to help welfare recipients get off welfare and become self-supporting."

Time Limits

Time limits represent the most straightforward way to reduce the welfare rolls and decrease the number of people relying on the government for their support. Unlike efforts to entice people off welfare by providing job training or child care or by allowing those who leave welfare to retain benefits such as health care and food stamps, welfare time limits simply dictate that certain individuals will lose their cash benefits on a specified date. Time limits represent the most radical and potentially the most important element in the 1996 welfare reform legislation, and surveys show that Americans generally support time limits for welfare recipients. Once again, however, when we probe beyond the basic questions of support or opposition to time limits, we see that Americans' attitudes are more complex, and their support more qualified, than might initially appear to be the case.

As the top section of table 8.3 shows, between half and three-quarters of Americans endorse a five-year limit on welfare receipt. A stricter two-year limit also receives strong support (from 57 percent to 69 percent of respondents), but support plummets if the two-year time limit is followed by a lifetime exclusion from welfare. Although generally supportive of welfare time limits, Americans also believe that the specific circumstances of individual welfare recipients need to be taken into account. For example, when asked whether they favor "a hard-and-fast cutoff for all able-bodied recipients after two years," or a "limit . . . applied on a case-by-case basis," 79 percent of respondents opted for the case-by-case approach (table 8.3). And when asked about a variety of specific circumstances, anywhere between half and three-quarters of the public felt that exceptions should be made for mothers who work part-time or have preschool children, people who are on welfare for the first time after working for many years, or those who live in areas of high unemployment (table 8.3).

The attitudes toward time limits found in table 8.3 show that most Americans favor continued government help for those welfare recipients who have demonstrated their commitment to the work ethic by enrolling

Table 8.3 Public Support for Welfare Time Limits

	Percentage Agree
Strict welfare time limits	
Limit welfare benefits to five years and do not allow people to get back on welfare for at least five years.[a]	50
Limit all adults to a total of five years on welfare.[b]	60
Limit to five years the amount of time a welfare recipient can receive cash payments.[c]	74
Cut off all benefits to people who had not found a job or become self-sufficient after two years.[d]	69
Limit welfare benefits to two years and do not allow people to get back on welfare for at least five years.[a]	57
Limit welfare benefits to two years and do not allow people to get back on welfare ever.[a]	23
Qualified welfare time limits	
If there were a two-year limit on welfare benefits, would you favor a hard-and-fast cutoff for all able-bodied recipients after two years, or do you think the limit should be applied on a case-by-case basis?[e] (percent saying case-by-case)	79
For each of the following cases, please tell me if the cutoff should apply to this person after two years on welfare, or if an exception should be made in this case . . . (percent saying exception)	
A mother on welfare who works part-time at a low-wage job.	77
A mother with preschool children.	72
Someone who has worked for many years and is on welfare for the first time.	59
Someone who lives in an area where the unemployment rate is more than 10%.	56
Someone who is in a job-training program but still reads at the seventh-grade level.[e]	53
Limit welfare recipients to a maximum of two years of benefits, after which those who are able to work would have to get a job or do community service.[f]	89
If benefits are cut off after two years, government should provide separate benefits to the children, even though their parents' benefits will have been cut off.[b]	78
Action to take when time limits are reached	
After a year or two, welfare recipients should stop receiving all benefits.	25
or	
Welfare recipients should continue to get benefits as long as they work for them.[g]	75

Table 8.3 (*Continued*)

	Percentage Agree
Action to take when time limits are reached (continued)	
After two years benefits would be ended for all able-bodied recipients, and the government would not provide any job. *or*	13
After two years, welfare recipients who have not found other employment would be required to work at a public service job.[e]	87
If government is going to cut off AFDC or welfare benefits after a specific period of time . . . should it . . .	
Simply end the family's benefits, including AFDC.	11
Make the parents do community service in exchange for welfare benefits.	62
Guarantee jobs to the parents after they are cut off welfare.[h]	27

Note: Results are based on national telephone surveys and exclude respondents saying "don't know" or providing no answer.

[a] *U.S. News and World Report* poll, November 1993.

[b] *CNN/USA Today* poll, December 1994.

[c] *Time*/CNN poll, March 1995.

[d] *CNN/USA Today* poll, May 1994.

[e] Peter D. Hart Associates poll, November 1993.

[f] *ABC/Washington Post* poll, March 1995.

[g] *CBS/New York Times* poll, December 1994.

[h] Henry J. Kaiser Foundation/Harvard School of Public Health poll, December 1994.

in job training, by working part-time at low wages, or simply by having a history of self-support. But this desire to help *deserving* welfare recipients does not preclude general support for time limits and work requirements, since Americans think that many—or even most—welfare recipients do not fall into the "deserving" category. Even in the case of undeserving welfare recipients, however, most Americans seem to feel that poor children cannot simply be abandoned. For example, 78 percent agreed that the government should provide separate benefits to the children if their parents' benefits have been cut off due to time limits.

The heated rhetoric surrounding debates over welfare reform reflects the emotional nature of the issue for many Americans. Arguments over welfare touch on some of our most cherished values and greatest concerns: individual responsibility, social compassion, the suffering of the poor, and the well-being of millions of children. Public opinion is often derided as being shallow or ill-informed. But when we look more closely we often find that apparent contradictions or inconsistencies reflect the public's sensitivity to the complexities of political issues. The attitudes expressed on surveys show that Americans are keenly aware of the complex nature of welfare and welfare reform. Although cynical toward welfare recipients and supportive of strong measures to limit welfare receipt by those who could be supporting themselves, the American public also displays a strong desire to help welfare recipients become self-supporting and a sensitivity to the differing situations that affect individual welfare recipients' abilities to do so.

Welfare Reform and Economic Self-Interest

For many politicians, the prime motive for welfare reform appears to be economic. But the public's enthusiasm for welfare reform stems from both a resentment toward welfare recipients who refuse to work and a desire to reward and facilitate self-support and self-responsibility. Consistent with the small role of economic self-interest in explaining opposition to welfare spending (chapter 2), the desire to save taxpayer dollars consistently emerges as a low priority in the public's thinking about welfare reform. For example, when a 1995 survey asked which of three goals for reforming welfare was most important, 66 percent of respondents chose "getting people into the workforce" and 20 percent chose "reducing out-of-wedlock births"; only 14 percent chose "reducing government spending" as the most important goal of welfare reform. Two other surveys asking respondents to choose among a variety of goals for welfare reform found that cutting costs or saving taxpayers money had even less priority, appealing to only 7 percent of Americans (table 8.4).

Far from viewing welfare reform as an opportunity to save money for themselves, most Americans say they would actually be willing to pay *more* in taxes to help the needy in general, and welfare recipients in particular. Table 8.5 reports results from survey questions that ask Americans whether they would be willing to pay higher taxes to support a variety of domestic policy goals. Although it is a pretty safe bet that few Americans like paying taxes or want to pay more, the results in table 8.5 suggest that most members of the public would be willing to do so if those taxes were to go toward social programs they value. For example, approximately two out of three Americans express a willingness to pay more in taxes to combat poverty and homelessness, and a similar percentage of the public would support more spending on a child care tax deduction for the poor even if it meant raising taxes. An increase in taxes for job training and education programs is slightly less

Table 8.4 Importance of Cutting Costs versus Other Goals for Welfare Reform

	Percentage Agree
Which of the following is the most important goal for reforming the welfare system?	
Getting people into the workforce	66
Reducing out-of-wedlock births	20
Reducing government spending[a]	14
What should the most important goal of welfare reform be? (up to two responses permitted)	
Help move people now on welfare into the workforce	52
End long-term dependence on welfare as a way of life	29
Eliminate fraud and abuse	28
Make sure poor children get the support they need	22
Save taxpayers money[b]	7
Which of the following goals of welfare reform is most important to you?	
Make people self-sufficient	93
Cut costs[c]	7

Note: Results are based on national telephone surveys and exclude respondents saying "don't know" or providing no answer.

[a] NBC/*Wall Street Journal* poll, August 1995.

[b] Hart/Teeter poll, November 1993.

[c] *Time*/CNN poll, May 1992.

popular, but even so, anywhere from 56 percent to 64 percent of Americans say they would be willing to pay more in taxes in order to expand these programs. Americans also express a willingness to pay higher taxes to provide health care for the poor. In one survey, 69 percent of Americans said they would pay more in taxes "to ensure that all poor people have access to medical care," and 88 percent would pay more for "feeding and providing medical care for very poor children."

These survey results are consistent with the broad support for the welfare state we saw in chapter 1. In this case, however, a higher standard is applied in gauging Americans' support for government social assistance. At least with regard to the aspects of the welfare state for which we have survey data, it seems that most Americans not only believe the government should be doing more and spending more, but they also indicate that they would be willing to pay higher taxes to achieve these ends. Fighting poverty and homelessness, and providing job training, education, public service jobs, and medical care for welfare recipients or poor people, are important enough to the American public

Table 8.5 The Public's Willingness to Pay Higher Taxes to Help the Needy

	Percentage Willing to Pay Higher Taxes
Poverty and homelessness	
Would you be willing to pay higher taxes for each of the following?	
Provide adequate health care for Americans	71
Improve the quality of the environment	71
Fight drugs	68
Improve the quality of public education	68
Reduce poverty	67
Reduce the amount of homelessness[a]	67
Would you be willing or not willing to pay more in taxes in order to have the government increase spending on homelessness?[b]	63
Would you, yourself, be willing to pay higher taxes to help reduce poverty and homelessness, or not?[c]	63
Would you favor more government spending on . . . even if it means raising taxes?	
Helping the homeless	72
A child care tax deduction for the poor[d]	67
Education and job training	
Would you support or oppose an increase in your own federal taxes to pay for job training and education programs that try to help people get off welfare?[e]	56
Would you be willing or unwilling to pay higher taxes to provide job training and public service jobs to help people get off welfare?[f]	59
Would you be willing or unwilling to pay more in taxes in order to provide job training and public service jobs for people on welfare so that they can get off welfare?[g]	64
Would you be willing or would you not be willing to pay higher taxes in order to provide job training for the unemployed?[h]	62
Medical care	
Would you be willing to pay higher taxes if the money was used for . . .	
Feeding and providing medical for very poor children	88
Fighting the war on drugs	81
Increasing benefits for retired people	78
Improving public schools in communities like yours[i]	74
If it meant an increase in your taxes, would you support or oppose an increase in government spending to ensure that all poor people have access to medical care?[j]	69

Table 8.5 (*Continued*)

	Percentage Willing to Pay Higher Taxes
Welfare	
How willing would you be to pay higher taxes if all of the added taxes were spent on . . . (percent saying very or somewhat willing)	
Fighting crime	80
The environment	71
Social Security	68
*Welfare*k	28

Note: Results are based on national telephone surveys and exclude respondents saying "don't know" or providing no answer.

aMarist Institute poll, February 1991.

bCBS News poll, January 1992.

cGallup poll, August 1992.

dHarris poll, February 1989.

eNBC News poll, January 1995.

fTimes Mirror poll, March 1994.

gCBS/*New York Times* poll, April 1995.

hNBC/*Wall Street Journal* poll, June 1994.

i*Time*/CNN poll, October 1989.

jGallup poll, January 1991.

kHarris poll, November 1994.

that they express a willingness to support higher taxes. (As table 8.5 shows, support is also high for tax increases to be spent on education, on improving the environment, and on fighting drugs.)

Of course, Americans do not favor an increase in taxes for every government activity. For example, in a 1994 survey only 41 percent of Americans supported higher taxes to help reduce the federal budget deficit,[18] and only one out of three said they would pay more to "improve our transportation and communication systems" or "provide aid to city and state governments."[19] Finally, reflecting the same desire to cut welfare expenditures that we examined in earlier chapters, only 28 percent said they would be willing to pay higher taxes if the money were to be spent on welfare (table 8.5).

Willingness to Help the Poor and the Limitations of Survey Data

Contrary to the widespread view that Americans' political preferences are shaped largely by calculations of personal economic gain or loss, we have repeatedly found that the American public supports greater efforts to help the needy, despite the economic costs these efforts entail. Americans say they want government to spend more money to help the poor, they indicate that saving tax dollars is a low priority for welfare reform, and they express a willingness to pay higher taxes themselves in order to reduce poverty and help people get off welfare. It is easy to believe that Americans want to see less poverty and that they would like government to make a larger and more effective effort to help the needy. But the skeptic may insist that, when push comes to shove, few people are really willing to make personal financial sacrifices to help those worse off. From this perspective, expressing support for higher taxes to help the poor may primarily reflect survey respondents' desire to appear caring and civic-minded to survey interviewers.

Experience teaches that we sometimes need to take people's responses to survey questions with a grain of salt. We know, for example, that "social desirability" pressures sometimes lead survey respondents to answer less than truthfully when sensitive issues are raised. Perhaps willingness to help the poor is one of these issues. In order not to appear callous, survey respondents may say they support higher taxes to help the poor when in fact they know full well that they would really prefer to keep their hard-earned money for themselves.

One way in which the honesty of survey respondents has been gauged is by comparing answers to traditional in-person or telephone surveys with responses to anonymous mail or "secret ballot" surveys that give the researcher no means of identifying any individual's answers, either at the time of the interview or later. One effort to assess the impact of social desirability effects compared responses to questions about nine different political issues obtained from in-person, telephone, and mail surveys in a Boston suburb. Seven of the issues showed no differences across type of survey, but this was not true for the two most socially sensitive questions. In this study (conducted in the early 1970s), 89 percent of mail survey respondents indicated that they favored legalizing abortion, compared with only 70 percent of those interviewed in person and 62 percent of those interviewed by telephone.[20] Similarly, 83 percent of those returning mail questionnaires said they favored "making birth control devices readily available to unmarried people," but in-person and telephone interviews found only 72 percent and 67 percent in favor, respectively.

Within the social context of the time, many respondents to the Boston study clearly felt uncomfortable indicating support for abortion or birth control to a stranger. But when they were able to express their views in an anonymous mail survey, reported levels of support increased. Using similar techniques, other studies have found that people tend to report fewer health problems, less alcohol consumption, and less permissive attitudes toward sex in face-to-face interviews than in anonymous self-administered questionnaires.[21]

Another area in which the honesty of survey responses has been studied is racial attitudes. As social norms against racial bigotry have grown over the past decades, some observers have come to believe that at least some of the apparent decline in antiblack prejudice is nothing more than a decrease in the willingness of whites to acknowledge their antiblack attitudes on surveys.[22] A variety of studies have tried to assess the extent to which survey measures of whites' racial attitudes are subject to social desirability effects. For example, Maria Krysan has conducted two studies in the tricounty area surrounding Detroit, Michigan. Krysan asked white respondents identical questions about their racial attitudes using either a face-to-face survey at the respondent's home or a mail survey with no interviewer involved.[23] For questions involving racial policy preferences or willingness to vote for a black candidate for president (but not for measures of "traditional prejudice" such as the belief that blacks have less inborn ability), Krysan often found more negative attitudes expressed on the mail survey than in the face-to-face interviews.

Using a very different technique, James Kuklinski and his colleagues have found similar results with regard to whites' attitudes toward race-based affirmative action.[24] They compared responses to two different question formats included in telephone interviews. Using the traditional approach, a random subset of white respondents was asked whether different aspects of affirmative action made them angry or upset. The remainder of the white respondents were asked the identical question, but in an "unobtrusive" manner such that the survey interviewer could not tell whether any individual respondent was angered or upset by these policies.[25] Consistent with Krysan's findings, Kuklinski found that whites expressed more anger over affirmative action when their responses were "private" than they did when they had to reveal their responses to the interviewer.[26]

Few studies of social desirability pressures in survey interviews have examined attitudes toward the needy. One exception, however, is found in one of Krysan's studies of racial attitudes described above, which also included two questions relating to assistance to the poor.[27] In face-to-face interviews, 65 percent of Krysan's respondents said they favored "giving businesses and industry special tax breaks for locating in poor and high unemployment areas," compared with 58 percent who supported the same proposal in the mail survey. On another question, 74 percent of face-to-face interviewees but only 60 percent of mail survey respondents said they favored "spending more money on the schools in poor neighborhoods especially for pre-school and early education programs." These differences, of 7 and 14 percentage points, do suggest that social desirability pressures lead some survey respondents to express a willingness to help the poor that conflicts with their true preferences.[28] But the differences between the face-to-face and mail surveys are modest, and in both of these questions most respondents continue to support increased assistance for the poor even in the more private mail survey. Furthermore, of the respondents who did not indicate support for these proposals, most said they "neither favor nor oppose" them. Only 14 percent of the mail survey respondents (and 16 percent of the face-to-face interviewees) opposed tax breaks for companies locating in poor neighborhoods, and only 16 percent of the mail respondents (and 13 percent of those interviewed face-to-face) opposed spending more for schools in poor neighborhoods.

Based on the two questions included in Krysan's study, we might conclude that typical telephone or face-to-face surveys do induce some respondents to overstate their level of support for efforts to help the poor, but that the impact of such social desirability pressures is modest. This conclusion is supported by another study that also compared support for the needy as assessed by two different data collection methods. During a 1992 election in Hamilton County, Ohio, voters were queried about a ballot proposal for a new county tax to provide home care services for elderly residents.[29] Voters emerging from polling places were either asked in person how they had voted on this socially desirable ballot proposal or given a clipboard with a questionnaire conspicuously marked "SECRET BALLOT (Please Do *Not* Sign Your Name)." Those respondents who were randomly selected to receive the "secret ballot" were instructed to fill out the questionnaire, fold it, and place it into a nearby box marked "SECRET BALLOT SURVEY." As expected, fewer voters were willing to acknowledge having voted against the tax for the elderly when their vote would be revealed to the interviewer, but the difference was small: 32 percent of those asked about their vote face-to-face said they had voted against the tax, compared with 38 percent of those completing secret ballots.[30]

Although this study did not ask about antipoverty efforts per se, it is nevertheless helpful in assessing social desirability effects in survey questions about the poor. The ballot proposal in question concerns assistance to a very sympathetic group (the elderly), and the kinds of assistance that would be provided by the proposed tax increase (e.g., home delivered meals, medical transportation, legal counseling) are services that Americans strongly support for the elderly.[31] Consequently, survey respondents are more likely to feel social pressure to say they favor this tax increase than they would feel if the money were to be put to more controversial uses. In addition, this study corresponds to the most "suspicious" results from the survey questions about poverty that we have examined: the claim to favor not just greater efforts or more government spending, but actual tax increases in order to help the poor.

This study of Hamilton County voters, however, differs in an important way from the typical telephone survey that asks about willingness to pay more taxes to help the poor. The respondents in this study were interviewed as they emerged from their polling place where most of them had just voted either in favor or in opposition to the tax proposal. For those who voted against the proposal, the social pressure to lie and claim to support it was counterbalanced by the undeniable fact of having just voted against the proposal. In a typical survey about a hypothetical tax increase, even respondents who in fact oppose such an increase can lie about their preferences without having to acknowledge to themselves quite so glaring a discrepancy between their survey response and their true beliefs (or behavior, as in this case).

In sum, the fairly meager data we have suggest that survey respondents do exaggerate their support for aid to the poor due to social desirability pressures. Nevertheless, it appears that the difference between the responses gathered in typical telephone or face-to-face surveys and those that would be obtained through a more private method of data collection is modest. The three comparisons discussed above found differences of 6, 7, and 14 percentage points between face-to-face and mail or secret ballot surveys. These differences are substantial enough to make weak opposition to a particular policy look like weak support. But where surveys indicate that public support for a given proposal to assist the poor is strong, it appears that measures of respondents' attitudes that lessen the problems of social desirability would continue to reflect support for those policies, albeit at somewhat lower levels.

Alternative Indicators of Americans' True Willingness to Help the Poor

Another way to assess Americans' true attitudes is to examine their behavior. Although individuals have only limited ability to influence the behavior of their government, they can take action on their own. Ample opportunities exist for Americans to help the needy through charities. Do they take advantage of these opportunities?

Standing beside America's reputation as a nation of rugged individualists is the perception of Americans as an unusually civic-minded people, eager to join in worthy causes and generous in sharing their resources with the less well-off. Alexis de Tocqueville, the most famous observer of American individualism, was equally impressed by Americans' propensity to join in collective endeavors, often with the aim of assisting those in need. Writing in the 1830s, Tocqueville marveled at the scope of voluntary associations in America: "There are not only commercial and industrial associations in which all take part, but others of a thousand different types—religious, moral, serious, futile, very general and very limited, immensely large and very minute. Americans combine to give fetes, found seminaries, build churches, distribute books, and send missionaries to the antipodes. Hospitals, prisons and schools take shape that way."[32]

More recent observers of American society have also been impressed by the wide array of voluntary efforts to help the needy. Robin Williams, for example, contrasted the historical generosity of Americans with the less generous nature of other societies: "The enormous range of relatively disinterested humanitarian activities in America—the commonplace Community Chest, the 'service club' activities, the public welfare agencies, the numerous private philanthropies, and so on—stands in striking contrast to the treatment meted out to 'the poor' and 'sturdy beggars' in many other parts of Western society within the past two centuries."[33]

Americans' embrace of voluntarism is reflected in comparative studies of organizational membership and voluntary work. One study, for example, surveyed residents of fifteen countries, asking respondents whether they belong to any voluntary associations, and if so, whether they currently do any voluntary unpaid work for those associations.[34] The highest level of association membership was found in the United States, where 73 percent of respondents said they belonged to at least one voluntary association. (The lowest level, at 30 percent, was found in Japan.) The United States also ranked high in the percentage of the population claiming to do unpaid work for a voluntary association (32 percent) but was edged out slightly by Canada, where 33 percent reported doing such work. (Once again Japan showed the lowest level of voluntary activity, with only 13 percent reporting doing unpaid work for a voluntary association.) The U.S. rankings did not change when the authors took into account differences among the countries in their populations' age, educational level, employment status, marital status, sex, and community size (although Japan did move up slightly when these other factors were taken into account).

Although America is certainly not alone in this regard, the tradition of charity and the sense of obligation toward the poor is firmly embedded in our culture. And just as the voluntarism that impressed Tocqueville has a long pedigree in American society, so too does the humanitarian prescription to help the needy. In his famous sermon of 1630, "A Model of Christian Charity," John Winthrop preached the importance of brotherly love and mutual support: "In this duty of love we must love brotherly without dissimulation, we must love one another with a pure heart fervently, we must bear one another's burdens, we must not look only on our own things but also on the things of our brethren."[35]

Americans' humanitarianism is still expressed in their high levels of participation in philanthropic causes. Large numbers of Americans actively participate in some kind of charitable organization, and even larger numbers donate money. In a recent survey, 41 percent of Americans reported being personally involved in a charity or social service activity such as helping the poor, the sick, or the elderly.[36] In the same survey, 60 percent of Americans reported that they had given money to church related charities in the past year, 70 percent reported having given to non–church related charities, and 74 percent said they had contributed food, clothing, or other property to a charitable organization within the past year.

We might expect to receive exaggerated reports of charitable activities in public opinion surveys. But self-reported contributions on Gallup surveys appear to be roughly compatible with charitable deductions claimed on income tax returns,[37] and IRS compliance studies show that taxpayers are remarkably honest about their claims of charitable contributions (97 percent of claimed charitable deductions can be documented by taxpayers).[38] In addition, cross-national surveys suggest that Americans are comparatively generous in their level of charitable donations. A 1991 survey asked people in five countries if they had made any donations to charity in the month before the survey, and if so, how much.[39] The Americans in this survey reported giving slightly less than the Canadians, but almost three times the amount given by Britons or Spaniards, and over four times that given by the French.[40]

Not all donations to charitable organizations go toward helping the needy, however. The single largest beneficiary of Americans' philanthropic largess is religious institutions, which receive about 44 percent of all charitable contributions.[41] While some of the money donated to these institutions is indeed used for programs to aid the needy, the larger part is used simply to maintain the institutions themselves, a clear benefit to those who donate, but of little value to poor people (other than those who happen to be members of a given congregation). Even considering the important role of religious institutions in charitable giving however, Americans do "put their money where their mouths are." The average American household's tax-deductible donations to charitable institutions totaled almost $700 in 1995,[42] and for the country as a whole, charitable contributions amount to a very sizable $144 billion annually.[43] In contrast, all levels of government together spend about $183 billion per year on nonmedical means-tested programs and another $161 billion on medical care for the poor. Federal, state, and local government spending for cash assistance—including AFDC, SSI, General Assistance, pensions for needy veterans, foster care, and the refunded portion of the EITC—amounts to only $84 billion per year.[44] In short, while the bulk of antipoverty spending in this country is provided by government, voluntary donations do represent a very substantial commitment of resources.

Personal Charity versus Government Assistance

Americans' generosity toward the less fortunate suggests that their expressed preference for more government spending to help the poor is not mere lip service. Of course, a willingness to donate to private charities does not necessarily imply a desire to see government take on greater responsibilities for helping the needy. Indeed, many argue that private charities are, in principle, a better means of helping the poor, either because they are more efficient or effective than government programs, or because they strengthen local communities by bringing volunteers together to work for the common good. (Of course, others argue that government is, in principle, a better means of helping the poor because it can redress the imbalance of resources among communities, because it has the scope of expertise and resources to meet widespread needs, or because it can be held accountable in ways that private charities cannot.)

Quite aside from these abstract arguments over the relative merits of government versus private provision, an individual's decision to donate money to help the poor is fundamentally different from the decision to support or oppose a tax increase for the same purpose. From the point of view of an individual concerned about poverty, government assistance has one tremendous advantage over private donations.

When an individual donates $50 to aid the needy, the needy become $50 better off. But when an individual supports legislation that taxes every citizen $50 to aid the needy, that $50 donation is multiplied millions-fold. For those who want to see spending increased for some particular cause, the benefit that results from a given level of tax increase (or a foregone tax decrease) is fantastically greater than the benefit that would derive from a single donation. At least for those Americans with no principled objection to government help for the poor, support for any given level of government expenditure—and its associated level of taxation—should be greater than willingness to make an individual donation of that same amount of money.

Assessing Americans' true willingness to pay more taxes to help the poor is a difficult task. Yet what we do know provides a strong challenge to the often-voiced opinion that the economic self-interest of middle-class voters leads them to oppose means-tested programs that benefit only the poor. On the contrary, the available evidence suggests that caring for the needy is an obligation that Americans both take upon themselves and place upon their government. To recapitulate: We saw in chapter 1 that Americans' desire to cut welfare spending is an exception to the otherwise strong support they express for the welfare state in general and for efforts to help the poor in particular. We saw in chapter 2 that popular support for social programs that benefit only the poor is nearly as great as support for similar programs that benefit all Americans. Chapter 2 also showed that—contrary to the self-interest hypothesis—public support for welfare spending rises rather than falls during economic hard times. In addition, the well-off express greater opposition to welfare than those with lower incomes, but these same well-off Americans are just as supportive of other means-tested programs that benefit only the poor. In this chapter we have seen that, across an array of programs to help the needy, Americans say not only that they want the government to spend more, but that they are willing to pay more in taxes to support these services. Finally, we have seen that Americans donate significant amounts of time and money to charitable causes.

The evidence that Americans support greater government efforts to help the poor is compelling. But if this account is true, why have politicians failed to respond? Why does the United States remain far behind most developed countries in the resources it devotes to helping the poor? I take up this question in chapter 9.

9

The Politics of the American Welfare State

The United States stands out among the world's industrialized countries in many ways, both good and bad. Among the less desirable characteristics that sets the United States apart is the ineffectiveness of its antipoverty policies. Government policies do less to reduce poverty in America than in almost any other industrialized nation. Figure 9.1 shows the combined impact of government taxes and transfer programs on the poverty levels of sixteen developed countries.[1] In twelve of these countries, government policies reduce the poverty rate by 60 percent to 80 percent. That is, of those who would be poor based on their market income alone, government programs lift between 60 percent and 80 percent out of poverty. In Canada and Great Britain, only 50 percent of those who would otherwise be poor are lifted above this threshold, while in Australia only 44 percent are raised above the poverty level. In the United States, which stands alone at the bottom of this ladder, poverty is reduced by only 29 percent as a consequence of government taxes and transfers.

Why Doesn't the American Government Do More to Help the Poor?

A full analysis of the political obstacles to a better-funded and more effective government antipoverty policy is beyond the scope of this book. But the brief account that follows can at least point to some of the factors that explain the persistence of our current rather feeble efforts to help the poor.

One reason that America has not devoted more resources to fighting poverty is the public's concern with the undeserving poor. Americans'

Figure 9.1   Percent Reduction in Poverty Due to Government Taxes and Transfer Programs

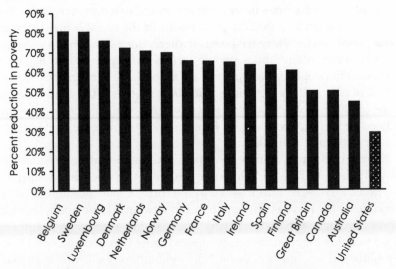

Source: Smeeding, "Financial Poverty in Developed Countries," table 7.

Notes: Poverty levels are based on 50% of each country's median disposable income. See page 262, note 1 for details of income, tax, and transfer calculations.

cynicism toward welfare recipients, sustained by misperceptions of the racial composition of the poverty population and negative stereotypes of blacks, limits the easiest and by many accounts most effective anti-poverty measure: giving money to those who lack it. The distinction between the deserving and the undeserving poor is an old one, as is the stereotype of blacks as lazy. But these two sets of attitudes became entwined in the mid-1960s when poor blacks first came to the widespread attention of the American media and the American public. The already existing belief that blacks were lazy contributed to the negative media coverage of the black poor over the ensuing decades, and this coverage has in turn helped to perpetuate the stereotype of blacks as lazy and the black poor as undeserving.

The portrayal of poverty in the news both reflects and reinforces the racial stereotypes that generate public opposition to welfare. I argued in earlier chapters that the media are instrumental in shaping public perceptions of the poor and that these perceptions have significant political consequences. For example, we saw in chapter 6 that even those Americans living in states with virtually no poor blacks exhibit the same misperceptions about the racial composition of the nation's poor as do those living in heavily black states. It is not personal experience, I concluded, but the mass media that generate these misperceptions. We also saw in chapter 6 that misperceptions of the racial composition of poor people and welfare recipients matter. Americans who think most welfare recipients (or poor people) are black express more negative views about people on welfare and are more likely to blame poverty on a lack of effort rather than on circumstances beyond the control of the poor (and this holds true even when we compare Americans who are otherwise identical with regard to age, sex, family income, and liberal/ conservative orientation).

Simply providing accurate information about the nature of America's poverty and welfare populations is unlikely to dispel public misperceptions. First, such information, in the form of statistics on the racial makeup of the poor, is already found in newsmagazine and television news coverage, although not very often. But as we saw in chapter 6, most people's perceptions are influenced more by vivid examples than by statistical information, even if the evidentiary value of the statistical information is far higher. For news stories on poverty, it is the specific poor people chosen as examples that are most likely to sway readers, and the race of these poor people is most often communicated by pictures.

To create a more accurate perception of the racial composition of the poor, news organizations must become far more conscious of the process of selecting the photographs or the specific poor people they will feature in their stories. The photo editors I interviewed had only the vaguest notion of the racial mix of poor people in the stories they had worked on over the years (and many expressed surprise when they learned how unbalanced their coverage was in this regard). But as we have seen, racial misrepresentation in the media extends beyond numerical inaccuracy. Just as important a consideration is how minorities are portrayed in any given category of news coverage.

One important step in raising the level of racial sensitivity in news coverage is to increase the representation of minorities in the newsroom. Although tremendous strides have been made over the past decades, minorities are still substantially underrepresented in the country's newsrooms, and progress toward integration has slowed to a crawl.[2] But it is not the sole responsibility of minority journalists to "monitor" the behavior of their news organizations in this regard. On the contrary, it is the responsibility of news professionals of all races to see to it that the news does not distort the social world by portraying certain social groups in unjustifiably negative ways.

In response to concerns over the images of minorities in the news, some news organizations have instituted "content audits" or "photo audits" to systematically track the way minorities (or women) are portrayed. For example, in 1988 the *Seattle Times* began to count photographs of minorities appearing in positive, neutral, and negative contexts, and it found that negative images of minorities outnumbered positive images by four to one.[3] In response to this dismal portrayal of minorities and the discussion and "consciousness raising" that ensued among the news staff, coverage changed. In the following year, positive images of minorities outnumbered negative images, and by 1990 the *Times* published twice as many photographs depicting minorities positively as negatively (a ratio that closely approximated the portrayal of whites in the *Times'* coverage). As the *Seattle Times'* experience shows, when a news organization makes the fair representation of different social groups a priority and takes concrete steps to monitor their own news content, substantial change can be accomplished in a short time.

The negative stereotypes of poor blacks reflected in and reinforced by the news media help to explain why Americans view welfare recipients with such suspicion and why the public sees welfare as a program of aid for the undeserving poor. But America not only offers meager welfare assistance, it also devotes fewer resources than most countries to those aspects of antipoverty policy that are not subject to concern about abuse by the undeserving. Indeed, even those antipoverty programs that enjoy wide popular support, such as job training, child care, and medical care for the needy, are funded at levels far too low to meet the needs of the poor (and far lower than levels in most other industrial countries).

In trying to account for the lack of effort and general ineffectiveness of U.S. antipoverty policy, we must acknowledge that the history of welfare reform shows that there has been an effort to move in directions that the public supports. Furthermore, after many failed attempts or minimal reforms, it appears that we are gradually doing more of the things to help the needy that Americans favor. For example, the value of the Earned Income Tax Credit (or EITC), which provides tax relief or cash grants to low-income workers, has increased dramatically in the past decade.[4] Unlike welfare, the EITC provides benefits only to the employed, thereby removing the suspicion that beneficiaries are shirkers who have chosen to live off the government rather than work for a living. Consequently, the EITC enjoys strong public support.[5] In addition to increasing funding for the EITC, the welfare reform legislation of 1996 increased funding for some of the support services for welfare recipients that the public favors (such as government-subsidized child care), while allowing states considerable latitude in deciding how much of their TANF block grants to devote to cash assistance and how much to education, job training, child care, and related services for the poor.

Recent changes in U.S. antipoverty policy have moved it somewhat more in the direction that opinion polls suggest the public favors. Nevertheless, overall funding remains low, and in the long term, the 1996 welfare reform legislation will likely reduce even further the resources devoted to helping the poor. One explanation for the relative paucity of spending to aid the poor is simply that poor people lack the power necessary to obtain more from government. Poor people are not only less likely to vote than are those with higher incomes, they are also less likely to contact elected officials, attend community meetings, work in political campaigns, take part in political protest activities, or donate money to political campaigns.[6] Occasionally, America's poor do rise up in mass protest over the conditions of their lives, and such protests can be effective in obtaining greater benefits from government, at least under the right conditions.[7] But the obstacles to collective political action by poor people are substantial and the poor themselves typically have little impact on the formation of government antipoverty policy.

In addition to having limited political resources, poor people and their sympathizers who try to expand government help for the needy must compete with other agendas and with organized interest groups that hold other priorities. As Senator Robert Dole put it, "There aren't any poor [people's] PACs."[8] From the pluralist perspective, political outcomes are shaped by the interplay among the various competing interest groups that represent the desires of different segments of the American public. But in E. E. Schattschneider's famous words, "The flaw in the pluralist heaven is that the heavenly chorus sings with a strong upper-class accent."[9]

While there may not be a "poor people's PAC," there are interest groups that advocate on behalf of the poor. In part, the lack of a more developed and better-funded antipoverty policy might be attributed to the lack of resources and hence the lack of effectiveness of such antipoverty interest groups. But another perspective on American politics explains the failure to enact the public's favored antipoverty agenda by pointing to the differences in the way average Americans and political elites think about poverty and welfare.

According to Steven Teles, the debate over welfare policy that has taken place over the past decades has been held hostage by the rather extreme positions staked out by elites on the political left and right.[10] Many on the left, he argues, defended existing cash assistance programs out of a conviction that the welfare system should not be used to enforce a particular pattern of behavior on welfare recipients (whether in regard to work, marriage, or childbearing). Maintaining benefit levels (or limiting their decline) became the primary objective of such thinkers.[11] At the same time, elites on the political right often adopted the view that the problems of the poor stem from the unfortunate choices of the poor themselves. From this perspective, welfare is seen as providing the means by which lazy or "dysfunctional" recipients can avoid work and responsibility, and consequently, the higher the benefits welfare provides, the more it undermines the work ethic of the poor.[12] As Teles points out, neither of these perspectives fits very well with the more centrist and nuanced views of the public. And more importantly, the polarized nature of elite debate has ensured that little headway could be made in reforming the existing welfare system (as exemplified by the simultaneous attacks on Nixon's Family Assistance Plan by the left and the right).

The polarization of political elites is especially problematic in a political system with many choke points. Unlike the more streamlined political structures of most European democracies, America's national political institutions contain numerous veto points at which potential legislation can be stopped. The division of powers between the executive and legislative branches, the bicameral legislature, the power of congressional committees through which bills must pass, and the weak control of the political parties over individual representatives all create opportunities for opponents to block proposed legislation.[13]

Another reason that American antipoverty policy seems to fall short of the public's desires might be that helping the poor is not a high enough priority among middle-class Americans to compel politicians to respond. That is, Americans might *prefer* to do more to help the poor (as I argued in the previous chapter) but may simply feel that the issue is not of great importance to them, given all the other pressing problems the country faces. One way to judge the importance of different issues is simply to ask Americans which issues they think most important. But while this approach can shed some light on the public's political priorities, we must interpret the results with caution, since we know that the survey responses to these questions are strongly influenced by the amount of media coverage an issue is currently receiving.[14]

One recent survey asked Americans to choose "the most important problem facing the United States at the present time" from among a list of five alternatives.[15] Of the five problems, the most frequently chosen were "decline in moral values" (32 percent of respondents) and "public institutions such as schools and hospitals not working well" (19 percent). Next in line was "the gap between the rich and the poor," which 14 percent of respondents chose as the most important problem facing the country, followed by "insecurity about safety from crime and violence" (12 percent) and "worries about economic security, including the loss of jobs to other countries" (11 percent). With the exception of the gap between rich and poor, all the problems in this list are issues that the public is widely thought to be concerned about. Thus the fact that concern with the gap between rich and poor was ranked in the middle of these five problems strongly indicates that Americans do assign a high priority to dealing with poverty and inequality. (And given the undeniable significance of the other problems on the list, it seems unlikely that respondents would have felt any social desirability pressure to name economic inequality as their most pressing concern.)

Another indication that poverty ranks fairly highly as a concern of the American public comes from surveys that allow respondents to name any issue they choose when asked about the most important problem facing the country. Figure 9.2 shows the average responses from all five of the CBS/*New York Times* surveys that asked this question during 1997 (the thirty-four issue categories listed are those used by the survey organization to code the responses to this open-ended question). The category of greatest interest is labeled "poverty/homelessness." Although concern about the poor might be reflected in responses coded into some of the other categories as well (such as "jobs/unemployment" or "economy"), the "poverty/homelessness" category clearly includes responses indicating concern with the condition of the least well-off.

As figure 9.2 shows, no problem was overwhelmingly chosen as the country's most important in 1997. Crime and drugs were the two most pressing concerns, mentioned by 11.6 percent and 8.4 percent of survey respondents, respectively. While poverty was clearly not the issue that Americans were most worried about in 1997, it nevertheless ranked quite highly compared with other issues that are more widely recognized as important to the American public. On average, 5.0 percent of survey respondents named poverty or homelessness as the country's most pressing problem, about the same number as those mentioning education (5.4 percent), and considerably more than those mentioning

Figure 9.2   Most Important Problem Facing the Country, 1997

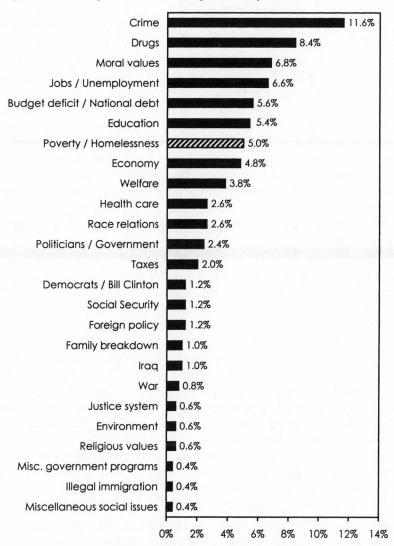

Percent naming each issue as the most important problem

Source: Average of all 1997 CBS/*New York Times* polls (1/10/97, 4/2/97, 6/10/97, 9/5/97, 11/23/97). Not shown are 9 responses that received less than 0.25% each, 13.4% naming miscellaneous (uncoded) issues, and 7.4% saying "don't know."

welfare (3.8 percent), health care (2.6 percent), taxes (2.0 percent), or illegal immigration (0.4 percent). Because responses to these "most important problem" questions are quite volatile, this evidence only suggests the priority that Americans attach to the problem of poverty. Nevertheless, it does present a challenge to the belief that America's failure to respond more forcefully to poverty results from the low priority the public places on helping the poor.

Finally, the political system has not produced the kind of antipoverty policy that the public prefers because the public's preferences have been consistently misread. In politics (as in many other areas of life) it is perceptions that count, and the perception that middle-class taxpayers will not support programs that help only the poor has made politicians reluctant to associate themselves with the effort to expand government assistance for the needy. In an otherwise unfavorable response to Republican efforts to trim the welfare state, the *St. Louis Post-Dispatch* wrote, "A hard-pressed middle class is tired of paying for aid to poor people who seem to be forever with us at great expense."[16] But as we have seen, this popular understanding of the sentiments of the American pubic is misguided. Most middle-class Americans, hard-pressed or otherwise, want to boost, not cut, assistance to the poor.

Welfare, of course, is another matter (as are food stamps, the other unpopular antipoverty program). And public opposition to welfare is important, not least because it points to the cynicism toward the undeserving poor that presents a significant (if exaggerated) political obstacle to antipoverty efforts. Attitudes toward welfare are also important because welfare has received disproportionate attention from the press and the public, despite the greater expenditures on other kinds of means-tested aid. But the public's real and strong opposition to welfare has been over-generalized, and the stark contrast between public opposition to welfare and public support of Social Security has been misinterpreted as an indicator that only those programs that directly benefit the middle class can enjoy popular support.

This widespread (and, I believe, profoundly mistaken) image of American citizens as primarily self-interested in their approach to politics is consistent with the deep cultural understandings that underlie American democracy. Our founding fathers viewed government as the mechanism by which competing interests could be tamed. And surely this is what much of politics is about—the pursuit of self-interest by the multiple factions that compose a society. But it is an impoverished understanding of politics that does not also recognize the importance of other motives. Civic pride, patriotic duty, a concern with justice, and a desire to help the least advantaged improve their lot can all conflict with individuals' pursuit of their material interests. Yet these nonmaterial values that Americans hold dear may be more important in understanding how the public thinks about politics than are calculations of self-interest narrowly understood. Political elites and organized interest groups battle over concrete benefits, but most ordinary Americans approach political questions by asking "which policy is best" not "which policy is best for me."

Policy Implications

Fighting poverty is not an easy task. The effort often involves tradeoffs between competing goals, and progress is increasingly hindered by global economic forces that bode ill for those with low education or skill levels.[17] How, then, should America respond to the challenge of poverty as we enter the new millennium? Clearly the costs and efficacy of alternative antipoverty policies must be our foremost concern. But the political viability of these alternatives is also an important consideration. There is little use in promoting antipoverty policies that stand no chance of acquiring the political support needed to become law.

One aspect of political viability concerns the public's attitudes toward proposed antipoverty programs. Of course public attitudes can and do change over time, in response both to changes in the social conditions that affect the country and to political leadership. Yet the history of Americans' attitudes toward welfare and welfare reform suggests an enduring set of concerns that the public brings to this debate.[18] Programs that fail to address these concerns or that are not oriented toward the antipoverty goals that the public embraces will be fighting an uphill political battle.

What lessons can we draw from the research reported here about the kinds of antipoverty programs the public is likely to support or oppose? What does this research suggest about the political viability of a more ambitious and effective government antipoverty effort? And finally, what obstacles stand in the way of a social welfare regime in the United States that is as successful at reducing poverty as those found in most of the world's other advanced industrial nations?

One lesson to be drawn from the work presented here is that an antipoverty program's race-neutral structure will not insulate it from racial politics. Most welfare recipients are not black, and welfare policies make no distinction between applicants based on racial or ethnic identity. But as we have seen, white Americans' thinking about welfare is thoroughly racialized: the perception that blacks lack commitment to the work ethic plays a central role in shaping whites' views of welfare and welfare recipients, and whites' perceptions of black welfare mothers are far better predictors of their attitudes toward poverty and welfare than are their perceptions of white welfare mothers. Responding to the lack of political support for race-targeted programs, some observers have called for a "surreptitious" social policy of combating racial inequality through race-neutral programs. In *The Truly Disadvantaged*, for example, William Julius Wilson urges liberals to adopt a "hidden agenda" of using race-neutral policies to address racial inequality.

Race-neutral programs *are* more popular among the American public than similar race-targeted programs.[19] But this difference stems from both racial and nonracial considerations. In addition to prejudice, self-interest, and racial stereotypes, the belief that scarce resources such as jobs or college admissions should not be allocated based on group membership may motivate whites' rejection of race-targeted programs. (It is interesting to note in this context that—depending on how the question is phrased—most women reject affirmative action programs for women.[20] Women's opposition to sex-based affirmative action obviously cannot stem from group self-interest, nor is it plausible to suggest that prejudice against women is at work. Instead, it would appear that a general aversion to group-based benefits lies behind their opposition.) Thus race-targeted policies can be rejected on nonracial grounds just as race-neutral policies can be rejected on the basis of racial attitudes. The politics of antipoverty policy is simply too complex to support the contention that a race-neutral structure can "deracialize" this debate. As long as blacks and other minorities remain disproportionately poor, it is unlikely that antipoverty policy can ever be divorced from racial politics.

Despite the unavoidable link between poverty and race, antipoverty programs do vary in the extent to which they evoke racial stereotypes. The association of antipoverty programs with minorities may depress support among whites, but as we have seen, this association is not an insurmountable barrier. Even programs strongly associated with blacks can enjoy high levels of popular approval if the programs are seen as providing benefits to those who are trying to help themselves. Race-based opposition to antipoverty programs emerges not simply from the perception that a program's beneficiaries are minorities, but from the perception that a program's beneficiaries are *undeserving minorities* who prefer to live off the government rather than work. Because the belief that blacks lack commitment to the work ethic remains widespread among white Americans, programs (like welfare) that are seen as undermining the work ethic and rewarding idleness will fall prey to the politics of racial stereotyping. But even highly racially identified programs can gain strong support among whites, as long as the programs are perceived as helping poor people to better support themselves. As we saw in chapter 7, most whites believe that Head Start and job training programs benefit primarily minorities, yet both of these programs receive overwhelming support from the American public.

In a period in which race and racial politics are never out of the headlines for long, few may be surprised that whites' opposition to welfare reflects their views of blacks. More surprising, I suspect, is the fact that public support is nevertheless strong for antipoverty programs that assist the "deserving poor."[21] Education, job training, job creation, welfare-to-work programs, the minimum wage, the Earned Income Tax Credit, health care, child care, housing assistance, subsidized transportation to work, and other benefits for the poor all enjoy substantial support among Americans. In dramatic contrast with welfare, the public wants more, not less government effort along these lines. Many of these programs receive widespread public support because they promise to enable poor people to better meet their own needs. For most Americans, poverty is only "solved" when people are able to earn their own way out of the ranks of the poor. "Human capital" programs, including education, job training, and "work readiness" programs, aim to combat poverty by increasing the ability of poor people to succeed in the labor market.

One reason human capital approaches to poverty are popular is because they benefit the deserving poor. But in the long run these programs may also help to decrease reliance on government assistance. Increasing government spending to move welfare recipients into the workforce may cost more in the short run but may save taxpayer dollars in the long run. Thus not only humanitarian concern for the deserving poor, but enlightened self-interest, might contribute to the popularity of these antipoverty programs.

Yet enlightened self-interest, as an explanation for public support of antipoverty spending, should not be pushed too far. We saw in chapter 2 the wide variety of evidence against the notion that economic self-interest plays an important role in explaining attitudes toward poverty and welfare. In addition, many popular antipoverty programs hold no such promise of a future "payoff" for taxpayers. For example, the Earned Income Tax Credit provides extra cash to people who are already supporting themselves. This surely improves the quality of recipients' lives and may raise them out of the ranks of the working poor. But the EITC does not hold much promise of increasing the earning power of its beneficiaries. Similarly, housing assistance and health care improve the lives of the needy, but seem quite unlikely to save taxpayers money in either the short run or the long run. Enlightened self-interest may be an *additional* reason for the popularity of some anti-poverty programs, but it can hardly be relied upon as an explanation for the public's desire to do more to help the poor.

Contrary, perhaps, to popular belief, Americans are not clamoring for cutbacks in government efforts to help the poor. Instead, most Americans want government to spend more on these programs, and most say they are willing to pay higher taxes in order to boost spending for the needy. But public concern does not, in itself, generate political responses. Politicians and other political elites must mobilize public opinion. The diffuse desire to help the deserving poor must be translated into policy proposals that can be debated in concrete terms. The 1996 welfare reforms represented a small step toward bringing antipoverty policy more into line with public desires. But those reforms responded primarily to Americans' cynicism toward welfare recipients and their desire to cut welfare benefits to the undeserving. Only token efforts were made in the 1996 legislation to satisfy the positive desires of the American public to *increase* spending for the deserving poor.

The 1996 welfare bill thus represents a half-finished agenda. The crucial question is whether political leaders will take the more difficult (because more costly) steps that the public also supports. As I write the concluding pages of this book, America's antipoverty policy is poised between a past that has been abandoned and a future that is still unformed. With the demise of AFDC, the decades-old federal guarantee of cash support for poor children is gone. Welfare has been cut back, time limits have been imposed, and states have been freed to impose a variety of restrictions on welfare receipt. For now, our economy is performing well and unemployment is at historic lows. But what will happen when unemployment rises (as it inevitably will) and suffering among the poor increases? How will the public and political leaders respond?

The findings in this book suggest that, when hard times come, the public will not turn its back on the poor, but will support even more strongly the expansion of government antipoverty efforts. Yet the history of the American welfare state suggests that government will likely fail to respond in a meaningful way to the growing needs of the poor; if so, the blame will lie in a failure of political leadership, not in a lack of concern for the poor among the American people.

Appendix

Chapter Two

Family Income, Demographics, and Opposition to Welfare Spending (text figure 2.5)

Table A.1 shows that the relationships between family income levels and welfare spending preferences shown in figure 2.5 (and reflected in the first regression model in table A.1) remain virtually unchanged when controls for race, sex, age, education, and region are introduced.

Family Income, Previous Welfare Receipt, Welfare Attitudes, and Opposition to Welfare Spending

The first two models in table A.2 show that most of the impact of family income on opposition to welfare spending can be accounted for by the lower levels of past welfare receipt experienced by higher-income respondents. The third model shows that an additional portion of this impact can be attributed to the greater support for welfare time limits found among those with higher incomes. The second model also shows that, when both past history of welfare receipt and current family income are considered simultaneously, history of welfare receipt is a far more powerful predictor of current attitudes toward welfare spending than is current family income.

Table A.1 Family Income, Demographics, and Opposition to Welfare Spending (results in this table reflect the relationships shown in figure 2.5)

	Regression Coefficient	Standard Error	Standardized Regression Coefficient	P Value
First regression model ($R^2 = .04$)				
Income: $10,000 to $19,999	.13	.01	.10	.001
Income: $20,000 to $29,999	.21	.01	.15	.001
Income: $30,000 to $39,999	.25	.01	.18	.001
Income: $40,000 to $49,999	.28	.01	.19	.001
Income: $50,000 to $59,999	.26	.02	.13	.001
Income: $60,000 to $69,999	.28	.02	.13	.001
Income: $70,000 and over	.32	.01	.22	.001
Second regression model ($R^2 = .06$)				
Income: $10,000 to $19,999	.12	.01	.09	.001
Income: $20,000 to $29,999	.19	.01	.14	.001
Income: $30,000 to $39,999	.23	.01	.16	.001
Income: $40,000 to $49,999	.26	.02	.18	.001
Income: $50,000 to $59,999	.24	.02	.12	.001
Income: $60,000 to $69,999	.26	.02	.12	.001
Income: $70,000 and over	.30	.02	.20	.001
Region (south)	−.01	.01	−.01	.38
Sex (female)	−.01	.01	−.01	.23
Education	−.01	.01	−.03	.001
Race (black)	−.24	.01	−.15	.001
Age: 30 to 39	.05	.01	.04	.001
Age: 40 to 49	.04	.01	.03	.001
Age: 50 to 59	.06	.01	.04	.001
Age: 60 to 69	.07	.01	.05	.001
Age: 70 and over	.07	.01	.04	.001

Source: General Social Survey, 1973–1994. N = 17,781.

Notes: The dependent variable in these analyses is opposition to welfare spending scored 1 for decrease spending and 0 for increase or maintain spending. Income has been converted into 1995 dollars.

Table A.2 Family Income, Previous Welfare Receipt, Welfare Attitudes, and Opposition
to Welfare Spending

	Regression Coefficient	Standard Error	Standardized Regression Coefficient	P Value
First regression model (R² = .01)				
Family income	.19	.08	.11	.02
Second regression model (R² = .07)				
Family income	.08	.08	.05	.30
Ever received welfare	−.27	.05	−.24	.001
Third regression model (R² = .10)				
Family income	.06	.08	.03	.43
Ever received welfare	−.25	.05	−.22	.001
Favors a time limit for welfare mothers	.21	.05	.17	.001

Source: CBS/*New York Times* poll, December 1994. *N* = 533.

Notes: Dependent variable is scored 1 for decrease welfare spending and 0 for maintain
or increase spending. All predictors are scored from 0 to 1. Family income coded in five
categories from "under $15,000" to "$75,000 and over." Questions were worded as follows: "Have you or any member of your family ever received food stamps or other welfare benefits?" "Do you favor or oppose limiting how long mothers with young children
can receive welfare benefits?"

Chapter Three

Indices of Racial Attitudes and Welfare Support from the 1986 National Election Study (text figure 3.4)

The items used to measure racial attitudes were combined into indices
based on an exploratory factor analysis with oblique rotation.[1] To con-
struct the indices shown in figure 3.4, the component variables were
first rescored to range from 0 to 1 (with 1 indicating more negative attitudes toward blacks) and then averaged. Cronbach's alpha reliability
for the indices is .65 for "blacks lack work ethic," .76 for "blacks are
innately inferior," .56 for "helping blacks is not government's job," and
.77 for opposition to affirmative action. Unlike these five indices of racial attitudes, the combined index of welfare attitudes includes two
variables with very different response scoring (i.e., the three-point scale
of spending preferences for food stamps and the 100-point feeling thermometer for welfare recipients). Therefore the two questions were first
rescored so that a high value indicates opposition to welfare; the questions were then standardized and averaged. The alpha reliability for the
resulting scale is .62.

Table A.3 Stereotypes of Social Groups and Opposition to Welfare Spending (results from this table are summarized in figure 3.3)

	Regression Coefficient	Standard Error	Standardized Regression Coefficient	P Value
Assessed individually				
Perception of blacks as lazy	.46	.13	.14	.001
Age	.27	.13	.08	.05
Sex	−.01	.06	−.01	.80
Region	.01	.08	.01	.89
Education	−.02	.22	−.00	.92
Family income	.56	.12	.20	.001
$N = 626, R^2 = .07$				
Perception of Hispanics as lazy	.24	.14	.07	.65
Age	.29	.14	.09	.04
Sex	−.05	.06	−.03	.41
Region	.05	.08	.02	.55
Education	−.08	.23	−.02	.73
Family income	.64	.13	.22	.001
$N = 600, R^2 = .06$				
Perception of Asians as lazy	.05	.13	.02	.71
Age	.29	.14	.09	.04
Sex	−.04	.06	−.03	.53
Region	.03	.08	.02	.69
Education	−.09	.23	−.02	.68
Family income	.62	.13	.21	.001
$N = 597, R^2 = .05$				
Perception of whites as lazy	.00	.15	.00	.98
Age	.35	.13	.11	.01
Sex	−.03	.06	−.02	.63
Region	.02	.08	.01	.81
Education	−.11	.22	−.02	.63
Family income	.61	.13	.21	.001
$N = 631, R^2 = .05$				
Assessed simultaneously				
Perception of blacks as lazy	.52	.15	.16	.001
Perception of Hispanics as lazy	.06	.16	.02	.70
Perception of Asians as lazy	−.14	.15	−.04	.35
Perception of whites as lazy	−.05	.16	−.01	.76
Age	.24	.14	.07	.09
Sex	−.03	.06	−.02	.60
Region	.03	.08	.01	.74
Education	.00	.23	.00	.99
Family income	.58	.13	.20	.001
$N = 579, R^2 = .07$				

Source: General Social Survey, 1994.

Notes: The dependent variable is scored −1, 0, or 1 for increase, maintain, and decrease welfare spending. All predictors are scored from 0 to 1, with high scores for female and southerner.

Racial Attitudes and Opposition to Welfare Spending (text table 3.2)

Table A.4 shows the detailed regression results that are summarized in table 3.2.[2] One complicating factor in these analyses concerns the use of the 100-point feeling thermometers as both independent and dependent variables. The feeling thermometers are particularly susceptible to correlated measurement error because respondents use these response scales in idiosyncratic (but consistent) ways.[3] Responses to the feeling thermometers present a problem analogous to acquiescent response bias, in that some respondents give consistently high scores on feeling thermometers and others consistently low scores, irrespective of the individual or social group being rated. Consequently, statistical associ-

Table A.4 Racial Attitudes and Opposition to Welfare Spending (results from this table are summarized in table 3.2)

	Regression Coefficient	Standard Error	Standardized Regression Coefficient	P Value
Cut spending for food stamps				
"Blacks lack work ethic"	20.1	7.3	.16	.006
"Blacks are innately inferior"	−4.3	9.1	−.02	.63
Negative feelings toward blacks	0.7	8.9	.00	.94
"Helping blacks is not government's job"	11.2	5.2	.12	.03
Opposition to affirmative action	14.8	7.4	.12	.05
"Civil rights leaders push too fast"	14.2	7.0	.12	.05
$N = 381, R^2 = .38$				
Negative feelings toward welfare recipients				
"Blacks lack work ethic"	14.3	4.4	.19	.001
"Blacks are innately inferior"	5.1	5.3	.05	.34
Negative feelings toward blacks	8.7	5.7	.09	.13
"Helping blacks is not government's job"	1.4	3.1	.03	.65
Opposition to affirmative action	8.5	4.5	.11	.06
"Civil rights leaders push too fast"	4.3	4.1	.06	.29
Average thermometer rating	−0.4	0.1	−.20	.001
$N = 373, R^2 = .20$				

(continued)

Table A.4 (*Continued*)

	Regression Coefficient	Standard Error	Standardized Regression Coefficient	P Value
Combined index				
"Blacks lack work ethic"	17.2	4.7	.21	.001
"Blacks are innately inferior"	−0.2	5.8	−.00	.97
Negative feelings toward blacks	3.1	6.2	.03	.62
"Helping blacks is not government's job"	4.1	3.3	.07	.21
Opposition to affirmative action	10.4	4.8	.13	.03
"Civil rights leaders push too fast"	11.7	4.5	.15	.01
Average thermometer rating	−0.3	0.1	−.14	.01
$N = 357$, $R^2 = .23$				

Source: National Election Study, 1986.

Notes: Dependent variables are scored from 0 to 100, with high scores indicating negative attitudes toward food stamps or welfare recipients. Predictors are scored from 0 to 1, with high scores indicating negative attitudes toward blacks. Analyses include white respondents only.

ations among all thermometer ratings are biased in a positive direction, artificially inflating associations among items with true positive correlations and depressing associations among items with true negative correlations. In the analyses in table A.4, the consequence is artificial inflation of the association between feelings toward blacks and feelings toward welfare recipients. To compensate for this consequence of correlated measurement error, I constructed an independent measure of thermometer response tendency and entered it into the regression analysis along with the substantive predictors. Feeling thermometer response tendencies were measured by averaging respondents' ratings of liberals, conservatives, Democrats, and Republicans; those with high average scores across this set of four target groups tend to give higher thermometer ratings irrespective of target, while those with low average scores tend in the opposite direction. This method variable (labeled "average thermometer rating" in table A.4) is used in the two regression analyses in which the feeling thermometer serves as a dependent variable.

Chapter Four

Question Wording, Response Coding, and Scale Construction for Questions from the National Race and Politics Study
(text tables 4.1–4.3)

Welfare spending: "Suppose you had a say in making up the federal budget, would you prefer to see more spent, less spent, or the same amount of money spent on welfare as it has been?" 0 = More spent, 50 = Kept the same, 100 = Less spent.

Age: Age in years recoded to range from 0 to 1.

Sex: 0 = male, 1 = female.

Region: 0 = non-South, 1 = South.

Education: "What is the highest grade or year of school you completed?" 0 = Eighth grade or lower, 0.2 = Some high school, 0.4 = High school graduate (or GED), 0.6 = Some college, 0.8 = College graduate, 1.0 = Some graduate work or graduate degree.

Marital status: 0 = not currently married, 1 = currently married.

Family income: "Think of the income BEFORE taxes of all members of your household living with you now. Include income from all sources, including wages, dividends, interest, pensions, and other sources." Responses coded in 13 categories from less than $10,000 (scored 0) to more than $70,000 (scored 1).

Liberal/conservative ideology: NES-style seven-point branching measure ranging from strong liberal (scored 0) to strong conservative (scored 1). Respondents who do not think of themselves as liberal or conservative are assigned the middle position along with moderates (scored 0.5).

Party identification: NES-style seven-point branching measure ranging from strong Democrat (scored 0) to strong Republican (scored 1). Respondents who express no partisan preference are assigned the middle position along with independents (scored 0.5).

Individualism: "The government in Washington tries to do too many things that should be left up to individuals and private businesses." 0 = Disagree strongly, .33 = Disagree somewhat, .67 = Agree somewhat, 1 = Agree strongly.

Perception of blacks as lazy: "Now I'll read a few words that people sometimes use to describe blacks. Of course, no word fits absolutely everybody, but, as I read each one, please tell me using a number from 0 to 10 how well you think it describes blacks as a group. If you think it's a very good description of most blacks, give it a 10. If you feel a word is a very inaccurate description of most blacks, give it a 0."

Respondents' scores for "hardworking" are subtracted from their scores for "lazy." The index is then rescaled to range from 0 (most hardworking) to 1 (most lazy). Cronbach's alpha reliability coefficient for this scale is .35.

Perception of welfare recipients as undeserving: "Most people on welfare could get by without it if they really tried." 0 = Disagree strongly, .33 = Disagree somewhat, .67 = Agree somewhat, 1 = Agree strongly. "Most people on welfare would rather be working than taking money from the government." 0 = Disagree strongly, .33 = Disagree somewhat, .67 = Agree somewhat, 1 = Agree strongly. Respondents' scores for the second question are subtracted from their scores for the first question. The index is then rescaled to range from 0 (most undeserving) to 1 (most deserving). Cronbach's alpha reliability coefficient for this scale is .49.

Welfare mother experiment: "Now think about a (black/white) woman in her early thirties. She is a high school (graduate/drop out) with a ten year old child and she has been on welfare for the past year. How likely is it that she will have more children in order to get a bigger welfare check?" 0 = Not at all likely, .33 = Somewhat unlikely, .67 = Somewhat likely, 1 = Very likely. "How likely do you think it is that she will really try hard to find a job in the next year?" 0 = Not at all likely, .33 = Somewhat unlikely, .67 = Somewhat likely, 1 = Very likely. Respondents' scores for the second question are subtracted from their scores for the first question. The index is then rescaled to range from 0 (most positive perception) to 1 (most negative). Cronbach's alpha reliability coefficient for this scale is .61.

Question Wording and Response Coding for Questions from the National Race and Politics Study (text figure 4.3)

Opposition to welfare spending: see "Welfare spending" in section above.

Government should help the poor by giving them money: "When people can't support themselves, the government should help by giving them enough money to meet their basic needs." 0 = Agree strongly, .33 = Agree somewhat, .67 = Disagree somewhat, 1 = Disagree strongly.

Most people on welfare would rather be working: see "Perception of welfare recipients as undeserving" above.

Welfare costs too much: "The high cost of welfare puts too big a burden on the average taxpayer." 0 = Disagree strongly, .33 = Disagree somewhat, .67 = Agree somewhat, 1 = Agree strongly.

Table A.5 Predictors of Opposition to Welfare Spending (results from this table are summarized in table 4.1)

	Regression Coefficient	Standard Error	Standardized Regression Coefficient	P Value
First regression model ($R^2 = .01$)				
Age	16.4	5.6	.09	.003
Sex	−1.6	2.5	−.02	.51
Region	1.1	3.1	.01	.71
Second regression model ($R^2 = .03$)				
Age	11.4	5.7	.06	.04
Sex	−1.4	2.5	−.02	.56
Region	0.4	3.1	.00	.88
Education	−7.7	5.4	−.05	.15
Marital status	10.5	2.6	.13	.001
Third regression model ($R^2 = .04$)				
Age	13.1	5.7	.07	.02
Sex	−0.8	2.5	−.01	.74
Region	1.1	3.0	.01	.71
Education	−13.5	5.7	−.08	.02
Marital status	8.4	2.7	.10	.002
Family income	13.9	4.5	.11	.002
Fourth regression model ($R^2 = .09$)				
Age	12.7	5.7	.07	.03
Sex	0.5	2.4	.01	.84
Region	−1.2	3.0	−.01	.69
Education	−10.8	5.6	−.06	.06
Marital status	7.0	2.6	.09	.01
Family income	11.8	4.4	.09	.01
Liberal/conservative ideology	18.0	4.8	.13	.001
Party identification	14.1	3.8	.12	.001
Individualism	15.5	4.2	.11	.001
Fifth regression model ($R^2 = .13$)				
Age	10.8	5.6	.06	.06
Sex	0.4	2.4	.01	.85
Region	−3.1	2.9	−.03	.30
Education	−5.2	5.5	−.03	.35
Marital status	6.4	2.6	.08	.02
Family income	12.6	4.3	.10	.004
Liberal/conservative ideology	15.8	4.7	.11	.001
Party identification	13.0	3.7	.11	.001
Individualism	15.0	4.2	.11	.001
Perception of blacks as lazy	40.0	6.6	.19	.001

(continued)

Table A.5 (Continued)

	Regression Coefficient	Standard Error	Standardized Regression Coefficient	P Value
Sixth regression model (R² = .18)				
Age	18.3	5.5	.10	.001
Sex	0.8	2.3	.01	.73
Region	−4.3	2.9	−.04	.13
Education	0.1	5.4	.00	.98
Marital status	5.5	2.5	.07	.03
Family income	13.0	4.2	.10	.003
Liberal/conservative ideology	12.9	4.6	.09	.005
Party identification	11.0	3.6	.10	.003
Individualism	10.4	4.1	.08	.02
Perception of blacks as lazy	23.7	6.7	.11	.001
Perception of welfare recipients as undeserving	41.7	5.4	.25	.001

Source: National Race and Politics Study, 1991. $N = 996$ for all equations.

Notes: Dependent variable is scored 0, 50, or 100 for increase, maintain, or decrease welfare spending. All predictors are scored from 0 to 1, with high scores for female, southerner, married, conservative, and Republican. Analyses include nonblack respondents only.

Most people on welfare could get by without it: see "Perception of welfare recipients as undeserving" above.

Lazy welfare recipients make me angry: "Now I'll read a list of problems facing the country. As I read each one, please use a number from zero to ten to tell me how angry it makes you. If something doesn't bother you at all, give it a zero. On the other hand, if the situation makes you extremely angry or upset, give it a ten. (Feel free to use any number between zero and ten, but remember, the more something angers or upsets you, the higher the number you should give it.) . . . How about: A man who collects welfare because he is too lazy to get a job?" Responses are rescored to range from 0 (least angry) to 1 (most angry).

People are poor because they don't try hard enough: "What do you think makes most poor people poor? Most of them are poor because . . ." 0 = They don't get the training and education they need; 1 = They don't try hard enough to get ahead; .5 = Both statements are wrong.

Most people who don't succeed in life are lazy: "Most people who don't succeed in life are just plain lazy." 0 = Disagree strongly, .33 = Disagree somewhat, .67 = Agree somewhat, 1 = Agree strongly.

Table A.6 Predictors of the Perception That Welfare Recipients Are Undeserving (results from this table are summarized in table 4.2)

	Regression Coefficient	Standard Error	Standardized Regression Coefficient	P Value
First regression model ($R^2 = .02$)				
Age	−11.0	3.3	−.10	.001
Sex	−1.0	1.5	−.02	.51
Region	6.4	1.8	.11	.001
Second regression model ($R^2 = .06$)				
Age	−15.0	3.3	−.14	.001
Sex	−1.5	1.4	−.03	.31
Region	6.1	1.8	.11	.001
Education	−20.4	3.2	−.20	.001
Marital status	3.3	1.5	.07	.04
Third regression model ($R^2 = .06$)				
Age	−15.0	3.4	−.14	.001
Sex	−1.5	1.5	−.03	.30
Region	6.1	1.8	.10	.001
Education	−20.1	3.4	−.20	.001
Marital status	3.3	1.6	.07	.04
Family income	−0.5	2.7	−.01	.84
Fourth regression model ($R^2 = .11$)				
Age	−16.2	3.4	−.15	.001
Sex	−0.8	1.4	−.02	.56
Region	4.7	1.8	.08	.01
Education	−18.3	3.3	−.18	.001
Marital status	2.7	1.6	.06	.08
Family income	−1.8	2.6	−.02	.50
Liberal/conservative ideology	9.0	2.8	.11	.002
Party identification	5.8	2.2	.08	.01
Individualism	11.6	2.5	.14	.001
Fifth regression model ($R^2 = .20$)				
Age	−18.1	3.2	−.17	.001
Sex	−0.9	1.4	−.02	.52
Region	2.9	1.7	.05	.09
Education	−12.9	3.2	−.13	.001
Marital status	2.1	1.5	.04	.15
Family income	−1.0	2.5	−.01	.69
Liberal/conservative ideology	6.9	2.7	.08	.01
Party identification	4.7	2.1	.07	.03
Individualism	11.1	2.4	.14	.001
Perception of blacks as lazy	39.1	3.8	.31	.001

Source: National Race and Politics Study, 1991. $N = 996$ for all equations.

Notes: Dependent variable is scored 0, 50, or 100 for increase, maintain, or decrease welfare spending. All predictors are scored from 0 to 1, with high scores for female, southerner, married, conservative, and Republican. Analyses include nonblack respondents only.

Table A.7 Predictors of the Perception That Blacks Are Lazy (results from this table are summarized in table 4.2)

	Regression Coefficient	Standard Error	Standardized Regression Coefficient	P Value
First regression model (R^2 = .02)				
Age	7.5	2.6	.09	.004
Sex	0.3	1.2	.01	.79
Region	5.4	1.4	.12	.001
Second regression model (R^2 = .06)				
Age	4.9	2.6	.06	.06
Sex	0.0	1.1	.00	.94
Region	5.3	1.4	.12	.001
Education	−15.0	2.5	−.19	.001
Marital status	1.7	1.2	.04	.17
Third regression model (R^2 = .06)				
Age	4.7	2.6	.06	.08
Sex	−0.2	1.1	−.00	.89
Region	5.2	1.4	.11	.001
Education	−14.3	2.6	−.18	.001
Marital status	1.9	1.3	.05	.13
Family income	−1.7	2.1	−.03	.43
Fourth regression model (R^2 = .07)				
Age	4.8	2.7	.06	.08
Sex	0.1	1.1	.00	.91
Region	4.7	1.4	.10	.001
Education	−13.8	2.6	−.17	.001
Marital status	1.5	1.3	.04	.24
Family income	−1.9	2.1	−.03	.36
Liberal/conservative ideology	5.4	2.3	.08	.02
Party identification	2.8	1.8	.05	.13
Individualism	1.4	2.0	.02	.50

Source: National Race and Politics Study, 1991. N = 996 for all equations.

Notes: Dependent variable is scored 0, 50, or 100 for increase, maintain, or decrease welfare spending. All predictors are scored from 0 to 1, with high scores for female, southerner, married, conservative, and Republican. Analyses include nonblack respondents only.

The Welfare Mother Experiment (text table 4.3)

To ensure that any random differences between the two experimental groups assigned to the black and white welfare mother experiment were not wrongly attributed to the effects of the experimental treatment itself, I constrained the variance/covariance matrices for the other variables in this series of regression equations to be equal. Consequently, the regression coefficients (and associated statistics) are identical for the two experimental groups for causal levels I through IV of the analysis. Table A.8 shows these results only once, but it contains the two different sets of results for the two experimental groups for level V.

Table A.8 Predictors of Opposition to Welfare Spending: The Welfare Mother Experiment (results from this table are summarized in table 4.3)

	Regression Coefficient	Standard Error	Standardized Regression Coefficient	P Value
First regression model (R^2 = .01)				
Age	15.1	5.9	.09	.01
Sex	−0.3	2.6	−.00	.91
Region	4.7	3.0	.05	.12
Second regression model (R^2 = .02)				
Age	10.3	6.0	.06	.09
Sex	−0.2	2.6	−.00	.94
Region	3.9	3.0	.04	.20
Education	−9.0	5.5	−.06	.10
Marital status	8.4	2.7	.10	.003
Third regression model (R^2 = .03)				
Age	12.2	6.0	.07	.05
Sex	0.3	2.6	.00	.90
Region	4.2	3.0	.05	.17
Education	−14.3	5.8	−.09	.02
Marital status	6.8	2.8	.08	.02
Family income	12.3	4.8	.10	.01
Fourth regression model (R^2 = .07)				
Age	11.5	6.1	.07	.06
Sex	1.3	2.6	.02	.60
Region	2.4	3.0	.03	.43
Education	−13.2	5.8	−.08	.03
Marital status	5.0	2.8	.06	.08
Family income	11.0	4.7	.09	.02
Liberal/conservative ideology	15.1	5.0	.11	.003
Party identification	11.9	4.0	.10	.004
Individualism	11.4	4.6	.08	.02
Fifth regression model for white welfare mother (R^2 = .08)				
Age	12.0	6.0	.07	.05
Sex	1.7	2.5	.02	.50
Region	1.9	3.0	.02	.53
Education	−9.9	5.8	−.06	.09
Marital status	5.5	2.8	.07	.05
Family income	11.3	4.7	.09	.02
Liberal/conservative ideology	14.5	5.0	.10	.004
Party identification	11.6	4.0	.10	.004
Individualism	10.0	4.6	.07	.03
Negative views of white welfare mother	15.9	5.0	.11	.002

(continued)

Table A.8 (*Continued*)

	Regression Coefficient	Standard Error	Standardized Regression Coefficient	P Value
Fifth regression model for black welfare mother ($R^2 = .10$)				
Age	11.1	5.9	.06	.06
Sex	1.2	2.5	.02	.64
Region	0.0	3.0	.00	.99
Education	−9.4	5.7	−.06	.10
Marital status	4.8	2.7	.06	.08
Family income	11.3	4.6	.09	.02
Liberal/conservative ideology	13.2	4.9	.09	.01
Party identification	13.3	4.0	.12	.001
Individualism	9.6	4.5	.07	.04
Negative views of black welfare mother	30.0	5.0	.20	.001

Source: National Race and Politics Study, 1991. $N = 879$ for all equations.

Notes: Dependent variable is scored 0, 50, or 100 for increase, maintain, or decrease welfare spending. All predictors are scored from 0 to 1, with high scores for female, southerner, married, conservative, and Republican. Analyses include nonblack respondents only.

Table A.9 Accounting for the Impact of Age on Opposition to Welfare Spending (results from this table are summarized in chapter 4, under "Predicting Opposition to Welfare")

	Regression Coefficient	Standard Error	Standardized Regression Coefficient	P Value
First regression model ($R^2 = .01$)				
Age	14.6	6.6	.09	.03
Second regression model ($R^2 = .08$)				
Age	4.5	6.5	.03	.49
Welfare encourages out-of-wedlock births	10.0	2.1	.21	.001
Welfare discourages pregnant girls from marrying	6.2	2.4	.12	.01

Source: General Social Survey, 1986. $N = 608$ for both equations.

Notes: Dependent variable is scored 0, 50, or 100 for increase, maintain, or decrease welfare spending. All predictors are scored from 0 to 1. Analyses include nonblack respondents only.

Chapter Six

Perceptions of the Race of Welfare Recipients (extension of table 6.1)

The regression analyses in table A.10 apply multivariate controls to the relationships reported in table 6.1. In all cases, the dependent variables,

Table A.10 Assessing the Impact of Perceptions of the Race of Welfare Recipients with and without Multivariate Controls (extension of table 6.1)

	Regression Coefficient	Standard Error	Standardized Regression Coefficient	P Value
Q1. What is more to blame when people are on welfare, lack of effort or circumstances beyond their control?				
First regression model (R^2 = .08)				
Most welfare recipients are white/black	.28	.05	.28	.001
Second regression model (R^2 = .11)				
Most welfare recipients are white/black	.28	.05	.27	.001
Age	−.003	.001	−.14	.02
Sex	.04	.05	.04	.41
Education	−.005	.03	−.01	.85
Family income	.02	.02	.05	.34
Liberal/conservative ideology	−.05	.04	−.08	.16
Q2. Do most people on welfare want to work?				
First regression model (R^2 = .06)				
Most welfare recipients are white/black	−.26	.04	−.24	.001
Second regression model (R^2 = .08)				
Most welfare recipients are white/black	−.23	.04	−.22	.001
Age	.001	.001	.05	.20
Sex	−.004	.04	−.00	.92
Education	−.06	.02	−.12	.01
Family income	.02	.02	.04	.38
Liberal/conservative ideology	.06	.03	.08	.05
Q3. Do most people on welfare really need it?				
First regression model (R^2 = .02)				
Most welfare recipients are white/black	.14	.04	.13	.002
Second regression model (R^2 = .05)				
Most welfare recipients are white/black	.12	.04	.12	.006
Age	.002	.001	.06	.17
Sex	−.03	.04	−.03	.51
Education	.06	.02	.13	.005
Family income	−.02	.02	−.05	.22
Liberal/conservative ideology	−.07	.03	−.10	.02

Source: CBS/New York Times poll, December 1994.

Notes: Analysis limited to nonblack respondents only. N = 334, 595, and 601 for the three different sets of analyses (the first set has a smaller sample size because the question was asked of only a random half of the respondents). Variables are coded with high scores for female, conservative, most welfare recipients are white, "circumstances beyond their control," "most people on welfare don't want to work," and "most people on welfare really need it."

as well as the independent variable of interest—whether respondents think most welfare recipients are black or most welfare recipients are white—are coded from 0 to 1. In each of the three sets of analyses, the impact of racial perceptions of welfare recipients remains nearly as strong after controls are introduced in the second regression model, indicating that the relationships shown in table 6.1 are not an artifact of respondents' demographic characteristics or ideological orientations.

Chapter Seven

Alternative Stereotypes of Blacks and Opposition to Welfare Spending (text figure 7.1)

Table A.11 Alternative Stereotypes of Blacks and Opposition to Welfare Spending (results from this table are summarized in figure 7.1)

	Regression Coefficient	Standard Error	Standardized Regression Coefficient	P Value
Assessed individually				
Perception of blacks as lazy	.49	.09	.13	.000
Age	.11	.08	.04	.15
Sex	−.09	.04	−.06	.03
Region	−.04	.04	−.02	.34
Education	.33	.13	.07	.01
Family income	.19	.08	.07	.02
$N = 1{,}550, R^2 = .04$				
Perception of blacks as unintelligent	.29	.10	.07	.004
Age	.15	.08	.05	.07
Sex	−.10	.04	−.07	.02
Region	−.04	.04	−.02	.38
Education	.30	.13	.07	.02
Family income	.17	.08	.07	.03
$N = 1{,}537, R^2 = .03$				
Perception of blacks as violent	.22	.09	.06	.02
Age	.17	.08	.06	.04
Sex	−.10	.04	−.07	.02
Region	−.04	.04	−.02	.34
Education	.30	.13	.07	.02
Family income	.20	.08	.08	.01
$N = 1{,}542, R^2 = .03$				

(continued)

Table A.11 (*Continued*)

	Regression Coefficient	Standard Error	Standardized Regression Coefficient	P Value
Assessed simultaneously				
Perception of blacks as lazy	.46	.11	.13	.000
Perception of blacks as unintelligent	.03	.12	.01	.78
Perception of blacks as violent	.04	.10	.01	.73
Age	.12	.08	.04	.14
Sex	−.09	.04	−.06	.03
Region	−.04	.04	−.03	.27
Education	.34	.13	.08	.01
Family income	.18	.08	.07	.02
$N = 1,527$, $R^2 = .04$				

Source: National Election Study, 1992.

Notes: The dependent variable is scored −1, 0, or 1 for increase, maintain, or decrease welfare spending. All predictors are scored from 0 to 1, with high scores for female and southerner. Analyses include white respondents only.

Chapter Eight

Racial Attitudes and Spending Preferences for Welfare and Unemployment (text figure 8.1)

Table A.12 Racial Attitudes and Spending Preferences for Welfare and Unemployment (these analyses reflect the relationships shown in figure 8.1)

	Regression Coefficient	Standard Error	Standardized Regression Coefficient	P Value
Spending for welfare				
Blacks just need to try harder	−19.1	2.8	−.16	.001
$N = 1,786$, $R^2 = .03$				
Spending for unemployment				
Blacks just need to try harder	−5.6	2.6	−.05	.03
$N = 1,829$, $R^2 = .003$				

Source: National Election Study, 1992.

Notes: Dependent variables are scored 0, 50, or 100 for increase, maintain, or decrease welfare spending. The independent variable ranges from 0 for strongly disagree to 1 for strongly agree with the following statement: "If blacks would only try harder they could be just as well off as whites." Analyses include white respondents only.

Notes

Introduction

1. "Annual Message to Congress on the State of the Union, January 22, 1971," Richard M. Nixon, *Public Papers of the Presidents of the United States: Richard Nixon, 1971* (Washington, D.C.: GPO, 1972), p. 51.

2. "The President's News Conference of August 6, 1977," Jimmy Carter, *Public Papers of the Presidents of the United States: Jimmy Carter, 1977 (Book II—June 25 to December 31, 1977)* (Washington, D.C.: GPO, 1978), p. 1443.

3. Franklin D. Roosevelt, "Annual Message to Congress, January 4, 1935," in *The Public Papers and Addresses of Franklin D. Roosevelt,* vol. 4 (New York: Random House, 1938), p. 19.

Chapter One

1. In the United States, social spending currently accounts for 65 percent of all government spending. U.S. Bureau of the Census, *Statistical Abstract of the United States: 1997* (Washington, D.C., 1997), pp. 299, 373, tables 477 and 578. European Community data indicate that social spending represents between 51 percent and 70 percent of all government spending in Belgium, Denmark, Germany, Spain, France, Ireland, Italy, and the United Kingdom. Portugal, in which social spending accounts for 47 percent of government expenditures, is the only country of those with available data that devotes less than half of its government budget to social spending. Statistical Office of the European Communities, *General Government Accounts and Statistics: 1981–1992* (Luxembourg, 1994).

2. U.S. Bureau of the Census, *Historical Statistics of the United States* (Washington, D.C., 1960), pp. 14, 74, cited in Daniel Bell, *The Coming of Post-industrial Society: A Venture in Social Forecasting* (New York: Basic Books, 1973), p. 124.

3. Cited in Bell, *Post-industrial Society,* p. 130.

4. Arnold J. Heidenheimer, Hugh Heclo, and Carolyn Teich Adams, *Comparative Public Policy: The Politics of Social Choice in Europe and America* (New York: St. Martin's Press, 1975), p. 189.

5. Organization for Economic Cooperation and Development, *New Orientations in Social Policy,* Social Policy Studies, no. 12 (Paris: Organization for Economic Cooperation and Development, 1994), pp. 59–60; see figure 1.4 for details.

6. U.S. Bureau of the Census, *Statistical Abstract: 1997,* pp. 299, 373, tables 477 and 578.

7. Ibid., p. 373, table 578.

8. Harold L. Wilensky, *The Welfare State and Equality: Structural and Ideological Roots of Public Expenditures* (Berkeley: University of California Press, 1975), p. 5.

9. U.S. House of Representatives, *Background Material and Data on Programs within the Jurisdiction of the Committee on Ways and Means, 1996* ("1996 Green Book"), table 8-28.

10. U.S. Bureau of the Census, *Statistical Abstract: 1997*, p. 375, table 582.

11. Ibid.

12. James T. Patterson, *America's Struggle against Poverty, 1900–1994* (Cambridge: Harvard University Press, 1994), p. 68.

13. Ibid.

14. U.S. Bureau of the Census, *Statistical Abstract of the United States: 1974* (Washington, D.C., 1975), p. 297, table 471.

15. U.S. Bureau of the Census, *Historical Statistics of the United States, Colonial Times to 1970* (Washington, D.C., 1975), series H346–367, p. 356.

16. Patterson, *America's Struggle against Poverty, 1900–1994*, p. 86.

17. These figures are in constant 1997 dollars. U.S. Bureau of the Census, *Statistical Abstract of the United States: 1966* (Washington, D.C., 1967), p. 304; U.S. Bureau of the Census, *Statistical Abstract of the United States: 1977* (Washington, D.C., 1977), p. 319.

18. U.S. Bureau of the Census, *Statistical Abstract: 1966*, p. 304; U.S. Bureau of the Census, *Statistical Abstract of the United States: 1995* (Washington, D.C., 1995); U.S. Bureau of the Census, *Historical Income Tables—Families*, 1995 (http://www.census.gov/hhes/income/histinc/incfamdet.html).

19. Lyndon B. Johnson, *Public Papers of the Presidents of the United States: Lyndon B. Johnson, 1963–64*, vol. 1 (Washington D.C.: GPO, 1965), p. 112, cited in Irwin Unger, *The Best of Intentions: The Triumph and Failure of the Great Society under Kennedy, Johnson, and Nixon* (New York: Doubleday, 1996), p. 79.

20. Christopher Jencks, *Rethinking Social Policy* (Cambridge: Harvard University Press, 1992), pp. 72–73. Note that the value Jencks assigns to any given noncash benefit is not the same as the cost to the government of providing that benefit, nor the same as the cost to a poor family of acquiring that same benefit in the market. For example, private medical insurance equivalent to Medicaid would cost many thousands of dollars a year. But a Medicaid recipient cannot sell his or her Medicaid policy, or trade it for food or housing. Basing the value of a benefit on what it would cost to purchase the benefit on the market assumes, quite unrealistically, that the beneficiary would in fact make such a purchase if he or she were given the equivalent amount of cash. Since the true value of the benefit may be much less than its market value, using the market value leads to an unrealistically high adjusted income. Instead, Jencks follows the Census Bureau's approach of valuing noncash benefits based on the amount of money they save the recipient.

21. Mary Daly, "Labor Market Effects of Welfare Reform" (Federal Reserve Bank of San Francisco, Economic Letter no. 97-24, August 29, 1997).

22. Raymond Hernandez, "Most Dropped from Welfare Don't Get Jobs," *New York Times*, March 23, 1998, p. A1.

23. Daniel P. McMurrer, Isabel V. Sawhill, and Robert I. Lerman, "Welfare Reform and Opportunity in the Low-Wage Labor Market" (The Urban Institute, Opportunity in America Series, no. 5, July 1977).

24. See Greg J. Duncan, "Poverty and Social Assistance Dynamics in the United States, Canada, and Europe," in *Poverty, Inequality, and the Future of Social Policy*, ed. Katherine McFate, Roger Lawson, and William Julius Wilson (New York: Russell Sage Foundation, 1995).

25. See Siv Gustafsson, "Single Mothers in Sweden," in McFate, Lawson, and Wilson, *Poverty, Inequality, and Social Policy; The Economist*, March 12, 1994, p. 57.

26. Timothy M. Smeeding, "Briefing: Cross-National Perspectives on Trends in Child Poverty and the Effectiveness of Government Policies in Preventing Child Poverty in the 1980s" (paper presented at the George Washington University Forum, Washington, D.C.,

February 25, 1991); this paper is cited in Katherine McFate, Timothy Smeeding, and Lee Rainwater, "Markets and States: Poverty Trends and Transfer System Effectiveness in the 1980s," in McFate, Lawson, and Wilson, *Poverty, Inequality, and Social Policy*, p. 59.

27. See Lars Bjorn, "Labor Parties, Economic Growth, and Redistribution in Five Capitalist Democracies," *Comparative Social Research* 2 (1979): 93–128; Francis G. Castles, "The Impact of Parties on Public Expenditures," in *The Impact of Parties*, ed. Francis G. Castles (Beverly Hills: Sage Publications, 1982); Michael Shalev, "The Social Democratic Model and Beyond: Two Generations of Comparative Research on the Welfare State," *Comparative Social Research* 6 (1983): 315–51.

28. See Frances G. Castles, *The Working Class and Welfare: Reflections on the Political Development of the Welfare State in Australia and New Zealand* (Sydney, Australia: Allen and Unwin, 1985); Bruce Headey, "Trade Unions and National Wage Policies," *Journal of Politics* 32 (1970): 407–39; Walter Korpi, *The Democratic Class Struggle* (Boston: Routledge and Kegan Paul, 1983).

29. See William Graebner, "Federalism in the Progressive Era: A Structural Interpretation of Reform," *Journal of American History* 64 (1977): 331–57; David Brian Robertson, "The Bias of American Federalism: The Limits of Welfare-State Development in the Progressive Era," *Journal of Policy History* 1 (1989): 261–91; Theda Skocpol, *Protecting Soldiers and Mothers: The Political Origins of Social Policy in the United States* (Cambridge: Harvard University Press, 1992).

30. Louis Hartz, *The Liberal Tradition in America: An Interpretation of American Political Thought since the Revolution* (San Diego: Harcourt Brace, 1955); Anthony King, "Ideas, Institutions, and the Policies of Governments: A Comparative Analysis," *British Journal of Political Science* 3, no. 3 (1973): 291–313; Daniel Levine, *Poverty and Society: The Growth of the American Welfare State in International Comparison* (New Brunswick, N.J.: Rutgers University Press, 1988).

31. For a review of this literature see Robert Y. Shapiro and Lawrence R. Jacobs, "The Relationship between Public Opinion and Public Policy: A Review," in *Political Behavior Annual*, vol. 2, ed. Samuel Long (Boulder: Westview Press, 1989).

32. Benjamin I. Page and Robert Y. Shapiro, "Effects of Public Opinion on Policy," *American Political Science Review* 77 (March 1983): 175–90; see also Alan D. Monroe, "Consistency between Public Preferences and National Policy Decisions," *American Politics Quarterly* 7 (January 1979): 3–19; Thomas Hartley and Bruce Russett, "Public Opinion and the Common Defense: Who Governs Military Spending in the United States?" *American Political Science Review* 86, no. 4 (December 1992): 905–15; John Zaller, *The Nature and Origins of Mass Opinion* (Cambridge: Cambridge University Press, 1992).

33. See Gerald C. Wright Jr., Robert S. Erikson, and John P. McIver, "Public Opinion and Policy Liberalism in the American States," *American Journal of Political Science* 31 (1987): 980–1001. Alaska, Hawaii, and Nevada were not included in the study—Alaska and Hawaii because they were excluded from the CBS/*New York Times* polls used for the analysis, and Nevada because of a "suspect reading on the ideology measure." Ibid., p. 985.

34. Tom W. Smith, "The Welfare State in Cross-National Perspective," *Public Opinion Quarterly* 51 no. 3 (fall 1987): 417. Another survey conducted in the United States, Austria, Germany, Italy, and the United Kingdom asked whether it should be the government's responsibility to provide a job to everyone who wants one, to provide health care for the sick, to provide a decent standard of living for the old, and to provide a decent standard of living for the unemployed. Once again, Americans proved to be the least supportive of government responsibility in all four areas compared with the other four nations surveyed. See ibid., p. 416.

35. Spending preferences are only partial and imperfect measures of public support.

For one thing, they reflect not only survey respondents' positive or negative views toward a given program area, but also their perceptions of current practices. For example, a respondent might strongly support Social Security but think current spending levels are adequate and therefore say that spending should be kept as it is. The same respondent might only weakly support government financial aid for college students but feel that current levels are very low and hence say spending should be increased. We must keep in mind, therefore, that spending preferences represent respondents' evaluations of current government efforts in each programmatic area rather than some absolute judgment of the desired level of government spending. Spending preferences nevertheless remain the best available measures of public attitudes toward the various aspects of the welfare state because nearly identical questions have been asked over a long period of time about a wide range of social programs.

36. See, for example, Robert Y. Shapiro and John T. Young, "Public Opinion and the Welfare State: The United States in Comparative Perspective," *Political Science Quarterly* 104, no. 1 (spring 1989): 59–89; Theodore R. Marmor, Jerry L. Mashaw, and Philip L. Harvey, *America's Misunderstood Welfare State: Persistent Myths, Enduring Realities* (New York: Basic Books, 1990); Fay Lomax Cook and Edith J. Barrett, *Support for the American Welfare State: The Views of Congress and the Public* (New York: Columbia University Press, 1992); Benjamin I. Page and Robert Y. Shapiro, *The Rational Public: Fifty Years of Trends in Americans' Policy Preferences* (Chicago: University of Chicago Press, 1992).

37. Cook and Barrett, *Support for the American Welfare State*, pp. 24–30.

38. For example, only 20 percent of households receiving food stamps have any reported earnings from employment. U.S. House of Representatives, *Background Material and Data on Programs within the Jurisdiction of the Committee on Ways and Means, 1994* ("1994 Green Book").

39. For example, see Lloyd A. Free and Hadley Cantril, *The Political Beliefs of Americans: A Study of Public Opinion* (New York: Simon and Schuster, 1968); Stanley Feldman and John Zaller, "The Political Culture of Ambivalence: Ideological Responses to the Welfare State," *American Journal of Political Science* 36 (1992): 268–307.

Chapter Two

1. See, for example, Donald R. Kinder and Lynn M. Sanders, *Divided by Color: Racial Politics and Democratic Ideals in the American Republic* (Chicago: University of Chicago Press, 1996), p. 137; Nathan Glazer, *The Limits of Social Policy* (Cambridge: Harvard University Press, 1988), p. 190; Marmor, Mashaw, and Harvey, *America's Misunderstood Welfare State*, p. 5; Herbert McClosky and John Zaller, *The American Ethos: Public Attitudes toward Capitalism and Democracy* (Cambridge: Harvard University Press, 1984), passim.

2. Marmor, Mashaw, and Harvey, *America's Misunderstood Welfare State*, p. 240.

3. Edmund Burke, *Reflections on the Revolution in France* (1790; reprint, Garden City, N.Y.: Anchor Press, 1973), p. 109.

4. Steven Lukes, *Individualism* (New York: Harper and Row, 1973).

5. Ibid., p. 26.

6. Alexis de Tocqueville, *Democracy in America* (1835; reprint, Garden City, N.Y.: Anchor Books, 1969), pp. 506, 671.

7. Ibid., p. 508.

8. Ibid., p. 645.

9. Yehoshua Arieli, *Individualism and Nationalism in American Ideology* (Cambridge: Harvard University Press, 1964), p. 282, quoting Ralph W. Emerson, "New England Reformers," in *Complete Writings* (New York: Wm H. Wise & Co., 1929), p. 318.

10. See, for example, Hartz, *The Liberal Tradition in America*; Robin M. Williams, *Ameri-

can Society: A Sociological Interpretation (New York: Knopf, 1951); Seymour Martin Lipset, *The First New Nation: The United States in Historical and Comparative Perspective* (New York: Norton, 1979); Robert N. Bellah et al., *Habits of the Heart: Individualism and Commitment in American Life* (Berkeley: University of California Press, 1985).

11. Frederick Jackson Turner, "Significance of the Frontier in American History," in *Annual Report of the American Historical Society, 1893* (Washington, D.C.: GPO, 1894), pp. 221–27.

12. Lipset, *The First New Nation*.

13. Hartz, *The Liberal Tradition*.

14. Leo Lowenthal, "Biographies in Popular Magazines," in *Radio Research*, ed. Paul F. Lazarsfeld and Frank N. Stanton (New York: Duell, Sloan and Pearce, 1944).

15. These figures represent average length of time receiving benefits for all AFDC cases opened between 1974 and 1987. Calculated from Peter Gottschalk, Sara McLanahan, and Gary D. Sandefur, "The Dynamics and Intergenerational Transmission of Poverty and Welfare Participation," in *Confronting Poverty: Prescriptions for Change*, ed. Sheldon H. Danziger, Gary D. Sandefur, and Daniel H. Weinberg (Cambridge: Harvard University Press, 1994), p. 95.

16. Ibid., p. 96.

17. CBS/*New York Times* survey, April 1995.

18. *Los Angeles Times* poll, April 1985.

19. Both figures are from the *Los Angeles Times* poll, April 1985.

20. This figure includes options 3 and 4 (table 2.3). Of the 77 percent of respondents in this group, over one-quarter are even more generous, opting for a program that provides a decent level of living for *all* who need it, and enough supporting services to allow them to achieve their full potentials.

21. Alexander Hamilton, James Madison, and John Jay, *The Federalist Papers* (1787–88; reprint, New York: Mentor, 1961), pp. 54, 110.

22. Ibid., p. 79.

23. Thomas R. Dye, *Politics in America* (New York: Prentice Hall, 1997), p. 1.

24. Jack Citrin and Donald Philip Green, "The Self-Interest Motive in American Public Opinion," *Research in Micropolitics* 3 (1990): 1–28; see also David O. Sears and Carolyn L. Funk, "The Role of Self-Interest in Social and Political Attitudes," *Advances in Experimental Social Psychology* 24 (1991): 1–91.

25. Citrin and Green, "The Self-Interest Motive," p. 14.

26. Angus Campbell et al., *The American Voter* (Chicago: University of Chicago Press, 1960), p. 205.

27. See Philip Arthur AuClaire, "Public Attitudes toward Social Welfare Expenditures," *Social Work* 29 (1984): 139–44; Cook and Barrett, *Support for the American Welfare State*; Richard M. Coughlin, "Social Policy and Ideology: Public Opinion in Eight Nations," *Comparative Social Research* 2 (1979): 3–40; Richard T. Curtin and Charles D. Cowan, "Public Attitudes toward Fiscal Programs," in *1972–1973 Surveys of Consumers*, ed. Burkhard Strumpel (Ann Arbor: University of Michigan, Institute for Social Research, 1975); Joe R. Feagin, "America's Welfare Stereotypes," *Social Science Quarterly* 52 (1972): 921–33; Joe R. Feagin, *Subordinating the Poor: Welfare and American Beliefs* (Englewood Cliffs, N.J.: Prentice-Hall, 1975); Yeheskel Hasenfeld and Jane A. Rafferty, "The Determinants of Public Attitudes toward the Welfare State," *Social Forces* 67 (1989): 1027–48; James R. Kluegel and Eliot R. Smith, *Beliefs about Inequality: Americans' Views of What Is and What Ought to Be* (New York: Aldine de Gruyter, 1986); Shapiro and Young, "Public Opinion and the Welfare State"; John B. Williamson, "Beliefs about the Motivation of the Poor and Attitudes toward Poverty Policy," *Social Problems* 21 (1974): 634–48.

28. Theda Skocpol, "Targeting within Universalism," in *The Urban Underclass*, ed. Christopher Jencks and Paul E. Peterson (Washington, D.C.: Brookings Institution, 1991), p. 432.

29. Robert Greenstein, "Universal and Targeted Approaches to Relieving Poverty: An Alternative View," in Jencks and Peterson, *The Urban Underclass*.

30. Mary R. Jackman and Robert W. Jackman, *Class Awareness in the United States* (Berkeley: University of California Press, 1983).

31. CBS/*New York Times* survey, October 15–18, 1991.

32. Times Mirror survey, "People, the Press, and Politics on the Eve of '92," October 31– November 10, 1991.

33. Times Mirror poll, October 25–30, 1995.

34. Cook and Barrett, *Support for the American Welfare State*, p. 62.

35. Although only poor people are eligible for Medicaid, one important group of Medicaid beneficiaries consists of the formerly nonpoor who have exhausted their financial resources and rely on Medicaid to pay for nursing-home care. To the extent that members of the middle class fear that they (or their parents) may one day belong to this group of Medicaid recipients, an element of self-interest may be involved in middle-class support for Medicaid. Nevertheless, only 5 percent of Medicaid recipients are nursing-home patients, and some portion of these were never members of the middle class. U.S. Bureau of the Census, *Statistical Abstract: 1995*, p. 116, table 166.

36. *Los Angeles Times* poll, January 19–22, 1995.

37. Lester Thurow, "Recession Plus Inflation Spells Stasis," *Christianity and Crisis* 41, no. 5 (March 30, 1981): 91–92.

38. U.S. Bureau of the Census, *Statistical Abstract of the United States: 1993* (Washington, D.C., 1993), p. 445, table 696.

39. Marmor, Mashaw, and Harvey, *America's Misunderstood Welfare State*, p. 85.

40. Michael Katz, *The Undeserving Poor: From the War on Poverty to the War on Welfare* (New York: Pantheon Books, 1989), p. 138.

41. William Julius Wilson, *The Truly Disadvantaged: The Inner City, the Underclass, and Public Policy* (Chicago: University of Chicago Press, 1987), p. 120.

42. The statistical test of the relationship shown in figure 2.1 consists of the regression of welfare spending preferences on (1) change in per capita GDP and (2) a dummy variable for the years 1983 through 1988 (see discussion of the mid-1980s in the text). An initial Durbin-Watson statistic of .54 suggested first-order autocorrelation of the errors, so a maximum likelihood (AR1) transformation was applied to the data. The resulting regression coefficients were 2.4 for GDP (s.e. $= .61; p < .001$) and -13.1 for the mid-1980s dummy variable (s.e. $= 5.3; p < .02$). The simple correlation of welfare spending preferences with GDP is .31 ($p = .15$); the partial correlation while controlling for the mid-1980s dummy is .55 ($p < .01$).

43. As measured by per capita GDP in constant dollars. U.S. Bureau of the Census, *Statistical Abstract: 1993*, p. 445, table 696.

44. On the growth of inequality in the 1980s, see Kevin Phillips, *The Politics of Rich and Poor: Wealth and the American Electorate in the Reagan Aftermath* (New York: Harper Collins, 1990) and Sheldon Danziger and Peter Gottschalk, *America Unequal* (Cambridge: Harvard University Press, 1995).

45. These data are from a 1984 survey of residents of South Bend, Indiana; for details see Diana C. Mutz and Jeffery J. Mondak, "Dimensions of Sociotropic Behavior: Group-Based Judgments of Fairness and Well-Being" (paper presented at the annual meeting of the Midwest Political Science Association, Chicago, April 6–8, 1995); Robert Huckfeldt and John Sprague, *Citizens, Politics, and Social Communication: Information and Influence in an Election Campaign* (New York: Cambridge University Press, 1995). The pattern of results

shown in figure 2.3 is consistent with a more limited set of questions from the University of Michigan's 1994 National Election Study, which is based on a nationwide sample of respondents. Warren E. Miller, *American National Election Study, 1984* [machine readable data file] (Ann Arbor: University of Michigan, Institute for Social Research, 1986).

46. Page and Shapiro, *The Rational Public*, p. 319.

47. The independent variable in this analysis is annual percent change in GDP measured in constant dollars; the dependent variable is the proportion of respondents saying welfare spending should be cut minus the proportion saying spending should be increased. Data from General Social Survey, Roper surveys, and CBS/*New York Times* survey (see figure 2.1 for details).

48. Based on self-reports from the General Social Survey. This question was asked on the 1987 General Social Survey; 1986 family income was converted into 1995 dollars.

49. *Los Angeles Times* poll, April 1985.

50. The asterisks in table 2.4 (and in tables elsewhere in the book) indicate the probability that the relationship observed in this particular survey sample does not exist in the population as a whole and appears in the survey data only because of the random error inherent in using a limited size sample to generalize to a larger population. Following convention, a single asterisk indicates a probability of less than five percent (expressed as "$p < .05$") that the observed relationship is due solely to chance. Similarly, two asterisks indicate that there is less than a one percent chance that the observed relationship is a fluke caused by sampling error, while three asterisks indicate that the likelihood of this is less than one-tenth of one percent. Note that these probabilities do not mean that the strength of the relationship is likely to be exactly the same among the whole population of American adults as it is in our sample, only that some relationship is very likely to exist and that the relationship is in the same direction as that found among the sample (for example, that those with higher incomes are more likely to believe that there are jobs available for anyone who is willing to work).

51. CBS/*New York Times* survey, December 6–9, 1994.

52. Of course, not everyone with a family income over $50,000 feels financially secure. For the most part, however, financial insecurity among Americans in this income bracket reflects a fear of downward mobility or income erosion that stops far short of the level of destitution at which one becomes eligible for welfare. The most significant exception to this generalization might be found among women with little work experience who would be hard pressed to support themselves (or themselves and their children) in the event of a divorce. Yet the impact of both family income and past welfare receipt is nearly identical for men and women, suggesting again that these factors influence welfare spending preferences because they reflect different sets of attitudes and experiences, not different calculations of economic self-interest.

53. Frances Fox Piven and Richard A. Cloward, *Regulating the Poor: The Functions of Public Welfare* (New York: Vintage, 1971), p. 35.

Chapter Three

1. The first of these figures is from the Times Mirror poll, June 1994; the second, from the Center for the Study of Policy Attitudes survey, October 1994. Both are cited in Steven Kull, *Fighting Poverty in America: A Study of American Public Attitudes* (Washington, D.C.: Center for the Study of Policy Attitudes, 1994).

2. Kull, *Fighting Poverty in America*, p. 8.

3. National Race and Politics Study, 1991. See chapter 4 for details.

4. *Los Angeles Times* poll, April 1985.

5. Beliefs about Social Stratification Survey, 1980; see Kluegel and Smith, *Beliefs about Inequality*, p. 153.

6. Time/CNN poll, conducted by Yankelovich/Clancy/Shulman, March 11–12, 1992.

7. These results are from the Indiana poll no. 15 (May 1990), conducted by the Indiana University Survey Center. Half of the respondents were asked, "As you probably know, poverty in America is a big problem. Some people in New York City are thinking of changing welfare programs so that welfare payments are linked to the cost of living. That way, if the cost of food, clothing and housing goes up, welfare payments will go up by the same amount. What do you think about New York City's plan? Are you strongly in favor of such a plan, somewhat in favor, somewhat opposed or strongly opposed to such a plan?" The other half of the respondents were asked the identical question except that Anchorage, Alaska, was substituted for New York City. These two versions did not produce significantly different results.

8. Harris poll no. 2621, February 1976.

9. In one survey respondents were asked whether they would support an additional one-cent-a-dollar sales tax to be used to help the poor. Fifty-seven percent of the sample said they would support such a tax, 40 percent were unsure, and only 3 percent said they opposed the tax. *Los Angeles Times* poll, April 1985.

10. In fact unemployment insurance is available only to workers laid off from a job, not those who quit or are fired for cause.

11. Katz, *The Undeserving Poor*, p. 13.

12. Ibid., pp. 5, 10.

13. Bob von Sternberg, "How Do You Solve Urban Poverty?" *Minneapolis/St. Paul Star Tribune*, October 27, 1996, p. 1A.

14. In 1993, 9.4 percent of white families and 31.3 percent of black families were poor. U.S. Bureau of the Census, *Statistical Abstract: 1995*, p. 484.

15. This figure is for 1995. Calculated from U.S. Bureau of the Census, *Statistical Abstract: 1995*, p. 18, and Steven A. Holmes, "U.S. Census Finds First Income Rise in Past Six Years," *New York Times*, September 27, 1996, p. A1.

16. National Race and Politics Study, 1991. See chapter 4 for details.

17. CBS/*New York Times* survey, 1994. Comparing public perceptions of the race of the poor with Census Bureau statistics suggests that African Americans have come to dominate public perceptions of the poor to a degree unjustified by the realities of American poverty. But comparing public perceptions with government statistics implies that a well-informed public ought to share the Census Bureau's understanding of the racial makeup of the poor. This follows, however, only if the public holds at least a roughly compatible understanding of who is to be included among the poor. Because poor blacks tend to be poorer than poor whites, a lower poverty line (the level of family income below which one is considered poor) would result in a higher proportion of African Americans among the poor, while a higher poverty line would result in a lower proportion of blacks. Thus if the public has a lower implicit poverty threshold than the government's official poverty line, public perceptions of the racial composition of the poor may not be as inaccurate as would otherwise appear to be the case. That is, if the public considers only the poorest of the "official poor" to be properly called poor, then their belief that half the poor are black would be less inaccurate. (The difference in the percentage black based on different poverty lines is not as great as one might expect, however. In 1993, for example, 26 percent of families with incomes below $15,000 (the approximate poverty level for a family of four) were black. In contrast, 32 percent of families with incomes below $10,000 were black, as were 36 percent of the very poorest families—those with money income of less than $5,000.)

All evidence, however, suggests that the public would count *more* of the population as poor than the government's poverty line would reflect (and consequently, the proportion of blacks would be even lower than the official figures indicate). When a recent survey informed respondents that the official poverty line for a family of four is now about $15,000 a year, 58 percent of respondents said the poverty line should be set higher, and only 7 percent said it should be set lower. (Fighting Poverty in America survey, 1994). When asked in another survey what the level of income should be below which a family of four could be considered poor, participants gave a median response that was about 15 percent higher than the official poverty line for a four-person family. (General Social Survey, 1993). Clearly, the discrepancy between the public's perception that half or more of poor people are black and the government's estimate of 29 percent cannot be attributed to different understandings of the meaning of "poor."

18. Data on poverty among Asian subgroups can be found on the *Asian & Pacific Islander American Health Forum* web site (http://www.igc.apc.org/apiahf/cenpa.html).

19. CBS News survey, October 1996.

20. The Census Bureau projects that the number of Hispanic Americans will surpass the number of African Americans sometime around 2010, and the proportion of black and Hispanic Americans who are poor is now about equal (U.S. Bureau of the Census, *Statistical Abstract: 1995*, p. 14; U.S. Bureau of the Census, *Statistical Abstract: 1997*, p. 476). These demographic changes may lead to changes in how Americans think about poverty and welfare, but as we will see in chapter 5, the connection between demographic realities and perceptions of the poor is a very loose one indeed.

21. See, for example, Richard A. Apostle et al., *The Anatomy of Racial Attitudes* (Berkeley: University of California Press, 1993); Lawrence Bobo, "Whites' Opposition to Busing: Symbolic Racism or Realistic Group Conflict?" *Journal of Personality and Social Psychology* 45 (1983): 1196–1210; John J. Woodmansee and Stuart W. Cook, "Dimensions of Verbal Racial Attitudes: Their Identification and Measurement," *Journal of Personality and Social Psychology* 7 (1967): 240–50; Lawrence Bobo and James R. Kluegel, "Opposition to Race-Targeting: Self-Interest, Stratification Ideology, or Racial Attitudes?" *American Sociological Review* 58 (1993): 443–64; Howard Schuman, Charlotte Steeh, and Lawrence Bobo, *Racial Attitudes in America: Trends and Interpretations* (Cambridge: Harvard University Press, 1985); David O. Sears, "Symbolic Racism," in *Eliminating Racism: Means and Controversies*, ed. Phyllis A. Katz and Dalmas A. Taylor (New York: Plenum, 1988); Paul M. Sniderman and Michael Gray Hagen, *Race and Inequality: A Study in American Values* (Chatham, N.J.: Chatham House, 1985).

22. The 1986 NES was a national, in-person survey conducted by the Center for Political Studies at the University of Michigan. See Warren E. Miller, *American National Election Study, 1986* (Ann Arbor: Inter-university Consortium for Political and Social Research, 1987). It included 2176 completed interviews and had a response rate of 67.7 percent. The survey used a split-ballot design, and most of the data analysis in this chapter is based on the "Form B" respondents only ("Form A" did not include most of the racial-attitude items of interest in this analysis).

23. On this point see Paul M. Sniderman et al., "A Test of Alternative Interpretations of the Contemporary Politics of Race: A Critical Examination of *Divided by Color*" (paper prepared at the annual meeting of the Midwest Political Science Association, Chicago, 1997); David O. Sears, Colette van Laar, and Mary Carrillo, "Is It Really Racism? The Origins of White Americans' Opposition to Race-Targeted Policies," *Public Opinion Quarterly* 61, no. 1 (spring 1997): 16–53.

24. For studies of black Americans' welfare attitudes see Lee Sigelman and Susan Welch, *Black Americans' Views of Racial Inequality: The Dream Deferred* (Cambridge: Cambridge University Press, 1991); Franklin D. Gilliam Jr. and Kenny J. Whitby, "Race, Class and Attitudes toward Social Welfare Spending: An Ethclass Interpretation," *Social Science Quarterly* 70, no. 1 (March 1989): 88–100.

25. These figures are based on combined data from the 1988 through 1994 General Social Surveys.

26. On attribution theory see Fritz Heider, *The Psychology of Interpersonal Relations* (New York: Wiley, 1958); Edward E. Jones and Keith E. Davis, "From Acts to Dispositions: The Attribution Process in Person Perception," in *Advances in Experimental Social Psychology*, vol. 7, ed. Leonard Berkowitz (New York: Academic Press, 1965). On the application of this theory to the study of public attitudes toward poverty see Lawrence Bobo and Ryan A. Smith, "Antipoverty Policy, Affirmative Action, and Racial Attitudes," in *Confronting Poverty: Prescriptions for Change*, ed. Sheldon H. Danziger, Gary D. Sandefur, and Daniel H. Weinberg (Cambridge: Harvard University Press, 1994); Feagin, *Subordinating the Poor*; Kluegel and Smith, *Beliefs about Inequality*; Thomas E. Nelson and Rosalee A. Clawson, "Poverty Attribution, Issue Framing, and Welfare Reform Opinion" (paper presented at the annual meeting of the American Political Science Association, San Francisco, August 29–September 1, 1996).

27. See George W. Stocking, *Race, Culture, and Evolution: Essays in the History of Anthropology* (New York: Free Press, 1968) on the history of biological racism.

28. Factor analysis indicates that these two questions—that blacks come from a less able race, and that God made the races different—tap a single underlying orientation and that respondents who agree with one of these statements are more likely to agree with the other (Martin Gilens, "Racial Attitudes and Opposition to Welfare," *Journal of Politics* 57, no. 4 [November 1995]: 994–1014). Nevertheless, the question about God is somewhat ambiguous with regard to the innate characteristics of blacks. In particular, some respondents might believe that God "made the races different" in a social rather than biological sense. That is, that God gave blacks a less desired position in society but that this racial inequality is not due to biological differences between blacks and whites.

29. On the nature of stereotypes see Daniel Bar-Tal et al., eds., *Stereotyping and Prejudice: Changing Conceptions* (New York: Springer-Verlag, 1989); James L. Hilton and William von Hippel, "Stereotypes," in *Annual Review of Psychology*, ed. Janet T. Spence, John M. Darley, and Donald J. Foss (Palo Alto, Calif.: Annual Reviews, 1996).

30. The argument that affective and cognitive elements of group orientations are distinct does not imply that they are unrelated, only that they are not determinative of one another. This implies that negative cognitions can exist alongside positive affect and vice versa, and that changes in cognitions may or may not be accompanied by congruent changes in affect. For discussion of the relationship between affect and cognition in social perception see Susan T. Fiske and Mark A. Pavelchak, "Category-Based versus Piecemeal-Based Affective Responses: Developments in Schema-Triggered Affect," in *Handbook of Motivation and Cognition*, ed. Richard M. Sorrentino and E. Tory Higgins (New York: Guilford, 1986); Klaus Fiedler and Joseph Forgas, eds., *Affect, Cognition, and Social Behavior: New Evidence and Integrative Attempts* (Toronto: C. J. Hogrefe, 1988); Joseph Forgas and Stephanie J. Moylan, "Affective Influences on Stereotype Judgments," *Cognition and Emotion* 5 (1991): 379–95.

Chapter Four

1. The National Race and Politics Study was directed by Paul M. Sniderman, Philip E. Tetlock, and Thomas Piazza, with support from the National Science Foundation (grant SES-8508937). Data were collected between February and November of 1991, using a two-phase sampling procedure based on area code and telephone prefix combinations from AT&T Bellcore tapes (for a discussion of the sampling methodology used in the survey see R. J. Casady and J. M. Lepkowski, "Optimal Allocation for Stratified Telephone Survey Designs," in *Proceedings of the Section on Survey Research Methods, American Statistical Association*, 1991). The NRPS produced 2,223 completed interviews with adult Americans

from the 48 contiguous states. The response rate for the survey was 65.3 percent. Respondents who completed the telephone interview were asked whether they would also be willing to complete a brief questionnaire sent in the mail. Of those respondents who completed telephone interviews, 1,942 were sent the mail-back questionnaire, and 1,198 actually completed and returned it.

In most respects both the full telephone sample and the mail-back subsample closely resemble the U.S. population. The raw survey data for both samples show, however, that women and young people are slightly underrepresented and those with no college education are substantially underrepresented. In both samples, the median income is slightly higher than that of the U.S. population. The Survey Research Center constructed sample weights reflecting the number of eligible adults in each household, the number of telephone numbers in each household, and respondents' sex, race, age, and education. The weighted data (used for all analyses of the NRPS) closely match the U.S. population in all respects. For a comparison of sample and population data, see Martin Gilens, " 'Race Coding' and White Opposition to Welfare," *American Political Science Review* 90, no. 3 (September 1996): 593–604.

2. Paul M. Sniderman and Edward G. Carmines, *Reaching Beyond Race* (Cambridge: Harvard University Press, 1997); Jon Hurwitz and Mark Peffley, *Perception and Prejudice: Race and Politics in the United States* (New Haven: Yale University Press, 1998). See also Paul M. Sniderman and Douglas B. Grob, "Innovations in Experimental Design in Attitude Surveys," *Annual Review of Sociology* 22 (1996): 377–99; Paul M. Sniderman et al., "Beyond Race: Social Justice as a Race Neutral Ideal," *American Journal of Political Science* 40, no. 1 (February 1996): 33–55; Martin Gilens, " 'Race Coding' and White Opposition to Welfare," *American Political Science Review* 90, no. 3 (September 1996): 593–604; Mark Peffley, Jon Hurwitz, and Paul M. Sniderman, "Racial Stereotypes and Whites' Political Views of Blacks in the Context of Welfare and Crime," *American Journal of Political Science* 41, no. 1 (January 1997): 30–60; James H. Kuklinski et al., "Racial Prejudice and Attitudes toward Affirmative Action," *American Journal of Political Science* 41, no. 2 (April 1997): 402–19; James H. Kuklinski, Michael D. Cobb, and Martin Gilens, "Racial Attitudes and the 'New South,' " *Journal of Politics* 59, no. 2 (May 1997): 323–49; Martin Gilens, Paul M. Sniderman, and James H. Kuklinski, "Affirmative Action and the Politics of Realignment," *British Journal of Political Science* 28, no. 1 (January 1998): 159–83.

3. For example, see Campbell et al., *The American Voter;* Michael M. Gant and Norman R. Luttbeg, "The Cognitive Utility of Partisanship," *Western Political Quarterly* 40 (September 1987): 499–518; Zaller, *Mass Opinion.*

4. See Bernard R. Berelson, Paul F. Lazarsfeld, and William N. McPhee, *Voting: A Study of Opinion Formation in a Presidential Campaign* (Chicago: University of Chicago Press, 1954).

5. See Cook and Barrett, *Support for the American Welfare State.*

6. See ibid.

7. See, for example, Martin Gilens, "The Gender Gap: Psychology, Social Structure, and Support for Reagan," *Berkeley Journal of Sociology* 29 (1984): 35–56; Mark Schlesinger and Caroline Heldman, "In a Different Choice?" (1997); Robert Y. Shapiro and Harpreet Mahajan, "Gender Differences in Policy Preferences: A Summary of Trends from the 1960s to the 1980s," *Public Opinion Quarterly* 50, no. 1 (spring 1986): 42–61.

8. See James M. Glaser and Martin Gilens, "Interregional Migration and Political Resocialization: A Study of Racial Attitudes under Pressure," *Public Opinion Quarterly* 61, no. 1 (spring 1997): 72–86; Kuklinski, Cobb, and Gilens, "Racial Attitudes and the 'New South' "; John Shelton Reed, *The Enduring South: Subcultural Persistence in Mass Society* (Chapel Hill: University of North Carolina Press, 1986).

9. On the stability of partisan identification see Donald Philip Green and Bradley Palm-

quist, "Of Artifacts and Partisan Instability," *American Journal of Political Science* 34 (1990): 871–902.

10. Edward G. Carmines and James A. Stimson, *Issue Evolution: Race and the Transformation of American Politics* (Princeton: Princeton University Press, 1989); Thomas Byrne Edsall and Mary D. Edsall, *Chain Reaction: The Impact of Race, Rights, and Taxes on American Politics* (New York: W. W. Norton, 1991).

11. Although it is not statistically distinguishable from zero, the estimated indirect impact of age in table 4.1 is slightly negative. This suggests that, were it not for differences in the more causally proximate variables in the model, older Americans would be even more opposed to welfare than we observe them to be (in other words, the direct effect of age is even larger—though very slightly—than its total effect).

12. Cook and Barrett use three variables to measure support for AFDC: respondents' satisfaction with tax dollars paying for AFDC, their willingness to write a letter opposing cutbacks in AFDC, and their willingness to pay higher taxes to avoid cutbacks in AFDC. *Support for the American Welfare State*, p. 196. They find that perceptions of recipient deservingness and program effectiveness are both significant predictors, as are current status as an AFDC recipient, party identification, and liberal/conservative orientation. Cook and Barrett's model lacks many of the predictors in my models, and my analysis lacks a measure of program effectiveness, which theirs includes. Insofar as our models overlap, however, they produce consistent findings. Cook and Barrett's measure of program effectiveness focuses on perceptions that AFDC creates dependency among its recipients, and they find this measure to be strongly correlated to their measure of recipient deservingness. Thus there is some reason to believe that similar perceptions of welfare and dependency may be reflected in my measure of welfare recipient deservingness.

13. Kluegel and Smith combine welfare spending preferences and perceptions of welfare recipients into a single dependent variable (*Beliefs about Inequality*, p. 160). Consistent with the results reported here, they find that racial attitudes and explanations for poverty are the most powerful predictors of their welfare attitudes measure. In particular, they find that support for welfare is highest among respondents who attribute poverty to structural factors such as low wages and a lack of jobs and lowest among those who attribute poverty to individual failings such as lack of effort or lack of thrift among the poor. These measures are broader than my indicator of whether welfare recipients are deserving, but they clearly tap into the same underlying judgments about the work ethic of the poor.

14. See Schuman, Steeh, and Bobo, *Racial Attitudes in America;* Glenn Firebaugh and Kenneth E. Davis, "Trends in Antiblack Prejudice, 1972–1984: Region and Cohort Effects," *American Journal of Sociology* 94, no. 2 (September 1988): 251–72.

15. For a discussion of the social desirability and consistency pressures that operate within the interview setting, see Howard Schuman and Stanley Presser, *Questions and Answers in Attitude Surveys* (San Diego: Academic Press, 1981).

16. See Thomas Piazza, Paul M. Sniderman, and Philip E. Tetlock, "Analysis of the Dynamics of Political Reasoning: A General-Purpose Computer-Assisted Methodology," in *Political Analysis*, ed. James A. Stimson (Ann Arbor: University of Michigan Press, 1989).

17. In addition, the hypothetical welfare mother is described to one random subsample as a high school graduate and to the other random subsample as a high school dropout. This experimental manipulation is orthogonal to the race of the hypothetical welfare mother, so that one-quarter of the respondents receive the "black dropout" version, one-quarter the "black graduate" version, one-quarter the "white dropout" version, and one-quarter the "white graduate" version. For the analyses in this chapter, the two educational variations are combined.

18. Cronbach's alpha for the welfare mother index is .61. Although the impact of whites'

responses to the black and white versions of the welfare mother questions differ dramatically (see below), the proportions of respondents with positive and negative perceptions hardly differ at all for the two different versions. For example, 70 percent of white respondents said that the hypothetical white welfare mother was likely to have more children in order to get a bigger welfare check while 66 percent thought this was true for the hypothetical black welfare mother. In evaluating this similarity of responses, it must be kept in mind that the hypothetical welfare mothers were described identically and in considerable detail with regard to age, education, number of children, and length of time on welfare. If respondents believe that these characteristics differ between real black and white welfare recipients (as indeed they do), they might hold more negative perceptions of what they believe to be a typical black welfare recipient than a typical white welfare recipient.

19. Although randomized assignment to experimental treatment groups (in this case the black and white versions of the welfare mother experiment) is used to ensure that respondents assigned to each group are as similar as possible in every way, some differences between randomly constructed groups are likely to emerge in any finite size sample. To decrease the likelihood that such randomly occurring differences between the experimental groups are responsible for the observed differences between the black and white welfare mother questions, the variance/covariance matrices of the other variables included in the analyses reported in table 4.3 are constrained to be equal for the two experimental groups. Consequently, the total effects of all predictor variables other than the welfare mother questions are identical for the two groups of respondents. Computationally, this is equivalent to estimating a single regression equation with an interaction term between attitudes toward welfare mothers and the random assignment to the black or white welfare mother condition. See appendix table A.8 for the full regression results from these analyses.

20. The only difference arises from the fact that the analysis in table 4.1 relied on some questions from the mail-back portion of the NRPS, which had fewer respondents.

21. U.S. House of Representatives, 1996 Green Book, table 8-28.

Chapter 5

1. U.S. Bureau of the Census, *Statistical Abstract: 1997*, p. 476, table 739; U.S. House of Representatives, 1996 Green Book, table 8-28.

2. See, for example, Hutchins Hapgood, *The Spirit of the Ghetto: Studies of the Jewish Quarter of New York* (New York: Funk and Wagnalls, 1902); Jacob Hollander, *Abolition of Poverty* (Boston: Houghton Mifflin, 1914); Robert Hunter, *Poverty* (n.p., 1904); Joseph Lee, *Constructive and Preventive Philanthropy* (New York: Macmillan, 1902); Amos Warner, *American Charities: A Study in Philanthropy and Economics* (New York: n.p., 1894).

3. Hunter, *Poverty*; for a discussion of Hunter and other early authors writing on American poverty see Patterson, *America's Struggle against Poverty, 1900–1994*.

4. Other popular early treatments of poverty similarly fail to mention blacks. These include Hollander, *Abolition of Poverty*; Maurice Parmalee, *Poverty and Social Progress* (New York: Macmillan, 1916); John Lewis Gillin, *Poverty and Dependency: Their Relief and Prevention* (New York: Appleton-Century, 1921); Robert W. Kelso, *Poverty* (New York: Longmans, Green, and Co., 1929).

5. Gilbert Osofsky, *Harlem: The Making of a Ghetto—Negro New York, 1890–1930* (New York: Harper and Row, 1966).

6. Ibid., p. 179.

7. I. M. Rubinow, *The Quest for Security* (New York: Henry Holt, 1934).

8. Herman P. Miller, "Changes in the Number and Composition of the Poor," in *Poverty in America*, ed. Margaret S. Gordon (Berkeley, Calif.: Chandler, 1965), p. 81.

9. U.S. Bureau of the Census, *Statistical Abstract of the United States: 1960* (Washington, D.C., 1961), p. 520.

10. This figures includes all stories on poor relief, food relief, almshouses, slums, unemployment relief, public welfare, and the poor.

11. James T. Patterson, *America's Struggle against Poverty, 1900–1985* (Cambridge: Harvard University Press, 1986), p. 126.

12. Debates still rage over the extent to which later antipoverty programs were a response to ghetto uprisings and growing black political strength, but most observers seem to agree that the Kennedy administration's antipoverty efforts had little to do with either placating blacks or cementing their political allegiance to the Democratic Party. See Katz, *The Undeserving Poor*, pp. 81–88; Patterson, *America's Struggle against Poverty, 1900–1994*, pp. 133–35.

13. August Meier and Elliott Redwick, *From Plantation to Ghetto* (New York: Hill and Wang, 1970), p. 213.

14. *Report of the National Advisory Commission on Civil Disorders*, p. 240, reprinted in Piven and Cloward, *Regulating the Poor*, p. 190.

15. Bobie Green Turner, *Federal/State Aid to Dependent Children Program and Its Benefits to Black Children in America, 1935–1985* (New York: Garland Publishing, 1993), pp. 249, 251.

16. Lyndon B. Johnson School of Public Affairs, *The Social Safety Net Reexamined: FDR to Reagan* (Austin: University of Texas, 1989), p. 75.

17. Robert C. Lieberman, "Race, Institutions, and the Administration of Social Policy," *Social Science History* 19, no. 4 (winter 1995): 521.

18. Alabama was an exception to this pattern, providing average monthly ADC benefits of $12.87 for black children and $14.44 for white children. Ibid.

19. Lyndon B. Johnson School of Public Affairs, *The Social Safety Net*, p. 76.

20. Ibid.

21. Turner, *Federal/State Aid to Dependent Children*, p. 108.

22. One reason that Social Security survivors' benefits disproportionately aided whites was that two occupations with large numbers of African Americans—agricultural and domestic workers—were initially excluded from the Social Security program.

23. Turner, *Federal/State Aid to Dependent Children*.

24. See Douglas A. Massey and Nancy A. Denton, *American Apartheid: Segregation and the Making of the Underclass* (Cambridge: Harvard University Press, 1993).

25. Harvard Sitkoff, *The Struggle for Black Equality, 1954–1992* (New York: Hill and Wang, 1993), p. 18.

26. See Gerald David Jaynes and Robin M. Williams Jr., eds., *A Common Destiny: Blacks and American Society* (Washington, D.C.: National Academy Press, 1989), p. 233.

27. Gareth Davies, *From Opportunity to Entitlement: The Transformation and Decline of Great Society Liberalism* (Lawrence: University Press of Kansas, 1996), pp. 56 ff. See also Dona Cooper Hamilton and Charles V. Hamilton, *The Dual Agenda: Race and Social Welfare Policies of Civil Rights Organizations* (New York: Columbia University Press, 1997).

28. Jack M. Bloom, *Class, Race, and the Civil Rights Movement* (Bloomington: Indiana University Press, 1987); Thomas R. Brooks, *Walls Come Tumbling Down: A History of the Civil Rights Movement, 1940–1970* (Englewood Cliffs, N.J.: Prentice-Hall, 1974).

29. Ibid.

30. Brooks, *Walls Come Tumbling Down*, p. 239.

31. Ibid., p. 245.

32. Sitkoff, *The Struggle for Black Equality*, p. 187.

33. Ibid., p. 189.

34. Kinder and Sanders, *Divided by Color*, p. 105.

35. See Sniderman et al., "A Critical Examination of *Divided by Color*"; Howard Schu-

man et al., *Racial Attitudes in America: Trends and Interpretations*, rev. ed. (Cambridge: Harvard University Press, 1997). While most racial attitudes on which we have data show either no change or a liberalization across the period of the mid- to late 1960s, the exception to this pattern concerns questions that tap whites' perceptions of the obstacles facing black Americans. In 1963, for example, 51 percent of whites said that blacks have as good a chance as whites to get any kind of job for which they are qualified. By 1978, 82 percent of whites expressed this view. Similarly, in 1963 only 19 percent of whites said that black people rather than white people are more to blame for the conditions in which blacks find themselves, but by 1968 this number had risen to 58 percent. For both surveys, see Schuman et al., *Racial Attitudes in America*, pp. 156–59. Although it is conceivable that the riots may have contributed to this change in whites' views, the lack of any conservative change in other aspects of racial attitudes makes this an unlikely explanation. A more plausible explanation is the demise of Jim Crow segregation and the landmark civil rights legislation of 1964 and 1965.

36. David O. Sears and John B. McConahay, *The Politics of Violence: The New Urban Blacks and the Watts Riot* (Boston: Houghton Mifflin, 1973), p. 169.

37. See Keith Kenney, "Effects of Still Photographs," *News Photographer* 47, no. 5 (May 1992): 41–42.

38. Of the 1203 stories on poverty published in these three magazines from 1960 through 1990, a random sample of 234 was examined for any specific mentions of the racial composition of the poor. Only 11 of these 234 stories (or 4.7 percent) gave any concrete information on the proportion of blacks among poor people, AFDC recipients, public housing tenants, or any other subgroup of the poor. Extrapolating from this sample to all of the poverty stories published during this thirty-one year period, we would expect each magazine to provide this kind of information approximately once every year and a half.

39. On the impact of photographs, see Doris Graber, "Television News without Pictures?" *Critical Studies in Mass Communication* 4 (March 1987): 74–78; Doris Graber, "Seeing Is Remembering: How Visuals Contribute to Learning from Television News," *Journal of Communication* 40 (1990): 134–55; Kenney, "Effects of Still Photographs." On the tendency to be swayed by specific examples rather than statistical information see Hans-Bernd Brosius and Anke Bathelt, "The Utility of Exemplars in Persuasive Communications," *Communication Research* 21, no. 1 (February 1994): 48–78; Ruth Hamill, Timothy DeCamp Wilson, and Richard E. Nisbett, "Insensitivity to Sample Bias: Generalizing from Atypical Cases," *Journal of Personality and Social Psychology* 39 (1980): 578–89; Dean C. Kazoleas, "A Comparison of the Persuasive Effectiveness of Qualitative versus Quantitative Evidence: A Test of Explanatory Hypotheses," *Communication Quarterly* 41, no. 1 (winter 1993): 40–50. For a general discussion of the importance of visual images in television news coverage of poverty see Robert M. Entman, "Television, Democratic Theory, and the Visual Construction of Poverty," *Research in Political Sociology* 7 (1995): 139–59.

40. The breakdown of detailed subject categories can be obtained from the author.

41. The reliability of the race coding was assessed by having two coders independently code a random sample of pictures. Using the picture as the unit of analysis, intercoder reliability for percent black in each picture was .87.

42. A difficult issue in the analysis of news photographs concerns the relative impact that different pictorial content might have on the reader. In particular, I had to decide whether photos depicting many poor people should be given more weight in the analysis than photos of one or a few poor people (and if so, by how much). The simplest approaches would have been to count each picture equally in calculating the racial portrayal of the poor, or alternatively to count each person pictured equally. But the first approach comes up short because it fails to assign greater weight to pictures with larger numbers

of poor people, while the second approach is problematic because it gives the same weight to the fiftieth person in a picture of a large group as it does to the sole individual in a picture of one poor person. In addition, counting each individual equally would allow a few pictures of large groups to dominate the results.

As a compromise, the number of poor people in a single picture is "capped" at twelve, and the race of these twelve people is constructed to be proportionate to the race of all the people in the picture. For example, if a picture contained ten poor whites and thirty poor blacks, it would be scored for analysis as containing three poor whites and nine poor blacks to maintain the percentage of blacks at 75 percent. Although this system is a fairly crude and imperfect compromise, it derives from the reasonable assumption that in general pictures with more people have a larger impact on readers' perceptions of the poor than do pictures with fewer people. Yet it also recognizes that this tendency has some limit, and that the impact of each individual within a large crowd is less than the impact of lone individuals or of individual people within a small group.

43. The figure for the average percentage of blacks among the poor includes only the years 1960 through 1992, since poverty data broken down by race are not available before 1960.

44. "Poverty, U.S.A.," *Newsweek*, February 17, 1964, pp. 19–38.

45. In addition to these fifty-four people for whom race could be identified, this story included four others of unidentifiable race.

46. "What's Going On in the Job Corps," *U.S. News and World Report*, July 26, 1965, pp. 57–60.

47. Schuman et al., *Racial Attitudes in America*.

48. For growth in welfare rolls see figure 1.2; welfare spending as a percentage of GNP is found in Marmor, Mashaw, and Harvey, *America's Misunderstood Welfare State*, p. 85.

49. See Patterson, *America's Struggle against Poverty, 1900–1994*, pp. 178–79, for a discussion of the growth of AFDC rolls during this period.

50. U.S. Bureau of the Census, *Statistical Abstract: 1993*, p. 415.

51. U.S. Department of Labor, *65th Annual Report: Fiscal Year 1977* (Washington, D.C., 1978), p. 117.

52. "Billions to Pay, and a Spreading Revolt," *Time*, September 1, 1975, p. 7.

53. U.S. Bureau of the Census, *Statistical Abstract: 1993*, pp. 445, 414; Patterson, *America's Struggle against Poverty, 1900–1994*, p. 211.

54. *Newsweek*, December 27, 1982, p. 12.

55. These figures for the "Hard-Luck Christmas" story reflect the raw numbers of poor people. The adjusted numbers of poor people, using a maximum of 12 poor people per picture (see note 42 above), are 3 blacks and 15 nonblacks. In this case the adjusted percentage black (3/18 = 17 percent) and the raw percentage black (17/90 = 19 percent) are quite similar.

56. Lawrence D. Maloney, Jeannye Thornton, and Benjamin M. Cole, "Poverty Trap: No Way Out?" *U.S. News and World Report*, August 16, 1982, pp. 31–35.

57. "The Hard-Luck Christmas of '82," *Newsweek*, December 27, 1982, p. 13.

58. The specific index entries in the *Readers' Guide to Periodical Literature* included in each of the subject categories in table 5.2 can be obtained from the author.

59. See Smith, "The Welfare State in Cross-National Perspective," 404–21; Cook and Barrett, *Support for the American Welfare State*.

60. Some argue that the very notion of an underclass is misguided at best and pernicious at worst (e.g., Adolph L. Reed, "The Underclass Myth," *Progressive* 55 (1991): 18–20), but this is not the place to debate the utility of this concept. Because the media have adopted the term "underclass," those interested in understanding public attitudes must acknowledge its importance, irrespective of our feelings about the desirability or undesirability of the concept.

61. Christopher Jencks and Paul E. Peterson, eds., *The Urban Underclass* (Washington, D.C.: Brookings Institution, 1991).

62. One such definition counts as members of the underclass only poor residents of census tracts with unusually high proportions of (1) welfare recipients, (2) female-headed households, (3) high school dropouts, and (4) unemployed working-age males. Erol R. Ricketts and Isabel V. Sawhill, "Defining and Measuring the Underclass," *Journal of Policy Analysis and Management* 7 (Winter 1988): 316–25. To qualify as an underclass area based on Ricketts and Sawhill's criteria, a census tract must be at least one standard deviation above the national average on all four of these characteristics. By this definition, only 5 percent of the American poor live in underclass areas, and 59 percent of the underclass is African American. However defined, it is clear that the American underclass contains substantial numbers of nonblacks, in contrast to the magazine underclass composed exclusively of African Americans.

63. "*Folio* 500: Circulation Figures for the 500 Top U.S. Magazines," *Folio: The Magazine for Magazine Management* 23, no. 12 (1994): 52. Readership is gauged by a Times Mirror survey of February 20, 1992, which asked, "I'd like to know how often, if ever, you read certain types of publications. For each that I read tell me if you read them regularly, sometimes, hardly ever or never. . . . News magazines such as *Time, U.S. News and World Report,* or *Newsweek.*" Twenty percent of respondents claimed to read such magazines regularly, 38 percent sometimes, 20 percent hardly ever, and 21 percent never.

64. See G. Cleveland Wilhoit and David H. Weaver, *The American Journalist: A Portrait of U.S. News People and Their Work* (Bloomington: Indiana University Press, 1991).

65. William G. Mayer, "Poll Trends: Trends in Media Usage," *Public Opinion Quarterly* 57, no. 4 (winter 1993): 593–611.

66. The search of television news stories was based on an electronic version of the *Vanderbilt Television News Index* that was generously provided by John Lynch, the Director of the Television News Archive at Vanderbilt University. A keyword search was used to identify all stories on poverty and related topics. A detailed classification of television news stories by index topic is available from the author.

67. Calculated from Paul A. Jargowsky and Mary Jo Bane, "Ghetto Poverty in the United States, 1970–1980," in *The Urban Underclass*, ed. Christopher Jencks and Paul E. Peterson (Washington, D.C.: Brookings Institution, 1991), p. 251.

Chapter 6

1. Walter Lippmann, *Public Opinion* (1922; reprint, New York: Macmillan, 1960), p. 79.

2. For example, see Shanto Iyengar and Donald R. Kinder, *News That Matters: Television and American Opinion* (Chicago: University of Chicago Press, 1987); Jon A. Krosnick and Donald R. Kinder, "Altering the Foundations of Support for the President through Priming," *American Political Science Review* 84, no. 2 (June 1990): 497–512; Everett M. Rogers and James W. Dearing, "Agenda Setting Research: Where Has It Been and Where Is It Going?" in *Communication Yearbook*, vol. 11, ed. James A. Anderson (Beverly Hills: Sage Publications, 1988); Shanto Iyengar, *Is Anyone Responsible? How Television Frames Political Issues* (Chicago: University of Chicago Press, 1991); W. Russell Neuman, Marion R. Just, and Ann N. Crigler, *Common Knowledge: News and the Construction of Political Meaning* (Chicago: University of Chicago Press, 1992); Lawrence Bartels, "Messages Received: The Political Impact of Media Exposure," *American Political Science Review* 87, no. 2 (June 1993): 267–85.

3. Ruth Hamill, Timothy DeCamp Wilson, and Richard E. Nisbett, "Insensitivity to Sample Bias: Generalizing from Atypical Cases," *Journal of Personality and Social Psychology* 39 (1980): 578–89.

4. Brosius and Bathelt, "Utility of Exemplars in Persuasive Communications"; Kazoleas, "Persuasive Effectiveness of Qualitative versus Quantitative Evidence." See also

Eugene Borgida and Richard E. Nisbett, "The Differential Impact of Abstract vs. Concrete Information on Decisions," *Journal of Applied Social Psychology* 7 (1977): 258–71; Zvi Ginossar and Yaacov Trope, "The Effects of Base Rates and Individuating Information on Judgments about Another Person," *Journal of Experimental Social Psychology* 16 (1980): 228–42; Daniel Kahneman and Amos Tversky, "On the Psychology of Prediction," *Psychological Review* 80 (1973): 237–51; Thomas R. Koballa, "Persuading Teachers to Reexamine the Innovative Elementary Science Programs of Yesterday: The Effects of Anecdotal versus Data-Summary Communications," *Journal of Research in Science Teaching* 23 (1986): 437–49; Richard E. Nisbett and Eugene Borgida, "Attribution and the Psychology of Prediction," *Journal of Personality and Social Psychology* 32 (1975): 932–43; Amos Tversky and Daniel Kahneman, "Belief in the Law of Small Numbers," *Psychological Bulletin* 76 (1971): 105–10. For contrary evidence, however, see Peter R. Dickson, "The Impact of Enriching Case and Statistical Information on Consumer Judgments," *Journal of Consumer Research* 8 (1982): 398–406; Gary L. Wells and John H. Harvey, "Do People Use Consensus Information in Making Causal Attributions?" *Journal of Personality and Social Psychology* 35 (1977): 279–93; E. James Baesler and Judee K. Burgoon, "The Temporal Effects of Story and Statistical Evidence on Belief Change," *Communication Research* 21, no. 5 (October 1994): 582–602.

5. Graber, "Seeing Is Remembering: How Visuals Contribute to Learning from Television News," *Journal of Communication* 40 (1990): 134–55.

6. Ibid., p. 146.

7. Iyengar and Kinder, *News That Matters*, p. 41.

8. Iyengar, *Is Anyone Responsible?*

9. Data on public perceptions come from the 1991 National Race and Politics Study (see chapter 4 for details). Figures for the true percentage of blacks among the poor are from the 1990 census. U.S. Bureau of the Census, *1990 Census of Population and Housing, Summary Tape File 3A (CD90-3c-1)* (Washington, D.C.: 1993).

10. CBS/*New York Times* survey, December 1994.

11. *Washington Post*/Kaiser Foundation/Harvard University survey, July 20–September 28, 1995. These figures are based on samples of 802 white and 451 black respondents. In 1991 the National Election Study (NES) conducted a pilot study that also asked respondents to estimate the proportion of blacks in the American population. On average, nonblack respondents guessed that African Americans accounted for 31 percent of all Americans, a fair bit higher than the 23 percent average for the *Washington Post* survey analyzed here. The reasons for this divergence are unclear, but it might reflect variation over time in perceptions of the population, differences in question order or context, or simply sampling error (with 802 and 373 nonblack respondents to the two surveys, the observed difference between 23 percent and 31 percent is not statistically significant). For an analysis of these NES data (including perceptions of the proportion of Hispanics and Jews in the American population) see Benjamin Highton and Raymond E. Wolfinger, "Memorandum to the Board of Overseers, National Election Studies: Estimating the Size of Minority Groups" (Berkeley, Calif., 1992).

12. The seven states in which blacks comprise more than 20 percent of the population include Maryland, North Carolina, South Carolina, Georgia, Alabama, Mississippi, and Louisiana; the nine states with populations less than 1 percent black are Maine, New Hampshire, Vermont, North Dakota, South Dakota, Montana, Idaho, Wyoming, and Utah. U.S. Bureau of the Census, *Statistical Abstract: 1995*, pp. 34, 36.

13. Lorelei Williams, "Wallflowers: Black Women in the Television Landscape" (senior essay, Yale University, Political Science and African American Studies, 1998).

14. Herbert J. Gans, *Deciding What's News: A Study of CBS Evening News, NBC Nightly News, Newsweek, and Time* (New York: Pantheon Books, 1979).

15. The ten largest metropolitan areas (based on 1980 population) and the percentage of blacks among the poor are: New York, 34.9 percent; Los Angeles, 13.0 percent; Chicago, 49.9 percent; San Francisco, 19.3 percent; Philadelphia, 45.4 percent; Detroit, 52.9 percent; Boston, 15.7 percent; Washington, 51.4 percent; Dallas, 32.4 percent; Houston, 33.6 percent. U.S. Bureau of the Census, *1990 Census of Population and Housing, Summary Tape File 3A.*

16. See Massey and Denton, *American Apartheid.*

17. See Wilson, *The Truly Disadvantaged,* p. 46.

18. See Jargowsky and Bane, "Ghetto Poverty," p. 251.

19. Richard Folkers, Associate Director (Photo Staff), *U.S. News and World Report,* telephone interview with author, October 8, 1993.

20. See, for example, Mark Fishman, *Manufacturing the News* (Austin: University of Texas Press, 1980); Todd Gitlin, *The Whole World Is Watching: Mass Media in the Making and Unmaking of the New Left* (Berkeley: University of California Press, 1980).

21. I am grateful to Guy Cooper and Stella Kramer at *Newsweek,* Richard L. Boeth and Mary Worrell-Bousquette at *Time,* and Richard Folkers and Sara Grosvenor at *U.S. News and World Report* for their time and cooperation. These telephone interviews were conducted in October 1993.

22. Not all of the photo editors I spoke with shared this concern about accuracy, however. Two of the editors responsible for "back-of-the-book" (i.e., softer news) stories stressed that the primary consideration was the "power" of the image, its human or emotional content. For these editors, the demographic characteristics of the poverty images was a distant consideration, when it was considered at all.

23. The two figures for the homeless reflect the racial composition of homeless people living in public places and homeless people staying in shelters, respectively. The figure for beneficiaries of means-tested government assistance benefits includes all people receiving AFDC, General Assistance, SSI, food stamps, Medicaid, or housing assistance. Many of the stories indexed under "public assistance" focus on AFDC, the beneficiaries of which were 39 percent black during this period. Sources for the percentage of African Americans in various subgroups of the poor include: for recipients of government housing benefits, U.S. Bureau of the Census, *Statistical Abstract: 1995,* p. 378; for the homeless, Kim Hopper and Norweeta G. Milburn, "Homelessness among African Americans: A Historical and Contemporary Perspective," in *Homelessness in America,* ed. Jim Baumohl (Phoenix: Oryx Press, 1996), p. 123; for poor children, U.S. Bureau of the Census, *Statistical Abstract: 1995,* p. 480; for all major means-tested government benefits, U.S. Bureau of the Census, *Statistical Abstract: 1995,* p. 378; for AFDC, U.S. House of Representatives, 1994 Green Book, p. 402.

24. The weighted figure for percentage of blacks among the poor (36 percent) is based on the percentages of all poor people pictured that fall into each of the nine subgroups of the poor shown in table 6.2. For example, since pictures of thirty-six poor people are found in stories on the underclass, this category is weighted 36/628, with the denominator being the total number of pictures indexed under one or more of these nine topics. (Note that 17 percent of the stories were indexed under more than one topic and that this analysis excludes fourteen stories that were not indexed under any of these topics.)

Figures for the true proportions of blacks among these different subgroups are as follows: *underclass* (60 percent black), the highest estimate offered in Ricketts and Sawhill, "Defining and Measuring the Underclass"; *poor people, Poverty* (29 percent black), the average proportion for the poor as a whole during this period; *housing programs* (40 percent black), all people living in public housing or government subsidized rental housing (U.S. Bureau of the Census, *Statistical Abstract: 1995,* p. 378); *homeless* (40 percent black), an average of the Census Bureau's 1990 "S-night" estimates for persons living in homeless shelters and persons living in public places (Hopper and Milburn, "Homelessness among African Americans"); *education* (38 percent black), children enrolled in Head Start (U.S. House of Representatives, 1994 Green Book); *poor children* (34 percent black), poor people under 18 years old (U.S. Bureau of the Census, *Statistical Abstract: 1995*, p. 480); *public assistance* (36 percent black), the average of the percentage black of AFDC recipients (39 percent, U.S. House of Representatives, 1994 Green Book) and the percentage black of all recipients of means-tested government aid (33 percent, U.S. Bureau of the Census, *Statistical Abstract: 1995*, p. 378); *employment programs* (31 percent black), adults enrolled in the Job Training Partnership Act, Title II-A programs (U.S. House of Representatives, 1996 Green Book, p. 930); *Medicaid* (34 percent black), all Medicaid recipients (U.S. Bureau of the Census, *Statistical Abstract: 1995*, p. 378).

25. See John F. Dovidio, Nancy Evans, and Richard B. Tyler, "Racial Stereotypes: The Contents of Their Cognitive Representations," *Journal of Experimental Social Psychology* 22 (1986): 22–37; Patricia G. Devine, "Stereotypes and Prejudice: Their Automatic and Controlled Components," *Journal of Personality and Social Psychology* 56 (1989): 5–18; Mahzarin R. Banaji, Curtis Hardin, and Alexander J. Rothman, "Implicit Stereotyping in Person Judgement," *Journal of Personality and Social Psychology* 65 (1993): 272–81.

26. See S. Robert Lichter and Stanley Rothman, "Media and Business Elites," *Public Opinion* 4, no. 5 (October/November 1981): 42–46; S. Robert Lichter, Stanley Rothman, and Linda S. Lichter, *The Media Elite* (Bethesda: Adler and Adler, 1986); David H. Weaver and G. Cleveland Wilhoit, *The American Journalist in the 1990s: U.S. News People at the End of an Era* (Mahwah, N.J.: Lawrence Erlbaum, 1996).

27. When the same question was asked in the 1991 Race and Politics Survey, 14 percent of respondents said whites are mostly to blame for blacks being worse off, 17 percent said blacks are mostly to blame, and 69 percent said that whites and blacks share the blame equally.

28. For these analyses each poor person pictured in newsmagazine poverty stories was coded as "working" or "not working" and as "under 18 years old," "between 18 and 64," or "over 64 years old." For this coding, textual information in the story and picture caption was used along with the picture itself. Intercoder reliability for under or over age 18 was .98, reliability for under or over age 64 was .95, and reliability for working status was .97. For further details of these analyses see Martin Gilens, "Race and Poverty in America: Public Misperceptions and the American News Media," *Public Opinion Quarterly* 60, no. 4 (winter 1996): 515–41.

29. Fay Lomax Cook, *Who Should Be Helped? Public Support for Social Services* (Beverly Hills: Sage Publications, 1979); Cook and Barrett, *Support for the American Welfare State.*

30. For these statistics on age, see U.S. Bureau of the Census, *Money Income and Poverty Status in the United States: 1989 (Advance Data from the March 1990 Current Population Survey),* Current Population Reports, Series P-60, no. 168 (Washington, D.C., 1990).

31. U.S. Bureau of the Census, *Poverty in the United States: 1988 and 1989,* Current Population Reports, Series P-60, no. 171 (Washington, D.C., 1990).

32. See, for example, Devine, "Stereotypes and Prejudice"; Banaji, Hardin, and Rothman, "Implicit Stereotyping in Person Judgement"; Russell H. Fazio et al., "Variability in Automatic Activation as an Unobtrusive Measure of Racial Attitudes: A Bona Fide Pipeline?" *Journal of Personality and Social Psychology* 69 (1995): 1013–27; Anthony G. Greenwald and Mahzarin R. Banaji, "Implicit Social Cognition: Attitudes, Self-Esteem, and Stereotypes," *Psychological Review* 102, no. 1 (January 1995): 4–27.

33. Devine, "Stereotypes and Prejudice."

34. For example, Fazio et al. found that white subjects varied in the extent to which they responded negatively to racial primes consisting of images of black faces, and that this

variation was related to subjects' racial beliefs as measured by surveys and to their inter-actions with a black experimenter. Fazio et al., "Variability in Automatic Activation."

Chapter 7

1. Ronald Takaki, *Iron Cages: Race and Culture in Nineteenth-Century America* (New York: Oxford University Press, 1990), p. 117.

2. Ibid., p. 113.

3. Ibid., p. 126.

4. Ibid., p. 119.

5. William Lloyd Garrison, *Thoughts on African Colonization* (Boston: Garrison and Knapp, 1832), p. 183, cited in George M. Frederickson, *The Black Image in the White Mind: The Debate on African American Character and Destiny, 1817-1914* (New York: Harper and Row, 1971), p. 36.

6. Daniel Katz and Kenneth W. Braly, "Racial Stereotypes of 100 College Students," *Journal of Abnormal and Social Psychology* 28 (1933): 280-90.

7. Students were asked to describe blacks, Chinese, English, Germans, Irish, Italians, Japanese, Jews, Turks, and "Americans."

8. See G. M. Gilbert, "Stereotype Persistence and Change among College Students," *Journal of Abnormal and Social Psychology* 46 (1951): 245-54; Marvin Karlins, Thomas L. Coffman, and Gary Walters, "On the Fading of Social Stereotypes: Studies in Three Generations of College Students," *Journal of Personality and Social Psychology* 13 (1969): 1-16.

9. General Social Survey, 1996.

10. Donald T. Campbell, "Stereotypes and the Perception of Group Differences," *American Psychologist* 22 (1967): 817-29.

11. Lippmann, *Public Opinion*, p. 122.

12. U.S. Bureau of the Census, *Statistical Abstract: 1997*, p. 397, table 620. The small over-all racial difference in labor force participation does mask larger differences among spe-cific age/sex subgroups of blacks and whites. For example, black and white women participate in the labor force at nearly identical rates (59.5 percent and 59.0 percent, re-spectively), but black men are somewhat less likely to be working or looking for work than are white men (69.0 percent versus 75.7 percent), and this differences appears to be greatest among the young. Cheryl Russell, *The Official Guide to Racial and Ethnic Diversity* (Ithaca: New Strategist Publications, 1996), pp. 134, 437. The factors contributing to racial differences in male labor force participation have been the subject of passionate debate, with some arguing that a "culture of nonwork" has evolved among the poor, and among poor young black males in particular. See, e.g., Lawrence M. Mead, *Beyond Entitlement: The Social Obligations of Citizenship* (New York: Free Press, 1986); Lawrence M. Mead, *The New Politics of Poverty: The Nonworking Poor in America* (New York: Basic Books, 1992). Others have argued that lower rates of black labor-force participation and higher rates of unemployment are caused not by a lack of desire to work but by "supply side" factors such as geographical or skills mismatches between the available jobs and the characteris-tics of black workers (or would-be workers) or by employer discrimination. See, e.g., Harry J. Holzer, "Black Employment Problems: New Evidence, Old Questions," *Journal of Policy Analysis and Management* 13, no. 4 (fall 1994): 699-722; Joleen Kirschenman and Katherine M. Neckerman, "We'd Love to Hire Them But . . ." in *The Urban Underclass*, ed. Christopher Jencks and Paul E. Peterson (Washington, D.C.: Brookings Institution, 1991); Wilson, *The Truly Disadvantaged*; William Julius Wilson, *When Work Disappears: The World of the New Urban Poor* (New York: Knopf, 1996). Studies of "reservation wages" (i.e., the lowest wage at which an unemployed person would be willing to take a job) suggest that,

as a group, unemployed blacks are willing to work for lower wages than are unemployed whites, and this holds true both for an unspecified job and for specific low-skill jobs such as cleaning, supermarket, or factory work. Holzer, "Black Employment Problems."

13. Annual Demographic Survey (March CPS Supplement), 1996.

14. For discussions of the cognitive functions of stereotypes see Roger Brown, *Social Psychology* (New York: Free Press, 1986); Hilton and von Hippel, "Stereotypes."

15. John Harding et al., "Prejudice and Ethnic Relations," in *Handbook of Social Psychology*, ed. Gardner Lindzen and Elliot Aronson (Reading, Mass.: Addison-Wesley, 1969); C. McCauley, C. Stitt, and M. Segal, "Stereotyping: From Prejudice to Prediction," *Psychological Bulletin* 87 (1980): 195-208; Mary R. Jackman and Mary Scheuer Senter, "Images of Social Groups: Categorical or Qualified?" *Public Opinion Quarterly* 44, no. 3 (fall 1980): 341-61.

16. Henri Tajfel and A. L. Wilkes, "Classification and Quantitative Judgement," *British Journal of Psychology* 54 (1963): 101-14.

17. Michael Billig and Henri Tajfel, "Social Categorization and Similarity in Intergroup Behavior," *European Journal of Social Psychology* 3 (1973): 27-52.

18. Thomas F. Pettigrew, "The Ultimate Attribution Error: Extending Allport's Cognitive Analysis of Prejudice," *Personality and Social Psychology Bulletin* 5 (1979): 461-76.

19. Georgette Wang and Jack McKillip, "Ethnic Identification and Judgements of an Accident," *Personality and Social Psychology Bulletin* 4 (1978): 296-99.

20. L. Diab, "National Stereotypes and the 'Reference Group' Concept," *Journal of Social Psychology* 57 (1962): 339-51; K. J. Gergen, "The Significance of Skin Color in Human Relations," *Daedalus* (1969): 390-406; Karlins, Coffman, and Walters, "On the Fading of Social Stereotypes."

21. J. McMurtry, *The Structure of Marx's World-View* (Princeton: Princeton University Press, 1978); D. Meyerson, *False Consciousness* (Oxford: Clarendon Press, 1991); John T. Jost and Mahzarin R. Banaji, "The Role of Stereotyping in System-Justification and the Production of False Consciousness," *British Journal of Social Psychology* 33 (1994): 1-27.

22. H. C. Triandis et al., "Stereotyping among Hispanics and Anglos: The Uniformity, Intensity, Direction, and Quality of Auto- and Heterostereotypes," *Journal of Cross-Cultural Psychology* 13 (1982): 409-26; John T. Jost, "Is It Time for a Theory of Outgroup Favoritism? A Comment on the Paper by Mullen, Brown, and Smith" (Yale University, 1993); Jost and Banaji, "The Role of Stereotyping in System-Justification."

23. Melvin J. Lerner, *The Belief in a Just World: A Fundamental Delusion* (New York: Plenum Press, 1980).

24. Kluegel and Smith, *Beliefs about Inequality*; Bobo and Smith, "Antipoverty Policy, Affirmative Action, and Racial Attitudes"; Nelson and Clawson, "Poverty Attribution."

25. Kluegel and Smith, *Beliefs about Inequality*, pp. 77, 79.

26. Ibid., p. 44.

27. The figure for 1942 is from Schuman, Steeh, and Bobo, *Racial Attitudes in America*, p. 74; the figure for 1995 is from a *Newsweek* poll of February 3.

28. Respectively, J. M. Jones, *Prejudice and Racism* (Reading, Mass.: Addison-Wesley, 1972), p. 61; Gordon W. Allport, *The Nature of Prejudice* (Reading, Mass.: Addison-Wesley, 1954), p. 9; Kinder and Sanders, *Divided by Color*, p. 109.

29. Harding et al., "Prejudice and Ethnic Relations"; Phyllis A. Katz, "The Acquisition of Racial Attitudes in Children," in *Towards the Elimination of Racism*, ed. Phyllis A. Katz (Elmsford, N.Y.: Pergamon Press, 1976); David O. Sears, "The Persistence of Early Political Predispositions," in *Review of Personality and Social Psychology*, ed. Ladd Wheeler and Phillip Shaver (Beverly Hills: Sage Publications, 1983), pp. 79-116; Diane Mackie and David Hamilton, *Affect, Cognition, and Stereotyping: Interactive Processes in Group Perception* (New York: Academic Press, 1993); Glaser and Gilens, "Interregional Migration and Political

Resocialization: A Study of Racial Attitudes under Pressure," *Public Opinion Quarterly* 61, no. 1 (spring 1997): 72–86.

30. John B. McConahay and Joseph C. Hough Jr., "Symbolic Racism," *Journal of Social Issues* 32 (1976): 23–45; David O. Sears, Carl P. Hensler, and Leslie K. Speer, "Whites' Opposition to 'Busing': Self-Interest or Symbolic Politics?" *American Political Science Review* 73 (1979): 369–84; Donald R. Kinder and David O. Sears, "Prejudice and Politics: Symbolic Racism versus Racial Threats to the Good Life," *Journal of Personality and Social Psychology* 40 (1981): 414–31; Sears, "Symbolic Racism"; Kinder and Sanders, *Divided by Color*; Sears, van Laar, and Carrillo, "Is It Really Racism?"

31. Bobo, "Whites' Opposition to Busing"; Lawrence Bobo, "Group Conflict, Prejudice, and the Paradox of Contemporary Racial Attitudes," in Katz and Taylor, *Eliminating Racism*; Bobo and Kluegel, "Opposition to Race-Targeting."

32. Paul M. Sniderman and Thomas Piazza, *The Scar of Race* (Cambridge: Harvard University Press, 1993); Sniderman et al., "A Critical Examination of *Divided by Color*"; Sniderman and Carmines, *Reaching Beyond Race*; Kuklinski et al., "Racial Prejudice and Attitudes toward Affirmative Action."

33. General Social Survey, February–April 1996.

34. John B. McConahay, "Modern Racism, Ambivalence, and the Modern Racism Scale," in *Prejudice, Discrimination, and Racism*, ed. John F. Dovidio and Samuel L. Gaertner (New York: Academic Press, 1986); Sears, "Symbolic Racism."

35. This approach to understanding the underlying "meaning" of a survey response by comparing its influence to that of related survey questions was used in the "welfare mother experiment" in chapter 4. In that case, the difference between the impact of otherwise identical questions about a black welfare mother and a white welfare mother revealed the importance of race in shaping whites' views on welfare. In this case three otherwise identical questions about the perceived qualities of black Americans reveals the importance of the specific cognitive content of the stereotype of blacks as lazy.

36. Sniderman and Piazza, *The Scar of Race*, pp. 92–97.

37. Lynn M. Sanders, "Racialized Interpretations of Economic Reality" (paper presented at the annual meeting of the American Political Science Association, San Francisco, August 29–September 1, 1996).

38. Times Mirror survey, 1995.

39. For example, 61 percent of respondents to the 1990 General Social Survey said spending for Head Start should be increased, and only 5 percent wanted spending for Head Start cut. In another poll, 60 percent of respondents said they would be willing to pay higher taxes in order to increase spending on job training programs, compared with 37 percent who were not willing to pay higher taxes for this purpose. NBC News/*Wall Street Journal* poll, June 1994.

40. Sanders, "Racialized Interpretations of Economic Reality," table 2.

41. CBS/*New York Times* poll, December 6, 1997. Percentages are based on the number of respondents who gave responses other than "don't know" or "no answer."

42. General Social Survey, 1990. These questions were asked of a random half of the survey respondents, with the other half being asked about identical policies that are income- rather than race-targeted (for example, "special college scholarships for children from economically disadvantaged backgrounds who maintain good grades" rather than "for black children who maintain good grades"). In each case the income-targeted program received higher support from white respondents. For college scholarships, the percentage in favor was 70 percent for the race-targeted and 91 percent for income-targeted versions; for preschool and early education programs the percentages in favor were 68 for the race-targeted and 86 for the income-targeted versions. For a discussion of whites' responses to these items see Bobo and Kluegel, "Opposition to Race-Targeting."

The greater popularity of the income-targeted versions is undoubtedly due to a number of factors. First, some white Americans *do* harbor a general antipathy toward blacks and will oppose even "opportunity enhancing" programs that aim to help them. Second, other white Americans may be generally sympathetic toward blacks but oppose programs that dispense benefits on the basis of racial group membership rather than individual need (for example, see Sniderman and Carmines, *Reaching Beyond Race*). Finally, some white Americans may have a positive desire to help blacks through race-targeted policies but an even stronger desire to help all poor people through income-targeted programs.

43. Simo Virtanen and Leonie Huddy offer a somewhat similar analysis of the impact of the lazy-black stereotype on whites' support for different types of race-targeted programs. They conclude, "Apparently, the belief that most blacks are unwilling to work hard does not affect support for programs targeted at deserving blacks who do not readily conform to this stereotype." Simo V. Virtanen and Leonie Huddy, "Old-Fashioned Racism and New Forms of Racial Prejudice," *Journal of Politics* 60, no. 2 (May 1998): 324.

44. The proportion of whites believing that most of the recipients of benefits from each program are minorities are 68 percent for welfare, 67 percent for food stamps, 68 percent for job training and job creation, and 80 percent for public housing. Sanders, "Racialized Interpretations of Economic Reality," table 2.

45. General Social Survey, 1990 and 1994 combined.

Chapter 8

1. U.S. House of Representatives, 1996 Green Book, table 8-23.

2. Orr used data from 1963 through 1972, and he found the predicted difference in average annual AFDC benefits for a state with an all-black AFDC caseload to be $400 lower than a state with no blacks receiving AFDC, measured in 1967 dollars. Larry L. Orr, "Income Transfers as a Public Good: An Application to A.F.D.C.," *The American Economic Review* 66, no. 3 (June 1976): 359–71. This figure represents $1936 in 1997 dollars.

3. Gerald C. Wright Jr., "Racism and Welfare Policy in America," *Social Science Quarterly* 57, no. 3 (December 1976): 718–30. See also Robert D. Plotnick and Richard F. Winters, "A Politico-Economic Theory of Income Redistribution," *American Political Science Review* 79, no. 2 (June 1985): 458–73, finding that the percentage of blacks on a state's AFDC caseload was associated with an antipoverty policy measure that combined AFDC benefit levels, Medicaid availability, and food stamps.

4. Christopher Howard, "A Bridge Too Far? Linking the Study of National and State-Level Social Policy in the United States" (paper presented at the annual meeting of the American Political Science Association, Washington, D.C., August 28–31, 1997).

5. For the impact of percent black on AFDC and unemployment insurance benefits, see ibid., table 3, model 2, and table 4, model 2, respectively.

6. U.S. Bureau of the Census, *Statistical Abstract: 1995*, p. 406.

7. U.S. Bureau of the Census, "Persons by Family Characteristics," 1960 Census of Population, PC(2)-4B (Washington, D.C., 1960), tables 1 and 19.

8. U.S. Bureau of the Census, "Marital Status and Living Arrangements: March 1994," Current Population Survey Reports (Washington, D.C., 1994).

9. The following discussion of welfare reform draws from Bruce S. Jansson, *The Reluctant Welfare State: A History of American Social Welfare Policies* (Pacific Grove, Calif.: Brooks/Cole, 1993); Marmor, Mashaw, and Harvey, *America's Misunderstood Welfare State*; Patterson, *America's Struggle against Poverty, 1900–1994*.

10. Jansson, *The Reluctant Welfare State*, p. 223.

11. See Danziger and Gottschalk, *America Unequal*.

12. The first of these requirements mandates that 75 percent of the two-parent families

on a state's welfare rolls must be working. To fulfill this requirement, at least 35 hours per week must be devoted to work between the two parents. A study by the Associated Press indicated that only half of the states were likely to meet this goal. See Jason DeParle, "Half the States Unlikely to Meet Goals on Welfare," *New York Times*, October 1, 1997, p. A1.

13. Daly, "Labor Market Effects of Welfare Reform."

14. For useful compendiums of survey questions on welfare reform see R. Kent Weaver, Robert Y. Shapiro, and Lawrence R. Jacobs, "Public Opinion on Welfare Reform: A Mandate for What?" in *Looking before We Leap: Social Science and Welfare Reform*, ed. R. Kent Weaver and William T. Dickens (Washington, D.C.: Brookings Institution, 1995); R. Kent Weaver, Robert Y. Shapiro, and Lawrence R. Jacobs, "Trends: Welfare," *Public Opinion Quarterly* 59, no. 4 (winter 1995): 606–27.

15. There is some indication that the belief that welfare mothers with young children should work has grown over the past few years. Weaver, Shapiro, and Jacobs show that the percentage of respondents favoring work requirements for mothers of young children grew from 45 percent in January 1994 to 64 percent in April 1995. "Public Opinion on Welfare Reform," 119; CBS/*New York Times* surveys. More recent surveys with the same question show the percentage favoring work requirements to be 59 percent in October 1995 and 67 percent in December of that year. (All results are from CBS/*New York Times* surveys, with figures based on the percentage of all respondents, including those who did not answer the question or said "don't know.") Some of this fluctuation is likely due simply to survey sampling error, but the differences (especially between the January 1994 survey and the three surveys conducted during 1995) may represent the impact of the national debate over welfare reform that took place during and after the 1994 midterm elections.

16. Associated Press poll, January 1997.

17. Respondents to the 1991 General Social Survey were asked how important different characteristics are for getting ahead in life. Ninety percent said "ambition" is "essential" or "very important," compared with 88 percent who answered the same way for "having a good education yourself," 88 percent for "hard work," 53 percent for "natural ability," 43 percent for "knowing the right people," 41 percent for "having well educated parents," and 18 percent for "coming from a wealthy family." Mail and telephone reinterviews of 1991 GSS respondents; February–April, 1992.

18. NBC News/*Wall Street Journal* poll, June 1994.

19. Thirty-four percent of respondents expressed a willingness to pay higher taxes to improve transportation and communication systems, while 31 percent said they would support higher taxes to help city and state governments. NBC News/*Wall Street Journal* poll, January 1993.

20. Frederick Wiseman, "Methodological Bias in Public Opinion Surveys," *Public Opinion Quarterly* 36, no. 1 (spring 1972): 105–8.

21. Reported in Seymour Sudman and Norman M. Bradburn, *Response Effects in Surveys: A Review and Synthesis* (Chicago: Aldine Publishing Co., 1974), pp. 40–47.

22. See, for example, Mary R. Jackman, "General and Applied Tolerance: Does Education Increase Commitment to Racial Integration?" *American Journal of Political Science* 22 (1978): 302–24; Mary R. Jackman and Michael J. Muha, "Education and Inter-group Attitudes: Moral Enlightenment, Superficial Democratic Commitment, or Ideological Refinement?" *American Sociological Review* 49 (1984): 751–69; Sears, "Symbolic Racism."

23. Maria Krysan et al., "Response Rates and Response Content in Mail versus Face-to-Face Surveys," *Public Opinion Quarterly* 58, no. 3 (fall 1994): 381–99; Maria Krysan, "Privacy and the Expression of White Racial Attitudes: A Comparison across Three Contexts" (Pennsylvania State University, December 1997). The second of these studies also included a modified version of the face-to-face interview in which answers to some of the

survey questions were obtained through a self-administered booklet that the respondent filled out during the course of the interview. At the conclusion of the interview the respondent placed this booklet in an envelope, sealed the envelope, and then returned the envelope to the interviewer. Results from this "modified" face-to-face technique were generally similar to those obtained from the standard version of the face-to-face interview.

24. Martin Gilens, Paul M. Sniderman, and James H. Kuklinski, "Affirmative Action and the Politics of Realignment," *British Journal of Political Science* 28, no. 1 (January 1998): 159–83; James H. Kuklinski et al., "Racial Prejudice and Attitudes toward Affirmative Action," *American Journal of Political Science* 41, no. 2 (April 1997): 402–19; James H. Kuklinski, Michael D. Cobb, and Martin Gilens, "Racial Attitudes and the 'New South,' " *Journal of Politics* 59, no. 2 (May 1997): 323–49; Paul M. Sniderman and Edward G. Carmines, *Reaching Beyond Race* (Cambridge: Harvard University Press, 1997).

25. Kuklinski and his colleagues used the following technique to "unobtrusively" measure white respondents' attitudes toward affirmative action. First, the sample of respondents was randomly divided into "baseline" and "treatment" groups, each of which was given a list of things that sometimes make people angry or upset (e.g., "corporations polluting the environment," or "the federal government increasing the tax on gasoline"). Respondents in each group were then asked to tell the interviewer how many of these things, *but not which ones*, make them angry or upset. The two groups were read an identical list of nonracial items, but for the treatment group only, a question about affirmative action was added to the list (i.e., "awarding college scholarships on the basis of race"). By subtracting the average number of items that angered respondents in the baseline group from the average number of items that angered those in the treatment group, the percentage of respondents that were angered by the affirmative action item could be determined. Although this technique reveals the percentage of people who are angered by affirmative action, it is impossible to tell which specific respondents found affirmative action objectionable. For details see the sources cited in the preceding note.

26. When racial attitudes are studied in the psychology laboratory, rather than with the large-scale population survey, additional techniques for assessing respondents' truthfulness can be employed. One set of experiments, for example, compared white students' racial attitudes as reported on a questionnaire under two conditions. Half the students (selected at random) were simply asked to indicate their attitudes toward blacks on a traditional survey. The other half were asked the same questions, but after being hooked up to what was supposedly a lie detector. Students who answered the survey while attached to the simulated lie detector expressed more negative attitudes toward blacks. See Faye Crosby, Stephanie Bromley, and Leonard Saxe, "Recent Unobtrusive Studies of Black and White Discrimination and Prejudice: A Literature Review," *Psychological Bulletin* 87, no. 3 (1980): 546–63; B. R. Schlenker et al., "The Bogus Pipeline and Stereotypes toward Blacks," *Journal of Psychology* 93 (1976): 319–29. For an example of the "bogus lie detector" method used to evaluate social desirability in reporting of sensitive behaviors, see Roger Tourangeau, Tom W. Smith, and Kenneth A. Rasinski, "Motivation to Report Sensitive Behaviors on Surveys: Evidence from a Bogus Pipeline Experiment," *Journal of Applied Social Psychology* 27, no. 3 (February 1997): 209–22. For other small-sample studies that attempt to assess the influence of social desirability on reports of racial attitudes see B. P. Allen, "Social Distance and Admiration Reactions of 'Unprejudiced' Whites," *Journal of Personality* 43 (1975): 709–26; C. S. Carver, D. C. Glass, and I. Katz, "Favorable Evaluations of Blacks and the Handicapped: Positive Prejudice, Unconscious Denial, or Social Desirability?" *Journal of Applied Social Psychology* 8 (1978): 97–106; Harold Sigall and Richard Page, "Current Stereotypes: A Little Fading, a Little Faking," *Journal of Personality and Social Psychology* 16 (1971): 252–58.

27. Krysan, "Privacy and the Expression of White Racial Attitudes," and personal communication with author, January 1998.

28. The 7 percentage point difference for the "tax breaks" question is not statistically significant at the .05 level (t = 1.60, d.f. = 470); the 14 percentage point difference for the "schools" question is significant at $p < .001$ (t = 3.25, d.f. = 474).

29. George F. Bishop and Bonnie S. Fisher, " 'Secret Ballots' and Self-Reports in an Exit-Poll Experiment," *Public Opinion Quarterly* 59, no. 4 (winter 1995): 568–88.

30. In this study, both the face-to-face interviews and the secret ballots indicated a larger vote for the elderly tax proposal than actually occurred. (The actual vote was 54 percent in favor, compared with 62 percent claiming to have voted in favor on the secret ballots, and 68 percent in face-to-face interviews. The latter percentages are based only on the number of people who did not deny voting on the proposal and were willing to participate in the survey.) This difference could be due to a social desirability effect that was operating even in the secret ballot survey. Despite the precautions taken by the researchers, some respondents may have feared that the poll-takers would somehow be able to identify them with their secret-ballot responses. An alternative explanation is that the exit-poll sampling as a whole was somewhat biased, and that the respondents to both the secret ballot and the face-to-face interview were somewhat more favorable toward the elderly tax proposal than nonsurveyed voters. This could occur if those who voted against the tax proposal were less likely to agree to participate in the study.

Evidence from another source suggests that a vestigial social desirability effect on the secret ballot results is an unlikely explanation of the discrepancy between the secret ballot and the actual vote. Studies comparing self-reported and actual votes in elections with black candidates (e.g., the election of Douglas Wilder as Virginia's governor) have found the secret ballot exit poll to accurately reflect the vote, even when whites' reluctance to acknowledge voting against a black candidate biased the results from face-to-face exit polls and from preelection telephone surveys. See Steven E. Finkel, Thomas M. Guterbock, and Marian J. Borg, "Race-of-Interviewer Effects in a Preelection Poll: Virginia 1989," *Public Opinion Quarterly* 55, no. 3 (fall 1991): 313–30.

31. See Cook, *Who Should Be Helped?* and Cook and Barrett, *Support for the American Welfare State.*

32. Tocqueville, *Democracy in America*, p. 513.

33. Robin M. Williams, *American Society: A Sociological Interpretation* (New York: Knopf, 1956), p. 400.

34. James E. Curtis, Edward G. Grabb, and Douglas E. Baer, "Voluntary Association Membership in Fifteen Countries: A Comparative Analysis," *American Sociological Review* 57 (April 1992): 143. The countries examined were Australia, Belgium, Canada, France, Great Britain, Ireland, Italy, Japan, Northern Ireland, the Netherlands, Norway, Spain, Sweden, the United States, and West Germany.

35. Quoted in Robert H. Bremner, *American Philanthropy* (Chicago: University of Chicago Press, 1960), p. 8.

36. All figures on charitable activities are from the Gallup poll, November 1989.

37. Calculated from Christopher Jencks, "Who Gives to What?" in *The Nonprofit Sector: A Research Handbook*, ed. Walter W. Powell (New Haven: Yale University Press, 1987), p. 323.

38. Charles Clotfelter, *Federal Tax Policy and Charitable Giving* (Chicago: University of Chicago Press, 1985).

39. Peter Halfpenny, "The 1991 International Survey of Giving," in *Researching the Voluntary Sector*, ed. Susan K. E. Saxon-Harrold and Jeremy Kendall (Tonbridge, England: Charities Aid Foundation, 1993).

40. Data were collected in each nation's currency and converted using purchasing-

power parity exchange rates. Ibid. Americans' higher level of charitable giving does not necessarily indicate that they are less selfish than people of other countries. In most European countries, the government assumes more responsibility for helping the poor, providing medical care, supporting the arts, and paying the costs of higher education. Thus Americans may give more because they perceive greater unmet needs in these areas. Nevertheless, Americans' willingness to step in and voluntarily give of their own resources to help others lends credibility to their professed willingness to pay higher taxes to assist the poor.

41. U.S. Bureau of the Census, *Statistical Abstract: 1997*, p. 392.

42. This figure represents the average contribution of all U.S. households in 1995, including the 31.5 percent of households that did not report any cash contributions (the average contribution for all households making some contribution was $1,017). Calculated from ibid., p. 391, tables 614 and 615.

43. Of this $144 billion, 88 percent comes from individuals and the remaining 12 percent from corporations and foundations. Calculated from ibid., pp. 391, 392, tables 614, 615, and 616.

44. Ibid., p. 375, table 582.

Chapter 9

1. Timothy M. Smeeding, "Financial Poverty in Developed Countries: The Evidence from LIS," working paper no. 155, Luxembourg Income Study, Luxembourg, April 1997. Only direct taxes are included in these calculations (i.e., income taxes, employee and employer payroll taxes, and "negative taxes" such as the EITC). Transfers include both means-tested and universal cash benefits (e.g., pensions, public assistance, family allowances) and near-cash benefits that are denominated in cash, such as food stamps or housing allowances. Indirect taxes such as consumption taxes (i.e., sales taxes or value added taxes), property taxes, and wealth taxes are not taken into account, nor are in-kind benefits such as medical care or education.

2. David K. Shipler, "Blacks in the Newsroom: Progress? Yes, But . . ." *Columbia Journalism Review*, May/June 1998, pp. 26–32.

3. For information on the *Seattle Times'* efforts to track and modify their portrayals of women and minorities I am indebted to Alex MacLeod and Gary Settle, the *Times'* Managing Editor and Photography Coach, respectively. In each year all news and feature photographs that appeared during a one-month period were examined (sports photographs and "head shots" of specific newsworthy individuals were excluded from these analyses).

4. Danziger and Gottschalk, *America Unequal.*

5. In one survey, 73 percent opposed "getting rid of the Earned Income Tax Credit, which reduces or cancels out income taxes for poor people who work, but make very little money." Times Mirror survey, September 28, 1995.

6. Sidney Verba et al., "Citizen Activity: Who Participates? What Do They Say?" *American Political Science Review* 87 (1993): 303–18; Sidney Verba, Kay Lehman Schlozman, and Henry E. Brady, *Voice and Equality: Civic Voluntarism in American Politics* (Cambridge: Harvard University Press, 1995).

7. Piven and Cloward, *Regulating the Poor;* Frances Fox Piven and Richard A. Cloward, *Poor People's Movements: Why They Succeed, How They Fail* (New York: Vintage, 1979); Susan Welch, "The Impact of Urban Riots on Urban Expenditures," *American Journal of Political Science* 19 (1975): 741–60; Robert B. Albritton, "Social Amelioration through Mass Insurgency? A Reexamination of the Piven and Cloward Thesis," *American Political Science Review* 73 (1979): 1003–11; Sanford F. Schram and J. Patrick Turbett, "Civil Disorder and the Welfare Explosion: A Two-Step Process," *American Sociological Review* 48 (1983): 408–14; Richard C. Fording, "The Conditional Effect of Violence as a Political Tactic: Mass

Insurgency, Welfare Generosity, and Electoral Context in the American States," *American Journal of Political Science* 41, no. 1 (January 1997): 1–29.

8. Quoted in Larry J. Sabato, *Paying for Elections: The Campaign Finance Thicket* (New York: Priority Press Publications, 1989), p. 16.

9. E. E. Schattschneider, *The Semisovereign People: A Realist's View of Democracy in America* (New York: Holt, Rinehart and Winston, 1960), p. 35.

10. Steven M. Teles, *Whose Welfare? A.F.D.C. and Elite Politics* (Lawrence: University Press of Kansas, 1996).

11. As examples of the liberal or egalitarian approach to welfare, Teles cites the work of Michael Katz (*In the Shadow of the Poorhouse: A Social History of Welfare in America* [New York: Basic Books, 1986]; *The Undeserving Poor*), Joel Handler (*The Moral Construction of Poverty: Welfare Reform in America* [Newbury Park, Calif.: Sage, 1991]), and Frances Fox Piven and Richard Cloward (*Regulating the Poor*).

12. Teles distinguishes between two versions of the conservative approach to welfare. The "hierarchist" or "culture of poverty" approach, as embodied in the work of Edward Banfield (*The Unheavenly City Revisited* [Boston: Little, Brown, 1974]) and Lawrence Mead (*Beyond Entitlement* and *The New Politics of Poverty*), identifies the "dysfunctional" culture of the poor as the reason for their self-destructive choices. In contrast, the "individualist" approach, most closely associated with Charles Murray (*Losing Ground: American Social Policy, 1950–1980* [New York: Basic Books, 1984]), blames the distorting incentives of the welfare state.

13. For a discussion of the impact of institutional structure on policy outcomes see R. Kent Weaver and Bert A. Rockman, *Do Institutions Matter? Government Capabilities in the United States and Abroad* (Washington, D.C.: Brookings Institution, 1993).

14. See, for example, Roy L. Behr and Shanto Iyengar, "Television News, Real-World Cues, and Changes in the Public Agenda," *Public Opinion Quarterly* 49, no. 1 (spring 1985): 38–57; Page and Shapiro, *The Rational Public*.

15. NBC News/*Wall Street Journal* survey, September 11, 1997.

16. John Bremner, "GOP, Business Misinterpreting Their 1994 Mandate," *St. Louis Post-Dispatch*, July 31, 1995, Business section, p. 12.

17. On the first of these difficulties see R. Kent Weaver and William T. Dickens, eds., *Looking before We Leap: Social Science and Welfare Reform* (Washington, D.C.: Brookings Institution, 1995); on the latter see Danziger and Gottschalk, *America Unequal*.

18. For more historically oriented overviews of public attitudes toward the poor see Hugh Heclo, "The Political Foundations of Antipoverty Policy," in *Fighting Poverty: What Works and What Doesn't*, ed. Sheldon H. Danziger and Daniel H. Weinberg (Cambridge: Harvard University Press, 1986); Patterson, *America's Struggle against Poverty, 1900–1994*.

19. For example, see Bobo and Kluegel, "Opposition to Race-Targeting."

20. For example, the 1996 General Social Survey asked respondents, "Some people say that because of past discrimination, women should be given preference in hiring and promotion. Others say that such preferences in hiring and promotion of women are wrong because it discriminate against men. What about your opinion—are you for or against preferential hiring and promotion of women?" In response to this question, 68 percent of women said they opposed preferential hiring and promotion, as did 72 percent of men. In another part of the survey, the identical question was asked with regard to preferential hiring and promotion of blacks. The responses to this question showed that women were also slightly less opposed than men to preferential treatment for blacks; 76 percent of women and 82 percent of men opposed race-based preferential treatment.

The fairly small differences in the public's opposition to sex-based and race-based affirmative action (which are similar to findings from other surveys; see Charlotte Steeh and Maria Krysan, "Trends: Affirmative Action and the Public, 1970–1995," *Public Opinion*

Quarterly 60, no. 1 [spring 1996]: 128–58) suggest that only a small part of the opposition to race-based preferences is racial in nature. Moreover, the similar male/female gap in opposition to race- and sex-based policies lends additional support to the view that the difference between men and women in opposition to sex-based affirmative action is not a consequence of individual or group-based self-interest. For very different evidence of the nonracial bases of opposition to affirmative action, see Gilens, Sniderman, and Kuklinski, "Affirmative Action and the Politics of Realignment."

21. In fact, empirical evidence supports this suspicion that most Americans underestimate the public's support for antipoverty spending. A national survey in 1994 asked respondents, "Do you think the average American is more supportive or less supportive of spending money on poverty-related programs than you are?" Kull, *Fighting Poverty in America*. If the public had accurate impressions of where their fellow citizens stood on this question, we would expect that the number of respondents replying that the average American is more supportive of antipoverty spending than they themselves would approximately equal the number replying that the average American is less supportive of antipoverty spending. In fact, the survey found that 51 percent of respondents thought the average American was less supportive, while only 20 percent thought the average American was more supportive (the remainder said "about the same" or "don't know"). Like the fictional residents of Garrison Keillor's Lake Wobegon, most Americans, it appears, believe that they are "above average" in their level of support for fighting poverty.

Appendix

1. See analysis in Martin Gilens, "Racial Attitudes and Opposition to Welfare," *Journal of Politics* 57, no. 4 (November 1995): 994–1014. Two changes are made from the analysis in "Racial Attitudes and Opposition to Welfare." First, two survey items are excluded, one each from the indices "Blacks lack work ethic" and "Helping blacks is not government's job." These exclusions provide greater theoretical clarity and result in a set of indices with more nearly equal reliabilities. Second, the feeling thermometer measuring warmth toward blacks is added to the analysis.

2. The small sample size in this analysis is due to both the split-ballot design of the 1986 National Election Study and the use of filter questions for some of the racial-attitude items (which results in higher levels of missing data).

3. Henry E. Brady, "The Perils of Survey Research: Inter-personally Incomparable Responses," *Political Methodology* 11, nos. 3–4 (1985): 269–91; Donald Philip Green, Susan Lee Goldman, and Peter Salovey, "Measurement Error Masks Bipolarity in Affect Ratings," *Journal of Personality and Social Psychology* 64 (1993): 1029–41.

Bibliography

Albritton, Robert B. "Social Amelioration through Mass Insurgency? A Reexamination of the Piven and Cloward Thesis." *American Political Science Review* 73 (1979): 1003–11.

Allen, B. P. "Social Distance and Admiration Reactions of 'Unprejudiced' Whites." *Journal of Personality* 43 (1975): 709–26.

Allport, Gordon W. *The Nature of Prejudice*. Reading, Mass.: Addison-Wesley, 1954.

Apostle, Richard A., Charles Y. Glock, Thomas Piazza, and Marjean Suelzle. *The Anatomy of Racial Attitudes*. Berkeley: University of California Press, 1983.

Arieli, Yehoshua. *Individualism and Nationalism in American Ideology*, p. 282. Cambridge: Harvard University Press, 1964. Quoting Ralph W. Emerson, "New England Reformers," in *Complete Writings* (New York: Wm H. Wise & Co., 1929), p. 318.

AuClaire, Philip Arthur. "Public Attitudes toward Social Welfare Expenditures." *Social Work* 29 (1984): 139–44.

Baesler, E. James, and Judee K. Burgoon. "The Temporal Effects of Story and Statistical Evidence on Belief Change." *Communication Research* 21, no. 5 (October 1994): 582–602.

Banaji, Mahzarin R., Curtis Hardin, and Alexander J. Rothman. "Implicit Stereotyping in Person Judgement." *Journal of Personality and Social Psychology* 65 (1993): 272–81.

Banfield, Edward. *The Unheavenly City Revisited*. Boston: Little, Brown, 1974.

Bar-Tal, Daniel, Carl F. Graumann, Arie W. Kruglanski, and Wolfgang Stroebe, eds. *Stereotyping and Prejudice: Changing Conceptions*. New York: Springer-Verlag, 1989.

Bartels, Lawrence. "Messages Received: The Political Impact of Media Exposure." *American Political Science Review* 87, no. 2 (June 1993): 267–85.

Baugher, Eleanor, and Leatha Lamison-White. *Poverty in the United States: 1995*. U. S. Bureau of the Census, Current Population Reports, Series P-60, no. 194. Washington, D.C., 1996.

Behr, Roy L., and Shanto Iyengar. "Television News, Real-World Cues, and Changes in the Public Agenda." *Public Opinion Quarterly* 49, no. 1 (spring 1985): 38–57.

Bell, Daniel. *The Coming of Post-industrial Society: A Venture in Social Forecasting*. New York: Basic Books, 1973.

Bellah, Robert N., Richard Madsen, William M. Sullivan, Ann Swidler, and Steven M. Tipton. *Habits of the Heart: Individualism and Commitment in American Life*. Berkeley: University of California Press, 1985.

Berelson, Bernard R., Paul F. Lazarsfeld, and William N. McPhee. *Voting: A Study of Opinion Formation in a Presidential Campaign*. Chicago: University of Chicago Press, 1954.

Billig, Michael, and Henri Tajfel. "Social Categorization and Similarity in Intergroup Behavior." *European Journal of Social Psychology* 3 (1973): 27–52.

Bishop, George F., and Bonnie S. Fisher. " 'Secret Ballots' and Self-Reports in an Exit-Poll Experiment." *Public Opinion Quarterly* 59, no. 4 (winter 1995): 568–88.

Bjorn, Lars. "Labor Parties, Economic Growth, and Redistribution in Five Capitalist Democracies." *Comparative Social Research* 2 (1979): 93–128.

Bloom, Jack M. *Class, Race, and the Civil Rights Movement*. Bloomington: Indiana University Press, 1987.

Bobo, Lawrence. "Whites' Opposition to Busing: Symbolic Racism or Realistic Group Conflict?" *Journal of Personality and Social Psychology* 45 (1983): 1196–1210.

———. "Group Conflict, Prejudice, and the Paradox of Contemporary Racial Attitudes." In *Eliminating Racism: Profiles in Controversy*, edited by Phyllis A. Katz and Dalmas A. Taylor. New York: Plenum, 1988.

Bobo, Lawrence, and James R. Kluegel. "Opposition to Race-Targeting: Self-Interest, Stratification Ideology, or Racial Attitudes?" *American Sociological Review* 58 (1993): 443–64.

Bobo, Lawrence, and Ryan A. Smith. "Antipoverty Policy, Affirmative Action, and Racial Attitudes." In *Confronting Poverty: Prescriptions for Change*, edited by Sheldon H. Danziger, Gary D. Sandefur, and Daniel H. Weinberg. Cambridge: Harvard University Press, 1994.

Borgida, Eugene, and Richard E. Nisbett. "The Differential Impact of Abstract vs. Concrete Information on Decisions." *Journal of Applied Social Psychology* 7 (1977): 258–71.

Brady, Henry E. "The Perils of Survey Research: Inter-personally Incomparable Responses." *Political Methodology* 11, nos. 3–4 (1985): 269–91.

Bremner, John. "GOP, Business Misinterpreting Their 1994 Mandate." *St. Louis Post-Dispatch*, July 31, 1995, Business section, 12.

Bremner, Robert H. *American Philanthropy*. Chicago: University of Chicago Press, 1960.

Brooks, Thomas R. *Walls Come Tumbling Down: A History of the Civil Rights Movement, 1940–1970*. Englewood Cliffs, N.J.: Prentice-Hall, 1974.

Brosius, Hans-Bernd, and Anke Bathelt. "The Utility of Exemplars in Persuasive Communications." *Communication Research* 21, no. 1 (February 1994): 48–78.

Brown, Roger. *Social Psychology*. New York: Free Press, 1986.

Burke, Edmund. *Reflections on the Revolution in France*. 1790. Reprint, Garden City, N.Y.: Anchor Press, 1973.

Campbell, Angus, Philip E. Converse, Warren E. Miller, and Donald E. Stokes. *The American Voter*. Chicago: University of Chicago Press, 1960.

Campbell, Donald T. "Stereotypes and the Perception of Group Differences." *American Psychologist* 22 (1967): 817–29.

Carmines, Edward G., and James A. Stimson. *Issue Evolution: Race and the Transformation of American Politics*. Princeton: Princeton University Press, 1989.

Carter, Jimmy. "The President's News Conference of August 6, 1977." In *Public Papers of the Presidents of the United States: Jimmy Carter, 1977 (Book II—June 25 to December 31, 1977)*. Washington, D.C.: GPO, 1978.

Carver, C. S., D. C. Glass, and I. Katz. "Favorable Evaluations of Blacks and the Handicapped: Positive Prejudice, Unconscious Denial, or Social Desirability?" *Journal of Applied Social Psychology* 8 (1978): 97–106.

Casady, R. J., and J. M. Lepkowski. "Optimal Allocation for Stratified Telephone Survey Designs." In *Proceedings of the Section on Survey Research Methods, American Statistical Association*, 1991.

Castles, Francis G. "The Impact of Parties on Public Expenditures." In *The Impact of Parties*, edited by Francis Castles. Beverly Hills: Sage Publications, 1982.

——. *The Working Class and Welfare: Reflections on the Political Development of the Welfare State in Australia and New Zealand.* Sydney, Australia: Allen and Unwin, 1985.

Citrin, Jack, and Donald Philip Green. "The Self-Interest Motive in American Public Opinion." *Research in Micropolitics* 3 (1990): 1–28.

Clotfelter, Charles. *Federal Tax Policy and Charitable Giving.* Chicago: University of Chicago Press, 1985.

Cook, Fay Lomax. *Who Should Be Helped? Public Support for Social Services.* Beverly Hills: Sage Publications, 1979.

Cook, Fay Lomax, and Edith J. Barrett. *Support for the American Welfare State: The Views of Congress and the Public.* New York: Columbia University Press, 1992.

Coughlin, Richard M. "Social Policy and Ideology: Public Opinion in Eight Nations." *Comparative Social Research* 2 (1979): 3–40.

Crosby, Faye, Stephanie Bromley, and Leonard Saxe. "Recent Unobtrusive Studies of Black and White Discrimination and Prejudice: A Literature Review." *Psychological Bulletin* 87, no. 3 (1980): 546–63.

Curtin, Richard T., and Charles D. Cowan. "Public Attitudes toward Fiscal Programs." In *1972–1973 Surveys of Consumers*, edited by Burkhard Strumpel. Ann Arbor: University of Michigan, Institute for Social Research, 1975.

Curtis, James E., Edward G. Grabb, and Douglas E. Baer. "Voluntary Association Membership in Fifteen Countries: A Comparative Analysis." *American Sociological Review* 57 (April 1992): 139–52.

Daly, Mary. "Labor Market Effects of Welfare Reform." Federal Reserve Bank of San Francisco, Economic Letter no. 97-24, August 29, 1997.

Danziger, Sheldon, and Peter Gottschalk. *America Unequal.* Cambridge: Harvard University Press, 1995.

Davies, Gareth. *From Opportunity to Entitlement: The Transformation and Decline of Great Society Liberalism.* Lawrence: University Press of Kansas, 1996.

DeParle, Jason. "Half the States Unlikely to Meet Goals on Welfare." *New York Times*, October 1, 1997, A1.

Devine, Patricia G. "Stereotypes and Prejudice: Their Automatic and Controlled Components." *Journal of Personality and Social Psychology* 56 (1989): 5–18.

Diab, L. "National Stereotypes and the 'Reference Group' Concept." *Journal of Social Psychology* 57 (1962): 339–51.

Dickson, Peter R. "The Impact of Enriching Case and Statistical Information on Consumer Judgments." *Journal of Consumer Research* 8 (1982): 398–406.

Dovidio, John F., Nancy Evans, and Richard B. Tyler. "Racial Stereotypes: The Contents of Their Cognitive Representations." *Journal of Experimental Social Psychology* 22 (1986): 22–37.

Duncan, Greg J. "Poverty and Social Assistance Dynamics in the United States, Canada, and Europe." In *Poverty, Inequality, and the Future of Social Policy*, edited by Katherine McFate, Roger Lawson, and William Julius Wilson. New York: Russell Sage Foundation, 1995.

Dye, Thomas R. *Politics in America.* New York: Prentice Hall, 1997.

The Economist 330, no. 7854 (March 12, 1994) 57.

Edsall, Thomas Byrne, and Mary D. Edsall. *Chain Reaction: The Impact of Race, Rights, and Taxes on American Politics.* New York: W. W. Norton, 1991.

Entman, Robert M. "Television, Democratic Theory, and the Visual Construction of Poverty." *Research in Political Sociology* 7 (1995): 139–59.

Fazio, Russell H., Joni R. Jackson, Bridget C. Dunton, and Carol J. Williams. "Variability in Automatic Activation as an Unobtrusive Measure of Racial Attitudes: A Bona Fide Pipeline?" *Journal of Personality and Social Psychology* 69 (1995): 1013–27.

Feagin, Joe R. "America's Welfare Stereotypes." *Social Science Quarterly* 52 (1972): 921–33.
———. *Subordinating the Poor: Welfare and American Beliefs*. Englewood Cliffs, N.J.: Prentice-Hall, 1975.

Feldman, Stanley, and John Zaller. "The Political Culture of Ambivalence: Ideological Responses to the Welfare State." *American Journal of Political Science* 36 (1992): 268–307.

Fiedler, Klaus, and Joseph Forgas, eds. *Affect, Cognition, and Social Behavior: New Evidence and Integrative Attempts*. Toronto: C. J. Hogrefe, 1988.

Finkel, Steven E., Thomas M. Guterbock, and Marian J. Borg. "Race-of-Interviewer Effects in a Preelection Poll: Virginia 1989." *Public Opinion Quarterly* 55, no. 3 (fall 1991): 313–30.

Firebaugh, Glenn, and Kenneth E. Davis. "Trends in Antiblack Prejudice, 1972–1984: Region and Cohort Effects." *American Journal of Sociology* 94, no. 2 (September 1988): 251–72.

Fishman, Mark. *Manufacturing the News*. Austin: University of Texas Press, 1980.

Fiske, Susan T., and Mark A. Pavelchak. "Category-Based versus Piecemeal-Based Affective Responses: Developments in Schema-Triggered Affect." In *Handbook of Motivation and Cognition*, edited by Richard M. Sorrentino and E. Tory Higgins. New York: Guilford, 1986.

"Folio 500: Circulation Figures for the 500 Top U.S. Magazines." *Folio: The Magazine for Magazine Management* 23, no. 12 (1994): 52.

Fording, Richard C. "The Conditional Effect of Violence as a Political Tactic: Mass Insurgency, Welfare Generosity, and Electoral Context in the American States." *American Journal of Political Science* 41, no. 1 (January 1997): 1–29.

Forgas, Joseph, and Stephanie J. Moylan. "Affective Influences on Stereotype Judgments." *Cognition and Emotion* 5 (1991): 379–95.

Free, Lloyd A., and Hadley Cantril. *The Political Beliefs of Americans: A Study of Public Opinion*. New York: Simon and Schuster, 1968.

Galbraith, John Kenneth. *The Affluent Society*. Boston: Houghton Mifflin, 1958.

Gans, Herbert J. *Deciding What's News: A Study of CBS Evening News, NBC Nightly News, Newsweek, and Time*. New York: Pantheon Books, 1979.

Gant, Michael M., and Norman R. Luttbeg. "The Cognitive Utility of Partisanship." *Western Political Quarterly* 40 (September 1987): 499–518.

Garrison, William Lloyd. *Thoughts on African Colonization*, 183. Boston: Garrison and Knapp, 1832. Cited in George M. Frederickson, *The Black Image in the White Mind: The Debate on African American Character and Destiny, 1817–1914* (New York: Harper and Row, 1971), 36.

Gergen, K. J. "The Significance of Skin Color in Human Relations." *Daedalus* (1969): 390–406.

Gilbert, G. M. "Stereotype Persistence and Change among College Students." *Journal of Abnormal and Social Psychology* 46 (1951): 245–54.

Gilens, Martin. "The Gender Gap: Psychology, Social Structure, and Support for Reagan." *Berkeley Journal of Sociology* 29 (1984): 35–56.

———. "Racial Attitudes and Opposition to Welfare." *Journal of Politics* 57, no. 4 (November 1995): 994–1014.

———. " 'Race Coding' and White Opposition to Welfare." *American Political Science Review* 90, no. 3 (September 1996): 593–604.

———. "Race and Poverty in America: Public Misperceptions and the American News Media." *Public Opinion Quarterly* 60, no. 4 (winter 1996): 515–41.

Gilens, Martin, Paul M. Sniderman, and James H. Kuklinski. "Affirmative Action and the Politics of Realignment." *British Journal of Political Science* 28, no. 1 (January 1998): 159–83.

Gilliam, Franklin D., Jr., and Kenny J. Whitby. "Race, Class, and Attitudes toward Social Welfare Spending: An Ethclass Interpretation." *Social Science Quarterly* 70, no. 1 (March 1989): 88–100.

Gillin, John Lewis. *Poverty and Dependency: Their Relief and Prevention.* New York: Appleton-Century, 1921.

Ginossar, Zvi, and Yaacov Trope. "The Effects of Base Rates and Individuating Information on Judgments about Another Person." *Journal of Experimental Social Psychology* 16 (1980): 228–42.

Gitlin, Todd. *The Whole World Is Watching: Mass Media in the Making and Unmaking of the New Left.* Berkeley: University of California Press, 1980.

Glaser, James M., and Martin Gilens. "Interregional Migration and Political Resocialization: A Study of Racial Attitudes under Pressure." *Public Opinion Quarterly* 61, no. 1 (spring 1997): 72–86.

Glazer, Nathan. *The Limits of Social Policy.* Cambridge: Harvard University Press, 1988.

Gottschalk, Peter, Sara McLanahan, and Gary D. Sandefur. "The Dynamics and Intergenerational Transmission of Poverty and Welfare Participation." In *Confronting Poverty: Prescriptions for Change,* edited by Sheldon H. Danziger, Gary D. Sandefur, and Daniel H. Weinberg. Cambridge: Harvard University Press, 1994.

Graber, Doris. "Television News without Pictures?" *Critical Studies in Mass Communication* 4 (March 1987): 74–78.

———. "Seeing Is Remembering: How Visuals Contribute to Learning from Television News." *Journal of Communication* 40 (1990): 134–55.

Graebner, William. "Federalism in the Progressive Era: A Structural Interpretation of Reform." *Journal of American History* 64 (1977): 331–57.

Green, Donald Philip, and Bradley Palmquist. "Of Artifacts and Partisan Instability." *American Journal of Political Science* 34 (1990): 871–902.

Green, Donald Philip, Susan Lee Goldman, and Peter Salovey. "Measurement Error Masks Bipolarity in Affect Ratings." *Journal of Personality and Social Psychology* 64 (1993): 1029–41.

Greenstein, Robert. "Universal and Targeted Approaches to Relieving Poverty: An Alternative View." In *The Urban Underclass,* edited by Christopher Jencks and Paul E. Peterson. Washington, D.C.: Brookings Institution, 1991.

Greenwald, Anthony G., and Mahzarin R. Banaji. "Implicit Social Cognition: Attitudes, Self-Esteem, and Stereotypes." *Psychological Review* 102, no. 1 (January 1995): 4–27.

Gustafsson, Siv. "Single Mothers in Sweden." In *Poverty, Inequality, and the Future of Social Policy,* edited by Katherine McFate, Roger Lawson, and William Julius Wilson. New York: Russell Sage Foundation, 1995.

Halfpenny, Peter. "The 1991 International Survey of Giving." In *Researching the Voluntary Sector,* edited by Susan K. E. Saxon-Harrold and Jeremy Kendall. Tonbridge, England: Charities Aid Foundation, 1993.

Hamill, Ruth, Timothy DeCamp Wilson, and Richard E. Nisbett. "Insensitivity to Sample Bias: Generalizing from Atypical Cases." *Journal of Personality and Social Psychology* 39 (1980): 578–89.

Hamilton, Alexander, James Madison, and John Jay. *The Federalist Papers.* 1787–88. Reprint, New York: Mentor, 1961.

Hamilton, Dona Cooper, and Charles V. Hamilton. *The Dual Agenda: Race and Social Welfare Policies of Civil Rights Organizations.* New York: Columbia University Press, 1997.

Handler, Joel. *The Moral Construction of Poverty: Welfare Reform in America.* Newbury Park, Calif.: Sage Publications, 1991.

Hapgood, Hutchins. *The Spirit of the Ghetto: Studies of the Jewish Quarter of New York.* New York: Funk and Wagnalls, 1902.

Harding, John, Harold Proshansky, Bernard Kutner, and Isidor Chein. "Prejudice and Ethnic Relations." In *Handbook of Social Psychology*, edited by Gardner Lindzen and Elliot Aronson. Reading, Mass.: Addison-Wesley, 1969.

Harrington, Michael. *The Other America: Poverty in the United States*. New York: Macmillan, 1962.

Hartley, Thomas, and Bruce Russett. "Public Opinion and the Common Defense: Who Governs Military Spending in the United States?" *American Political Science Review* 86, no. 4 (December 1992): 905–15.

Hartz, Louis. *The Liberal Tradition in America: An Interpretation of American Political Thought since the Revolution*. San Diego: Harcourt Brace Jovanovich, 1955.

Hasenfeld, Yeheskel, and Jane A. Rafferty. "The Determinants of Public Attitudes toward the Welfare State." *Social Forces* 67 (1989): 1027–48.

Headey, Bruce. "Trade Unions and National Wage Policies." *Journal of Politics* 32 (1970): 407–39.

Heclo, Hugh. "The Political Foundations of Antipoverty Policy." In *Fighting Poverty: What Works and What Doesn't*, edited by Sheldon H. Danziger and Daniel H. Weinberg. Cambridge: Harvard University Press, 1986.

Heidenheimer, Arnold J., Hugh Heclo, and Carolyn Teich Adams. *Comparative Public Policy: The Politics of Social Choice in Europe and America*. New York: St. Martin's Press, 1975.

Heider, Fritz. *The Psychology of Interpersonal Relations*. New York: Wiley, 1958.

Hernandez, Raymond. "Most Dropped from Welfare Don't Get Jobs." *New York Times*, March 23, 1998, A1.

Highton, Benjamin, and Raymond E. Wolfinger. "Memorandum to the Board of Overseers, National Election Studies: Estimating the Size of Minority Groups." Berkeley, Calif., 1992.

Hilton, James L., and William von Hippel. "Stereotypes." In *Annual Review of Psychology*, edited by Janet T. Spence, John M. Darley, and Donald J. Foss. Palo Alto, Calif.: Annual Reviews, 1996.

Hochschild, Jennifer L. *What's Fair? American Beliefs about Distributive Justice*. Cambridge: Harvard University Press, 1981.

———. *Facing Up to the American Dream: Race, Class, and the Soul of a Nation*. Princeton: Princeton University Press, 1995.

Holmes, Steven A. "U.S. Census Finds First Income Rise in Past Six Years." *New York Times*, September 27, 1996, A1.

Hollander, Jacob. *Abolition of Poverty*. Boston: Houghton Mifflin, 1914.

Holzer, Harry J. "Black Youth Nonemployment: Duration and Job Search." In *The Black Youth Employment Crisis*, edited by Richard B. Freeman and Harry J. Holzer. Chicago: University of Chicago Press, 1986.

———. "Black Employment Problems: New Evidence, Old Questions." *Journal of Policy Analysis and Management* 13, no. 4 (fall 1994): 699–722.

Hopper, Kim, and Norweeta G. Milburn. "Homelessness among African Americans: A Historical and Contemporary Perspective." In *Homelessness in America*, edited by Jim Baumohl. Phoenix: Oryx Press, 1996.

Howard, Christopher. "A Bridge Too Far? Linking the Study of National and State-Level Social Policy in the United States." Paper presented at the annual meeting of the American Political Science Association, Washington, D.C., August 28–31, 1997.

Huckfeldt, Robert, and John Sprague. *Citizens, Politics, and Social Communication: Information and Influence in an Election Campaign*. New York: Cambridge University Press, 1995.

Hunter, Robert. *Poverty*. N.p., 1904.

Hurwitz, Jon, and Mark Peffley. *Perception and Prejudice: Race and Politics in the United States*. New Haven: Yale University Press, 1998.

Iyengar, Shanto. *Is Anyone Responsible? How Television Frames Political Issues*. Chicago: University of Chicago Press, 1991.

Iyengar, Shanto, and Donald R. Kinder. *News That Matters: Television and American Opinion*. Chicago: University of Chicago Press, 1987.

Jackman, Mary R. "General and Applied Tolerance: Does Education Increase Commitment to Racial Integration?" *American Journal of Political Science* 22 (1978): 302–24.

Jackman, Mary R., and Robert W. Jackman. *Class Awareness in the United States*. Berkeley: University of California Press, 1983.

Jackman, Mary R., and Michael J. Muha. "Education and Inter-group Attitudes: Moral Enlightenment, Superficial Democratic Commitment, or Ideological Refinement?" *American Sociological Review* 49 (1984): 751–69.

Jackman, Mary R., and Mary Scheuer Senter. "Images of Social Groups: Categorical or Qualified?" *Public Opinion Quarterly* 44, no. 3 (fall 1980): 341–61.

Jansson, Bruce S. *The Reluctant Welfare State: A History of American Social Welfare Policies*. Pacific Grove, Calif.: Brooks/Cole, 1993.

Jargowsky, Paul A., and Mary Jo Bane. "Ghetto Poverty in the United States, 1970–1980." In *The Urban Underclass*, edited by Christopher Jencks and Paul E. Peterson. Washington, D.C.: Brookings Institution, 1991.

Jaynes, Gerald David, and Robin M. Williams, Jr., eds. *A Common Destiny: Blacks and American Society*. Washington, D.C.: National Academy Press, 1989.

Jencks, Christopher. "Who Gives to What?" In *The Nonprofit Sector: A Research Handbook*, edited by Walter W. Powell. New Haven: Yale University Press, 1987.

———. *Rethinking Social Policy*. Cambridge: Harvard University Press, 1992.

Jencks, Christopher, and Paul E. Peterson, eds. *The Urban Underclass*. Washington, D.C.: Brookings Institution, 1991.

Johnson, Lyndon B. *Public Papers of the Presidents of the United States: Lyndon B. Johnson, 1963–64*. Vol. 1. Washington, D.C.: GPO, 1965.

Johnson, Norman. *The Welfare State in Transition: The Theory and Practice of Welfare Pluralism*. Amherst: University of Massachusetts Press, 1987.

Jones, Edward E., and Keith E. Davis. "From Acts to Dispositions: The Attribution Process in Person Perception." In *Advances in Experimental Social Psychology*, vol. 7, edited by Leonard Berkowitz. New York: Academic Press, 1965.

Jones, J. M. *Prejudice and Racism*. Reading, Mass.: Addison-Wesley, 1972.

Jost, John T. "Is It Time for a Theory of Outgroup Favoritism? A Comment on the Paper by Mullen, Brown, and Smith." Yale University, 1993.

Jost, John T., and Mahzarin R. Banaji. "The Role of Stereotyping in System-Justification and the Production of False Consciousness." *British Journal of Social Psychology* 33 (1994): 1–27.

Kahneman, Daniel, and Amos Tversky. "On the Psychology of Prediction." *Psychological Review* 80 (1973): 237–51.

Karlins, Marvin, Thomas L. Coffman, and Gary Walters. "On the Fading of Social Stereotypes: Studies in Three Generations of College Students." *Journal of Personality and Social Psychology* 13 (1969): 1–16.

Katz, Daniel, and Kenneth W. Braly. "Racial Stereotypes of 100 College Students." *Journal of Abnormal and Social Psychology* 28 (1933): 280–90.

———. "Racial Prejudice and Racial Stereotypes." *Journal of Abnormal and Social Psychology* 30 (1935): 175–93.

Katz, Michael. *In the Shadow of the Poorhouse: A Social History of Welfare in America*. New York: Basic Books, 1986.

———. *The Undeserving Poor: From the War on Poverty to the War on Welfare*. New York: Pantheon Books, 1989.

Katz, Phyllis A. "The Acquisition of Racial Attitudes in Children." In *Towards the Elimination of Racism*, edited by Phyllis A. Katz. Elmsford, N.Y.: Pergamon Press, 1976.

Katz, Phyllis A., and Dalmas A. Taylor. *Eliminating Racism: Means and Controversies.* New York: Plenum, 1988.

Kazoleas, Dean C. "A Comparison of the Persuasive Effectiveness of Qualitative versus Quantitative Evidence: A Test of Explanatory Hypotheses." *Communication Quarterly* 41, no. 1 (winter 1993): 40–50.

Kelso, Robert W. *Poverty.* New York: Longmans, Green, and Co., 1929.

Kenney, Keith. "Effects of Still Photographs." *News Photographer* 47, no. 5 (May 1992): 41–42.

Kinder, Donald R., and Lynn M. Sanders. *Divided by Color: Racial Politics and Democratic Ideals in the American Republic.* Chicago: University of Chicago Press, 1996.

Kinder, Donald R., and David O. Sears. "Prejudice and Politics: Symbolic Racism versus Racial Threats to the Good Life." *Journal of Personality and Social Psychology* 40 (1981): 414–31.

King, Anthony. "Ideas, Institutions, and the Policies of Governments: A Comparative Analysis." *British Journal of Political Science* 3, no. 3 (1973): 291–313.

Kirschenman, Joleen, and Katherine M. Neckerman. "We'd Love to Hire Them But . . ." In *The Urban Underclass*, edited by Christopher Jencks and Paul E. Peterson. Washington, D.C.: Brookings Institution, 1991.

Kluegel, James R., and Eliot R. Smith. *Beliefs about Inequality: Americans' Views of What Is and What Ought to Be.* New York: Aldine de Gruyter, 1986.

Koballa, Thomas R. "Persuading Teachers to Reexamine the Innovative Elementary Science Programs of Yesterday: The Effects of Anecdotal versus Data-Summary Communications." *Journal of Research in Science Teaching* 23 (1986): 437–49.

Korpi, Walter. *The Democratic Class Struggle.* Boston: Routledge and Kegan Paul, 1983.

Krosnick, Jon A., and Donald R. Kinder. "Altering the Foundations of Support for the President through Priming." *American Political Science Review* 84, no. 2 (June 1990): 497–512.

Krysan, Maria. "Privacy and the Expression of White Racial Attitudes: A Comparison across Three Contexts." Pennsylvania State University, December 1997.

Krysan, Maria, Howard Schuman, Leslie Jo Scott, and Paul Beatty. "Response Rates and Response Content in Mail versus Face-to-Face Surveys." *Public Opinion Quarterly* 58, no. 3 (fall 1994): 381–99.

Kuklinski, James H., Michael D. Cobb, and Martin Gilens. "Racial Attitudes and the 'New South.'" *Journal of Politics* 59, no. 2 (May 1997): 323–49.

Kuklinski, James H., Paul M. Sniderman, Kathleen Knight, Thomas Piazza, Philip E. Tetlock, Gordon R. Lawrence, and Barbara Mellers. "Racial Prejudice and Attitudes toward Affirmative Action." *American Journal of Political Science* 41, no. 2 (April 1997): 402–19.

Kull, Steven. *Fighting Poverty in America: A Study of American Public Attitudes.* Washington, D.C.: Center for the Study of Policy Attitudes, 1994.

Lane, Jan-Erik, David McKay, and Kenneth Newton. *Political Data Handbook, OECD Countries.* Oxford: Oxford University Press, 1997.

Lee, Joseph. *Constructive and Preventive Philanthropy.* New York: Macmillan, 1902.

Lerner, Melvin J. *The Belief in a Just World: A Fundamental Delusion.* New York: Plenum Press, 1980.

Levine, Daniel. *Poverty and Society: The Growth of the American Welfare State in International Comparison.* New Brunswick, N.J.: Rutgers University Press, 1988.

Lichter, S. Robert, and Stanley Rothman. "Media and Business Elites." *Public Opinion* 4, no. 5 (October/November 1981): 42–46.

Lichter, S. Robert, Stanley Rothman, and Linda S. Lichter. *The Media Elite*. Bethesda: Adler and Adler, 1986.

Lieberman, Robert C. "Race, Institutions, and the Administration of Social Policy." *Social Science History* 19, no. 4 (winter 1995): 511–42.

Lippmann, Walter. *Public Opinion*. 1922. Reprint, New York: Macmillan, 1960.

Lipset, Seymour Martin. *The First New Nation: The United States in Historical and Comparative Perspective*. New York: Norton, 1979.

Lowenthal, Leo. "Biographies in Popular Magazines." In *Radio Research*, edited by Paul F. Lazarsfeld and Frank N. Stanton. New York: Duell, Sloan and Pearce, 1944.

Lukes, Steven. *Individualism*. New York: Harper and Row, 1973.

Lyndon B. Johnson School of Public Affairs. *The Social Safety Net Reexamined: FDR to Reagan*. Austin: University of Texas, 1989.

Mackie, Diane, and David Hamilton. *Affect, Cognition, and Stereotyping: Interactive Processes in Group Perception*. New York: Academic Press, 1993.

Marmor, Theodore R., Jerry L. Mashaw, and Philip L. Harvey. *America's Misunderstood Welfare State: Persistent Myths, Enduring Realities*. New York: Basic Books, 1990.

Massey, Douglas A., and Nancy A. Denton. *American Apartheid: Segregation and the Making of the Underclass*. Cambridge: Harvard University Press, 1993.

Mayer, William G. "Poll Trends: Trends in Media Usage." *Public Opinion Quarterly* 57, no. 4 (winter 1993): 593–611.

McCauley, C., C. Stitt, and M. Segal. "Stereotyping: From Prejudice to Prediction." *Psychological Bulletin* 87 (1980): 195–208.

McClosky, Herbert, and John Zaller. *The American Ethos: Public Attitudes toward Capitalism and Democracy*. Cambridge: Harvard University Press, 1984.

McConahay, John B. "Modern Racism, Ambivalence, and the Modern Racism Scale." In *Prejudice, Discrimination, and Racism*, edited by John F. Dovidio and Samuel L. Gaertner. New York: Academic Press, 1986.

McConahay, John B., and Joseph C. Hough, Jr. "Symbolic Racism." *Journal of Social Issues* 32 (1976): 23–45.

McFate, Katherine, Timothy Smeeding, and Lee Rainwater. "Markets and States: Poverty Trends and Transfer System Effectiveness in the 1980s." In *Poverty, Inequality, and the Future of Social Policy*, edited by Katherine McFate, Roger Lawson, and William Julius Wilson. New York: Russell Sage Foundation, 1995.

McMurrer, Daniel P., Isabel V. Sawhill, and Robert I. Lerman "Welfare Reform and Opportunity in the Low-Wage Labor Market." The Urban Institute, Opportunity in America Series, no. 5, July 1977.

McMurtry, J. *The Structure of Marx's World-View*. Princeton: Princeton University Press, 1978.

Mead, Lawrence M. *Beyond Entitlement: The Social Obligations of Citizenship*. New York: Free Press, 1986.

———. *The New Politics of Poverty: The Nonworking Poor in America*. New York: Basic Books, 1992.

Meier, August, and Elliott Redwick. *From Plantation to Ghetto*. New York: Hill and Wang, 1970.

Meyerson, D. *False Consciousness*. Oxford: Clarendon Press, 1991.

Miller, Herman P. "Changes in the Number and Composition of the Poor." In *Poverty in America*, edited by Margaret S. Gordon. Berkeley, Calif.: Chandler, 1965.

Miller, Warren E. *American National Election Study, 1984*. Machine readable data file. Ann Arbor: University of Michigan, Institute for Social Research, 1986.

———. *American National Election Study, 1986*. Ann Arbor: Inter-university Consortium for Political and Social Research, 1987.

Monroe, Alan D. "Consistency between Public Preferences and National Policy Decisions." *American Politics Quarterly* 7 (January 1979): 3–19.

Murray, Charles. *Losing Ground: American Social Policy, 1950–1980*. New York: Basic Books, 1984.

Mutz, Diana C., and Jeffery J. Mondak. "Dimensions of Sociotropic Behavior: Group-Based Judgments of Fairness and Well-Being." Paper presented at the annual meeting of the Midwest Political Science Association, Chicago, April 6–8, 1995.

Nelson, Thomas E., and Rosalee A. Clawson. "Poverty Attribution, Issue Framing, and Welfare Reform Opinion." Paper presented at the annual meeting of the American Political Science Association, San Francisco, August 29–September 1, 1996.

Neuman, W. Russell, Marion R. Just, and Ann N. Crigler. *Common Knowledge: News and the Construction of Political Meaning*. Chicago: University of Chicago Press, 1992.

Nisbett, Richard E., and Eugene Borgida. "Attribution and the Psychology of Prediction." *Journal of Personality and Social Psychology* 32 (1975): 932–43.

Nixon, Richard M. "Annual Message to Congress on the State of the Union." In *Public Papers of the Presidents of the United States: Richard Nixon, 1971*. Washington, D.C.: GPO, 1972.

Organization for Economic Cooperation and Development. *New Orientations in Social Policy*. Social Policy Studies, no. 12. Paris: Organization for Economic Cooperation and Development, 1994.

Orr, Larry L. "Income Transfers as a Public Good: An Application to A.F.D.C." *The American Economic Review* 66, no. 3 (June 1976): 359–71.

Osofsky, Gilbert. *Harlem: The Making of a Ghetto—Negro New York, 1890–1930*. New York: Harper and Row, 1966.

Page, Benjamin I., and Robert Y. Shapiro. "Effects of Public Opinion on Policy." *American Political Science Review* 77 (March 1983): 175–90.

———. *The Rational Public: Fifty Years of Trends in Americans' Policy Preferences*. Chicago: University of Chicago Press, 1992.

Parmalee, Maurice. *Poverty and Social Progress*. New York: Macmillan, 1916.

Patterson, James T. *America's Struggle against Poverty, 1900–1985*. Cambridge: Harvard University Press, 1986.

———. *America's Struggle against Poverty, 1900–1994*. Cambridge: Harvard University Press, 1994.

Peffley, Mark, Jon Hurwitz, and Paul M. Sniderman. "Racial Stereotypes and Whites' Political Views of Blacks in the Context of Welfare and Crime." *American Journal of Political Science* 41, no. 1 (January 1997): 30–60.

Pettigrew, Thomas F. "The Ultimate Attribution Error: Extending Allport's Cognitive Analysis of Prejudice." *Personality and Social Psychology Bulletin* 5 (1979): 461–76.

Phillips, Kevin. *The Politics of Rich and Poor: Wealth and the American Electorate in the Reagan Aftermath*. New York: Harper Collins, 1990.

Piazza, Thomas, Paul M. Sniderman, and Philip E. Tetlock. "Analysis of the Dynamics of Political Reasoning: A General-Purpose Computer-Assisted Methodology." In *Political Analysis*, edited by James A. Stimson. Ann Arbor: University of Michigan Press, 1989.

Piven, Frances Fox, and Richard A. Cloward. *Regulating the Poor: The Functions of Public Welfare*. New York: Vintage, 1971.

———. *Poor People's Movements: Why They Succeed, How They Fail*. New York: Vintage, 1979.

———. *Regulating the Poor: The Functions of Public Welfare*. 2d ed. New York: Vintage, 1993.

Plotnick, Robert D., and Richard F. Winters. "A Politico-Economic Theory of Income Redistribution." *American Political Science Review* 79, no. 2 (June 1985): 458–73.

Quadagno, Jill. *The Color of Welfare: How Racism Undermined the War on Poverty*. New York: Oxford University Press, 1994.

Reed, Adolph L. "The Underclass Myth." *Progressive* 55 (1991): 18–20.

Reed, John Shelton. *The Enduring South: Subcultural Persistence in Mass Society*. Chapel Hill: University of North Carolina Press, 1986.

Ricketts, Erol R., and Isabel V. Sawhill. "Defining and Measuring the Underclass." *Journal of Policy Analysis and Management* 7 (winter 1988): 316–25.

Robertson, David Brian. "The Bias of American Federalism: The Limits of Welfare-State Development in the Progressive Era." *Journal of Policy History* 1 (1989): 261–91.

Rogers, Everett M., and James W. Dearing. "Agenda Setting Research: Where Has It Been and Where Is It Going?" In *Communication Yearbook*, vol. 11, edited by James A. Anderson. Beverly Hills: Sage Publications, 1988.

Roosevelt, Franklin D., "Annual Message to Congress, January 4, 1935." In *The Public Papers and Addresses of Franklin D. Roosevelt*. Vol. 4. New York: Random House, 1938.

Rubinow, I. M. *The Quest for Security*. New York: Henry Holt, 1934.

Russell, Cheryl. *The Official Guide to Racial and Ethnic Diversity*. Ithaca: New Strategist Publications, 1996.

Sabato, Larry J. *Paying for Elections: The Campaign Finance Thicket*. New York: Priority Press Publications, 1989.

Sanders, Lynn M. "Racialized Interpretations of Economic Reality." Paper presented at the annual meeting of the American Political Science Association, San Francisco, August 29–September 1, 1996.

Schattschneider, E. E. *The Semisovereign People: A Realist's View of Democracy in America*. New York: Holt, Rinehart and Winston, 1960.

Schlenker, B. R., T. V. Bonoma, D. Hutchinson, and L. Burns. "The Bogus Pipeline and Stereotypes toward Blacks." *Journal of Psychology* 93 (1976): 319–29.

Schlesinger, Mark, and Caroline Heldman. "In a Different Choice?" Yale University, 1997.

Schram, Sanford F., and J. Patrick Turbett. "Civil Disorder and the Welfare Explosion: A Two-Step Process." *American Sociological Review* 48 (1983): 408–14.

Schuman, Howard, and Stanley Presser. *Questions and Answers in Attitude Surveys*. San Diego: Academic Press, 1981.

Schuman, Howard, Charlotte Steeh, and Lawrence Bobo. *Racial Attitudes in America: Trends and Interpretations*. Cambridge: Harvard University Press, 1985.

Schuman, Howard, Charlotte Steeh, Lawrence Bobo, and Maria Krysan. *Racial Attitudes in America: Trends and Interpretations*. Rev. ed. Cambridge: Harvard University Press, 1997.

Sears, David O. "The Persistence of Early Political Predispositions." In *Review of Personality and Social Psychology*, edited by Ladd Wheeler and Phillip Shaver. Beverly Hills: Sage Publications, 1983.

———. "Symbolic Racism." In *Eliminating Racism: Means and Controversies*, edited by Phyllis A. Katz and Dalmas A. Taylor. New York: Plenum, 1988.

Sears, David O., and Carolyn L. Funk. "The Role of Self-Interest in Social and Political Attitudes." *Advances in Experimental Social Psychology* 24 (1991): 1–91.

Sears, David O., Carl P. Hensler, and Leslie K. Speer. "Whites' Opposition to 'Busing': Self-Interest or Symbolic Politics?" *American Political Science Review* 73 (1979): 369–84.

Sears, David O., and John B. McConahay. *The Politics of Violence: The New Urban Blacks and the Watts Riot*. Boston: Houghton Mifflin, 1973.

Sears, David O., Colette van Laar, and Mary Carrillo. "Is It Really Racism? The Origins of White Americans' Opposition to Race-Targeted Policies." *Public Opinion Quarterly* 61, no. 1 (spring 1997): 16–53.

Shalev, Michael. "The Social Democratic Model and Beyond: Two Generations of Comparative Research on the Welfare State." *Comparative Social Research* 6 (1983): 315–51.

Shapiro, Robert Y., and Lawrence R. Jacobs. "The Relationship between Public Opinion and Public Policy: A Review." In *Political Behavior Annual*, vol. 2, ed. Samuel Long. Boulder: Westview Press, 1989.

Shapiro, Robert Y., and Harpreet Mahajan. "Gender Differences in Policy Preferences: A Summary of Trends from the 1960s to the 1980s." *Public Opinion Quarterly* 50, no. 1 (spring 1986): 42–61.

Shapiro, Robert Y., and John T. Young. "Public Opinion and the Welfare State: The United States in Comparative Perspective." *Political Science Quarterly* 104, no. 1 (spring 1989): 59–89.

Shipler, David K., "Blacks in the Newsroom: Progress? Yes, But . . ." *Columbia Journalism Review*, May/June 1998, 26–32.

Sigall, Harold, and Richard Page. "Current Stereotypes: A Little Fading, a Little Faking." *Journal of Personality and Social Psychology* 16 (1971): 252–58.

Sigelman, Lee, and Susan Welch. *Black Americans' Views of Racial Inequality: The Dream Deferred*. Cambridge: Cambridge University Press, 1991.

Sitkoff, Harvard. *The Struggle for Black Equality, 1954–1992*. New York: Hill and Wang, 1993.

Skocpol, Theda. "Targeting within Universalism." In *The Urban Underclass*, edited by Christopher Jencks and Paul E. Peterson. Washington, D.C.: Brookings Institution, 1991.

———. *Protecting Soldiers and Mothers: The Political Origins of Social Policy in the United States*. Cambridge: Harvard University Press, 1992.

Smeeding, Timothy M. "Briefing: Cross-National Perspectives on Trends in Child Poverty and the Effectiveness of Government Policies in Preventing Child Poverty in the 1980s." Paper presented to the George Washington University Forum, Washington, D.C., February 25, 1991.

———. "Financial Poverty in Developed Countries: The Evidence from LIS." Working paper no. 155, Luxembourg Income Study, Luxembourg, April 1997.

Smith, Tom W. "The Welfare State in Cross-National Perspective." *Public Opinion Quarterly* 51, no. 3 (fall 1987): 404–21.

Sniderman, Paul M., and Edward G. Carmines. *Reaching Beyond Race*. Cambridge: Harvard University Press, 1997.

Sniderman, Paul M., Edward G. Carmines, William Howell, and William Morgan. "A Test of Alternative Interpretations of the Contemporary Politics of Race: A Critical Examination of *Divided by Color*." Paper presented at the annual meeting of the Midwest Political Science Association, Chicago, 1997.

Sniderman, Paul M., Edward G. Carmines, Geoffrey C. Layman, and Michael Carter. "Beyond Race: Social Justice as a Race Neutral Ideal." *American Journal of Political Science* 40, no. 1 (February 1996): 33–55.

Sniderman, Paul M., and Douglas B. Grob. "Innovations in Experimental Design in Attitude Surveys." *Annual Review of Sociology* 22 (1996): 377–99.

Sniderman, Paul M., and Michael Gray Hagen. *Race and Inequality: A Study in American Values*. Chatham, N.J.: Chatham House, 1985.

Sniderman, Paul M., and Thomas Piazza. *The Scar of Race*. Cambridge: Harvard University Press, 1993.

Spears, R., and A. S. R. Manstead. "The Social Context of Stereotyping and Differentiation." *European Journal of Social Psychology* 19 (1989): 101–21.

Statistical Office of the European Communities. *General Government Accounts and Statistics: 1981–1992*. Luxembourg: Statistical Office of the European Communities, 1994.

Steeh, Charlotte, and Maria Krysan. "Trends: Affirmative Action and the Public, 1970–1995." *Public Opinion Quarterly* 60, no. 1 (spring 1996): 128–58.

Stocking, George W. *Race, Culture, and Evolution: Essays in the History of Anthropology*. New York: Free Press, 1968.

Sudman, Seymour, and Norman M. Bradburn. *Response Effects in Surveys: A Review and Synthesis*. Chicago: Aldine Publishing Co., 1974.

Tajfel, Henri, and A. L. Wilkes. "Classification and Quantitative Judgement." *British Journal of Psychology* 54 (1963): 101–14.

Takaki, Ronald. *Iron Cages: Race and Culture in Nineteenth-Century America*. New York: Oxford University Press, 1990.

Teles, Steven M. *Whose Welfare? A.F.D.C. and Elite Politics*. Lawrence: University Press of Kansas, 1996.

Thurow, Lester. "Recession Plus Inflation Spells Stasis." *Christianity and Crisis* 41, no. 5 (March 30, 1981): 91–92.

Tocqueville, Alexis de. *Democracy in America*. 1835. Reprint, Garden City, N.Y.: Anchor Books, 1969.

Tourangeau, Roger, Tom W. Smith, and Kenneth A. Rasinski. "Motivation to Report Sensitive Behaviors on Surveys: Evidence from a Bogus Pipeline Experiment." *Journal of Applied Social Psychology* 27, no. 3 (February 1997): 209–22.

Triandis, H. C., J. Lisansky, B. Setiadi, B. Chang, G. Marin, and H. Betancourt. "Stereotyping among Hispanics and Anglos: The Uniformity, Intensity, Direction, and Quality of Auto- and Heterostereotypes." *Journal of Cross-Cultural Psychology* 13 (1982): 409–26.

Turner, Bobie Green. *Federal/State Aid to Dependent Children Program and Its Benefits to Black Children in America, 1935–1985*. New York: Garland Publishing, 1993.

Turner, Frederick Jackson. "Significance of the Frontier in American History." In *Annual Report of the American Historical Society, 1893*. Washington, D.C.: GPO, 1894.

Tversky, Amos, and Daniel Kahneman. "Belief in the Law of Small Numbers." *Psychological Bulletin* 76 (1971): 105–10.

U.S. Bureau of the Census. *Historical Statistics of the United States*. Washington, D.C., 1960.

———. "Persons by Family Characteristics." 1960 Census of Population, PC(2)-4B. Washington, D.C., 1960.

———. *Statistical Abstract of the United States: 1960*. Washington, D.C., 1961.

———. *Statistical Abstract of the United States: 1966*. Washington, D.C., 1967.

———. *Historical Statistics of the United States, Colonial Times to 1970*. Washington, D.C., 1975.

———. *Statistical Abstract of the United States: 1974*. Washington, D.C., 1975.

———. *Statistical Abstract of the United States: 1977*. Washington, D.C., 1977.

———. *Poverty in the United States: 1988 and 1989*. Current Population Reports, Series P-60, no. 171. Washington, D.C., 1990.

———. *Money Income and Poverty Status in the United States: 1989*. Current Population Reports, Series P-60, no. 168. Washington, D.C., 1990.

———. *1990 Census of Population and Housing, Summary Tape File 3A (CD90-3c-1)*. Washington, D.C., 1993.

———. *Statistical Abstract of the United States: 1993*. Washington, D.C., 1993.

———. "Marital Status and Living Arrangements: March 1994." Current Population Survey Reports. Washington, D.C., 1994.

———. *Statistical Abstract of the United States: 1995*. Washington, D.C., 1995.

———. *Historical Income Tables—Families* (http://www.census.gov/hhes/income/histinc/incfamdet.html), 1995.

———. *Statistical Abstract of the United States: 1997*. Washington, D.C., 1997.

U.S. Department of Agriculture. *Rural Homelessness: Focusing on the Needs of the Rural Homeless*. Washington, D.C., 1996.

U.S. Department of Labor. *65th Annual Report: Fiscal Year 1977*. Washington, D.C., 1978.

U.S. House of Representatives. *Background Material and Data on Programs within the Jurisdiction of the Committee on Ways and Means, 1994* (the "Green Book"), 1994.

———. *Background Material and Data on Programs within the Jurisdiction of the Committee on Ways and Means, 1996* (the "Green Book"), 1996.

——. *Background Material and Data on Programs within the Jurisdiction of the Committee on Ways and Means, 1998* (the "Green Book"), 1998.

Unger, Irwin. *The Best of Intentions: The Triumph and Failure of the Great Society under Kennedy, Johnson, and Nixon.* New York: Doubleday, 1996.

Verba, Sidney, Kay Lehman Schlozman, and Henry E. Brady. *Voice and Equality: Civic Voluntarism in American Politics.* Cambridge: Harvard University Press, 1995.

Verba, Sidney, Kay Lehman Schlozman, Henry Brady, and Norman H. Nie. "Citizen Activity: Who Participates? What Do They Say?" *American Political Science Review* 87 (1993): 303–18.

Virtanen, Simo V., and Leonie Huddy. "Old-Fashioned Racism and New Forms of Racial Prejudice." *Journal of Politics* 60, no. 2 (May 1998): 311–32.

von Sternberg, Bob. "How Do You Solve Urban Poverty?" *Minneapolis/St. Paul Star Tribune*, October 27, 1996, 1A.

Wang, Georgette, and Jack McKillip. "Ethnic Identification and Judgements of an Accident." *Personality and Social Psychology Bulletin* 4 (1978): 296–99.

Warner, Amos. *American Charities: A Study in Philanthropy and Economics.* New York: n.p., 1894.

Waxman, Laura, and Remy Trupin. *A Status Report on Hunger and Homelessness in America's Cities.* Washington, D.C.: U.S. Conference of Mayors, 1997.

Weaver, David H., and G. Cleveland Wilhoit. *The American Journalist in the 1990s: U.S. News People at the End of an Era.* Mahwah, N.J.: Lawrence Erlbaum, 1996.

Weaver, R. Kent, and William T. Dickens, eds. *Looking before We Leap: Social Science and Welfare Reform.* Washington, D.C.: Brookings Institution, 1995.

Weaver, R. Kent, and Bert A. Rockman. *Do Institutions Matter? Government Capabilities in the United States and Abroad.* Washington, D.C.: Brookings Institution, 1993.

Weaver, R. Kent, Robert Y. Shapiro, and Lawrence R. Jacobs. "Public Opinion on Welfare Reform: A Mandate for What?" In *Looking before We Leap: Social Science and Welfare Reform*, edited by R. Kent Weaver and William T. Dickens. Washington, D.C.: Brookings Institution, 1995.

——. "Trends: Welfare." *Public Opinion Quarterly* 59, no. 4 (winter 1995): 606–27.

Welch, Susan. "The Impact of Urban Riots on Urban Expenditures." *American Journal of Political Science* 19 (1975): 741–60.

Wells, Gary L., and John H. Harvey. "Do People Use Consensus Information in Making Causal Attributions?" *Journal of Personality and Social Psychology* 35 (1977): 279–93.

Wilensky, Harold L. *The Welfare State and Equality: Structural and Ideological Roots of Public Expenditures.* Berkeley: University of California Press, 1975.

Wilhoit, G. Cleveland, and David H. Weaver. *The American Journalist: A Portrait of U.S. News People and Their Work.* Bloomington: Indiana University Press, 1991.

Williams, Lorelei. "Wallflowers: Black Women in the Television Landscape." Senior Essay in Political Science and African American Studies, Yale University, 1998.

Williams, Robin M. *American Society: A Sociological Interpretation.* New York: Knopf, 1951.

Williamson, John B. "Beliefs about the Motivation of the Poor and Attitudes toward Poverty Policy." *Social Problems* 21 (1974): 634–48.

Wilson, William Julius. *The Truly Disadvantaged: The Inner City, the Underclass, and Public Policy.* Chicago: University of Chicago Press, 1987.

——. *When Work Disappears: The World of the New Urban Poor.* New York: Knopf, 1996.

Wiseman, Frederick. "Methodological Bias in Public Opinion Surveys." *Public Opinion Quarterly* 36, no. 1 (spring 1972): 105–8.

Woodmansee, John J., and Stuart W. Cook. "Dimensions of Verbal Racial Attitudes: Their Identification and Measurement." *Journal of Personality and Social Psychology* 7 (1967): 240–50.

Wright, Gerald C., Jr. "Racism and Welfare Policy in America." *Social Science Quarterly* 57, no. 3 (December 1976): 718–30.

Wright, Gerald C., Jr., Robert S. Erikson, and John P. McIver. "Public Opinion and Policy Liberalism in the American States." *American Journal of Political Science* 31 (1987): 980–1001.

Zaller, John. *The Nature and Origins of Mass Opinion.* Cambridge: Cambridge University Press, 1992.

Index